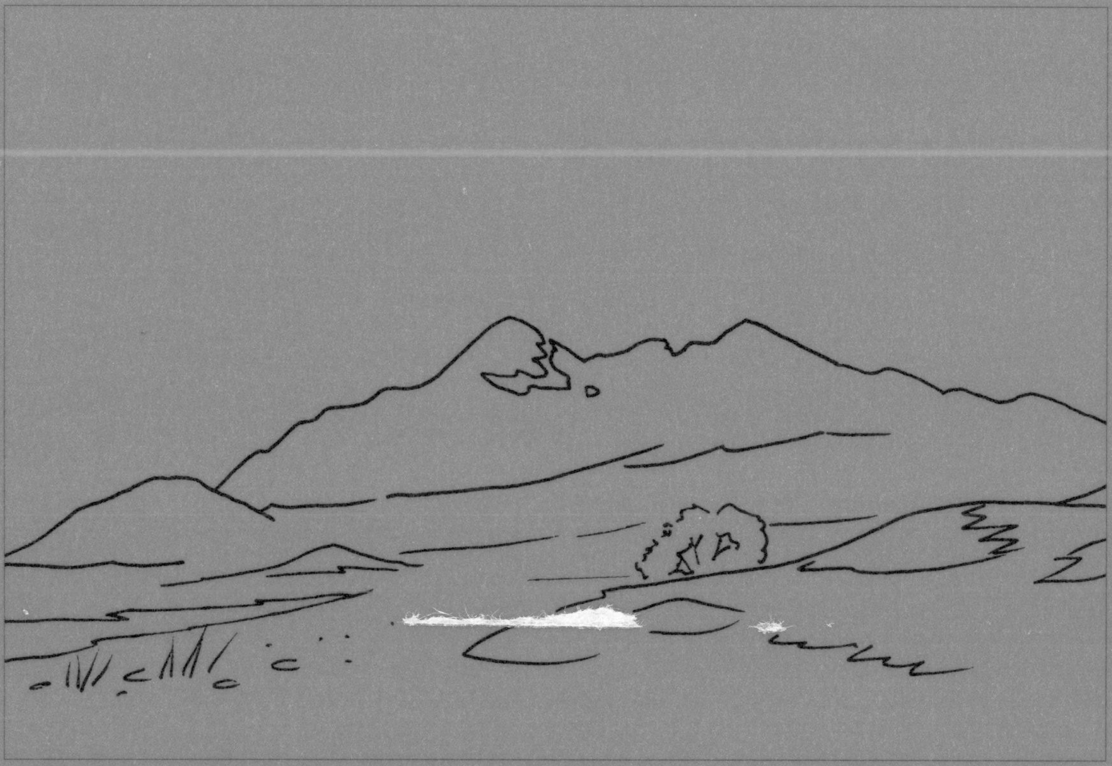

1

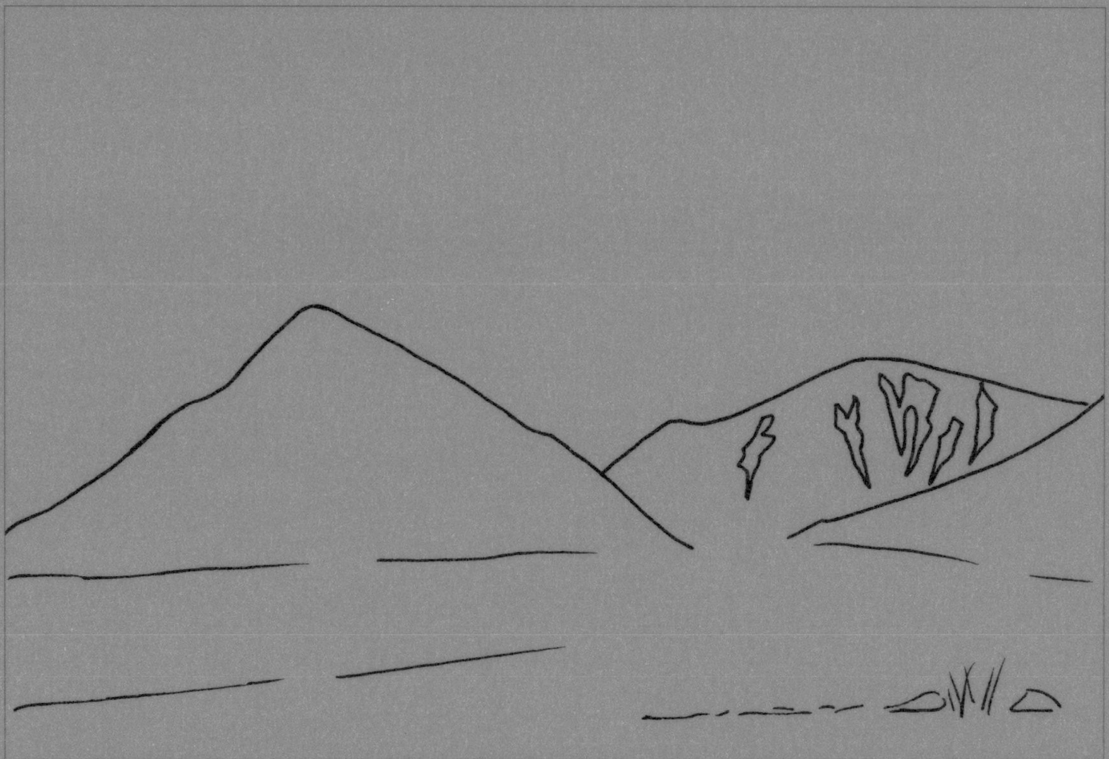

2

1

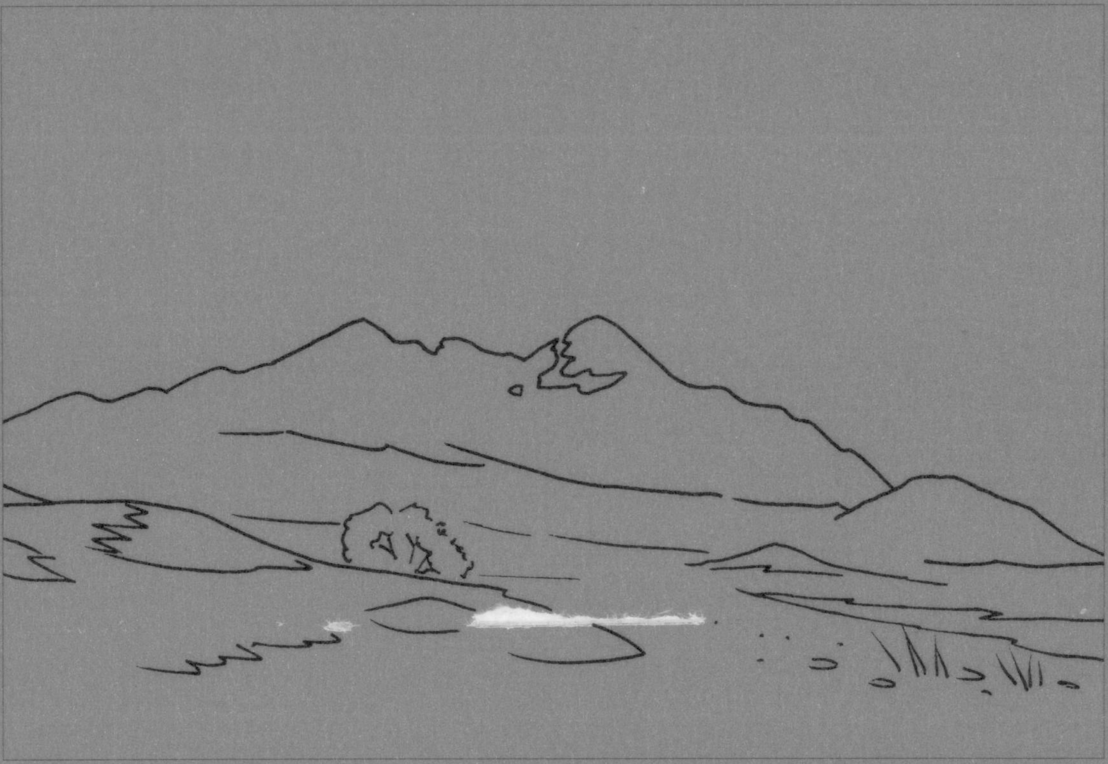

2

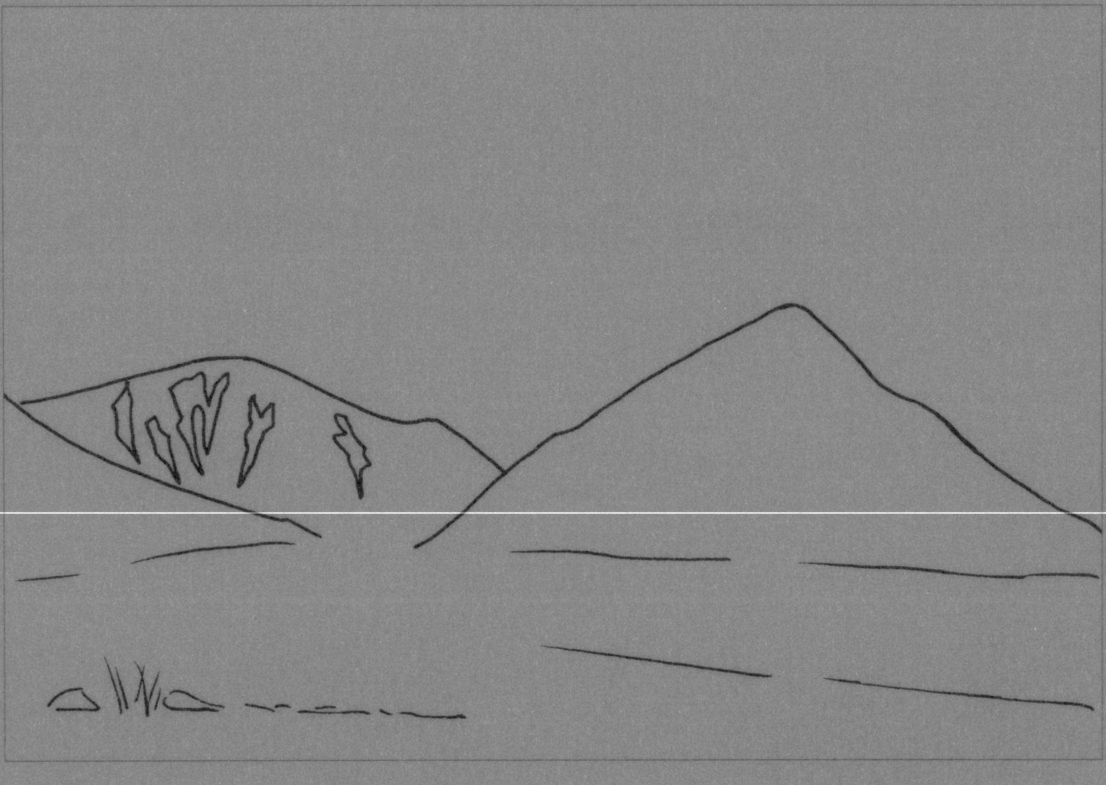

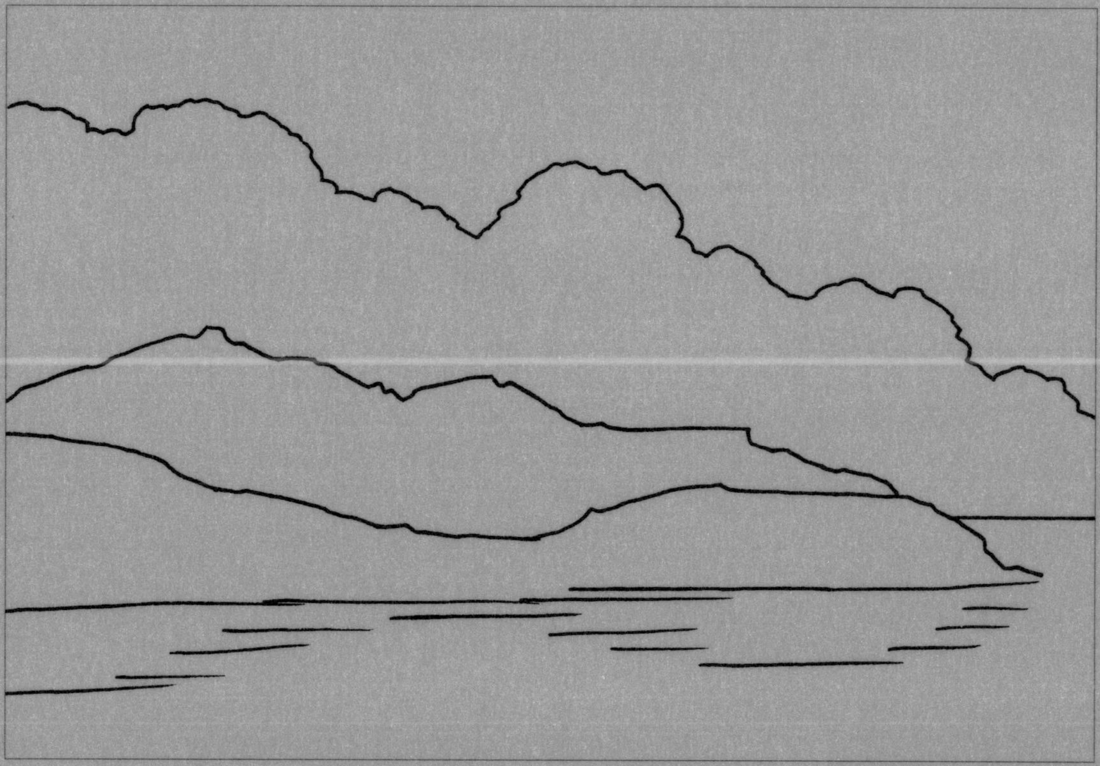

3

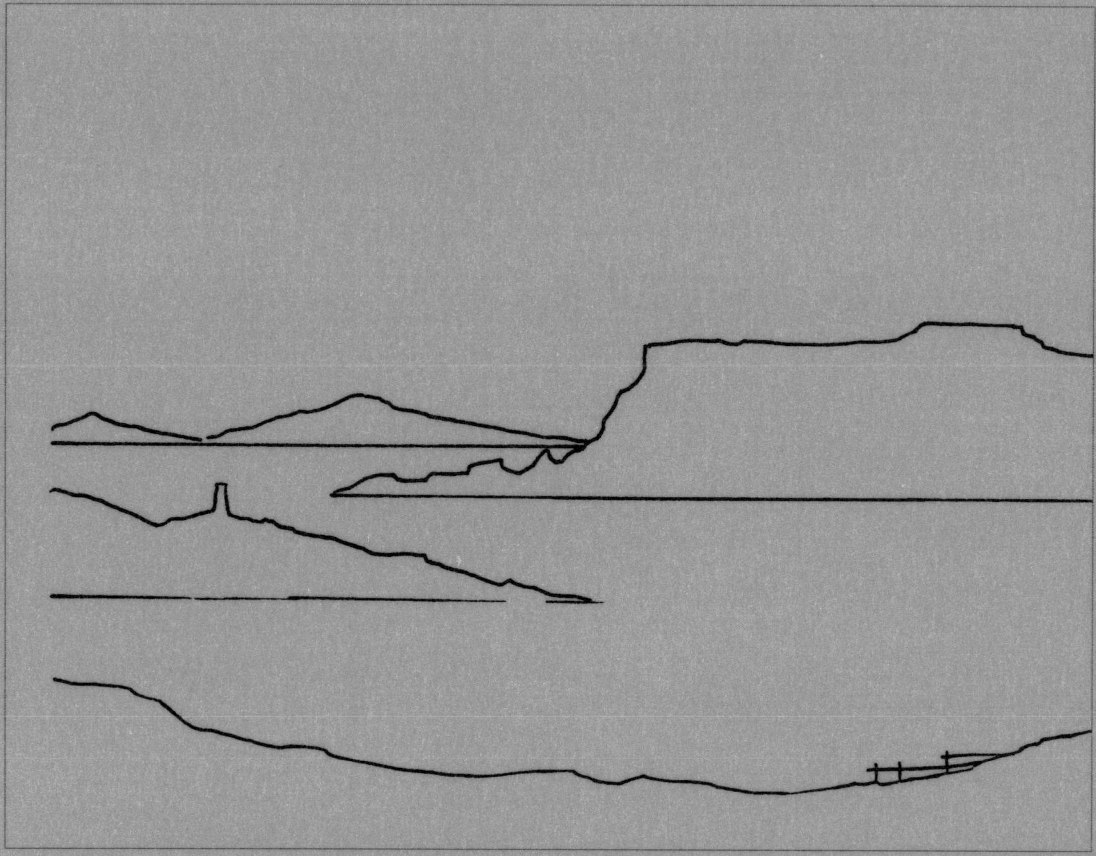

4

3

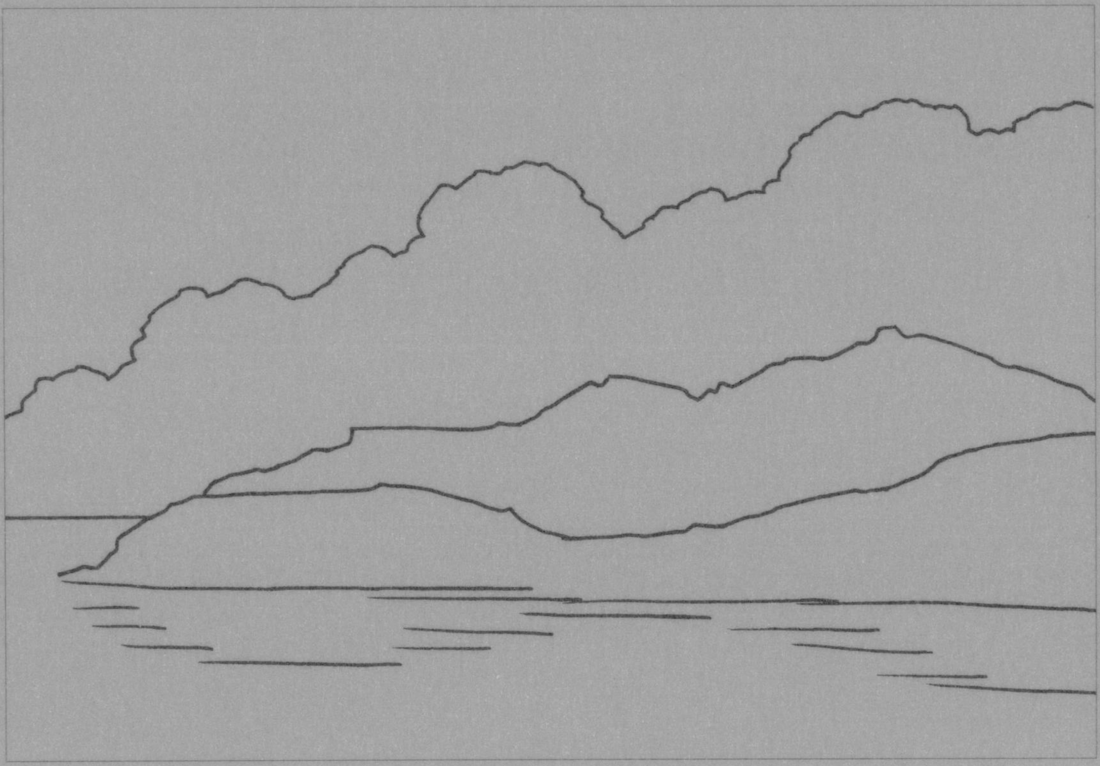

4

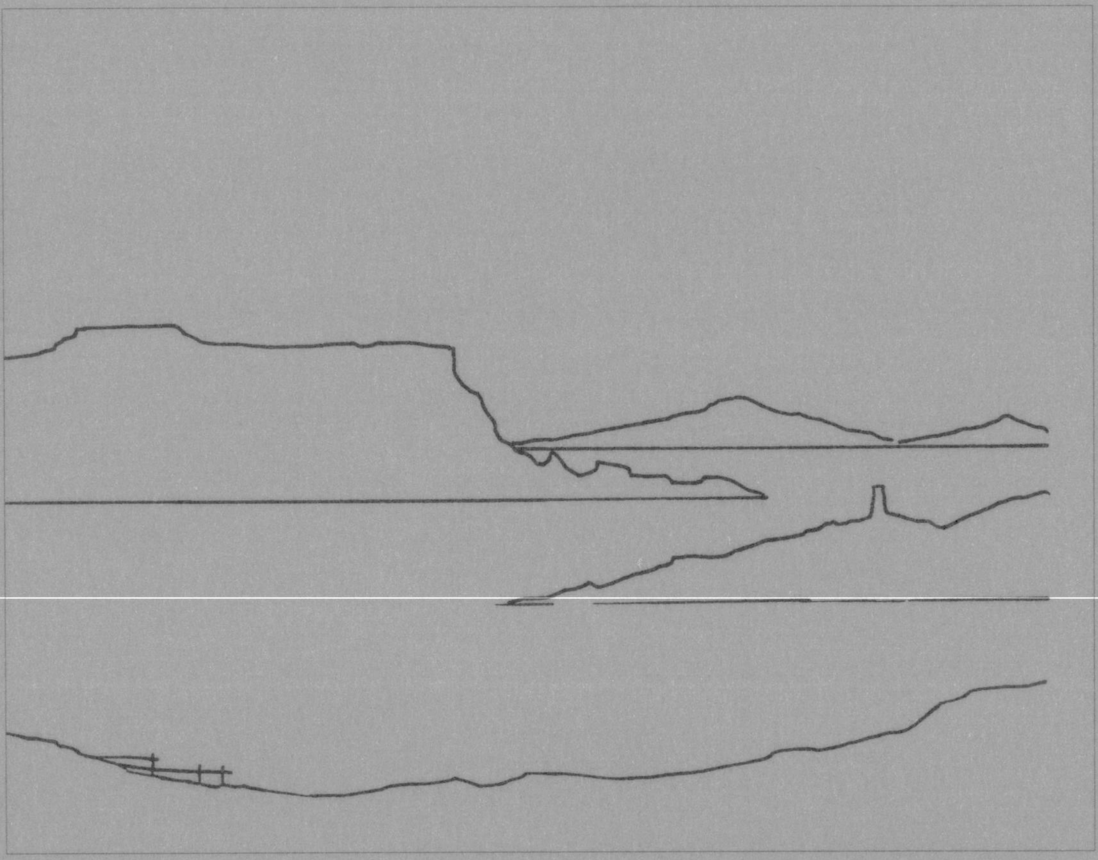

5

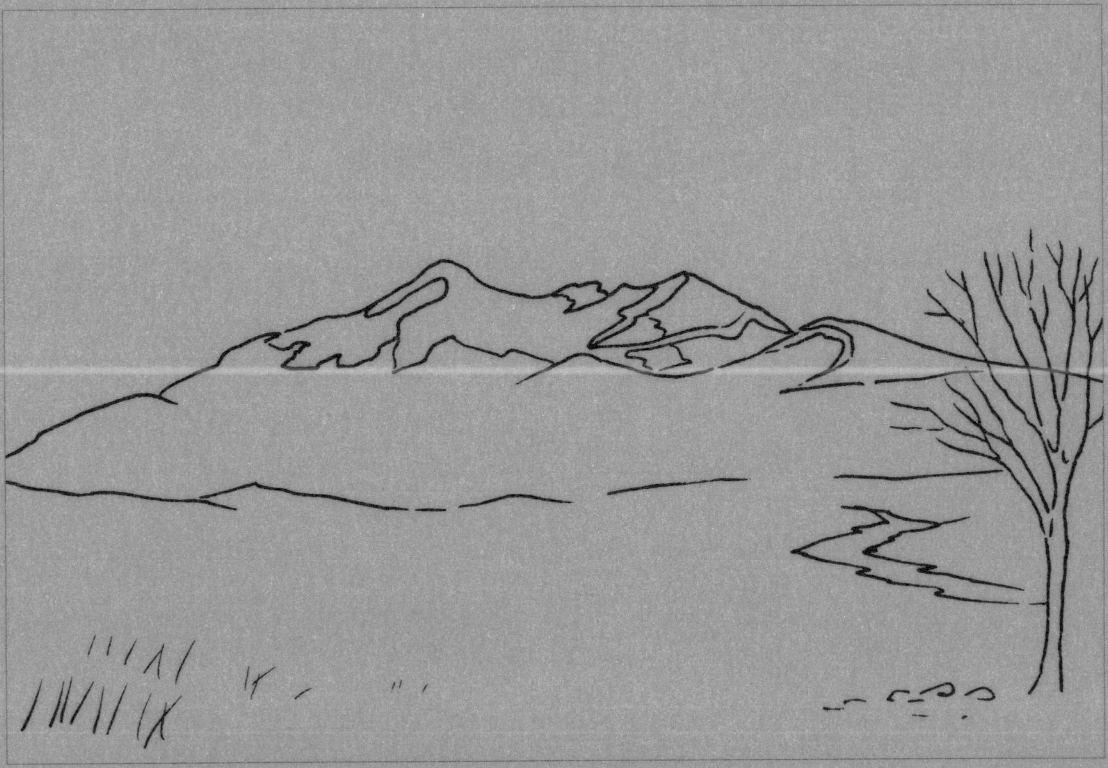

6

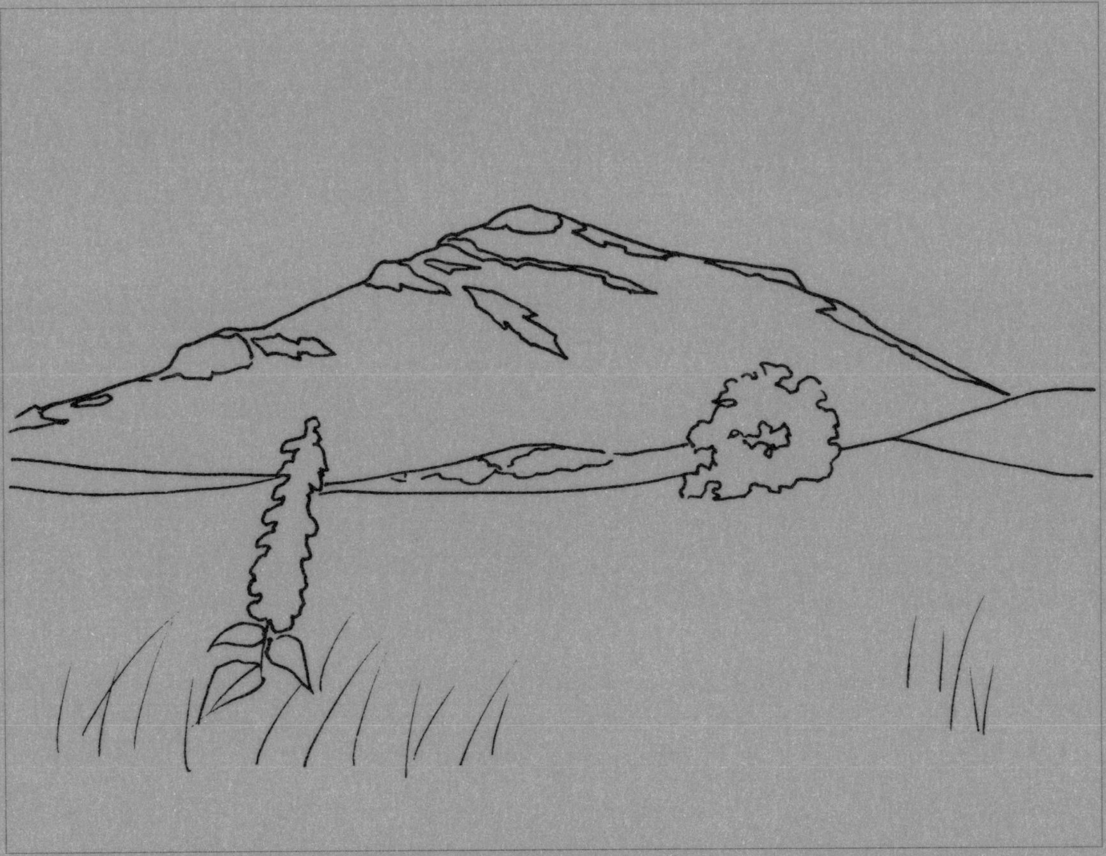

5

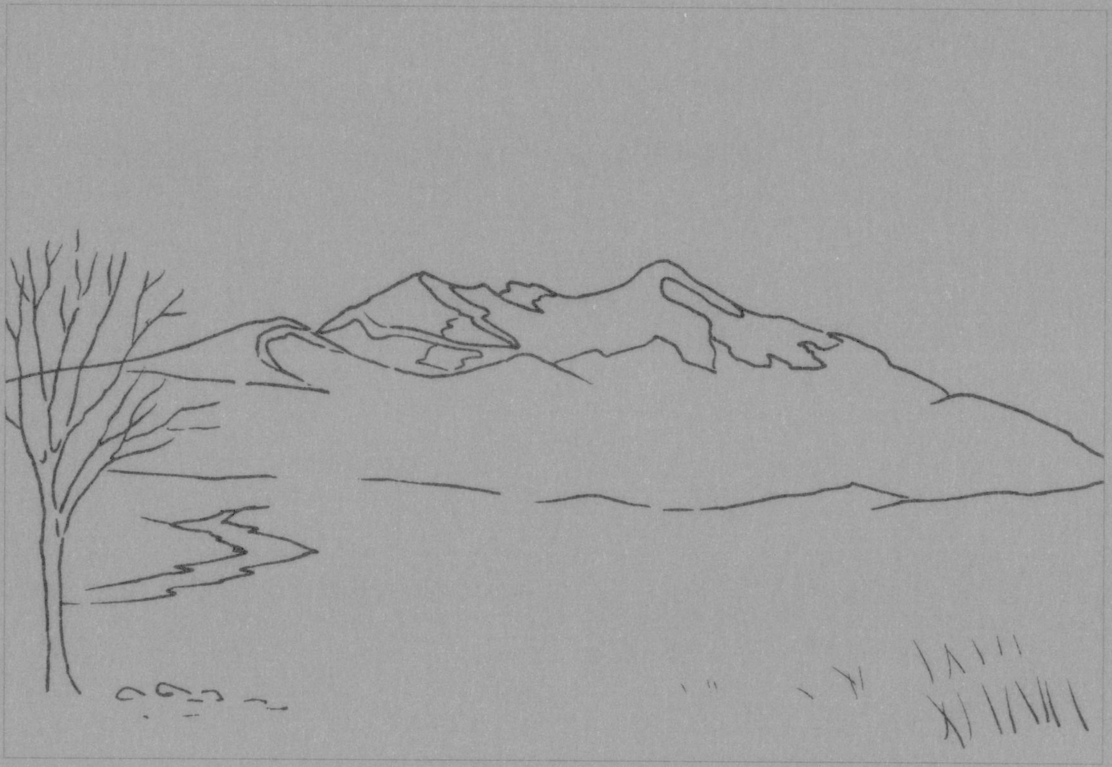

6

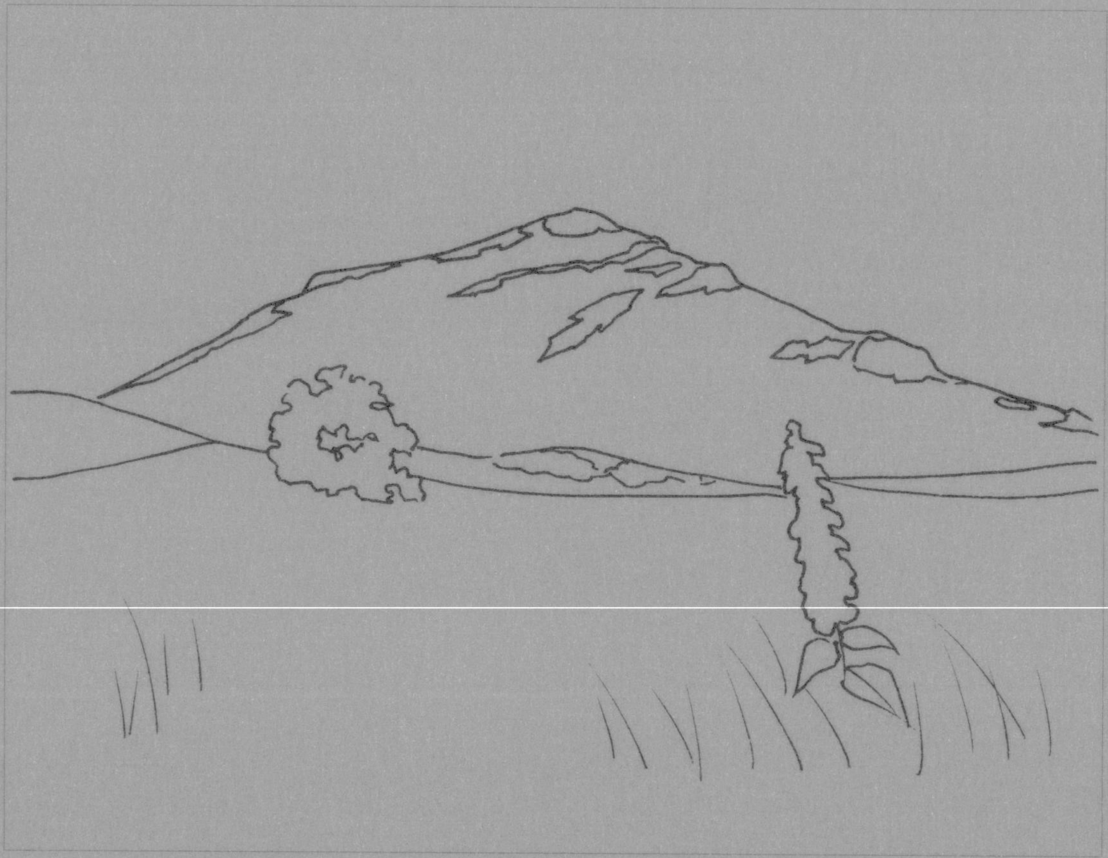

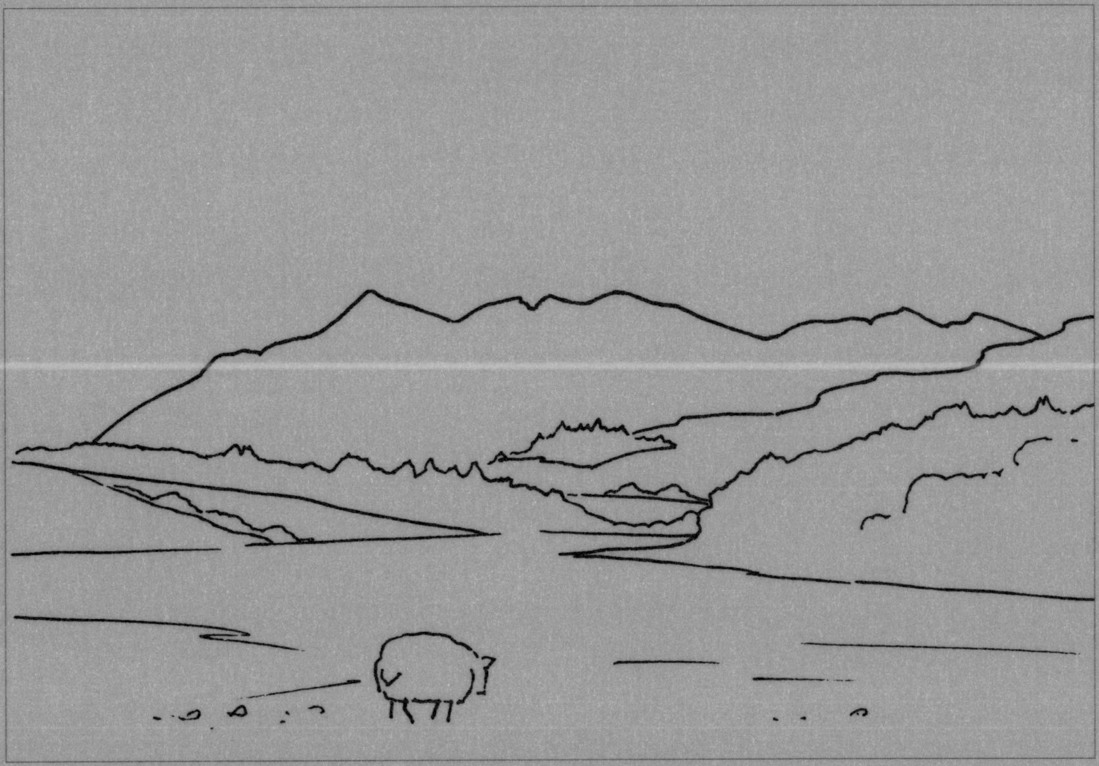

7

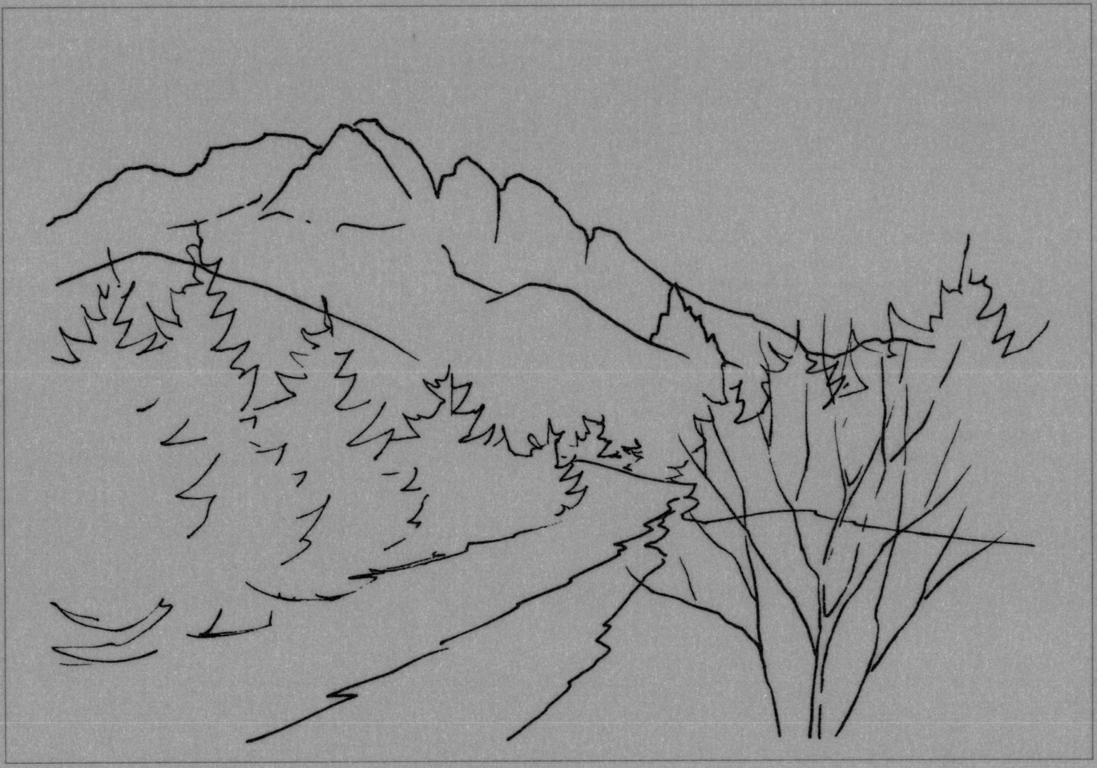

8

7

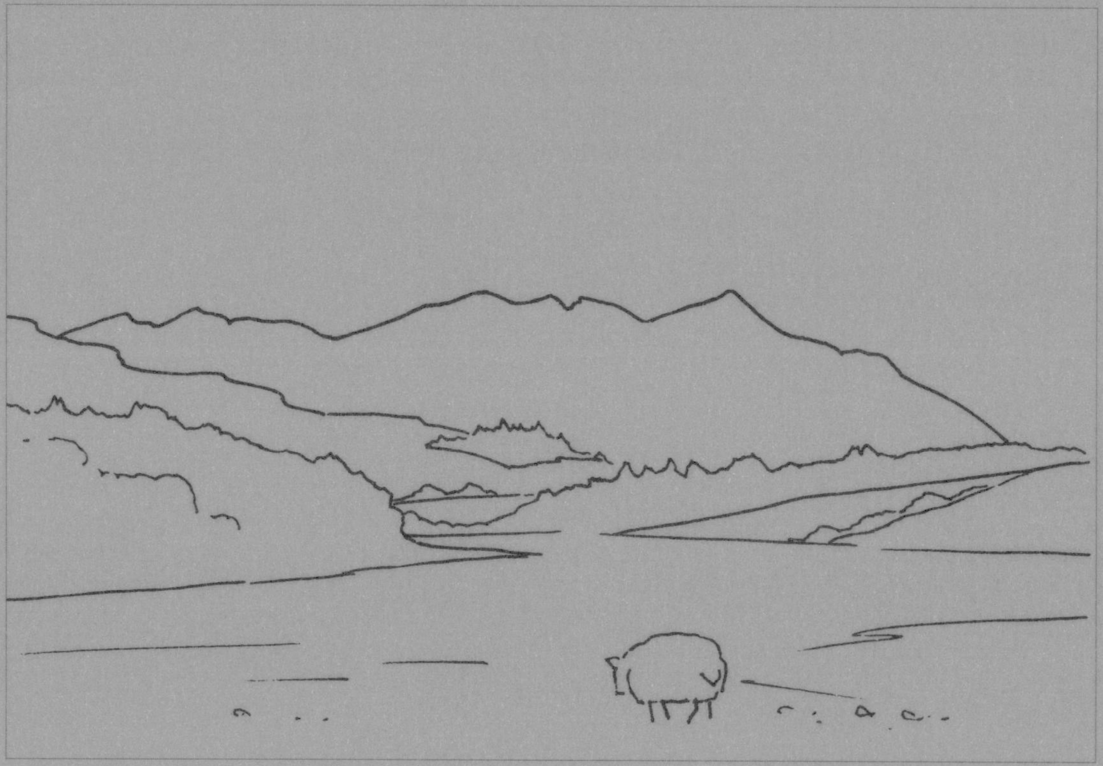

8

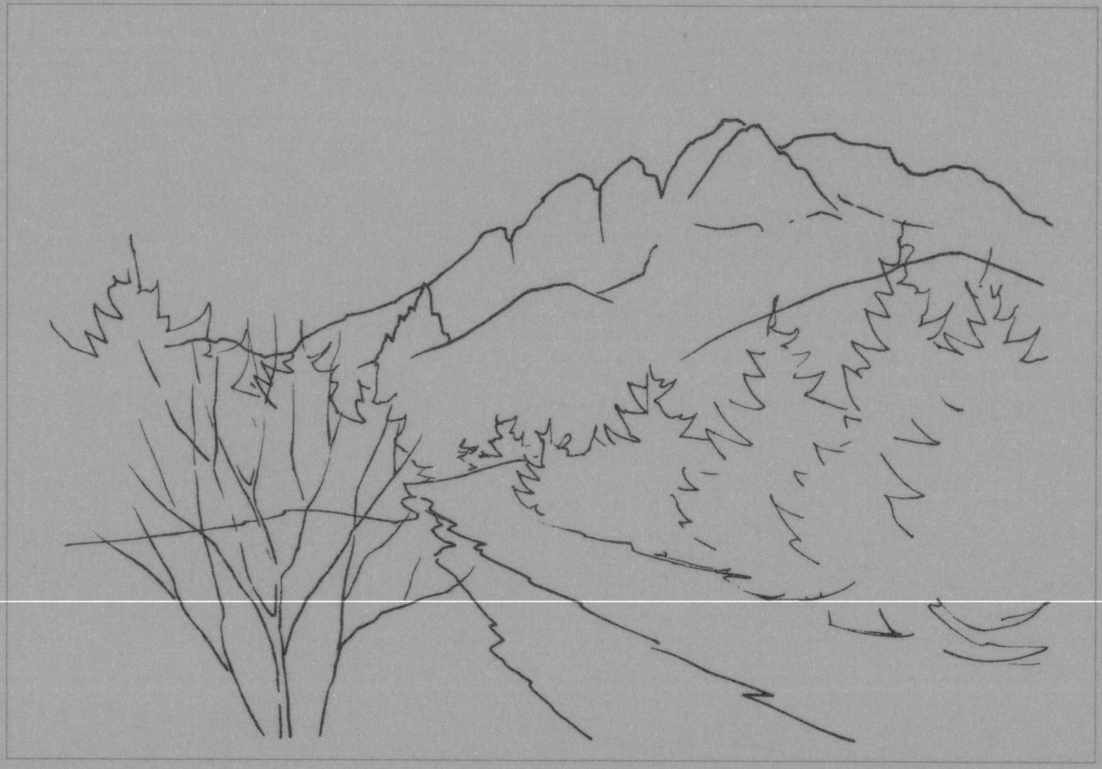

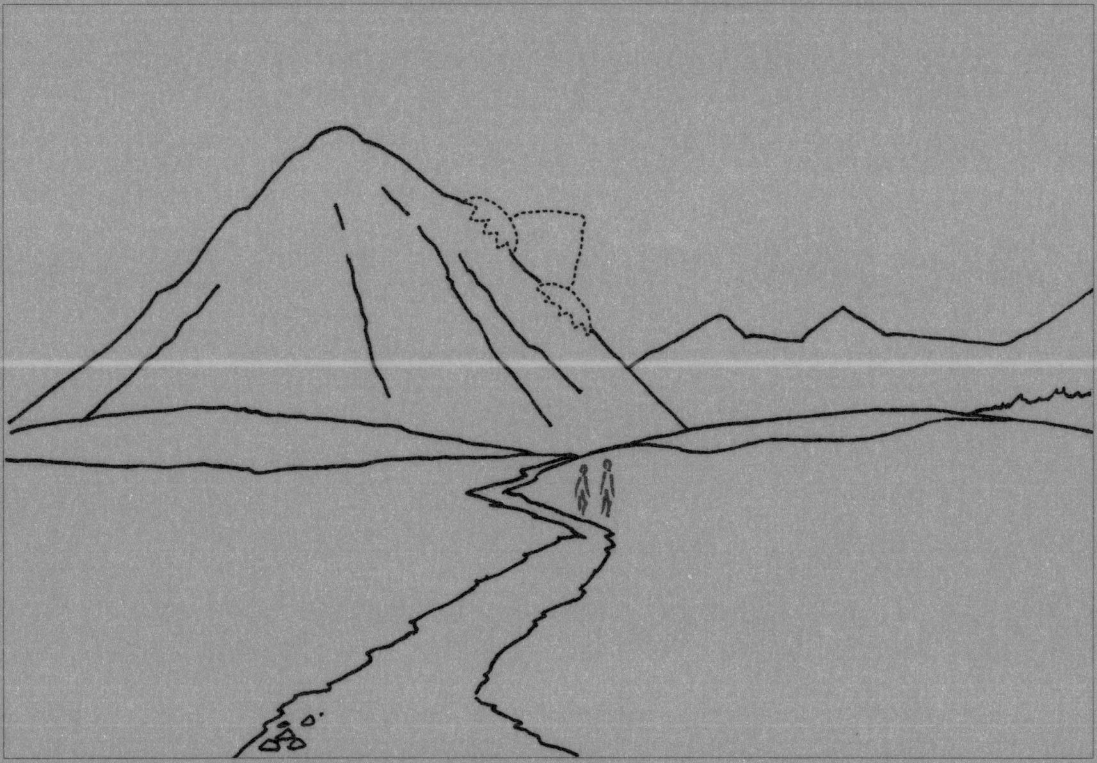

9

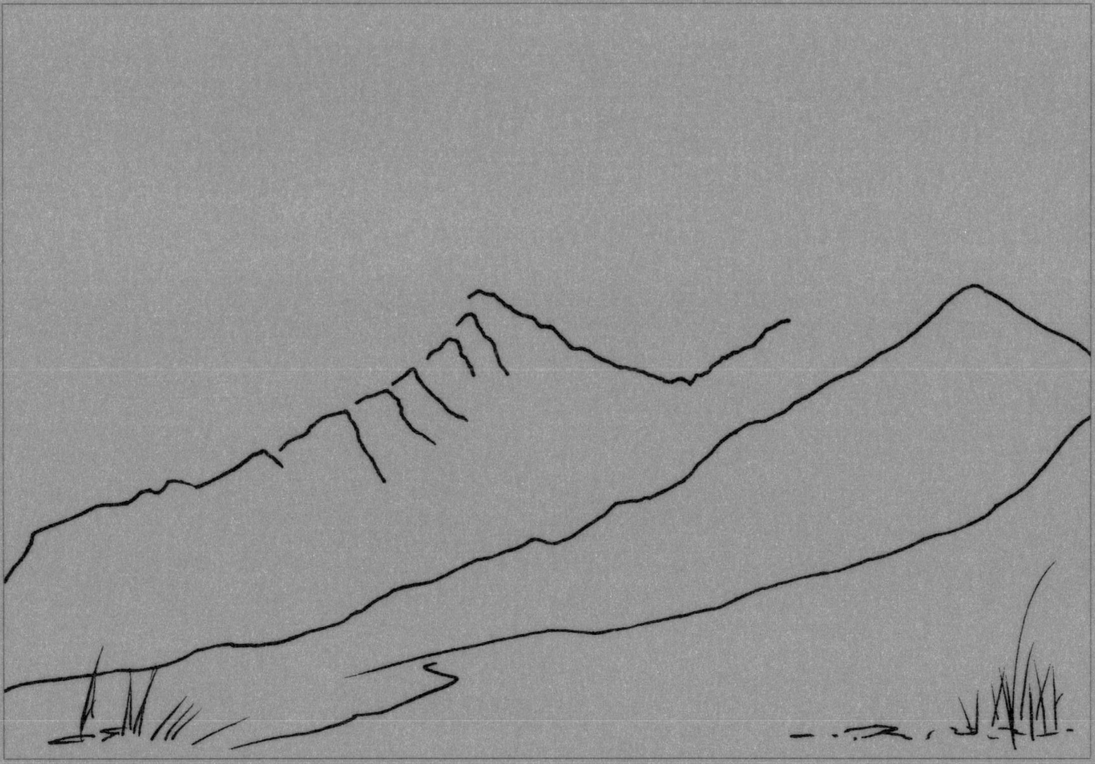

10

9

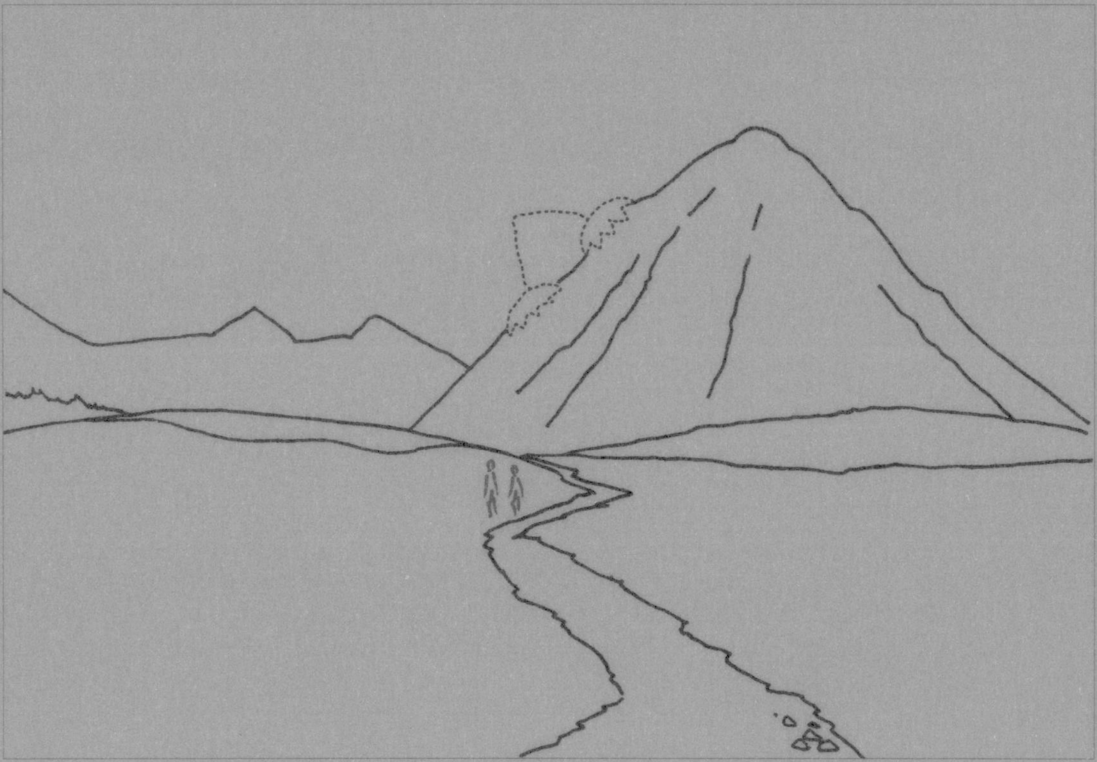

10

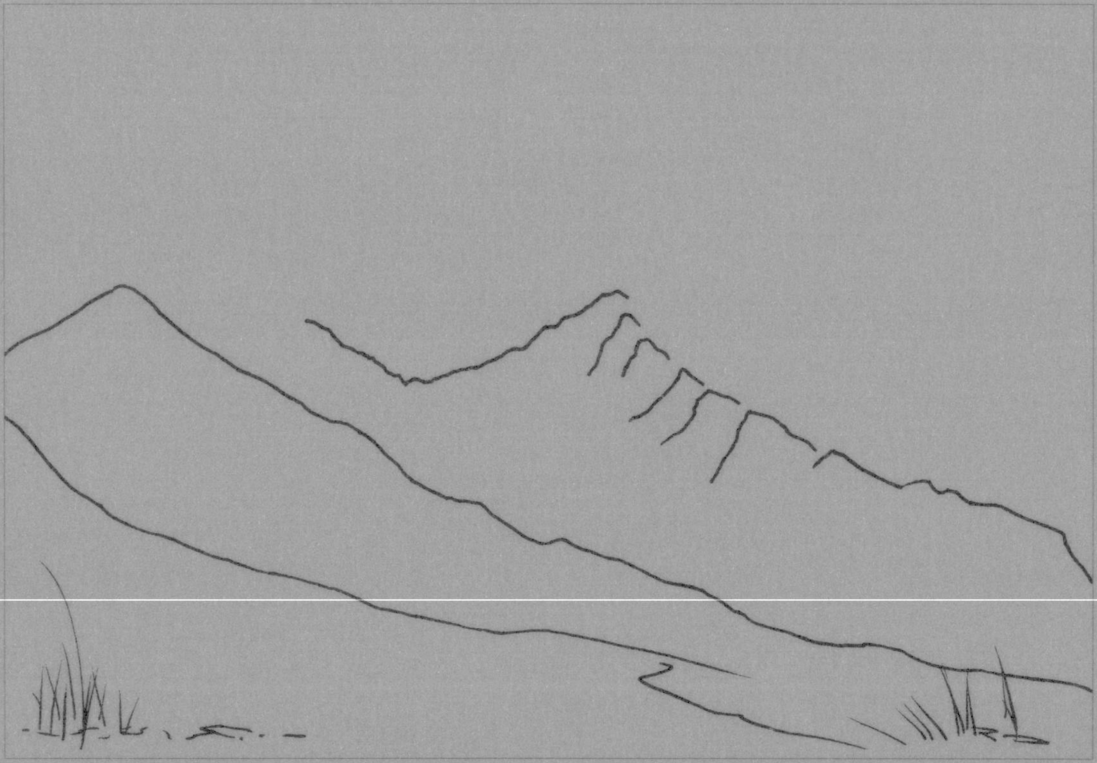

11

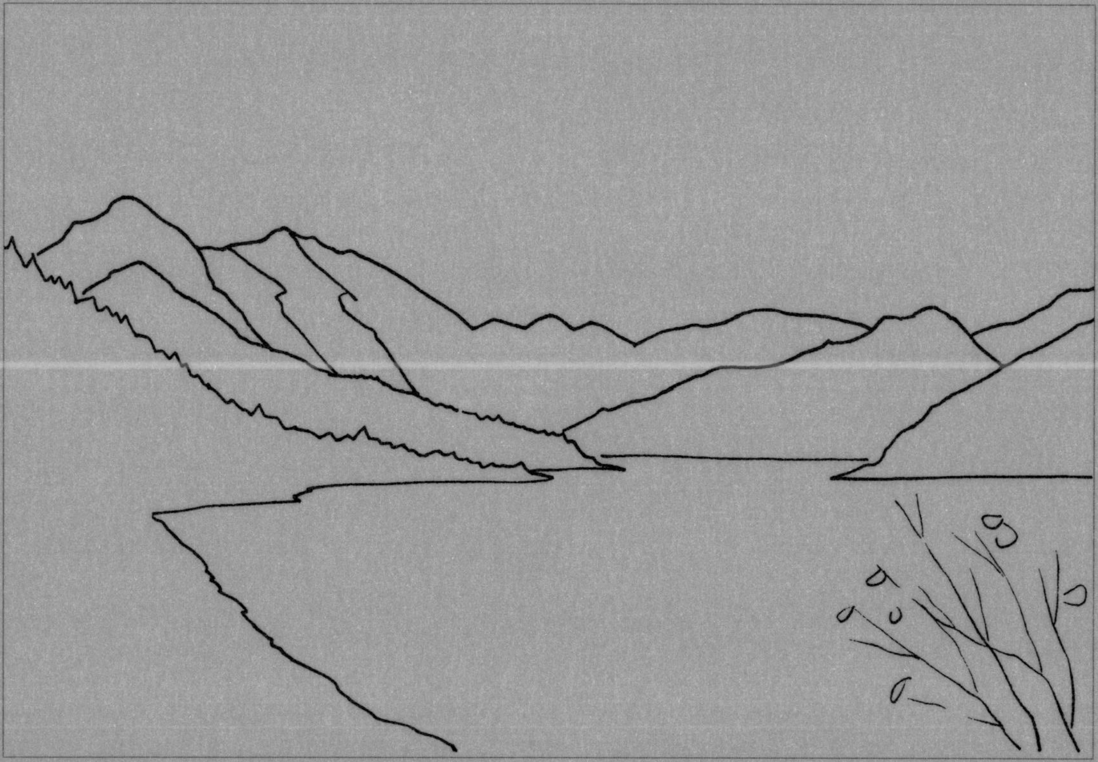

12

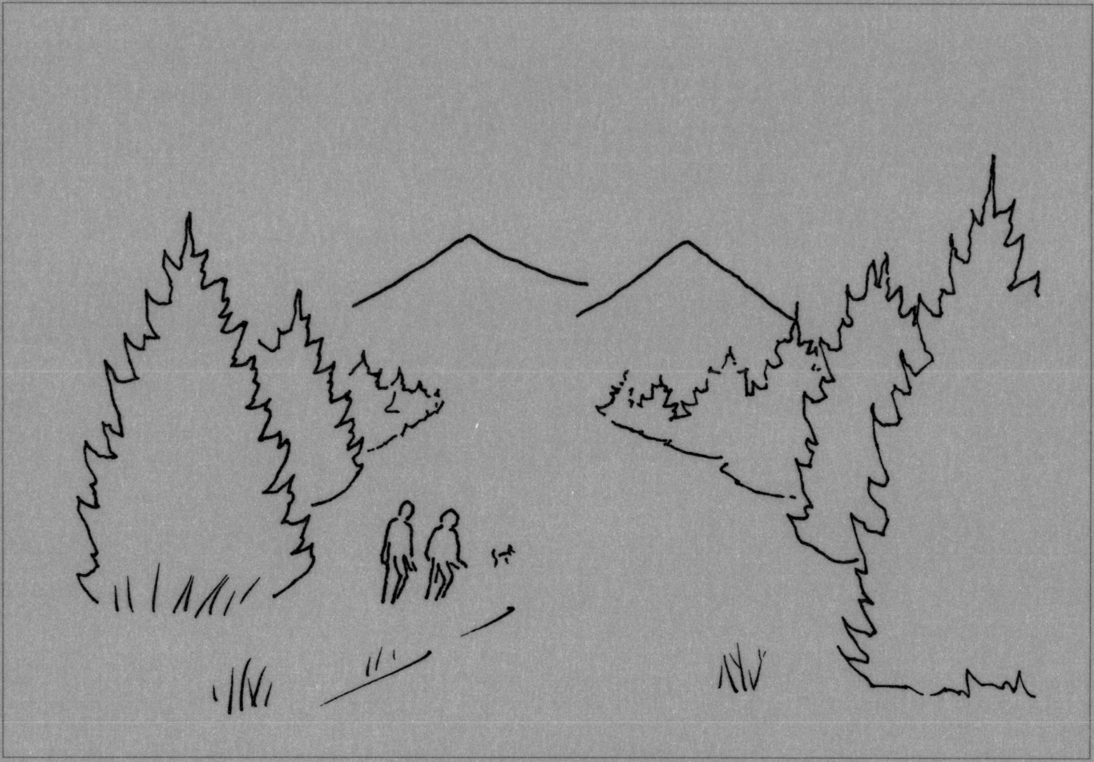

11

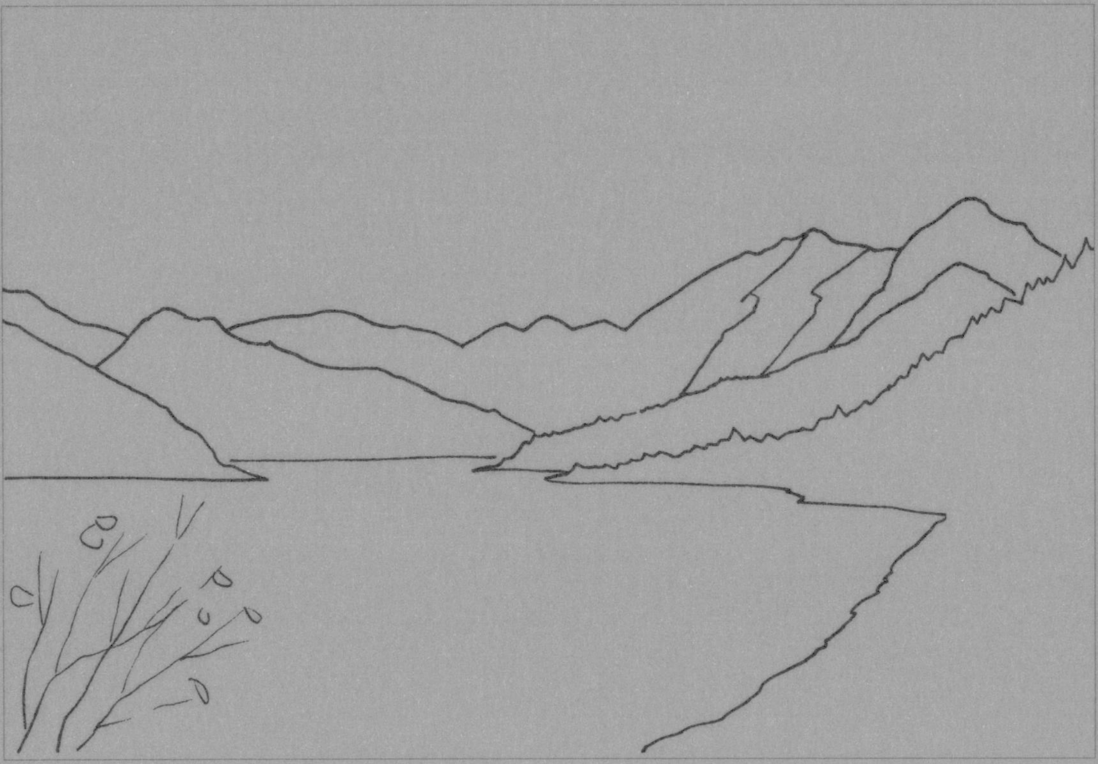

12

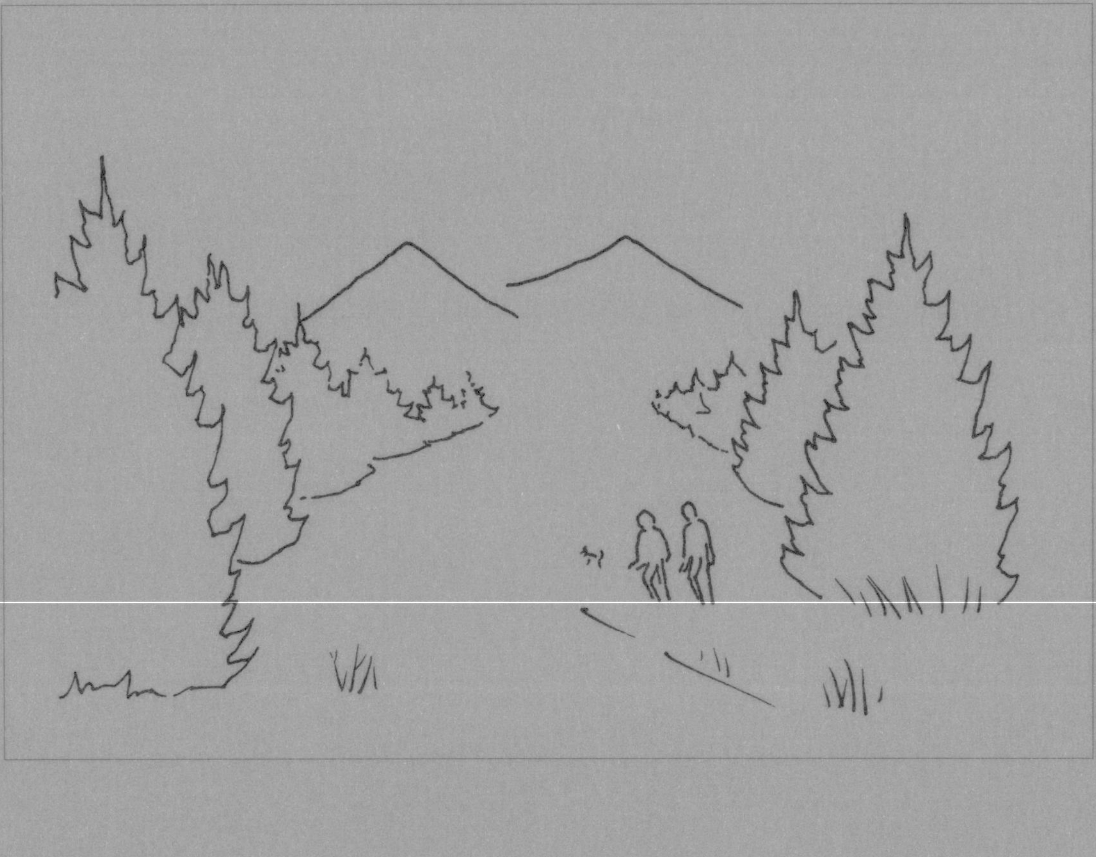

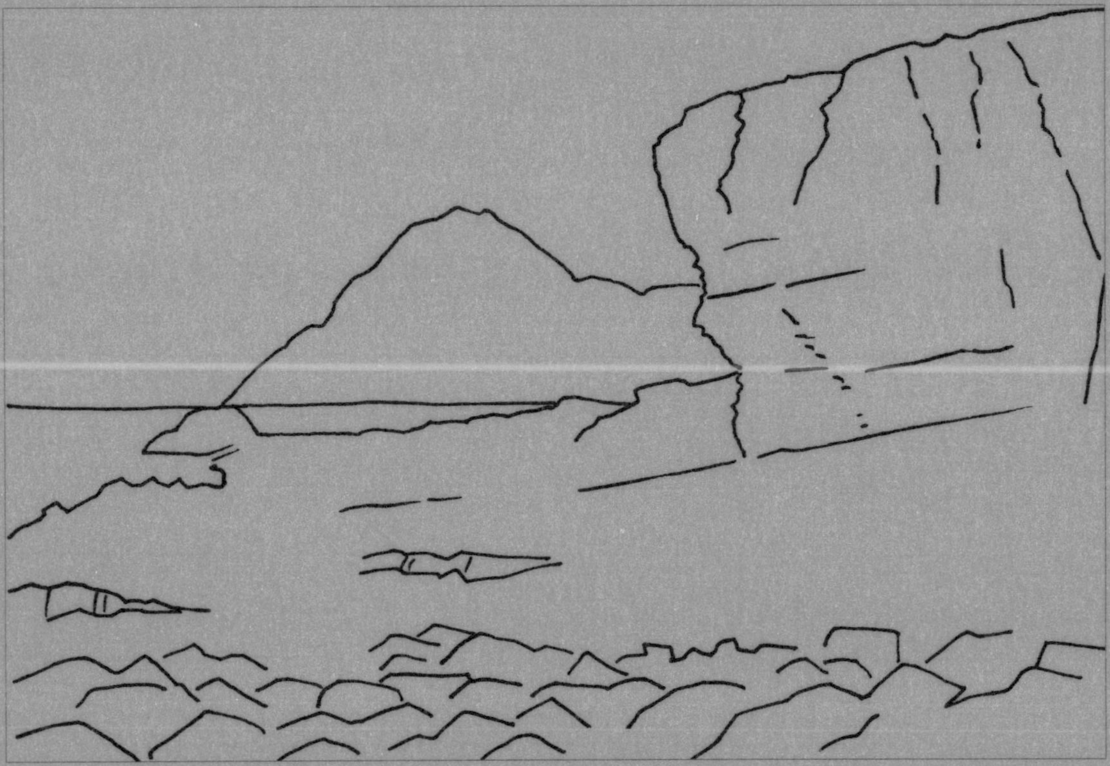

13

14

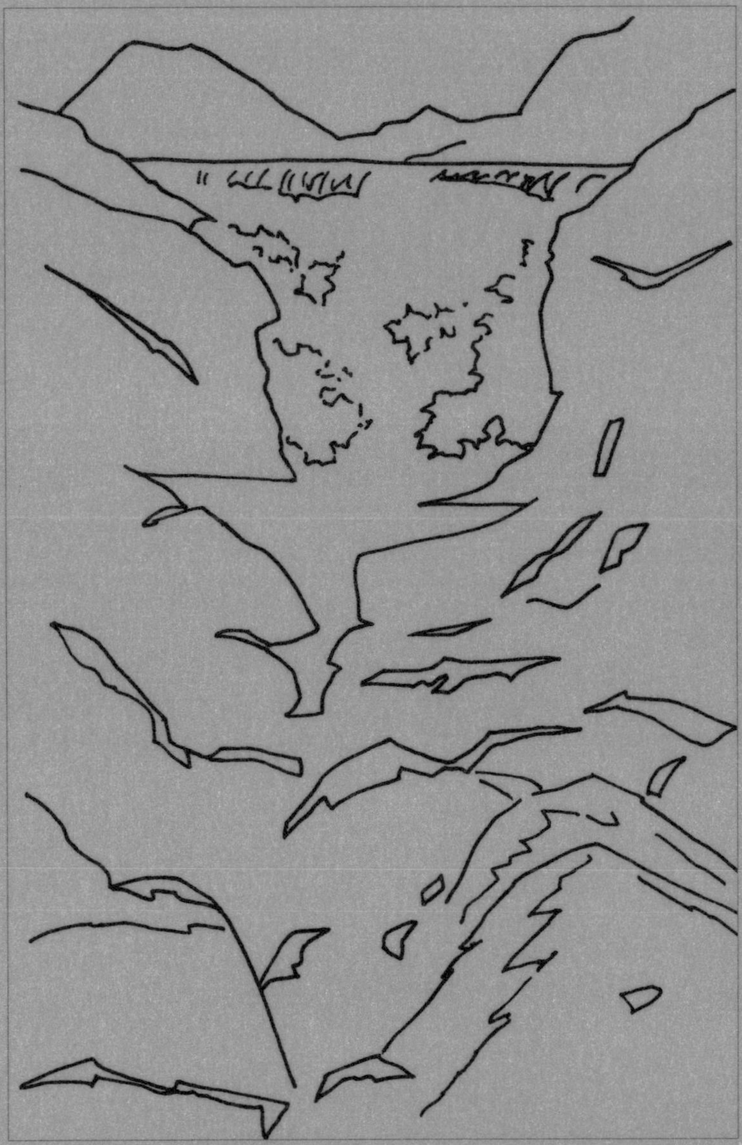

13

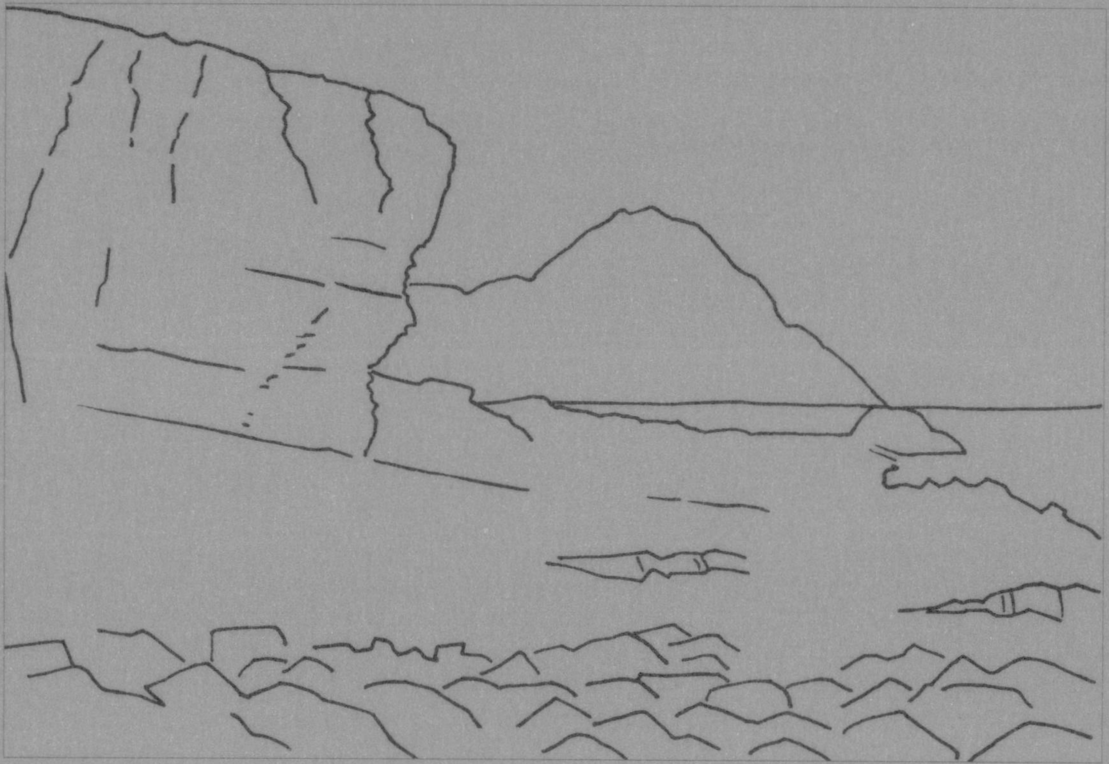

14

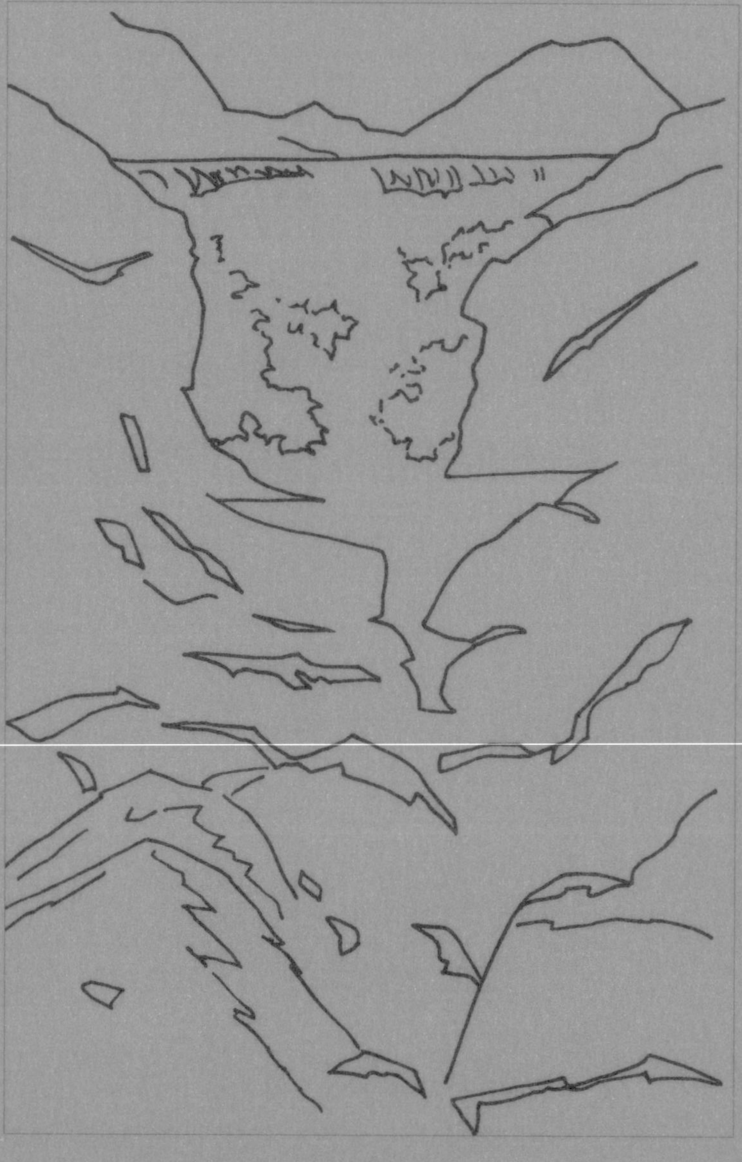

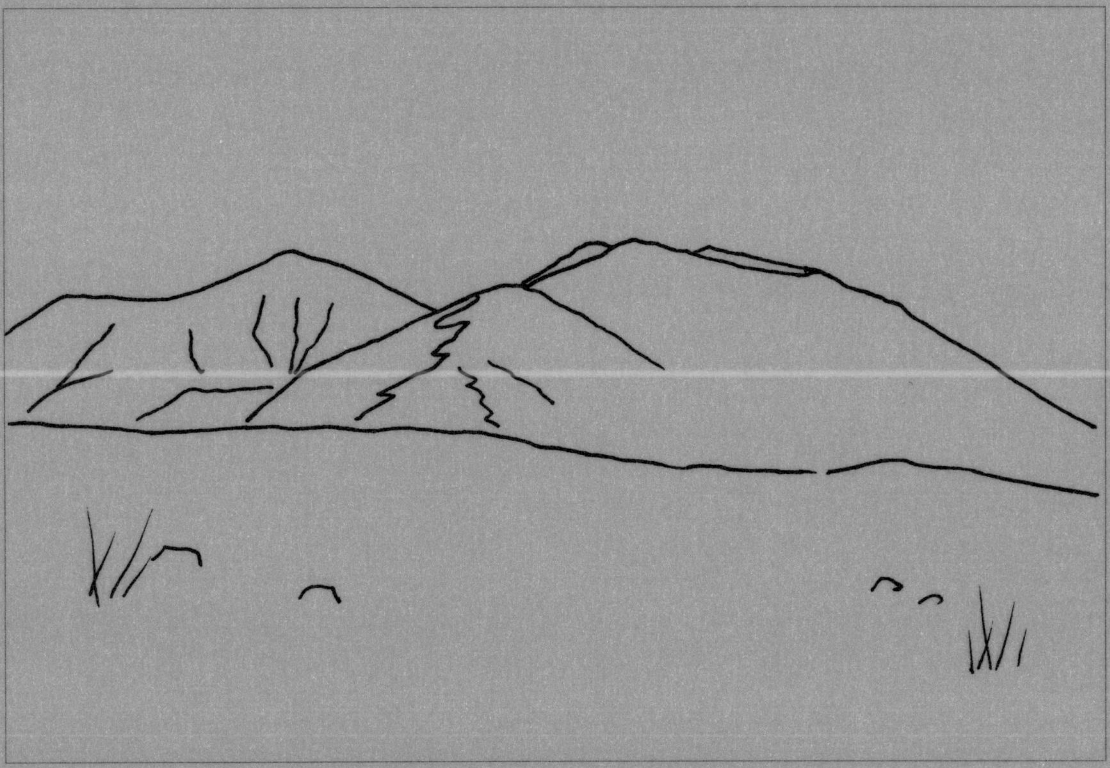

15

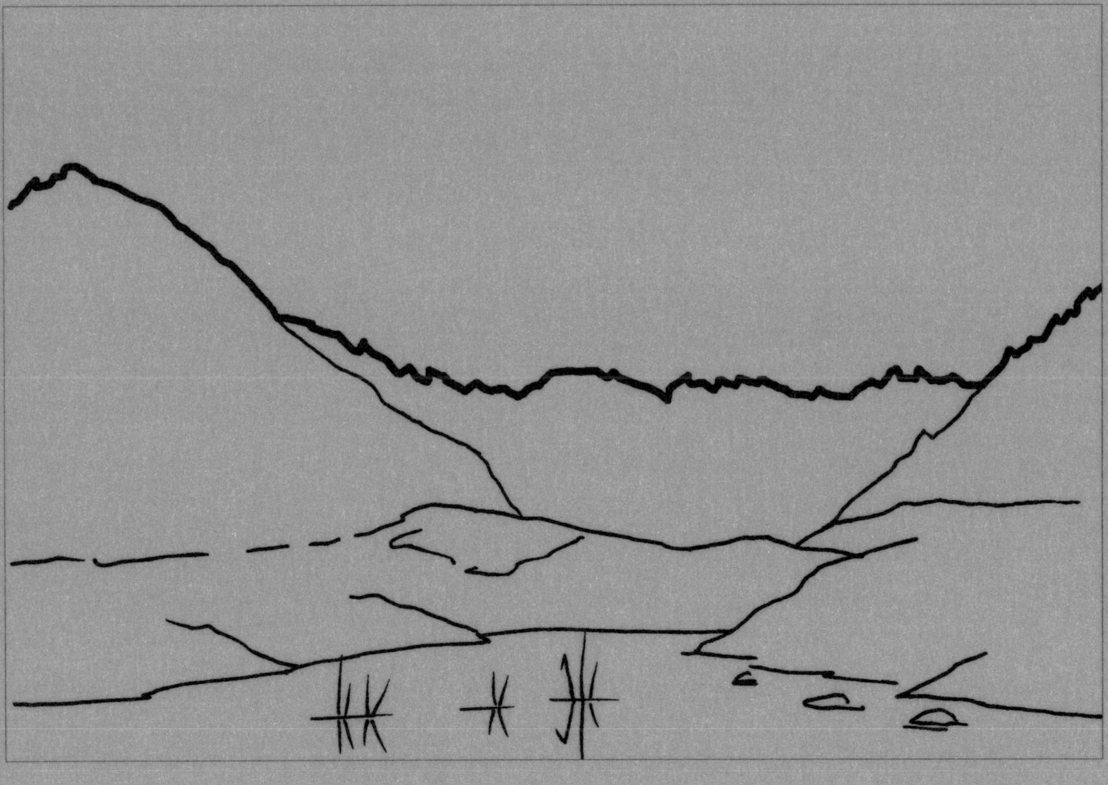

16

15

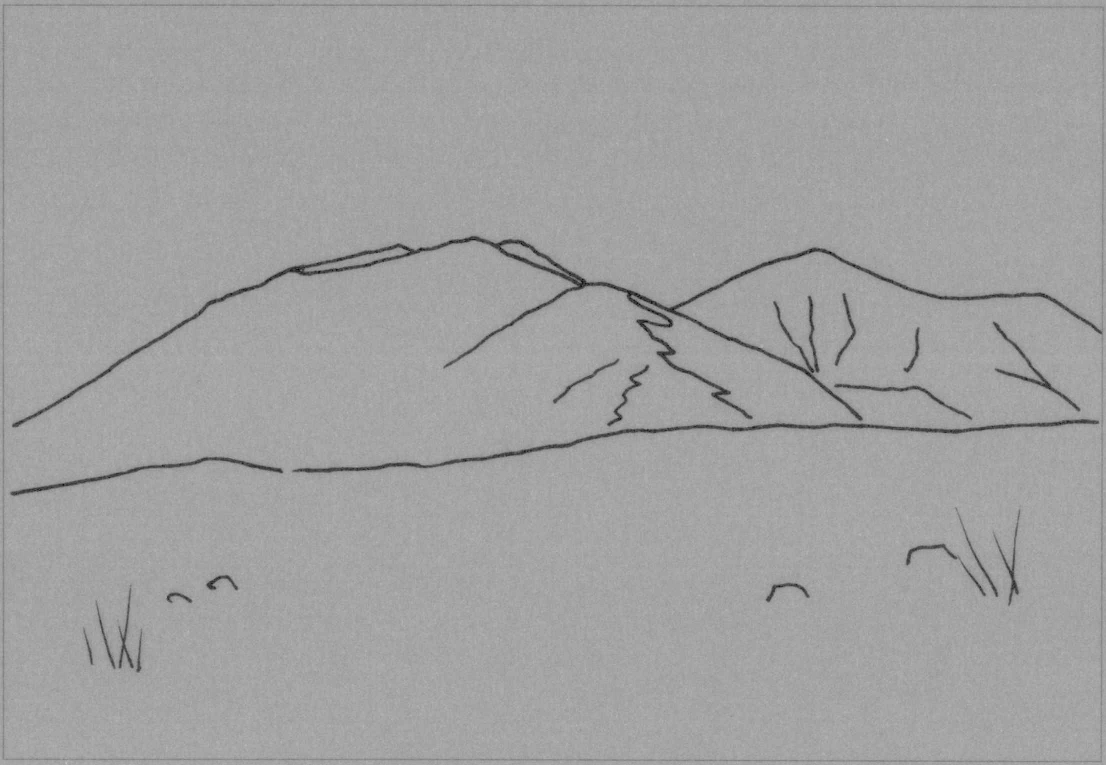

16

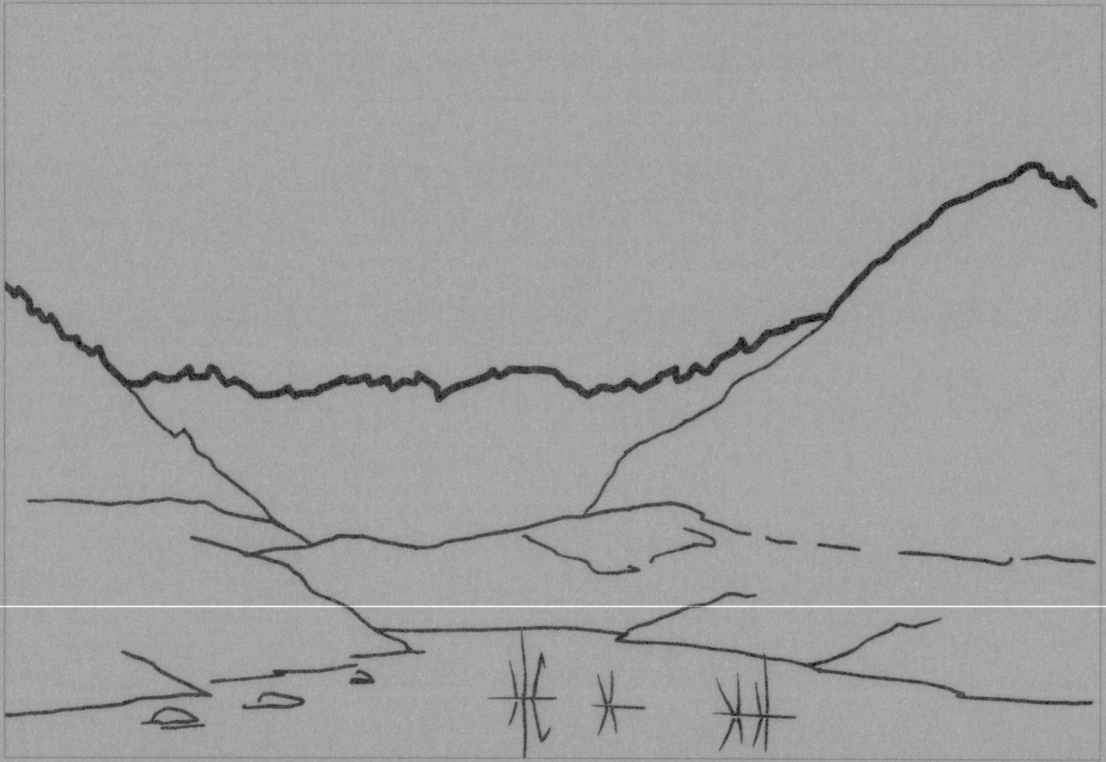

17

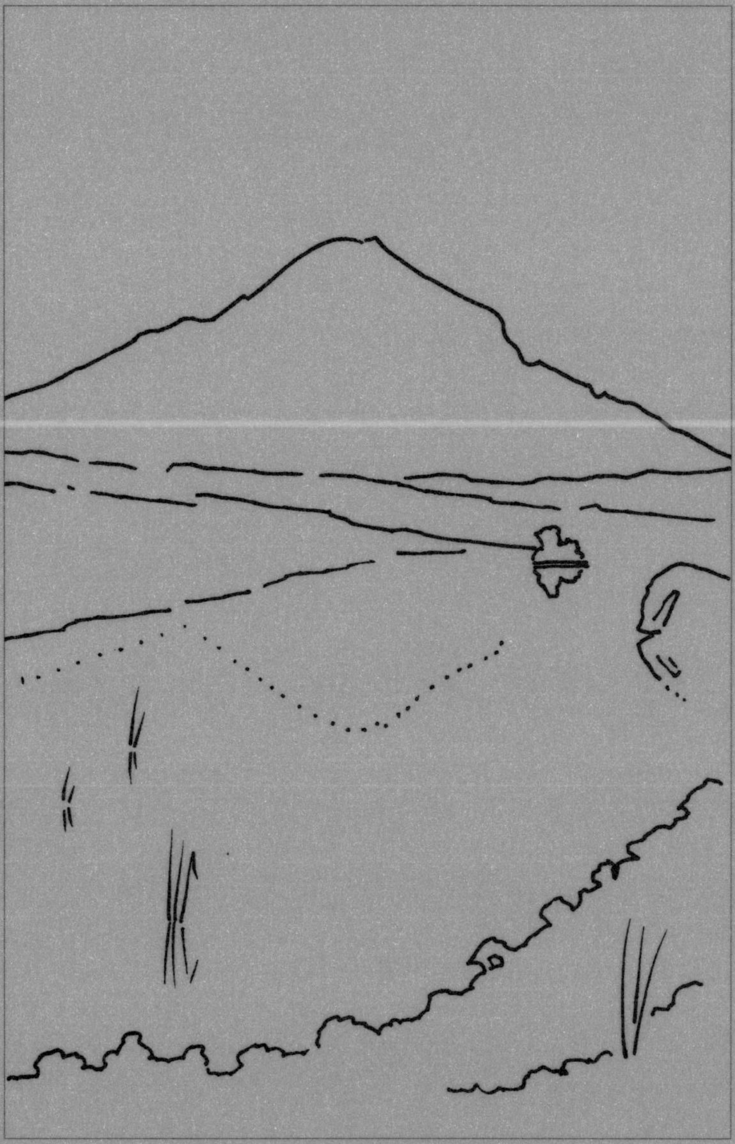

18

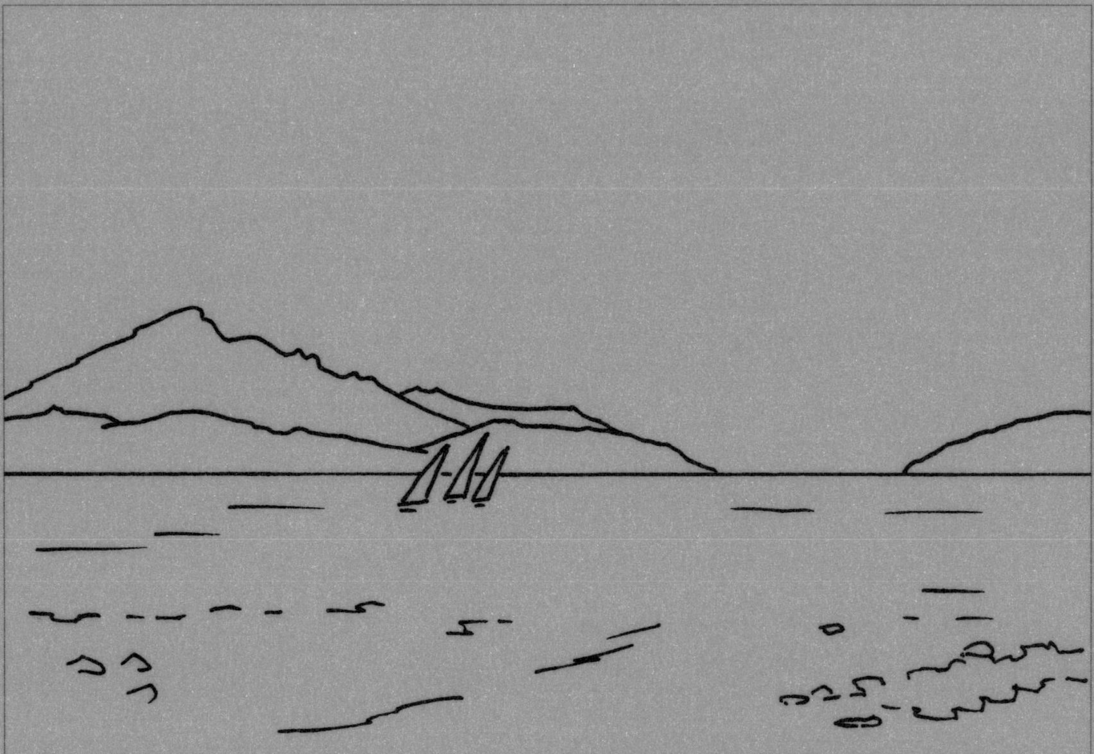

17

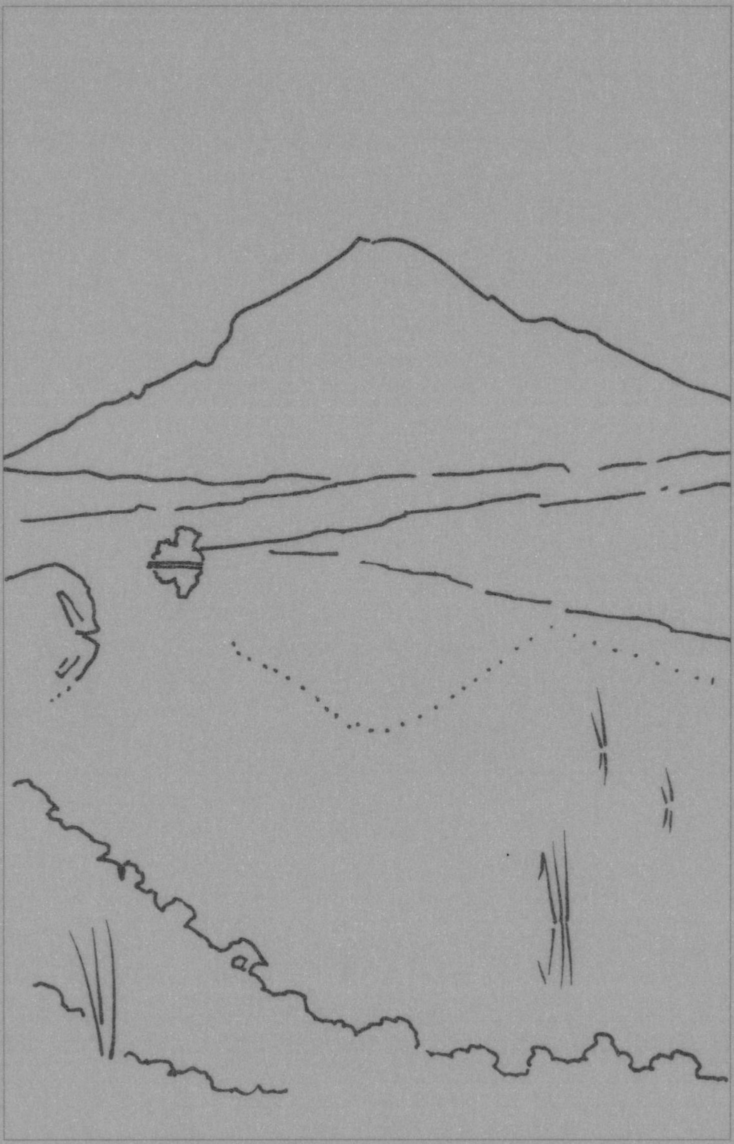

18

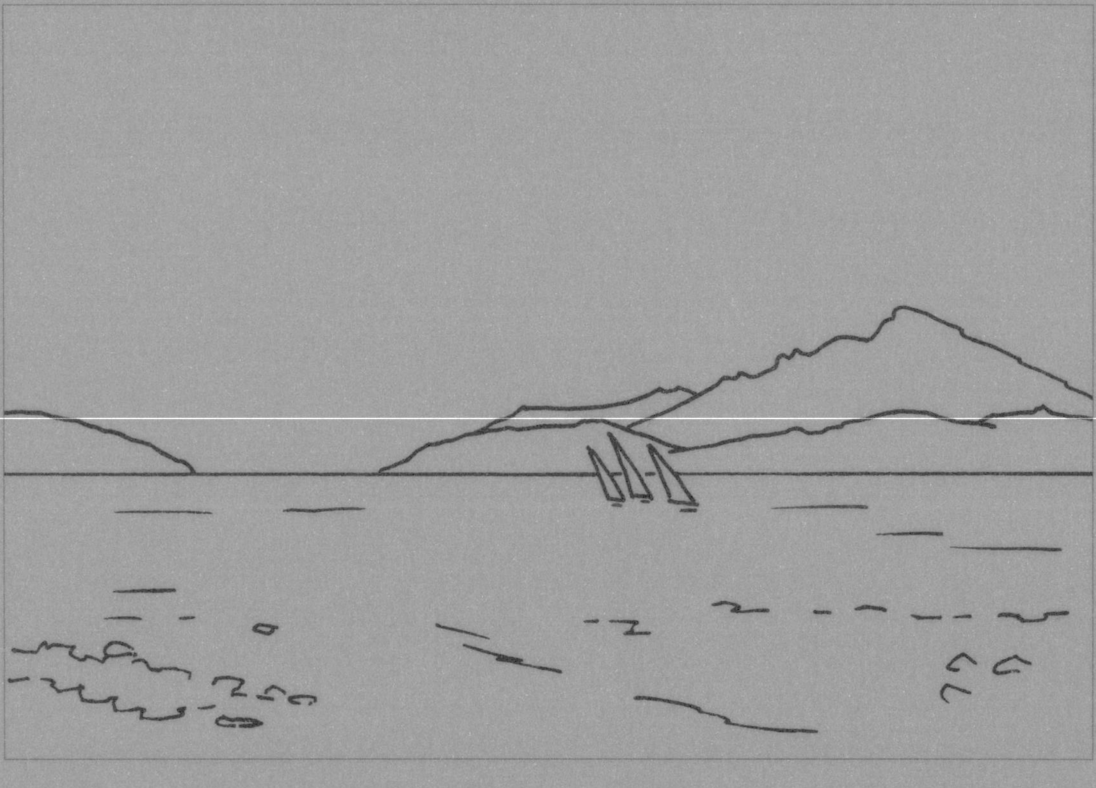

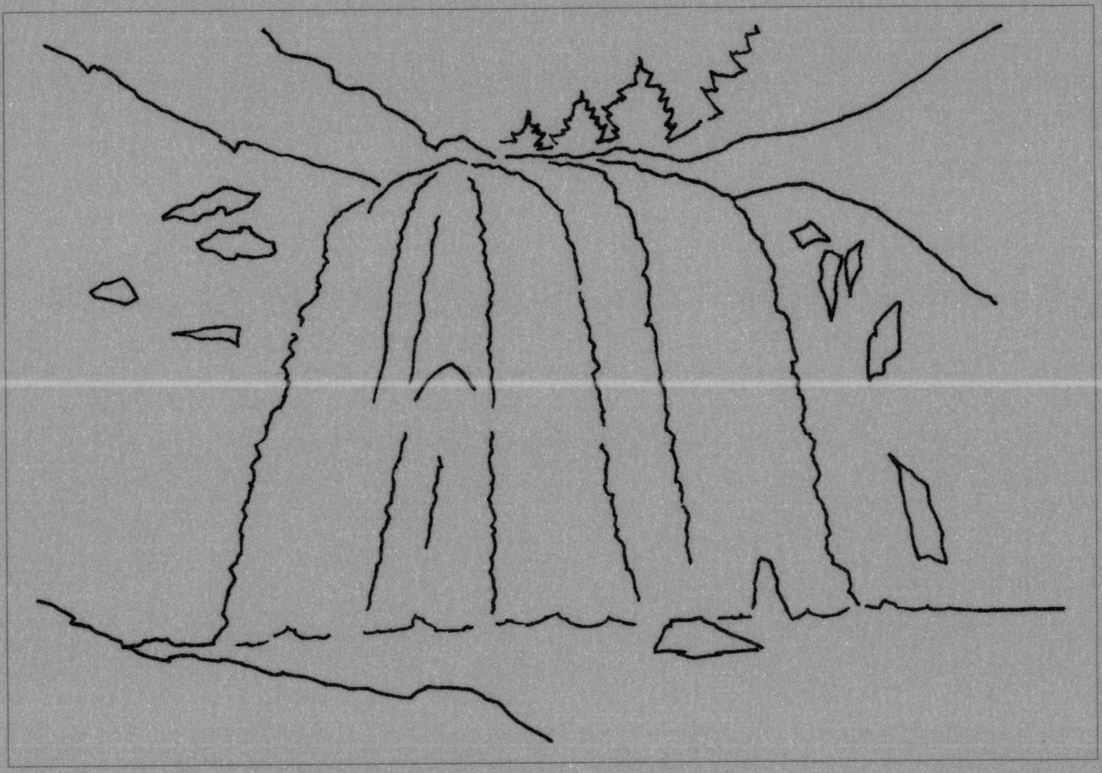

19

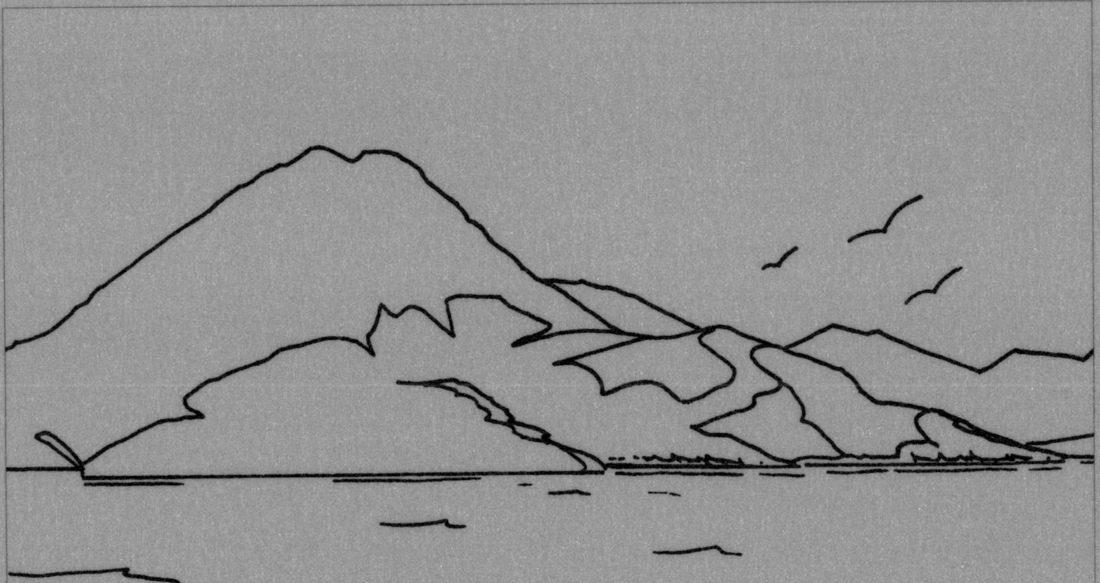

20

19

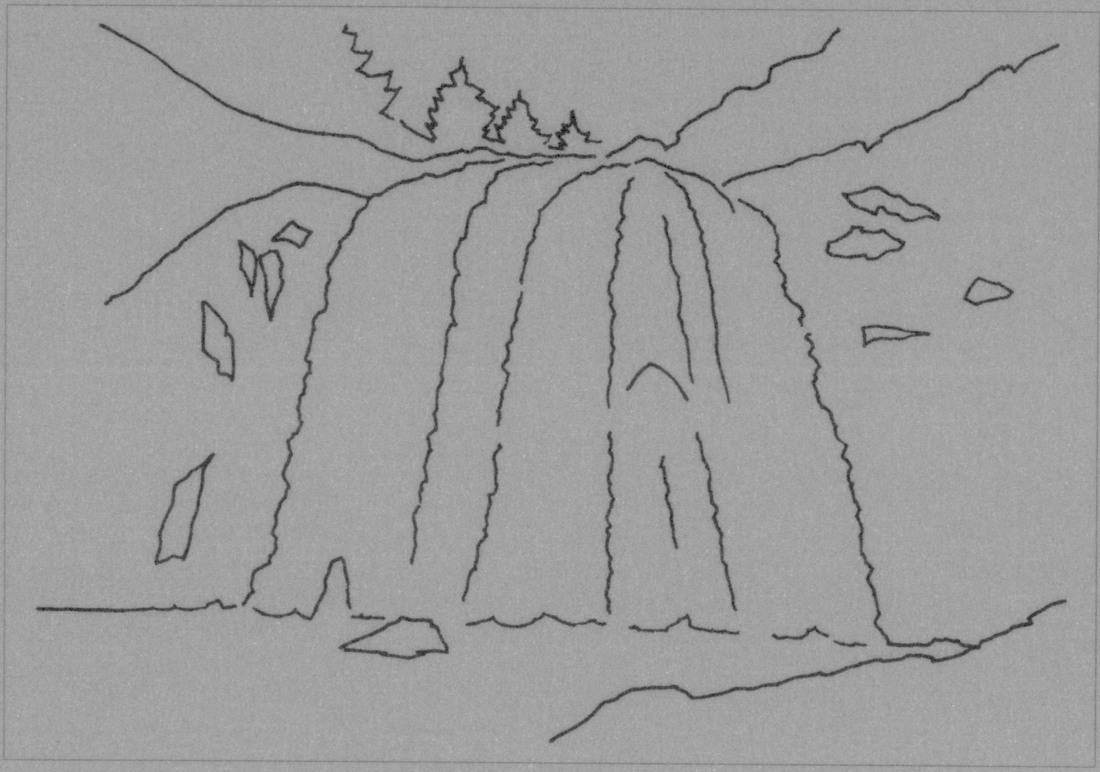

20

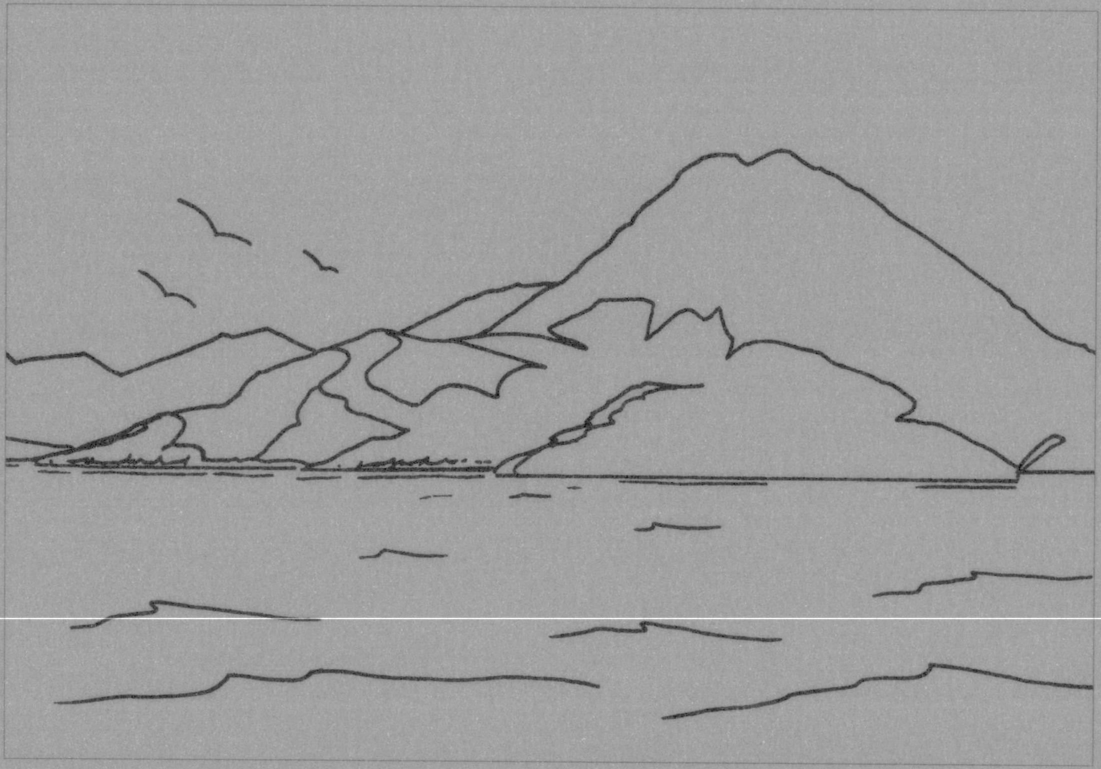

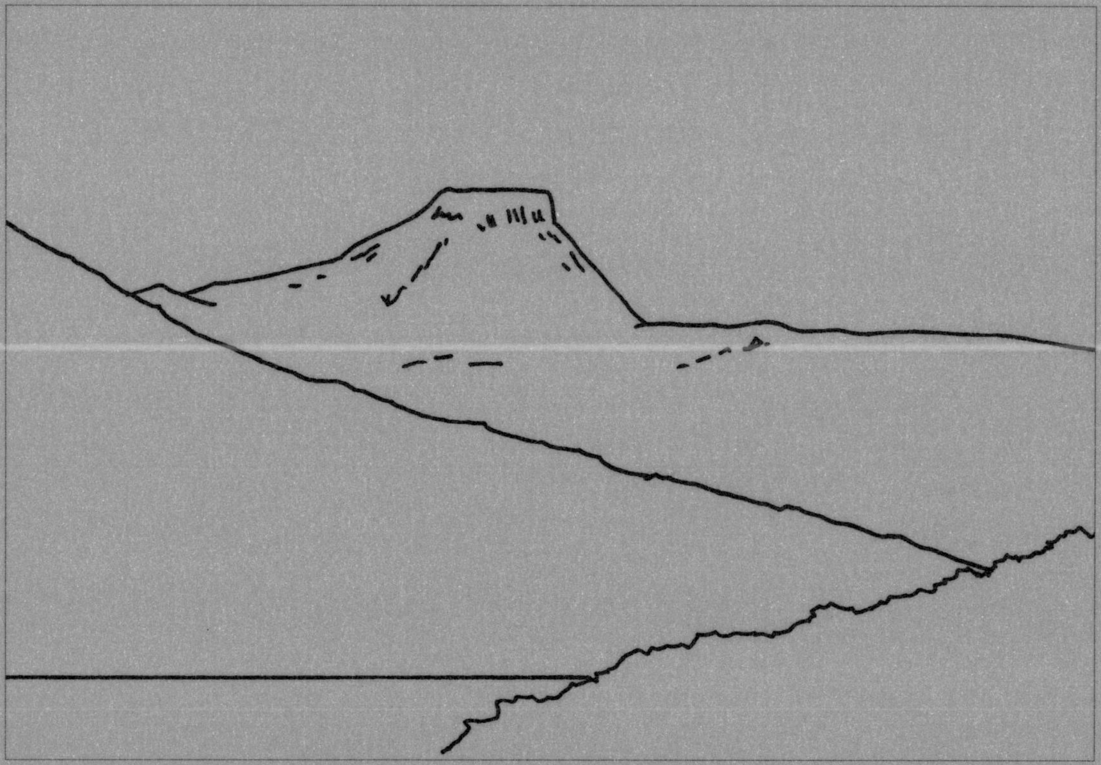

21

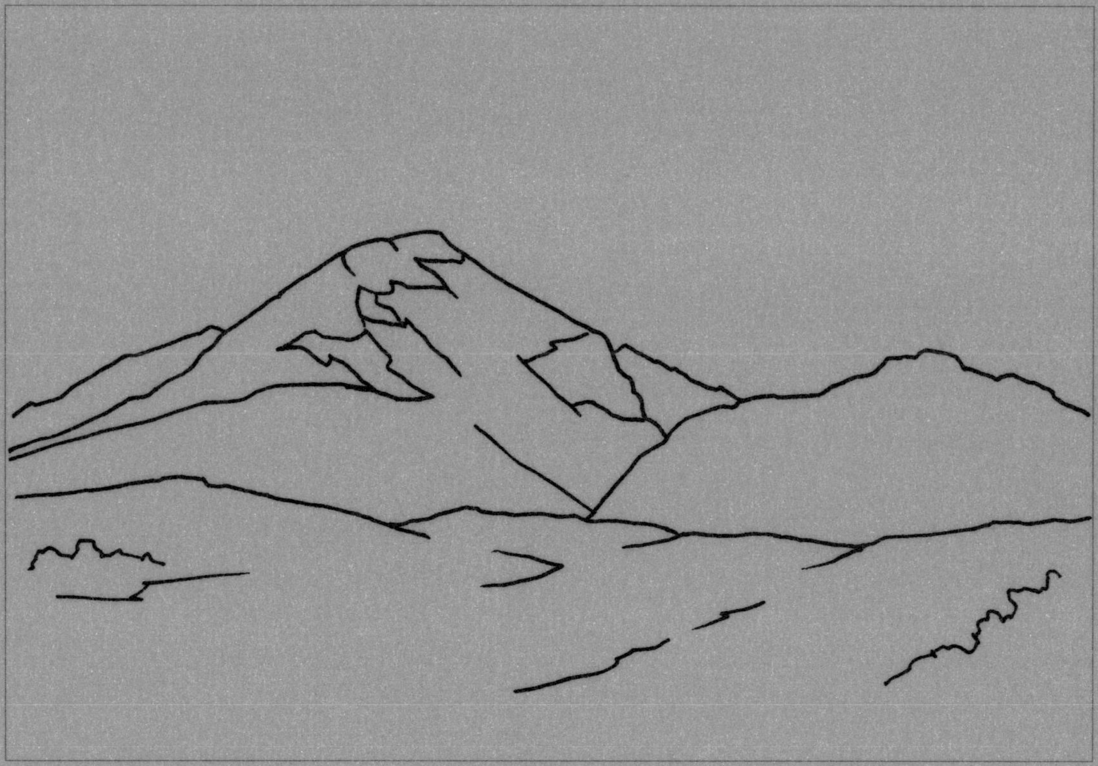

22

21

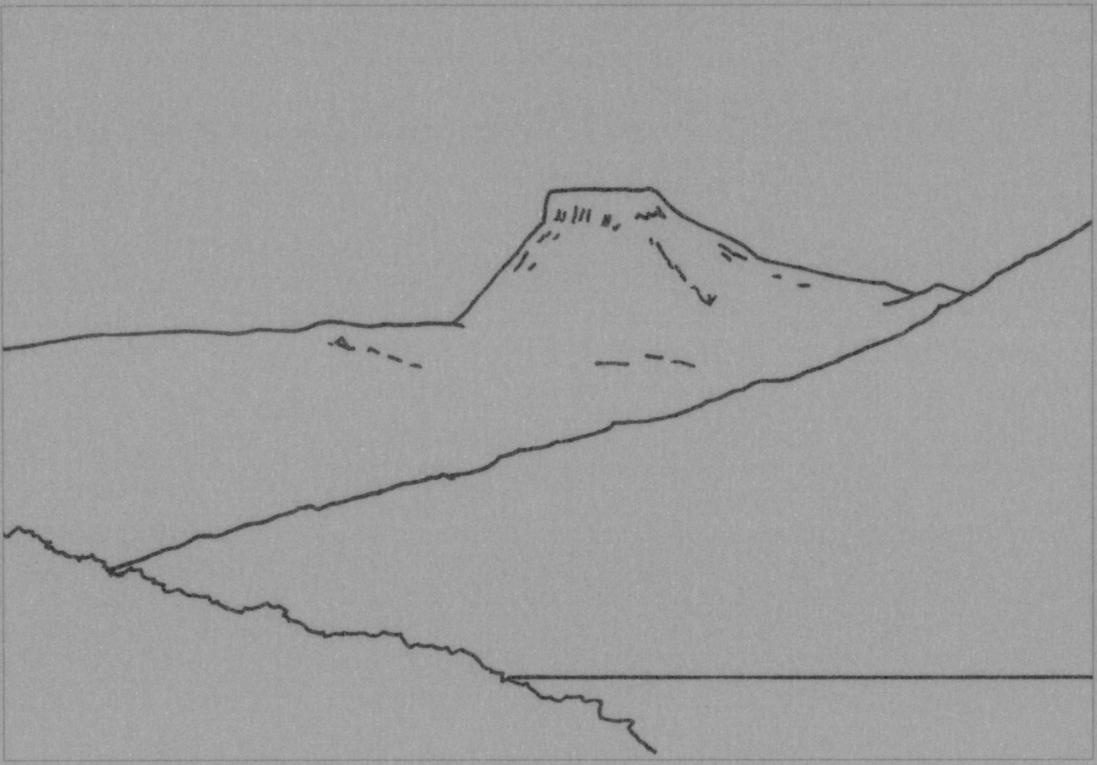

22

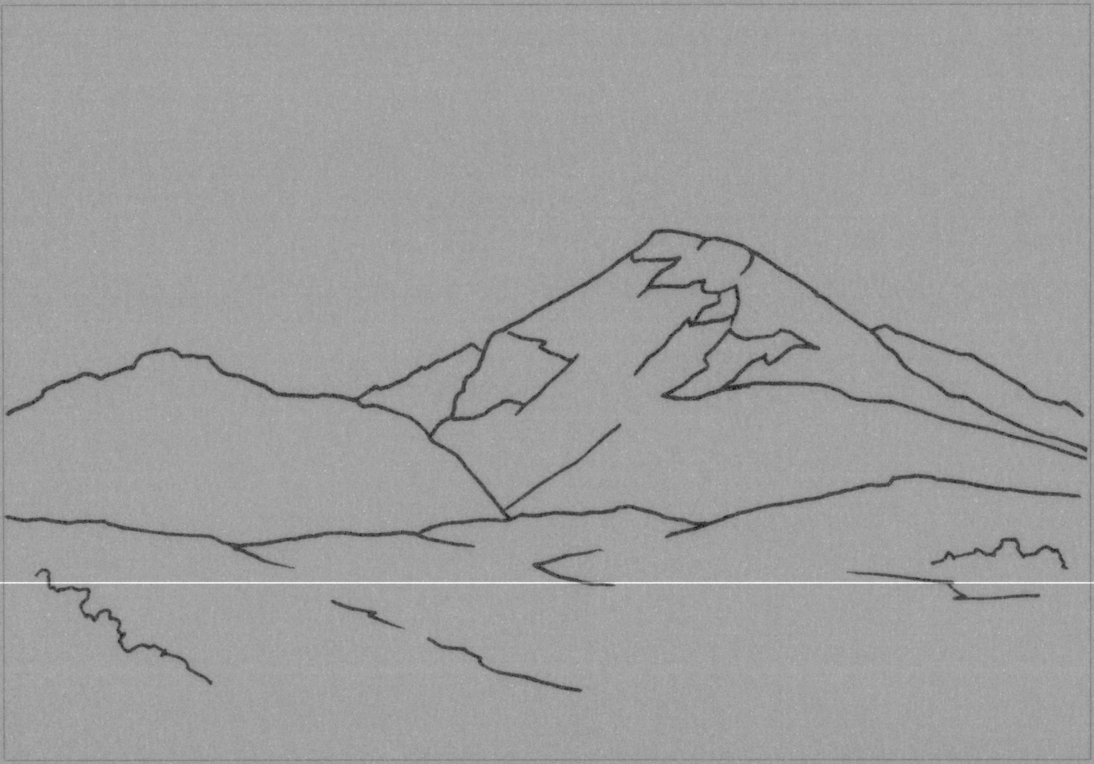

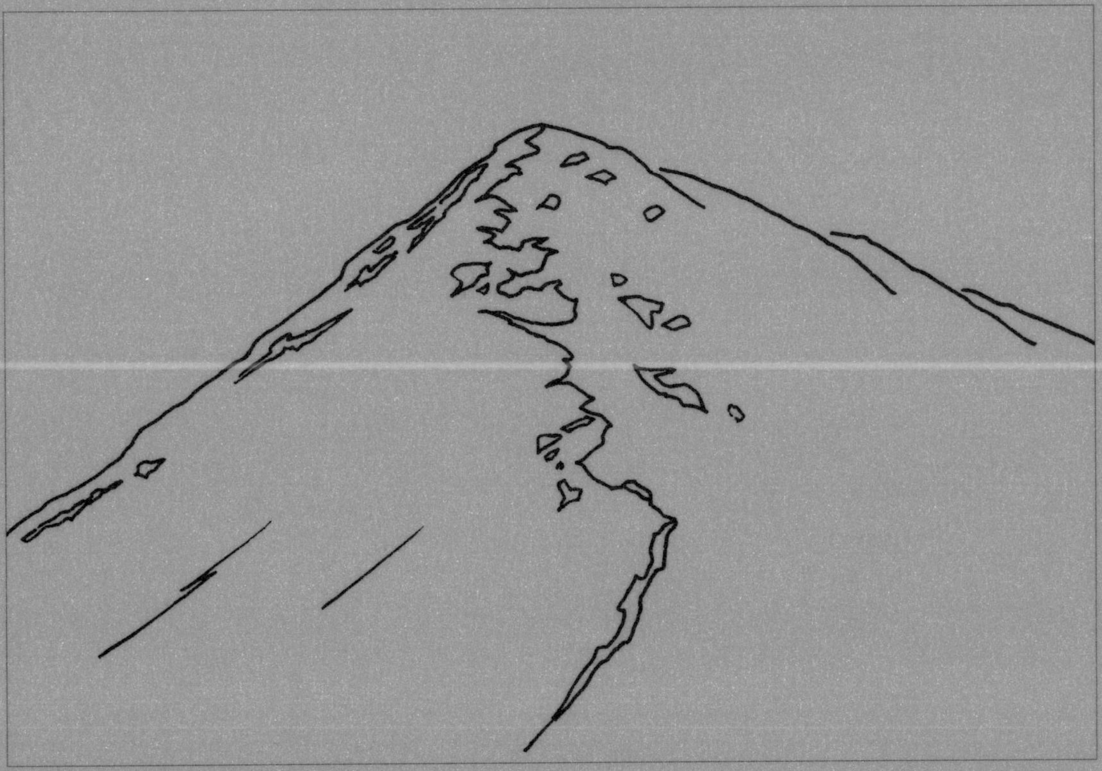

23

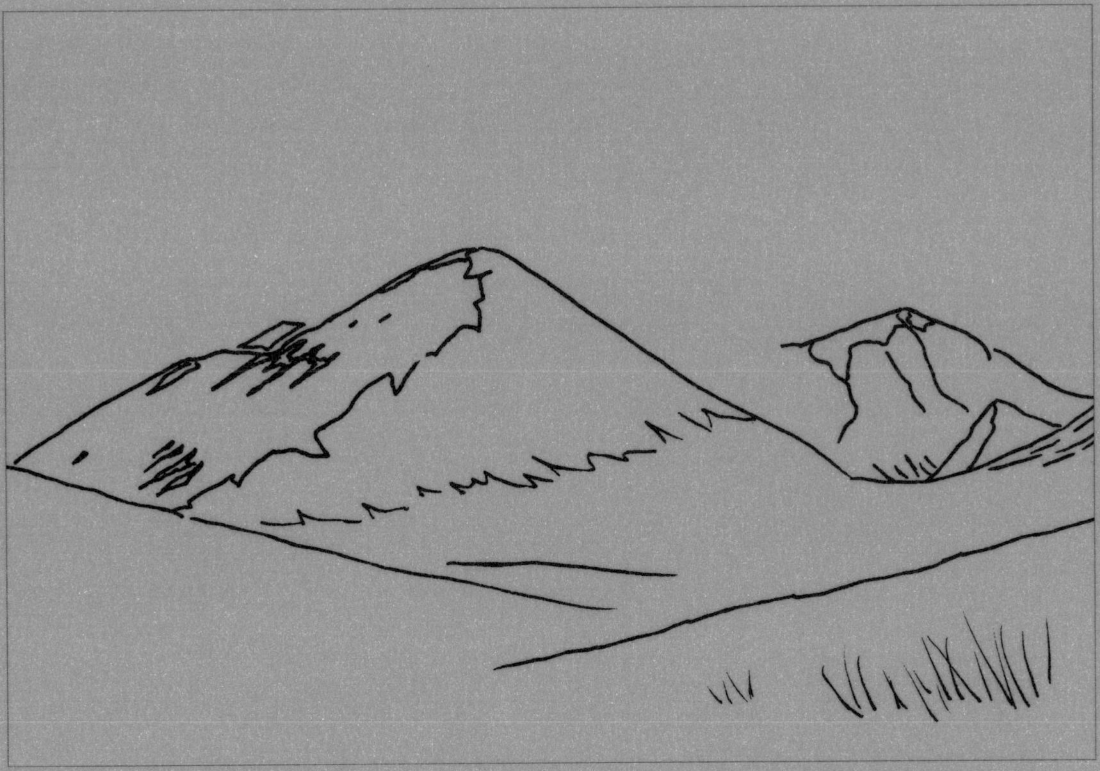

24

23

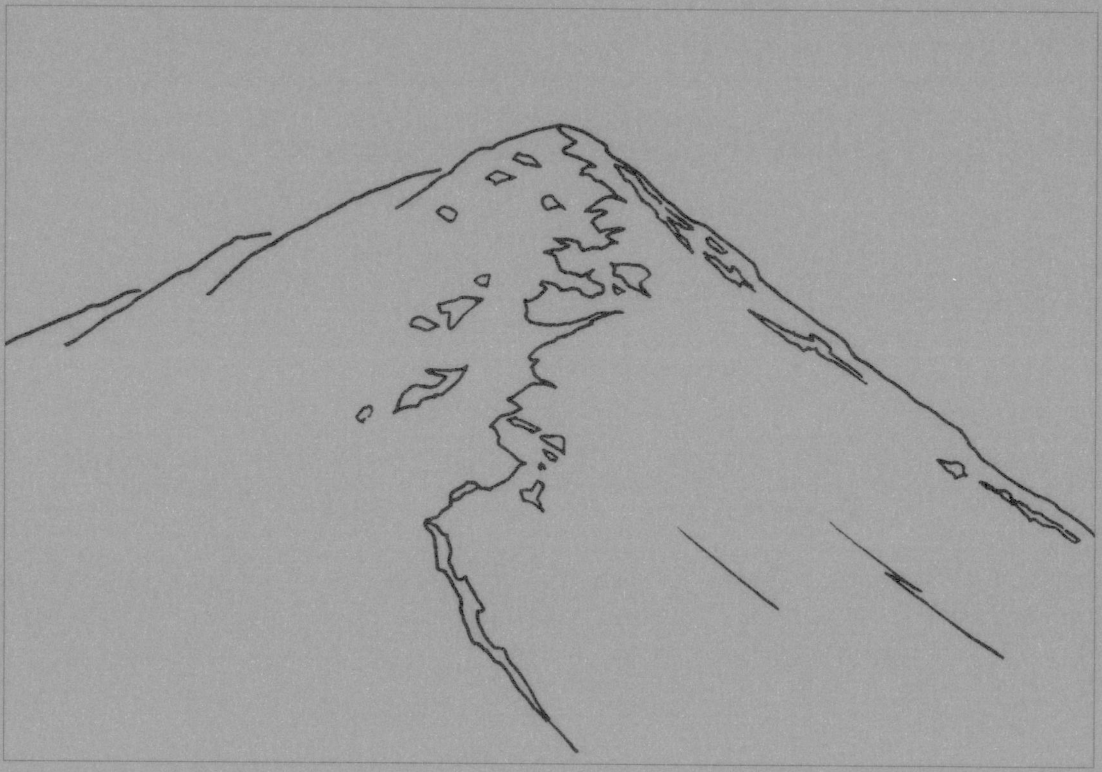

24

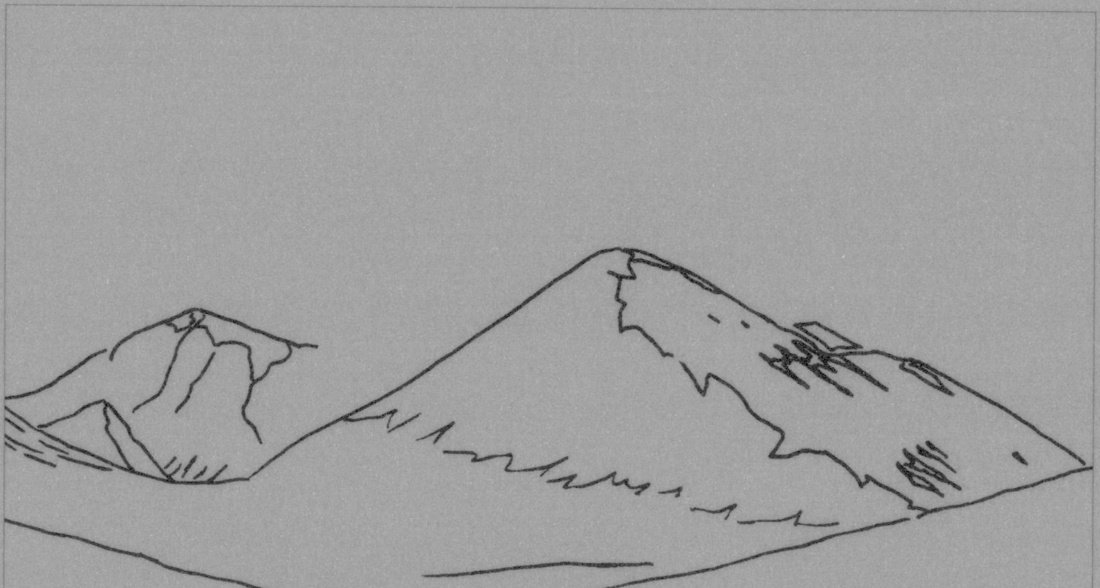

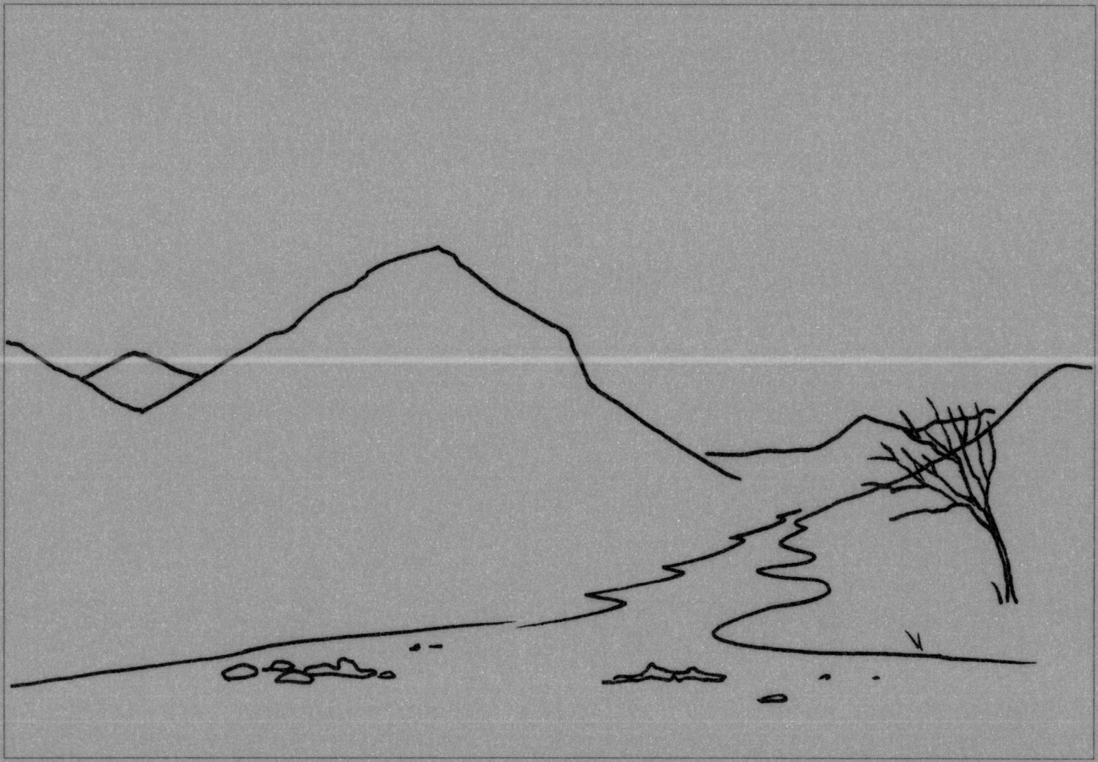
25

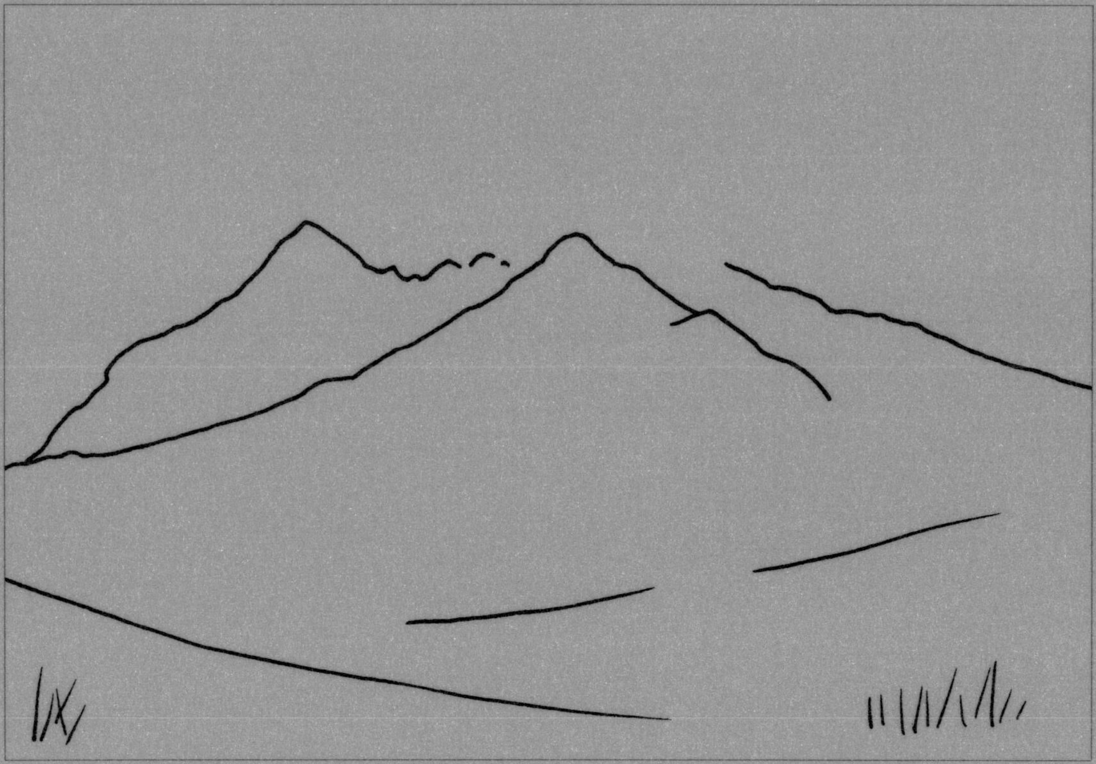
26

25

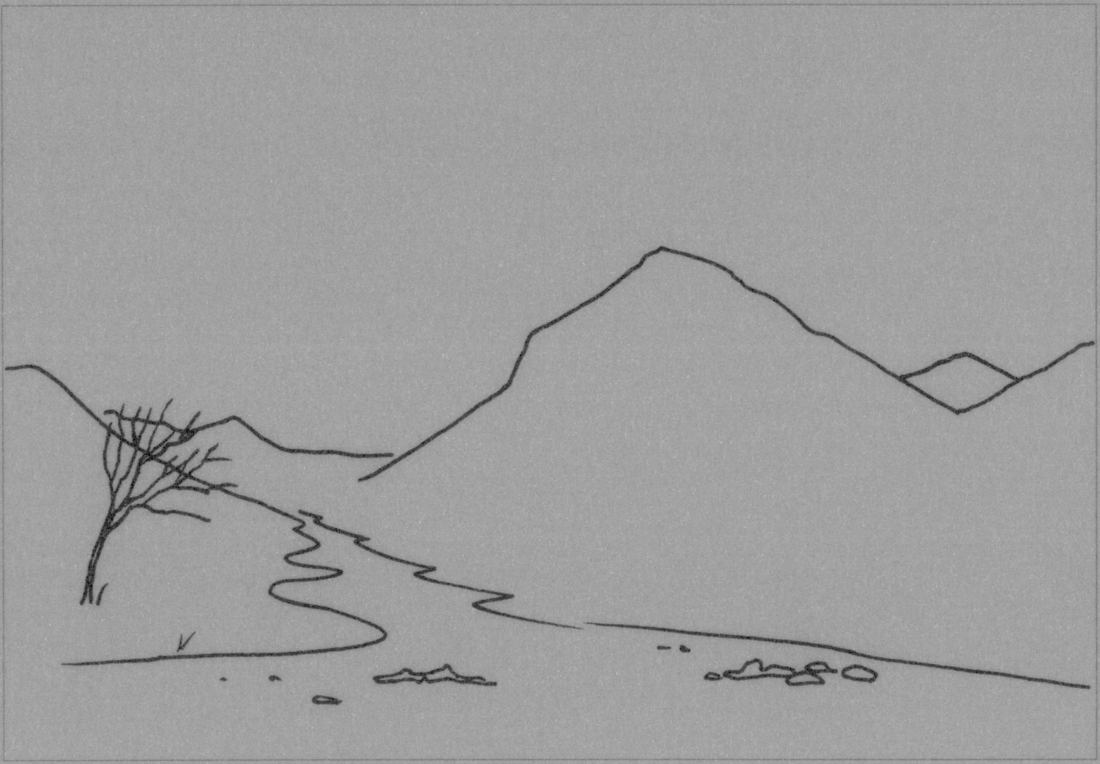

26

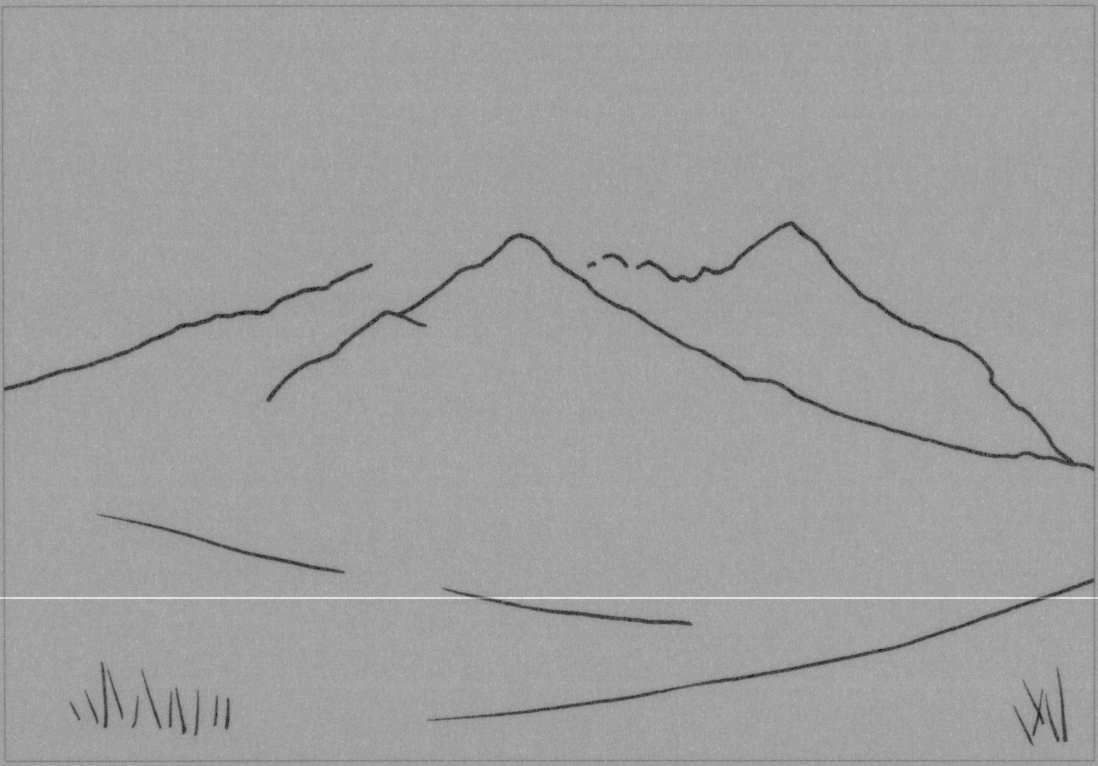

27

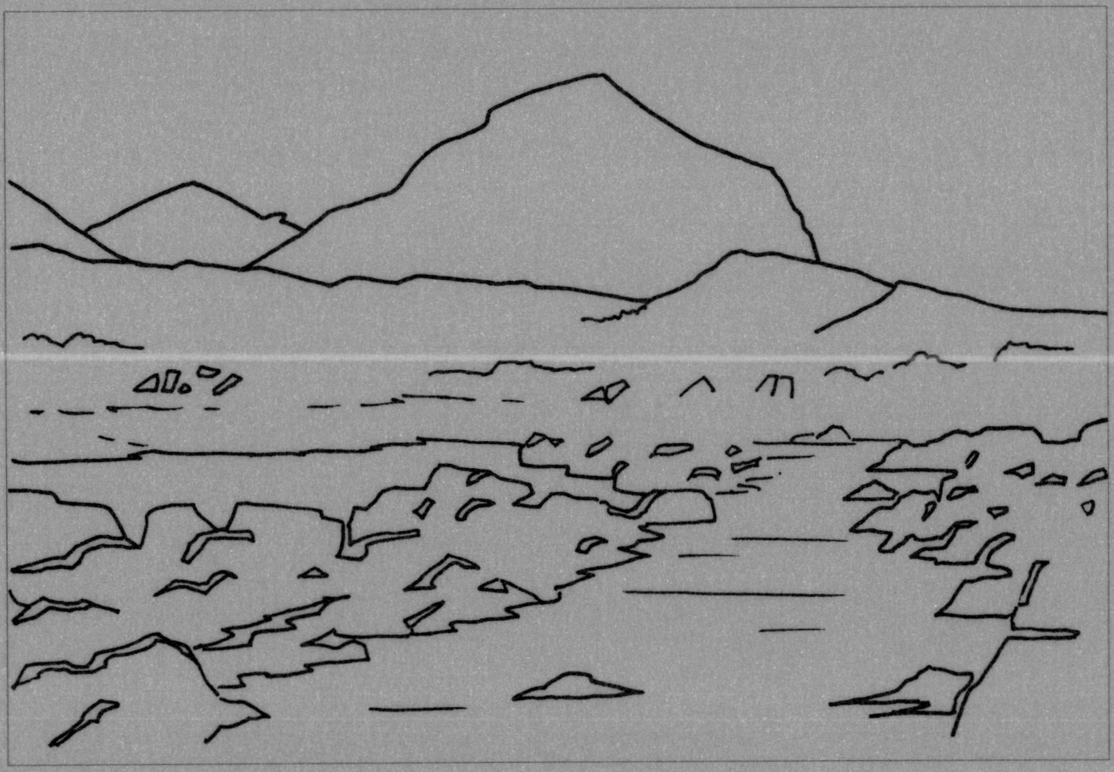

28

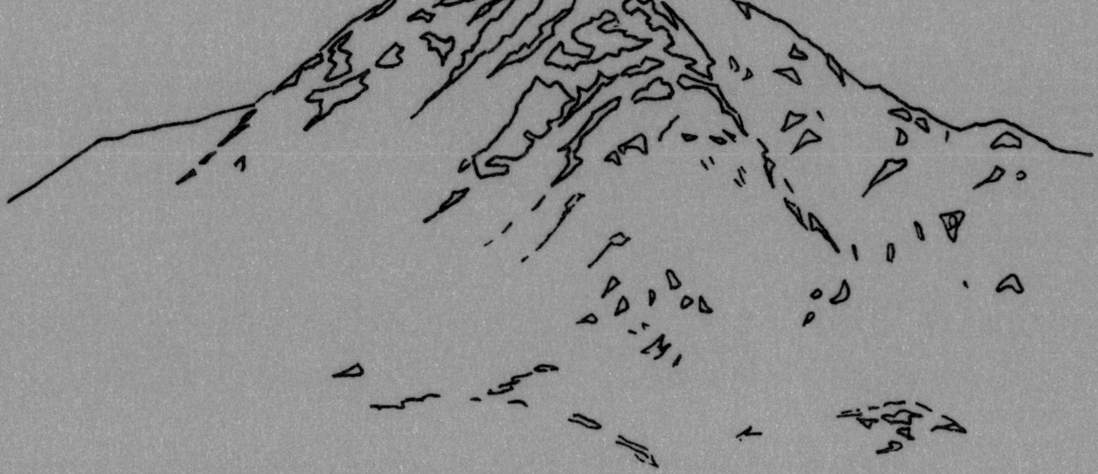

27

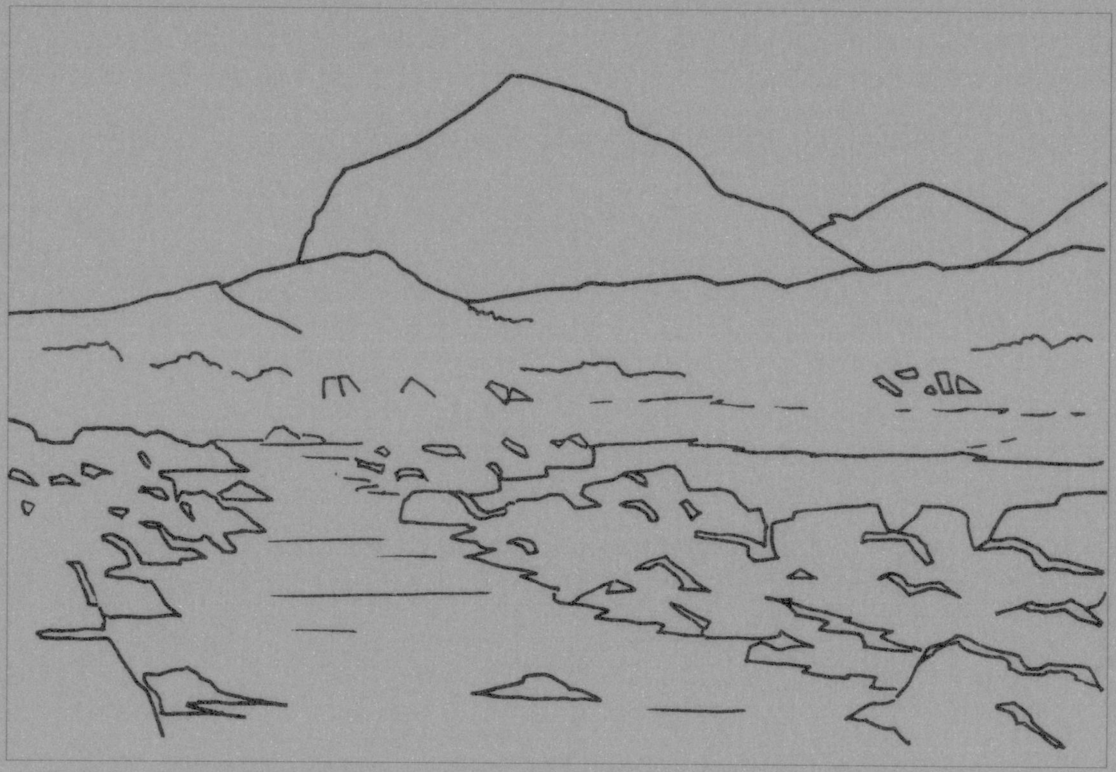

28

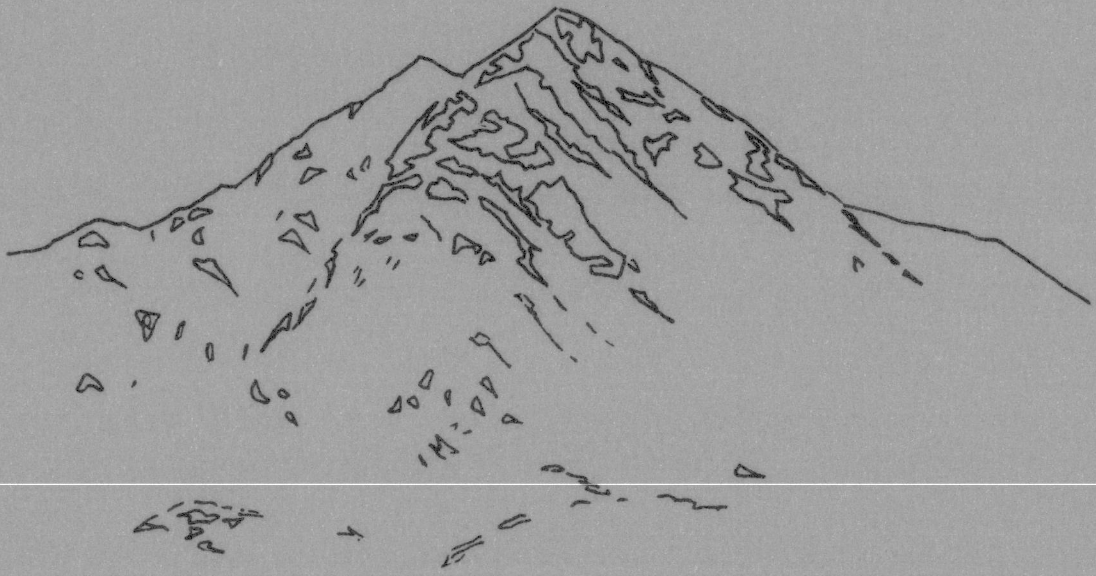

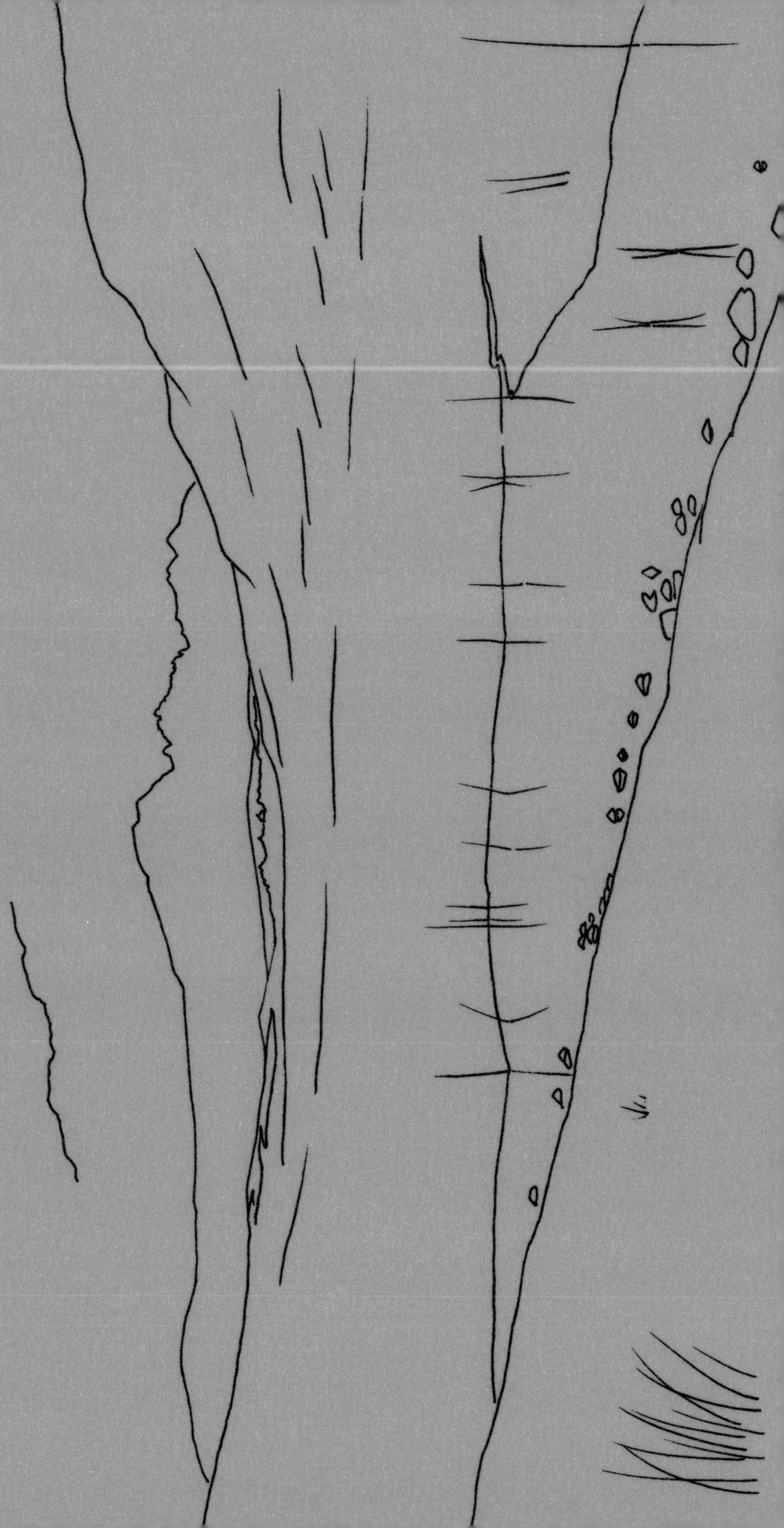

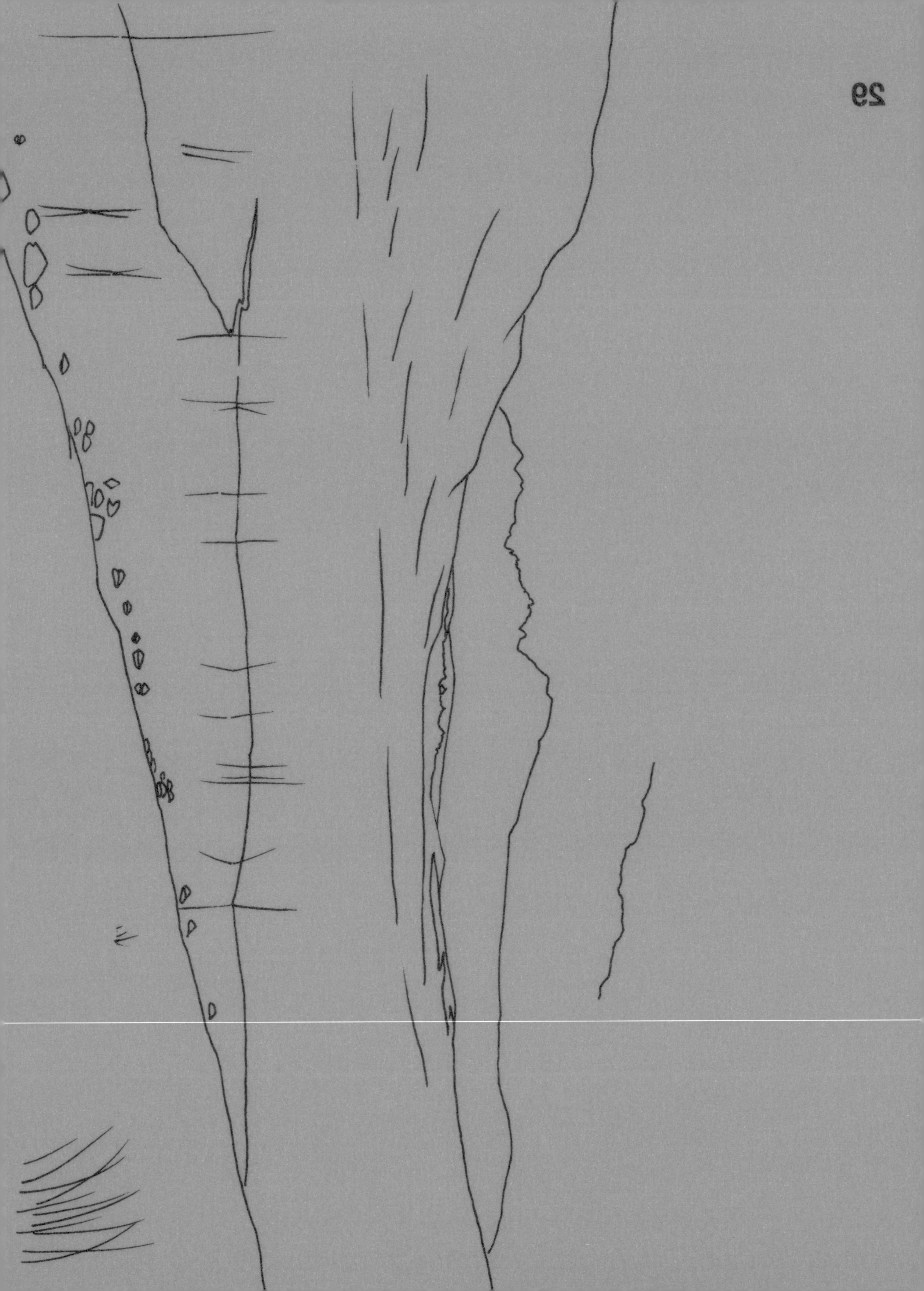

30

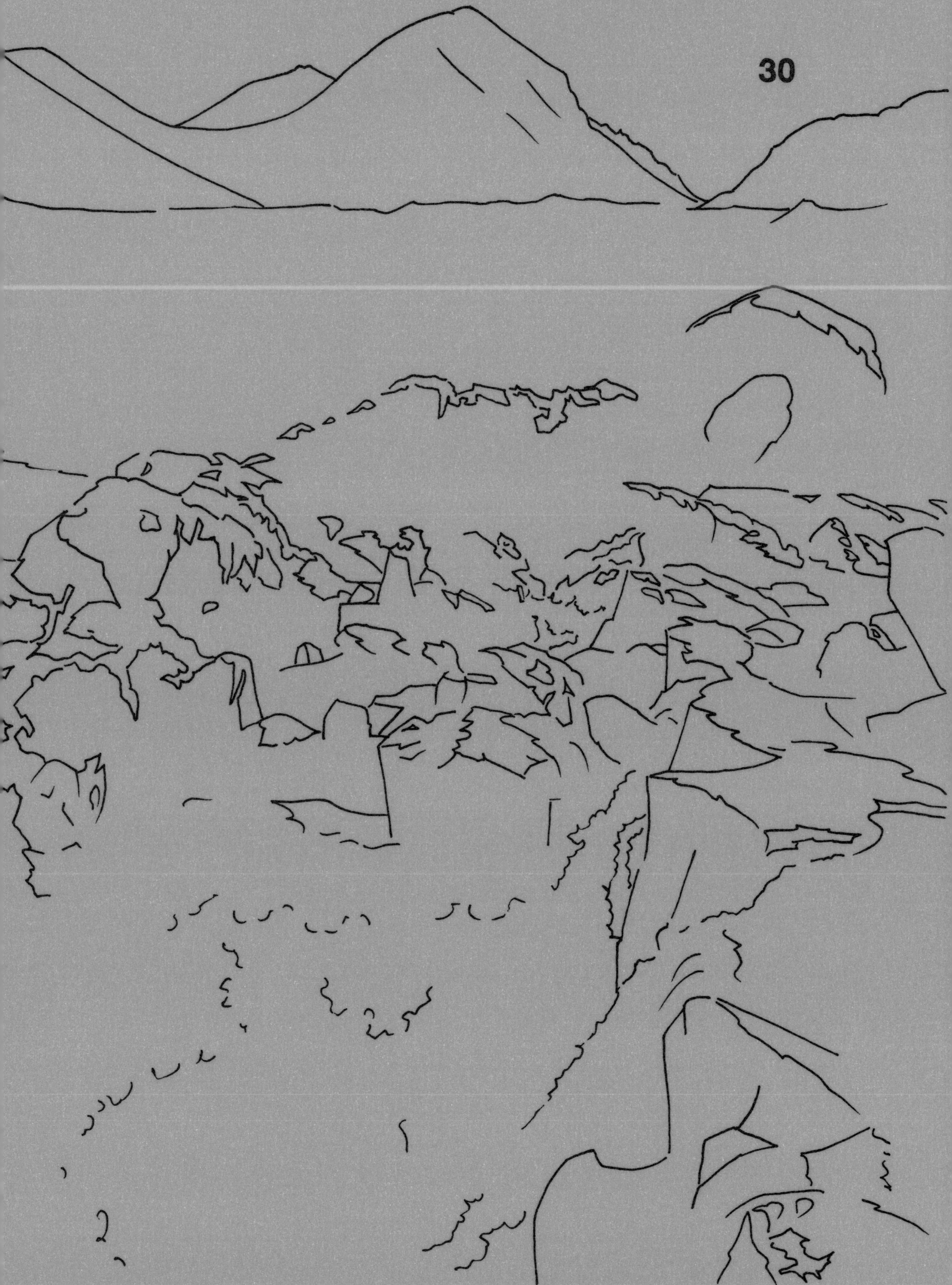

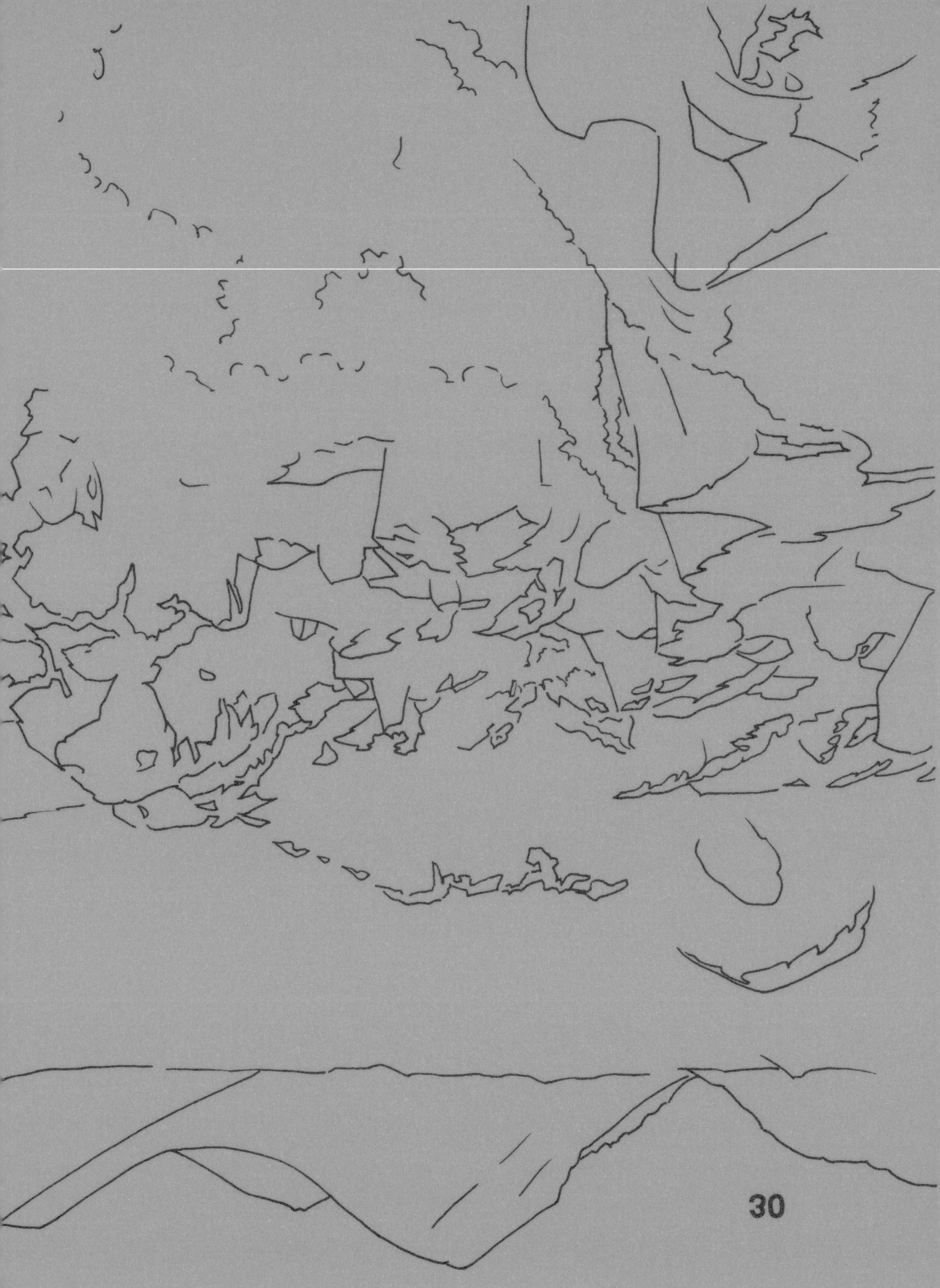

Ready to Paint in 30 Minutes

Mountain Scenes

in Watercolour

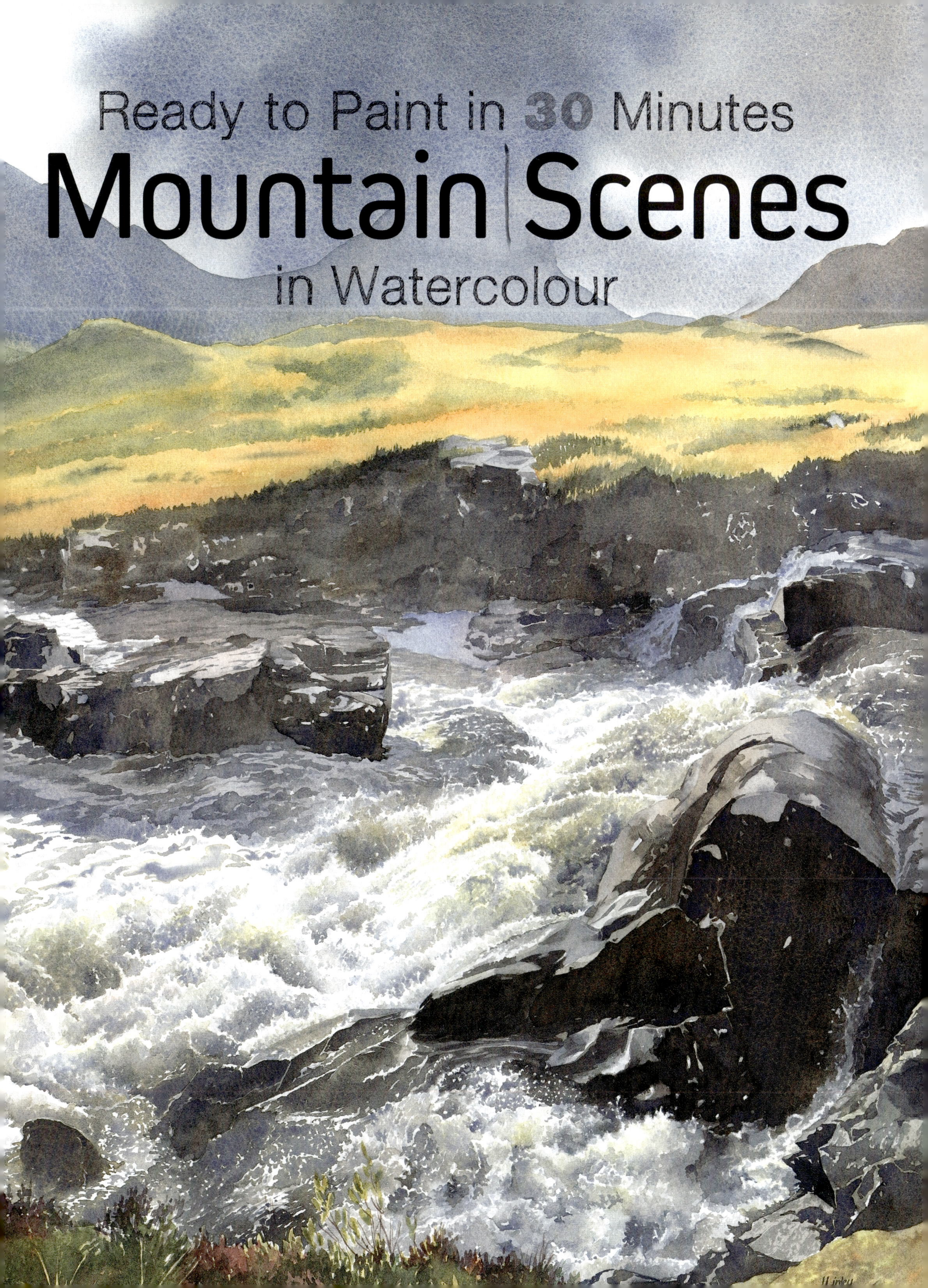

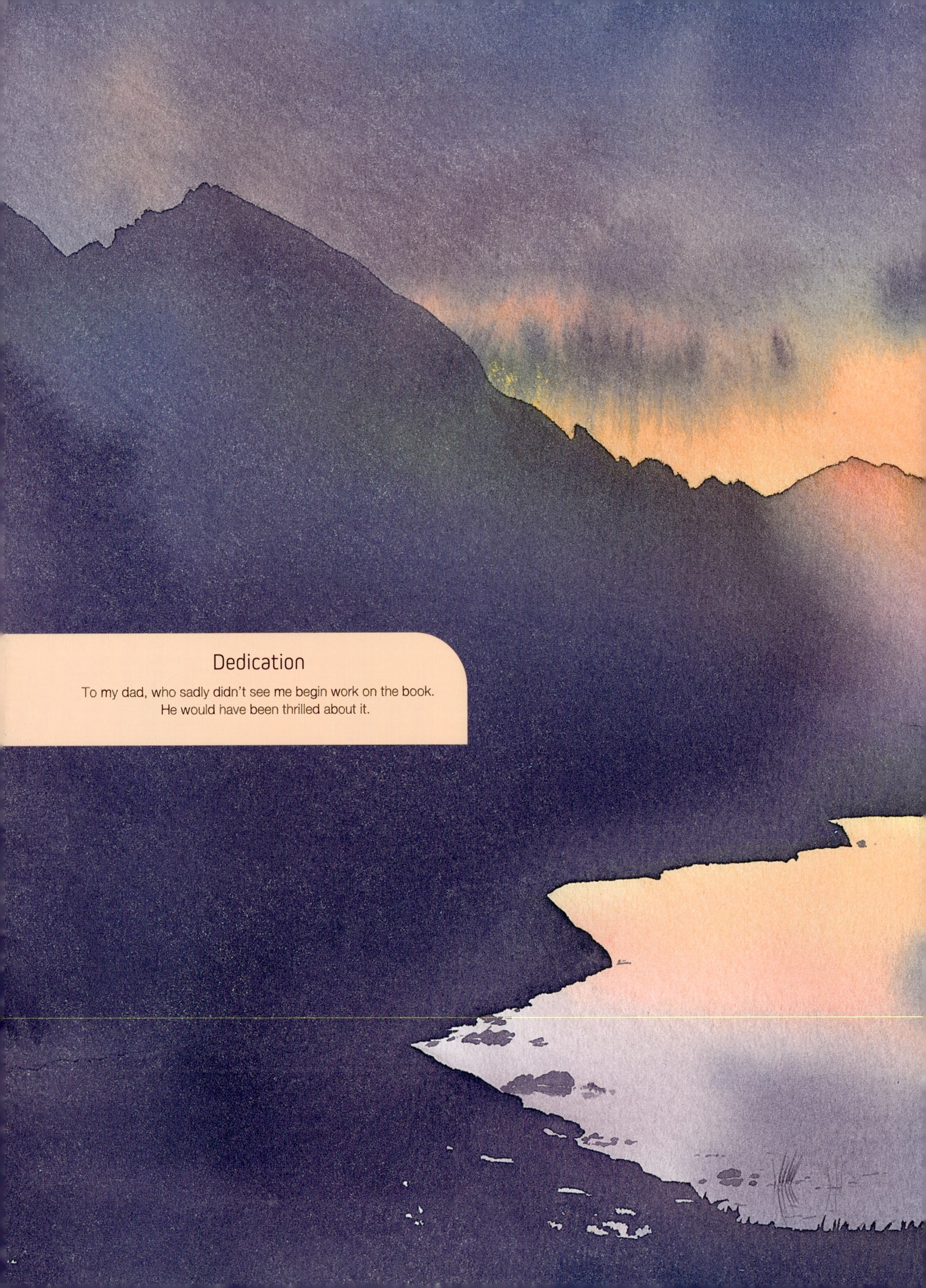

Dedication

To my dad, who sadly didn't see me begin work on the book.
He would have been thrilled about it.

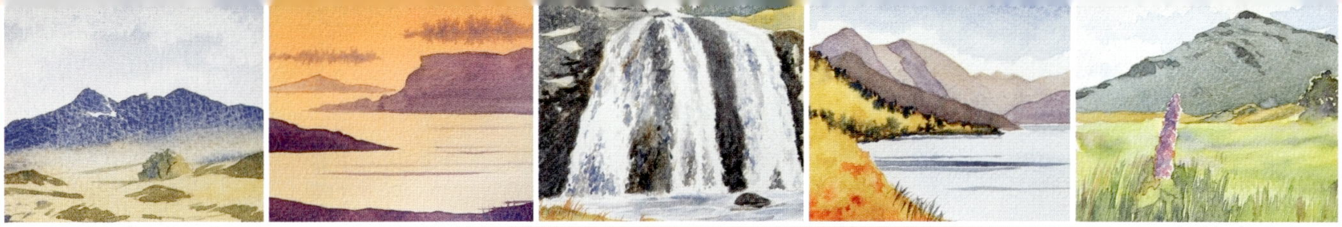

Ready to Paint in 30 Minutes

Mountain Scenes

in Watercolour

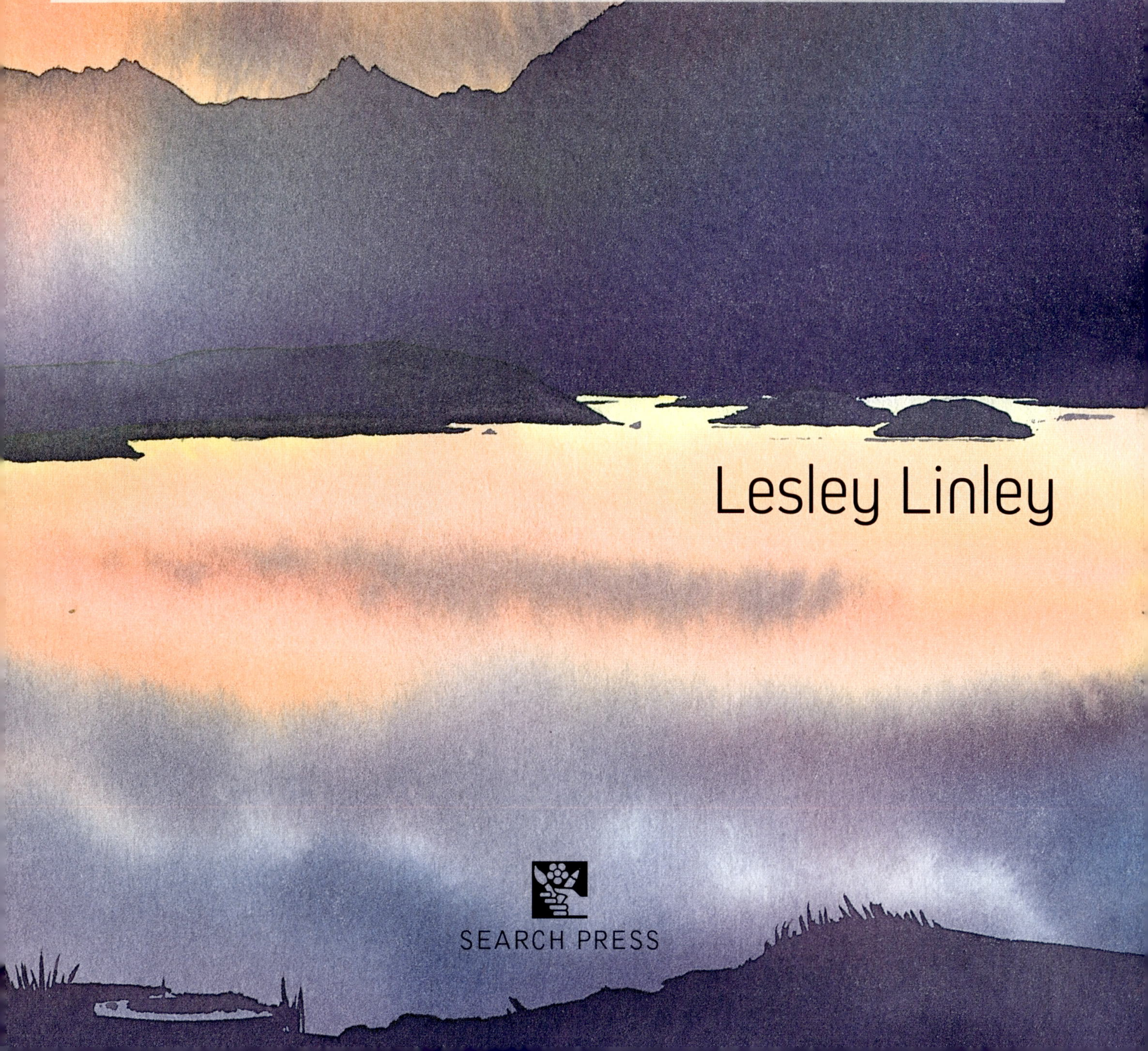

Lesley Linley

SEARCH PRESS

First published in 2020

Search Press Limited
Wellwood, North Farm Road,
Tunbridge Wells, Kent TN2 3DR

Photographs by Roddy Paine Photographic Studios

ISBN: 978-1-78221-686-5

Suppliers
If you have any difficulty obtaining any of the materials and equipment mentioned in this book, please visit the Search Press website: www.searchpress.com

Acknowledgements

To my family, especially my parents and husband, and my friends who have all shared the ups and downs in the life of an artist. To my students and fellow painters who encourage and inspire; to Gavin Sawyer at Roddy Paine Photographic Studios for his patience, and to my ever-cheerful editor Edward Ralph and the lovely team at Search Press. Thanks also to St Cuthberts Mill for providing some of the paper used in preparing for this book.

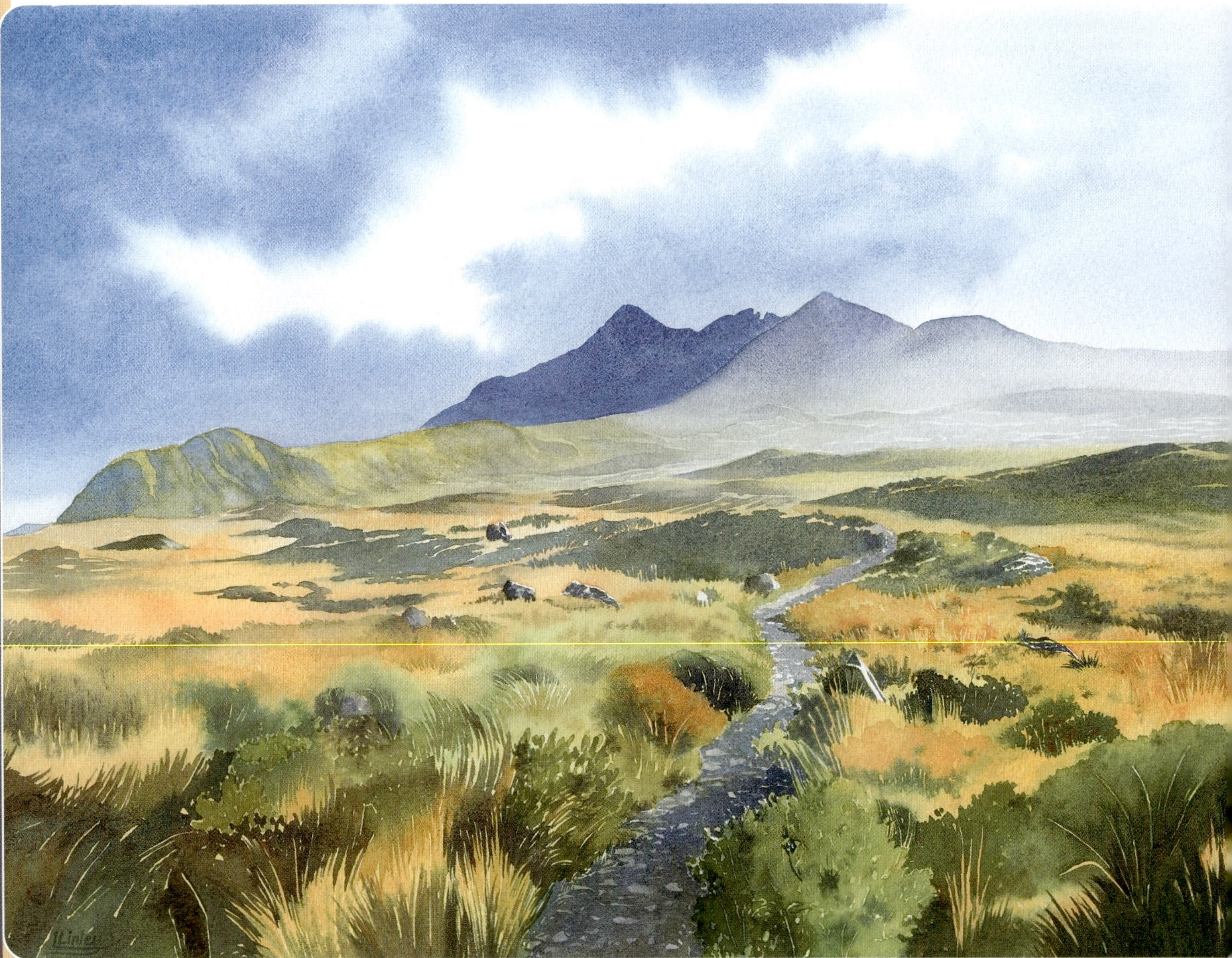

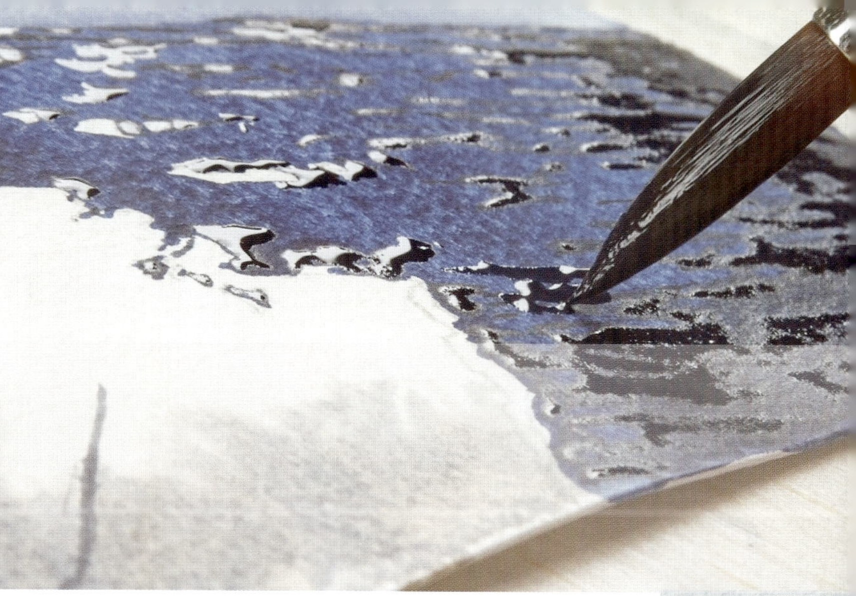

CONTENTS

INTRODUCTION

I have always enjoyed teaching beginners, sharing their delight when they achieve beyond their expectations, turning 'I can't' into 'I did'. The thrill I get from that hasn't diminished over the years. I believe that anyone can learn if they are prepared to watch and listen (or read) and practise, practise, practise.

It still surprises me that so many people expect to produce a masterpiece every time they pick up a brush; we need to continue to play, practise and experiment in order to develop our skills. The painting time suggested for these projects – 30 minutes – encourages you to stop before overworking your painting; there is often a freshness in practice pieces that is lost when we set out to produce a finished painting.

These 15 x 10cm (6 x 4in) projects allow you to learn in bitesize pieces by producing small paintings; look on them as sections of larger works. For the step-by-step exercises, read all the instructions for each project and have everything to hand before starting to paint. Unless told otherwise within the individual project text, allow each step to dry before beginning the next.

If your first attempt isn't too successful, you can try again – in fact, you will benefit from working through each project more than once. Perhaps revisit the book a few weeks or months after working through it. As you become more familiar with the processes, it will be easier to see how you can use them in your own paintings when you break away from the book to work on your own. At that stage, keep the book handy – it will offer reassurance if you're having 'a bad day'. Even the most experienced painter will have those occasionally.

None of these projects shows the only way, or the correct way, to paint; these are suggestions, methods that I've found work for me and for my students. Every artist has their own way of working, preferred method and choice of materials. Find out what suits you; if a method works for you, even if you've just invented it, it's not wrong, it's simply different. Eventually you'll learn what you like and can select the techniques and materials you will need to pursue your style and subject.

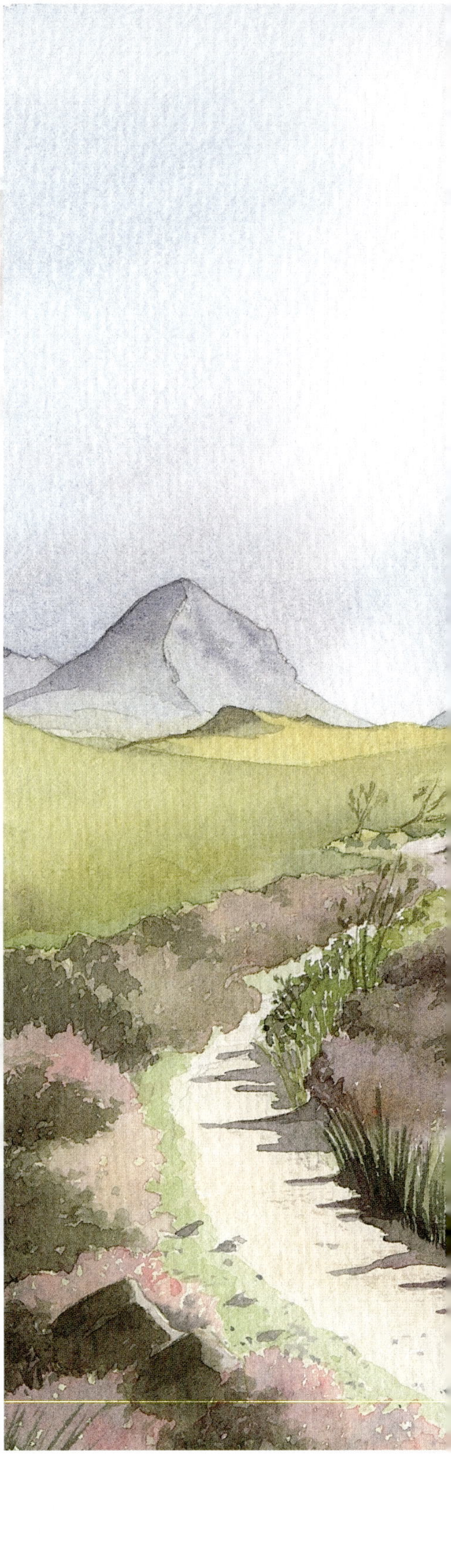

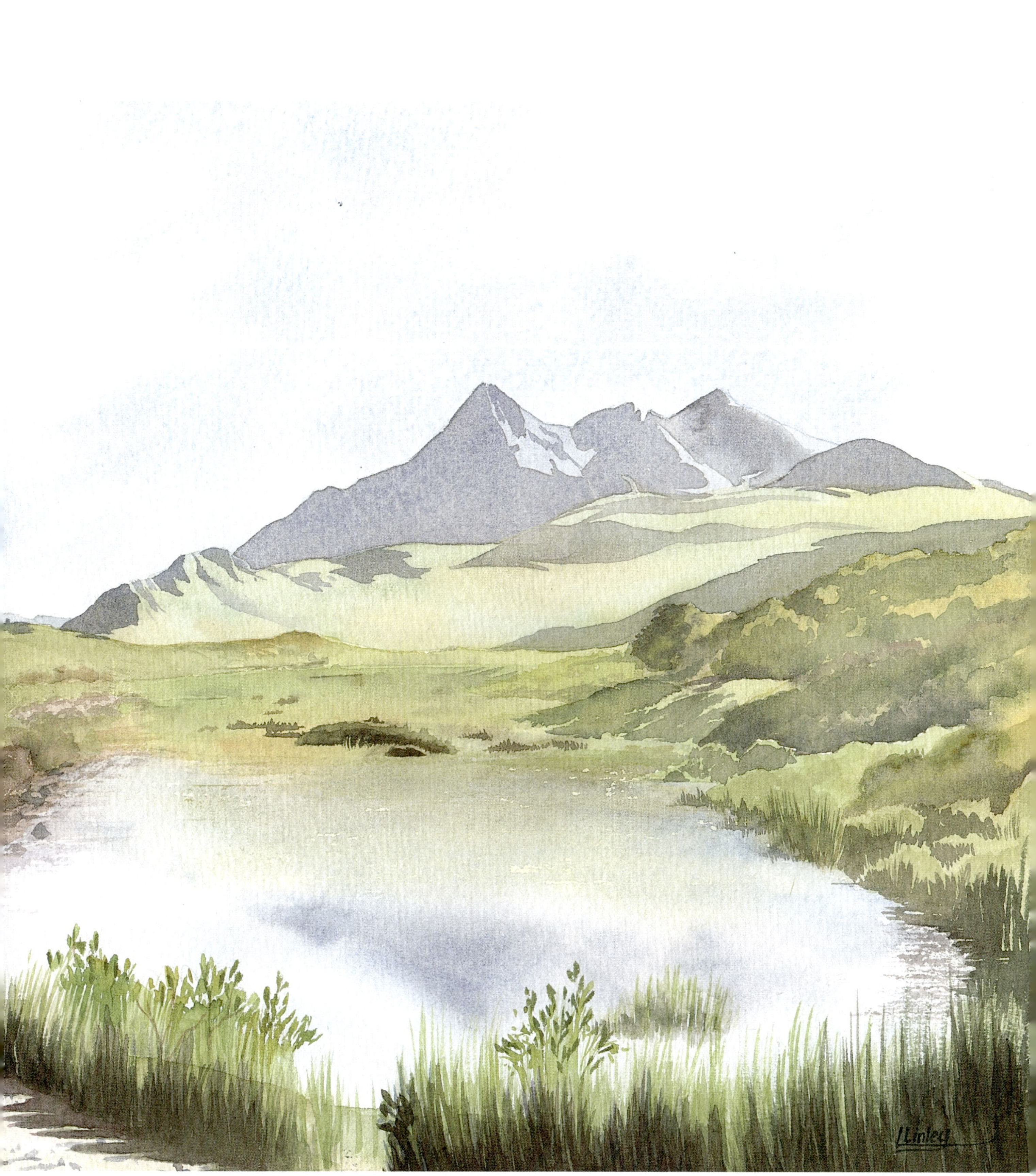

Cuillin Reflections

37 x 27cm (14½ x 10½in)

This painting is about calmness and tranquillity. The distant hills are painted in simple, fresh washes, with just enough detail to show the evening light casting soft shadows. The moorland foliage is painted with wet-on-dry and wet-in-wet techniques to suggest distance, and the diffused reflection in the shallow pool hints at the gentlest of breezes.

BASIC PAINTING EQUIPMENT

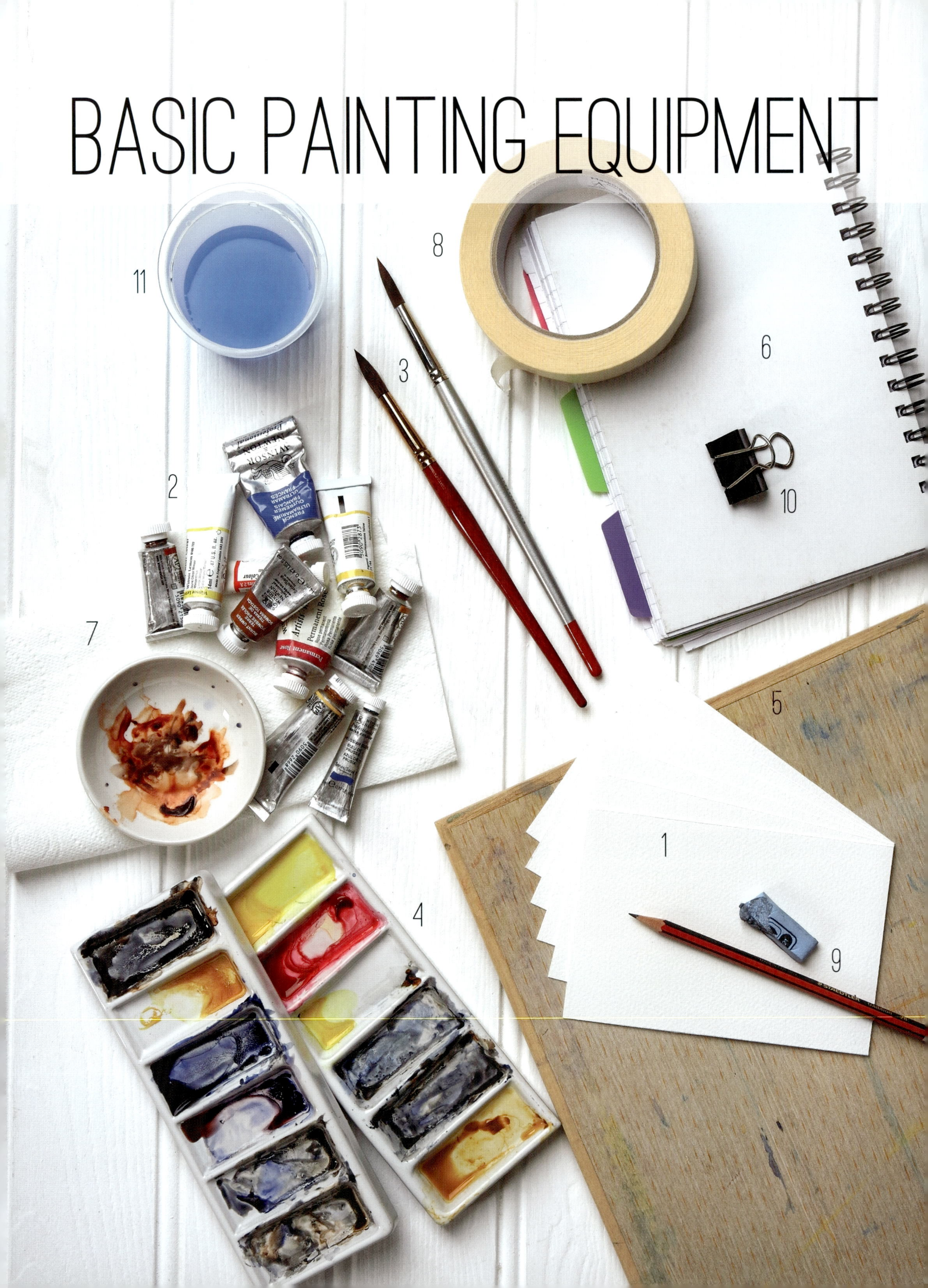

Too often we believe that the way to be a successful painter is to have every colour, gadget or brush available; the opposite is often the case. My advice has always been to buy good quality materials – just a few items to begin with – adding others as you find you need them. I don't believe it is helpful to use cheap materials for practice, as inferior quality often results in disappointment.

It's more pleasing – and encouraging – to use good quality materials; and all you really need is paint, paper and one brush.

1 Paper A 15 x 10cm (6 x 4in) pad or block of paper is ideal for the projects in this book, but you can also cut larger sheets down to size, which can be more economical. Find a paper you like and stick with it: you may not get the same results on a different brand. Use good quality paper from a reputable manufacturer. Lightweight papers are cheaper than heavyweights but will be more likely to cockle when wet. A good general-use paper is 300gsm (140lb) in weight, with a slightly textured surface known as Not, or Cold Pressed. When you begin to work on larger landscapes, you may like to try a Rough surface paper for more 'tooth' or texture.

2 Paints It's easy to get carried away, but a few well-chosen paints will suffice. Students' quality paints are an economical starting point, but try artists' quality as soon as you're able. You need less as artists' colours tend to be stronger and more vibrant. Tubes can be easier to use when you need a large volume of colour but for the small exercises in this book pans (solid blocks of paint that need to be wetted) would be fine; you can use a mixture of tubes and pans if you prefer. I put out paint as I plan to use it, using a paint box only to store 'end of tube' colours. Any paint left on your palette after a painting session can be used for practising brushstrokes, or warming up before beginning a painting.

3 Brushes One good-quality size 10 round brush with a good point will do the job of many brushes and will suffice for these projects. Buy the best you can afford; a high-quality brush made for watercolour painting from a reputable brand. Sable hair is expensive, but a good brush will last a long time if well looked after. The brush should be comfortable to hold: small brushes tend to have thin handles, larger brushes wider handles, and the length of handle can affect the balance in your hand. As you work, brushes will lose their point, but keep hold of older brushes – they can be useful for lifting colour washes or mixing.

4 Palette These are available in many sizes and types, in ceramic, plastic and metal. I prefer ceramic as it is particularly easy to clean. Small palettes and paint boxes rarely hold enough paint for a large wash so you may need extra containers for these. A white plate/saucer can be useful, as it allows you to see the colours you're mixing. I use a ceramic 'slant well' palette for small quantities and plates for larger volumes of paint.

5 Painting board A large, lightweight board is handy to lean upon, and will let you set your paper at an angle. This will help washes of paint to flow.

6 Notebook This will come in handy for recording your own notes. A well-maintained notebook will let you look back on what you tried and what happened. This is particularly handy when experimenting with colours and techniques.

7 Kitchen paper Useful for wiping brushes, lifting out paint, mopping up spills and cleaning palettes. Avoid coloured papers for lifting out as the colour may bleed.

8 Adhesive tape If you wish to hold paper down on a board, masking tape is useful, but if it's left on for long periods, it may leave a sticky residue. If you paint right up to the tape, you should leave your painting to dry before removing the tape or the paper may tear.

9 Pencil and eraser You will need a 2B pencil to transfer the tracings onto paper. Be careful to pencil lightly (the drawings shown in this book are intentionally heavier to help ensure you can see them). Scribble on scrap paper with a newly sharpened pencil to remove a too-sharp point so that you don't scratch the paper. I use a putty eraser for erasing pencil lines and removing surplus graphite from watercolour paper after tracing down. Erasers degrade over time, so buy small ones and replace them every year or two.

10 Metal clips An alternative to masking tape for securing your paper to a board.

11 Water pot A glass jar is useful. Alternatively, you can use a plastic water pot, which can be found in anti-spill versions. It is helpful to have several water pots, one for clean water to dilute your paint, and one or more pots for rinsing brushes.

MY COLOUR PALETTE

My basic palette (choice of colours) is based around Winsor & Newton's six-colour mixing system in professional (Artists') quality. This includes a warm and cool version of each primary colour, giving a wider range of colours from mixing than if just one red, yellow and blue were used.

The six colours are Winsor lemon, Winsor yellow, permanent rose, scarlet lake, French ultramarine and Winsor blue (green shade). In addition to these I use raw sienna, burnt umber, burnt sienna, quinacridone gold, Prussian blue and cobalt blue.

KNOW YOUR MATERIALS

People are often surprised when I suggest that they're struggling to achieve the result they require because they're using the wrong materials for the purpose. For example, they may be unaware that some colours behave differently from others, or that the choice of papers can influence results.

I use Saunders Waterford rag paper ('rag' means it is made from cotton, rather than wood fibre) for my paintings. The High White version (whiter than Traditional White) gives me the extra brightness I need because I don't use white paint; my white is simply the paper. The numerous layers I often paint mean that the paper needs to be durable.

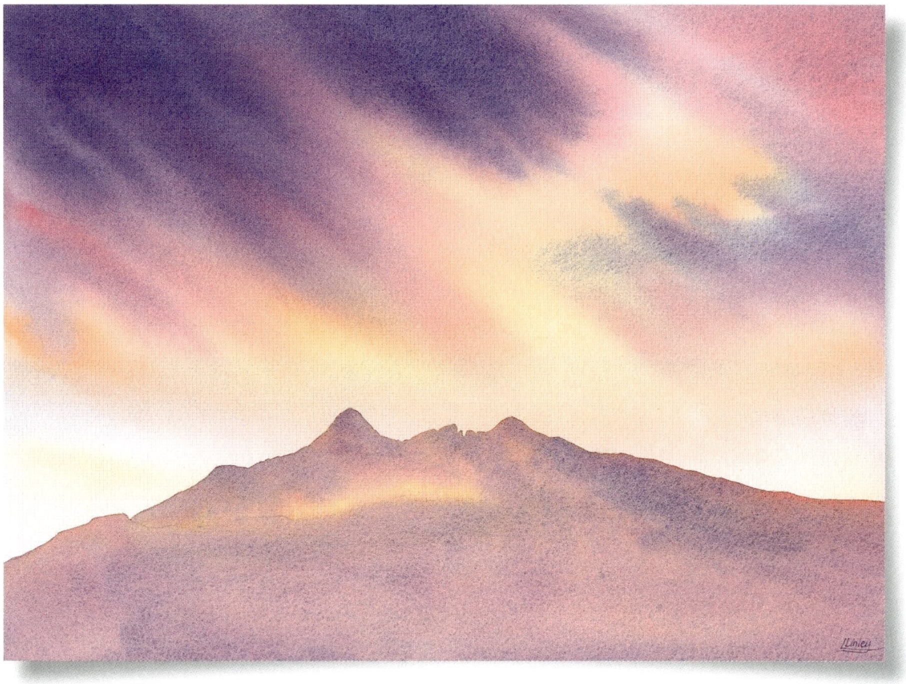

Cuillin Aurora

37 x 27cm (14½ x 10½in)

Just three colours were used here. Colourful washes such as this require practice and a certain amount of luck but choosing colours carefully, and knowing how they work together, can influence the outcome. The hills were painted wet on dry with colour flooded onto the paper and blended a little to give a slightly variegated glaze.

I use a dozen colours (see the box on page 9) and know how they behave on my paper. Knowing which mixes give bright colours and which give subdued colours will save a lot of disappointment. I often combine French ultramarine with burnt umber to produce an interesting natural grey mix; these colours work well for me for rocks, clouds or water. Mixing two colours rather than buying a ready-mixed uniform grey means that I'm able to have a variety of shades of blue/brown in the warm and cool greys that form, rather than simply different tones of the same colour.

This part of the book is showing you how to play with your materials – and have fun while you paint! It isn't difficult to learn how your materials handle and experimenting can be very enjoyable; write down what you did in your notebook: the colours (including manufacturer and quality); the techniques; the paper… what happened? Try the same method with different colours, or a different method with the same colours.

Besides the tools described, you'll need to develop two more things for success: drawing skills and observational skills. While this book provides tracings to help you, to make progress as an artist you will need drawing skills. Drawing can be enormous fun and will also help your observational skills. For the latter, you'll get more out of everyday life if you learn to really look at, and take note of, what is around you. Really look: don't assume that you already know. Whether it's a grey day, a blue sky, or your break-time cup of coffee, you'll find there's a lot more to it than a cursory glance reveals.

LARGER PAPER

If you have difficulty working on small pieces of paper, simply draw 15 x 10cm (6 x 4in) rectangles on a larger sheet of watercolour paper, leaving a little space in between them.

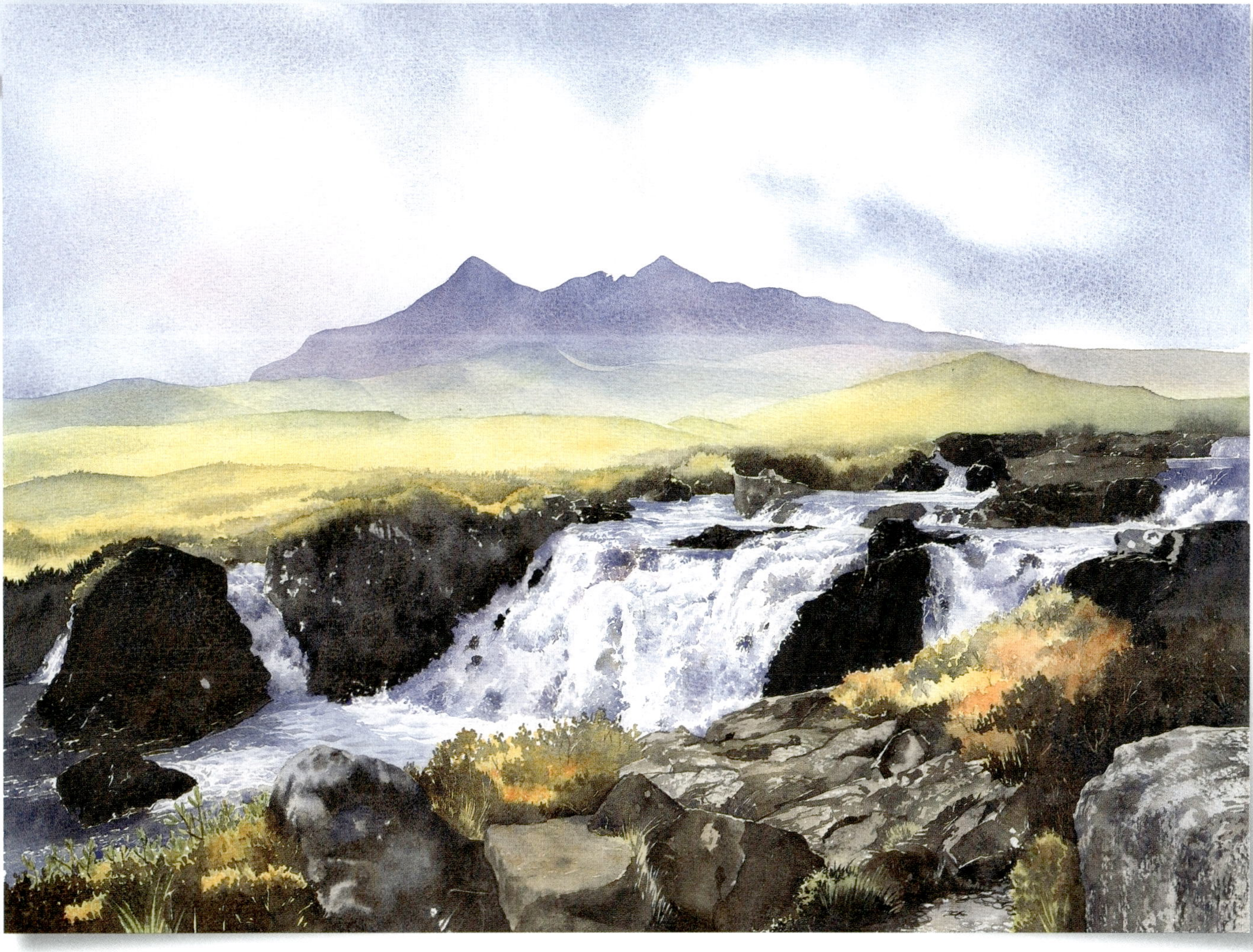

Autumn Colour in the Cuillin

55 x 37cm (22 x 14½in)

The mountains have been painted simply, in colours that increase the impression of distance. The waterfall and foreground are more colourful with darker tones and plenty of detail. The paper needed to be able to take several washes and allow lifting out without breaking down.

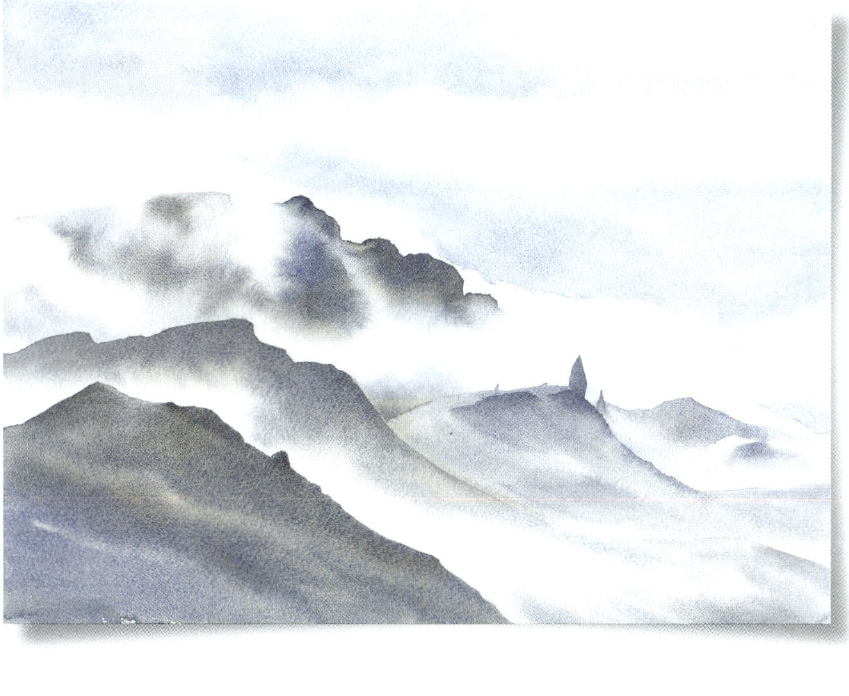

Storr Mists

37 x 27cm (14½ x 10½in)

I loved to watch mist encircle these peaks as it fell from the ridge, revealing contours not seen when the hills were in silhouette. Much of this painting was done wet-in-wet for misty effects. The crisp 'found' edges at the hill tops were painted wet on dry but softened below to create lost edges as they merge with the mist.

YOU WILL NEED

Paint colours: Prussian blue

Brushes: size 10 round

Brushstrokes

Before buying a large number of brushes, I recommend that you get to know what you can achieve with a single, good-quality size 10 round brush. The doodles I've suggested here resulted from a challenge that I set myself many years ago, which was to achieve effects with a single brush that are often thought to require numerous specialist brushes.

Half an hour of playing with a brush is useful to find out what can be achieved and is a relaxing introduction to watercolour. Improving your brush handling skills will certainly not be wasted time.

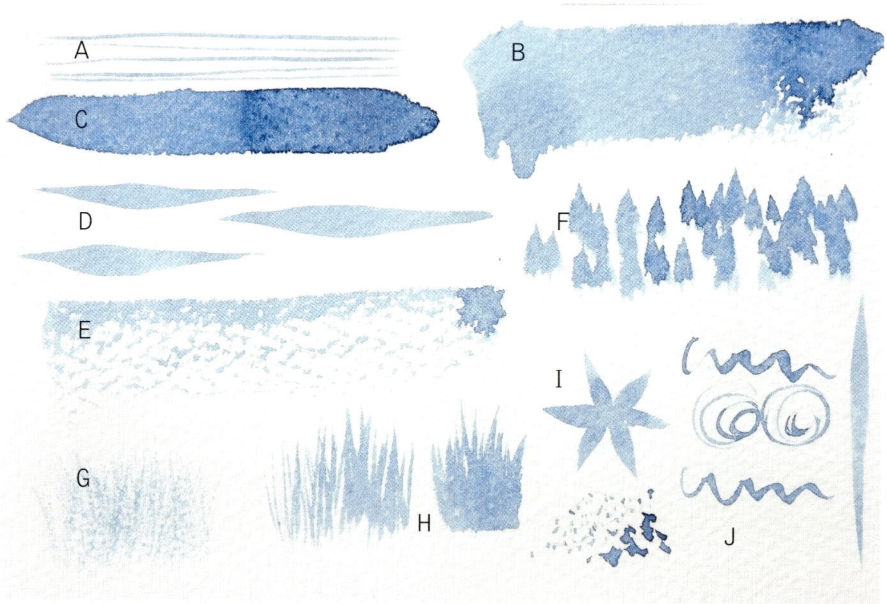

USING YOUR BRUSH

Prepare some well-diluted paint, and place your paper on a board. Using just your size 10 round brush, try to make all the strokes shown above. The most important marks (A–E) are explained in more detail opposite; but experiment to see whether you can create the other marks (the 'Other marks' box opposite provides some starting points):

A – Fine lines
B – Broad lines
C – Very broad lines
D – Tapering strokes
E – Drybrush
F – Gentle jabs
G – Broken lines
H – Grasses
I – Flower
J – Dots, swirls and squiggles

Technique: Preparing your paint

The clue is in the name but isn't explained on the packaging; watercolour paint should be mixed (diluted) with water; it should flow when mixed and not need to be physically spread as you would when applying emulsion paint.

Watercolours become paler as they dry so when preparing your paints, you need to make your colours/tones stronger to begin with to allow for this.

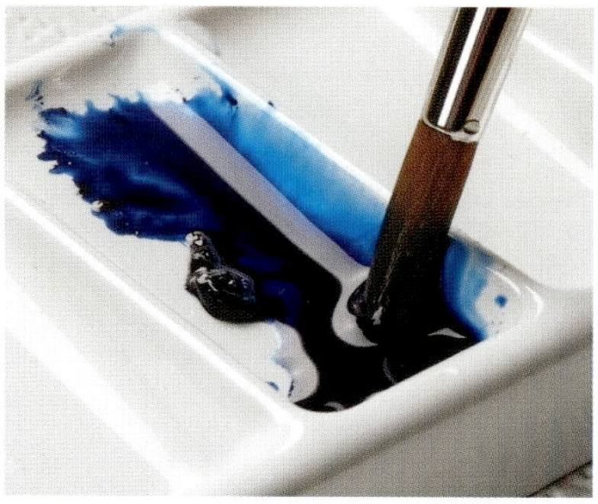

1 Squeeze out a small amount of paint into a space on your palette. Wet a size 10 round brush and add water by gently brushing the brush over the paint.

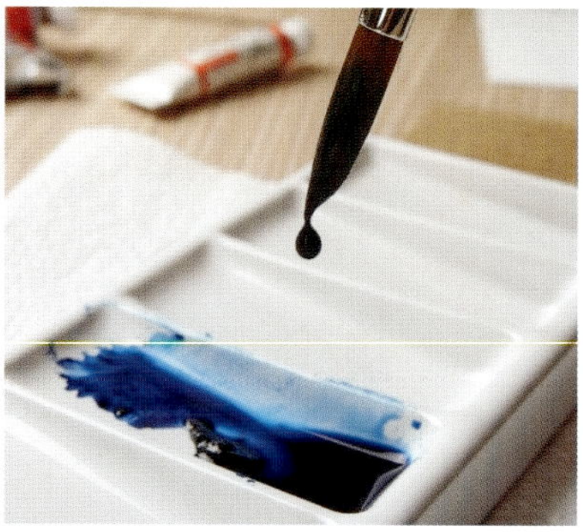

2 Continue until the mix forms a drop which drips off your brush when held up like this.

BRUSH TECHNIQUES

These five simple marks are hugely versatile, so taking the time to practise them will give you confidence for the other projects in the book.

BRUSH CARE

- Never put a dry brush into paint: always dampen it first.
- Wash your brush thoroughly after use, in cold water. Use your fingers to reshape it to a point, then leave to dry. Once dry, I store my brushes in a pot with the tips upright so that the hairs will not get spoiled.
- Never leave your brush standing on its tip, whether in water or not, the tip will be spoiled and it is very unlikely that you will be able to straighten it.

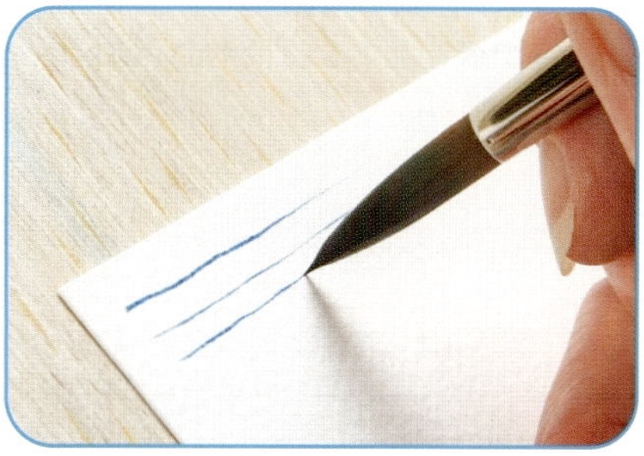

(A) Fine lines

For fine lines you shouldn't have too much paint on your brush because a fully loaded brush (that is, about to drip) doesn't form a fine point. First dampen your brush and check that it makes a good point when twirled on kitchen paper/ palette or rolled between your finger and thumb. Hold the brush upright and lightly draw the brush across the surface of the paper. Practise adjusting your lightness of touch, and the amount of paint in the brush, until you get the finest lines possible with that brush.

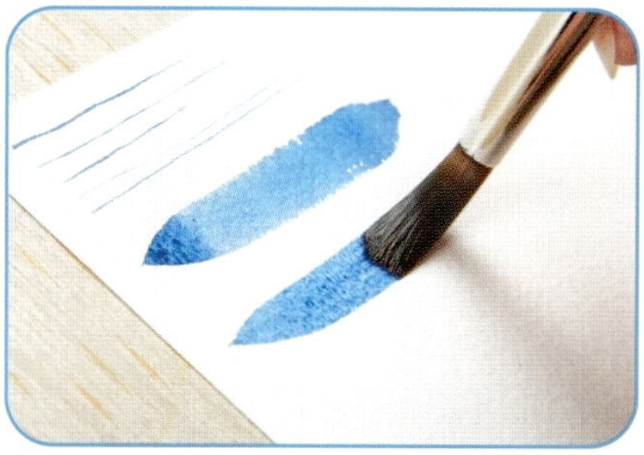

(B) Broad lines

For broad lines, load your brush (dip and pick up plenty of the paint). Holding the brush upright, press down gently so that the hairs point left (reverse if left-handed) and sweep the brush sideways across the paper, pressing down to get the full width of the brush.

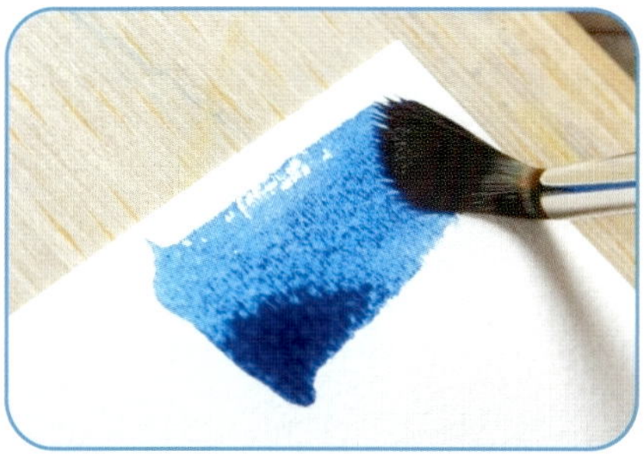

(C) Very broad lines

For a very broad line, load your brush, press it down onto the paper with the hairs facing away from you, and move it sideways to get a stroke that is the length of the hairs. Your brush will soon run out of paint and will then give a broken line – this is used for the drybrush technique (right).

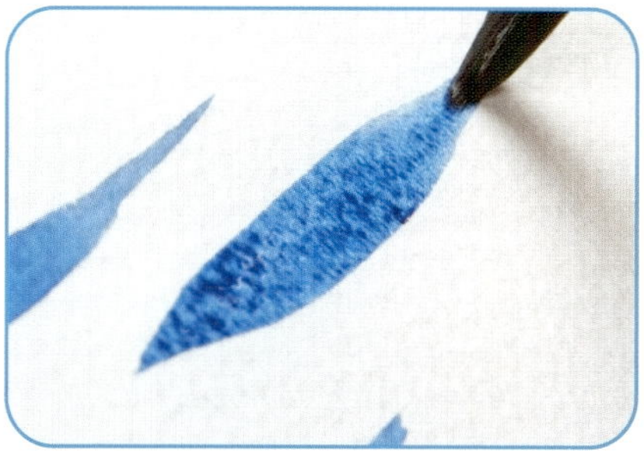

(D) Tapering strokes

Useful for ripples or willowy marks. Load your brush, then wipe it on your palette to remove a little paint (we want a fine point to begin the stroke). Hold your brush upright, moving sideways before you touch the paper, and touch down lightly. Then, still moving, increase the pressure to get a wider stroke. Finally, gently release the pressure (still moving across the paper) and lift off. When done well, this stroke has a lovely rhythmical feel.

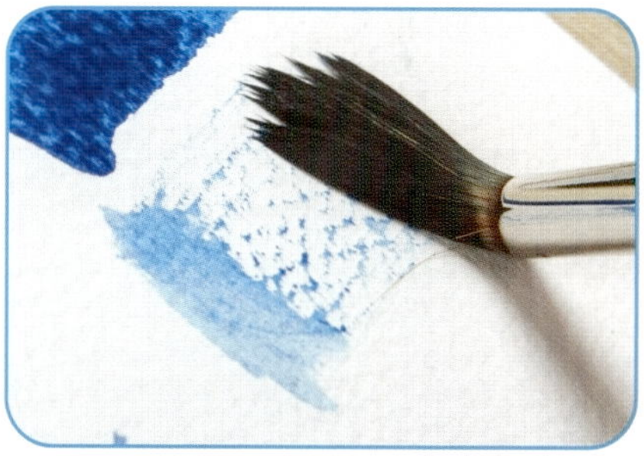

(E) Drybrush

Giving a broken line effect, suitable for sparkle on the sea, for example, drybrush is a versatile technique. Make a broad sideways mark with a brush that has little paint in it, i.e. the paint has begun to run out. If you have difficulty with this technique, you may find it helps to hold the brush flat, as if you're about to roll it across the table, and gently skim across the paper. Your paper needs to be held flat.

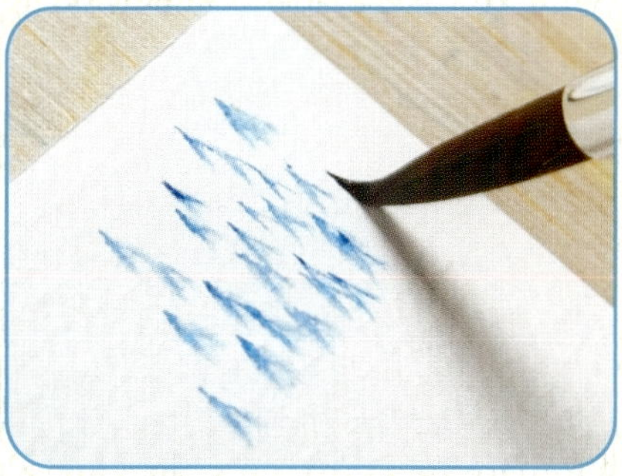

OTHER MARKS

What mark does your brush make if jabbed gently at the paper? This brush gave me a rough leaf shape (left). Try rotating your brush in your fingers to see if you get the same pattern if you turn it. Try with varying amounts of paint and pressure. Dots, swirls and squiggles (right) are most easily made with the brush held upright.

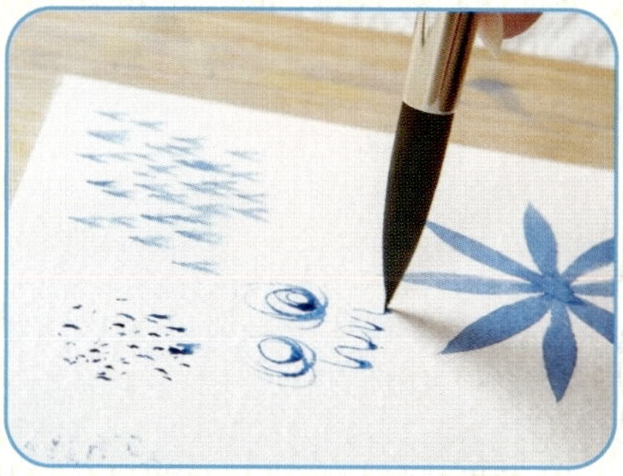

YOU WILL NEED

Paint colours: Prussian blue, permanent rose

Brushes: size 10 round

PREPARING A WASH

When preparing a wash, put water into the palette and add colour to it until you have the correct strength of colour. Experiment with clean water to find the amount you need to wet your sheet of paper. You can then allow the paper to dry and reuse it, knowing how much water you'll need for a wash.

When you begin to work on larger paintings you may be surprised at just how much paint you'll need for a full page. Try half a teaspoon of water as a starting point for the 15 x 10cm (6 x 4in) size of painting in this book. Remember that the brush will take up quite a lot of paint, and allow for that.

Washes

Being able to create a good wash is a basic watercolour skill. A wash is simply an area of paper covered with diluted paint. For best results, do this simply and directly, using plenty of the diluted paint. The result should be free of streaks and almost 'glow' as the paper shows through a thin wash.

Good paper is essential for a successful wash; cheap papers may cockle or disintegrate. You can, however, practise multiple washes on one sheet of good paper, by allowing each to dry thoroughly before applying the next.

A wash should only be worked into or added to while it is still damp enough to shine. If you add paint once the shine subsides, the effect is similar to when a drop of water falls from your brush onto your damp painting; you will get a blotchy watermark or 'backrun'. This occurs because the paper has already absorbed some of the water from the first wash. A common beginner's mistake is to fuss too much; if, for instance, you notice a small fleck of paper unpainted, the temptation is to go back and paint it, but you may create a backrun where the new paint displaces the paint in the first wash. Leave it to dry before doing anything.

Technique: **Flat wash**

A flat wash is a basic wash that will help you understand the importance of having plenty of paint prepared, applying it generously and leaving it to dry. The colour and tone of the paint should be the same throughout the wash. Don't wash the brush in between strokes, as this will dilute your paint.

Before you begin, secure your paper to a board, and set it at a slight slope in order to help the paint flow. Mix a little more paint than you think you'll need.

Holding the brush upright as you paint each stroke allows the paint to almost fall from the brush. If your brush starts to run out of paint before you get to the other side of the paper, quickly dip again and continue; try to use a large enough brush so that this doesn't happen.

Don't worry about the little pool or bead of paint that forms at the lower edge of the wash; this prevents the paint from drying too quickly and allows the next stroke to blend smoothly into it.

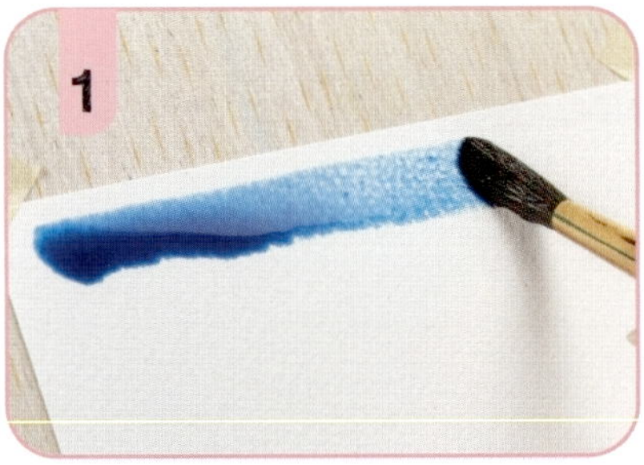

1 Starting from the top of your paper, load your brush with paint dilute enough to form a drop at the brush tip. Draw it in a broad stroke from left to right (right to left if you're left-handed).

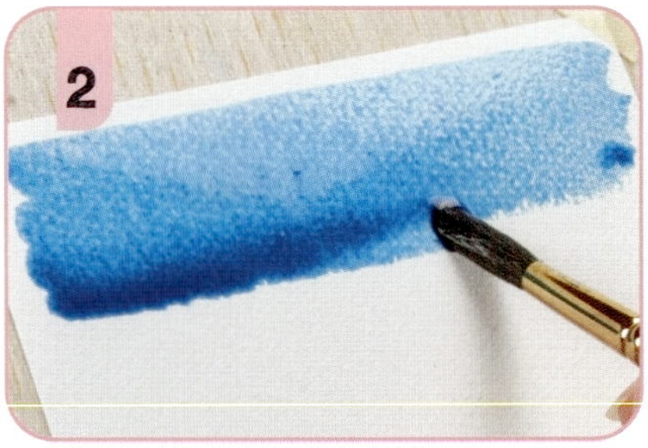

2 Lift the brush away, then make another stroke from left to right, overlapping the previous, still wet, one. This helps to avoid streaks.

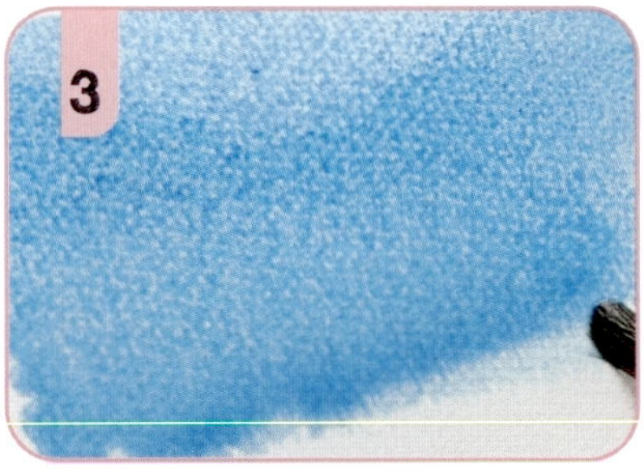

3 When you have painted as much as you wish to paint, dab your brush on kitchen paper to remove excess moisture and create a thirsty brush; use the tip of the brush to 'drink' any colour that is pooling at the edge. Don't press too hard or you may create a pale area in your work.

SIMPLE LANDSCAPE

Although the ability to produce a flat wash is a desirable skill, the graduated wash will be more commonly used in a landscape painting, as skies and landscapes vary in tone and colour. Tone is the lightness or darkness of a colour. A sky will normally (but not always) be paler at the horizon, as will land, so your stronger tones and colours will normally be at the top and bottom of your painting.

You can dilute the paint as you go or prepare different dilutions in your palette and use paler/weaker ones as you work down the paper. The method for applying paint to paper is the same as for a flat wash.

For land you could rotate your paper 180 degrees (so that it is upside-down) so that you can still work dark to light. Unless sky and land are to merge together you'd let the sky dry before painting the land.

You can also paint a graduated wash that changes in colour and tone by gradually introducing the second colour into the mix, and variegated washes where several colours are used.

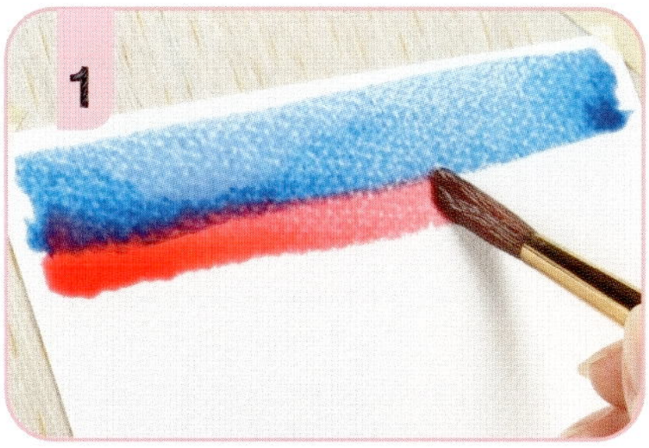

1 Start the graduated wash with a broad stroke of Prussian blue. While wet, quickly rinse your brush, then load it with permanent rose for the second stroke.

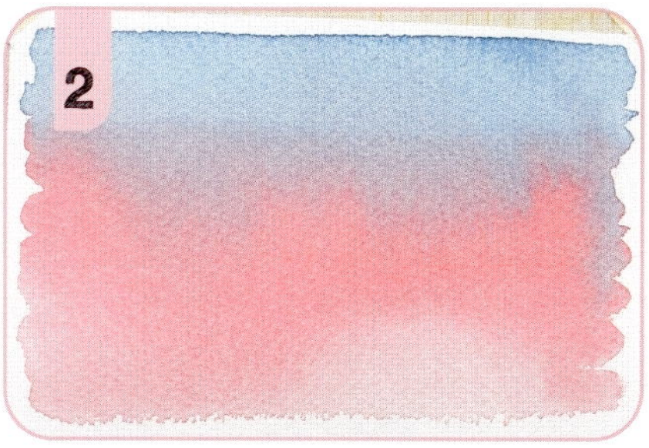

2 Work down to the bottom of the paper, as for a flat wash. Allow to dry thoroughly.

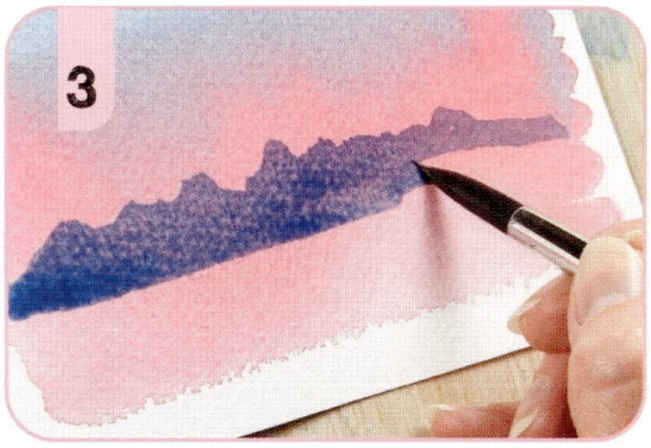

3 Use Prussian blue to paint a simple wiggly line as a mountain range, then fill in down to a flat line (the horizon). This is effectively an area of flat wash laid over the top of the previous wash.

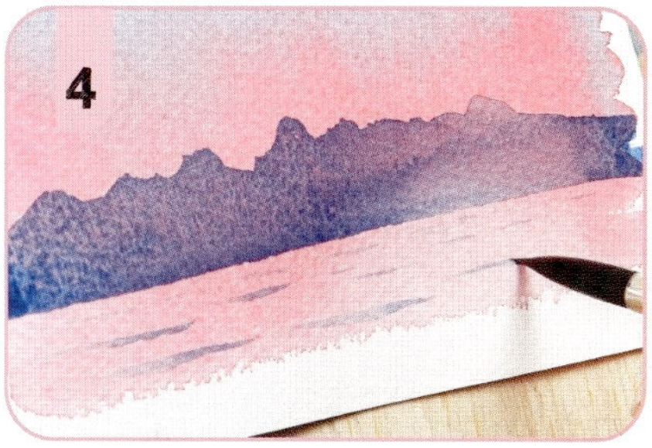

4 Use the point of your brush to add some lines as ripples in the water to finish your first mountain landscape.

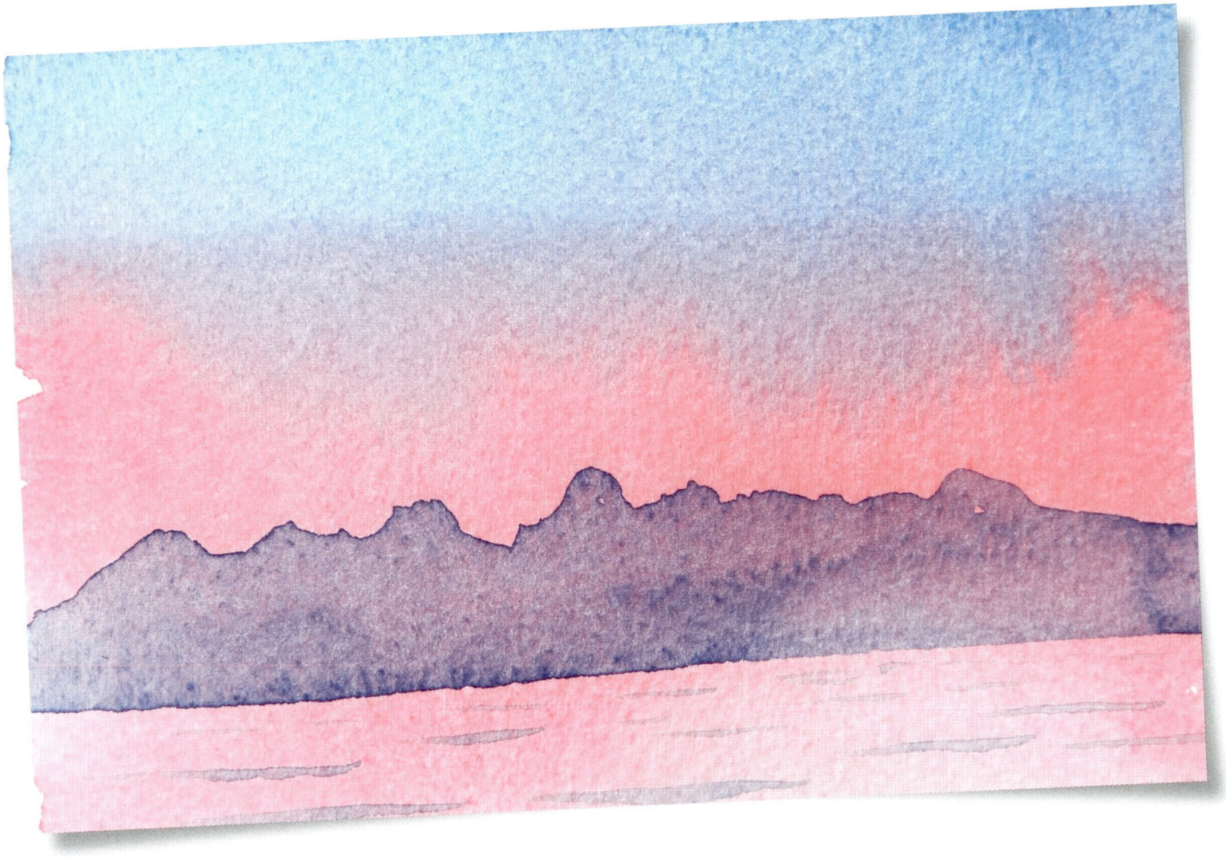

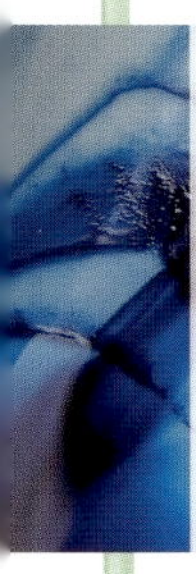

YOU WILL NEED

Paint colours: Winsor lemon, Winsor yellow, permanent rose, scarlet lake, Winsor blue (green shade), French ultramarine

Brushes: size 10 round

Colour mixing

You'll learn more about colour mixing if you explore what you can make from a few basics than if you buy every colour available. In fact, there is no such thing as the 'right colours' – what you choose depends on the subject you are painting and your own taste. These exercises are here to help you choose a few to begin with.

MIXING BASICS

The primary colours of red, yellow, and blue cannot be mixed from other colours but many colours can be made from them. There are a number of ways to do this with watercolour; either in the palette, prior to applying it to the paper, or on the paper itself.

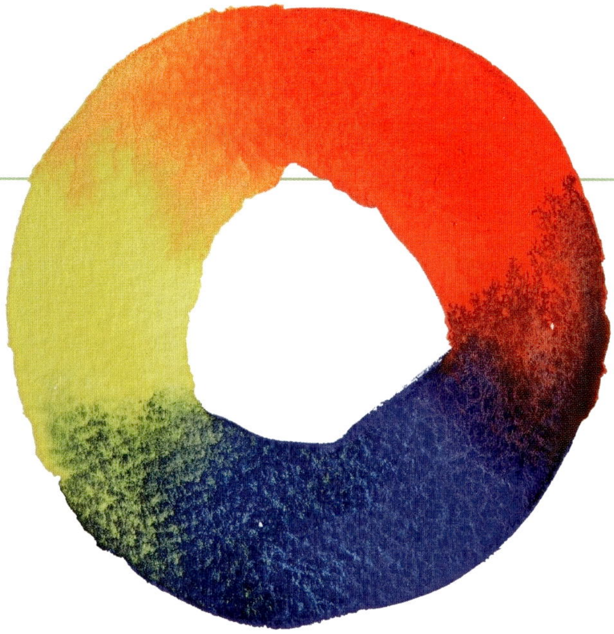

Technique: **Wet in wet**

The technique of allowing one colour to blend into another on the paper is called wet in wet. In the example to the right, areas of red, yellow and blue were painted. While wet, the areas were drawn together with the brush and allowed to bleed together, creating areas of orange, green, and purple where the different colours mix on the paper.

Orange, green and purple are the secondary colours, which are the result of combining two primary colours. The precise hues you create will depend on the primary colours you use. Try painting a version using a different red, blue and yellow trio.

Technique: **Glazing**

You can also create mixes of colours on the paper by overlaying a weak wash of transparent colour over another dry wash.

This is called glazing, and it can be a very effective way to create a colour that 'glows' or has a transparency that would not be achieved by other methods. The order in which your colours are laid onto the paper affects the end result: try this for yourself.

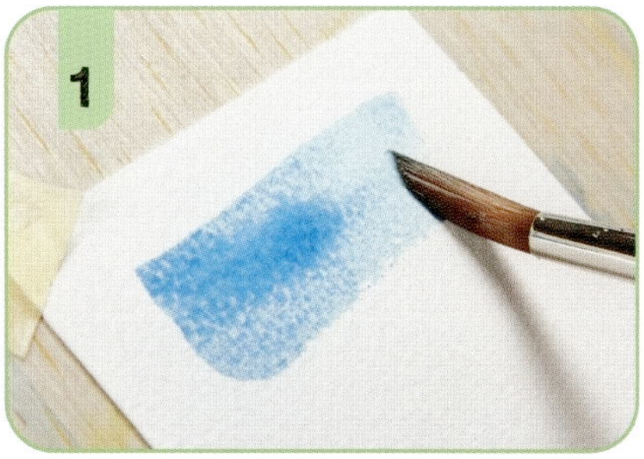

1 Prepare and apply your first colour to the paper.

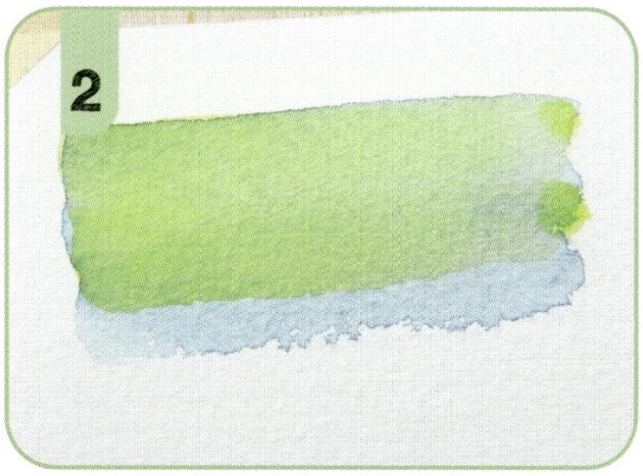

2 Allow to dry completely, then paint your second colour over the top to create the mix. The yellow applied here appears green, as some of the blue below shows through.

Technique: **Mixing in the palette**

Mixing in this way lets you create uniform mixes. Always add dark to light when mixing, and do so cautiously; a tiny amount of a strong colour can soon overpower a weaker or paler colour.

Tip

Change your rinsing water frequently; you won't get clear fresh colours if you're not washing your brush properly.

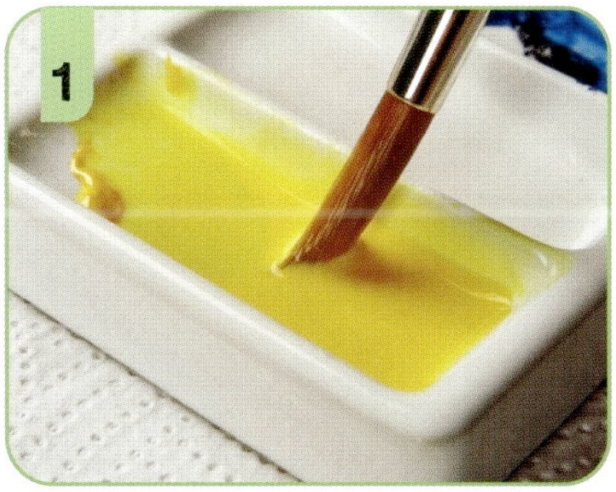

1 Prepare a well of a light colour – such as Winsor yellow – as described on page 12.

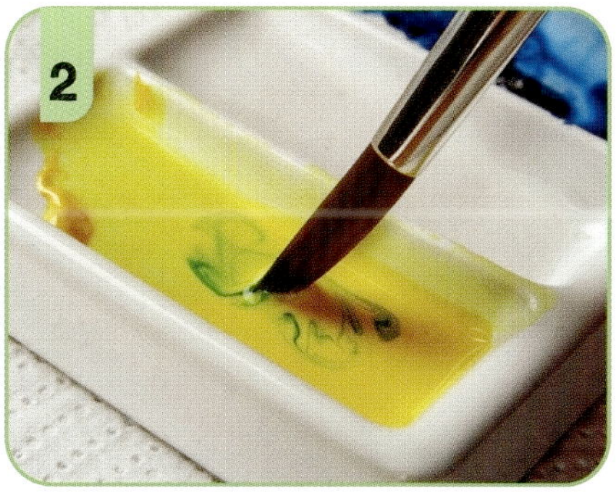

2 Clean the brush and pick up a small amount of a darker colour – Prussian blue, here – into the well.

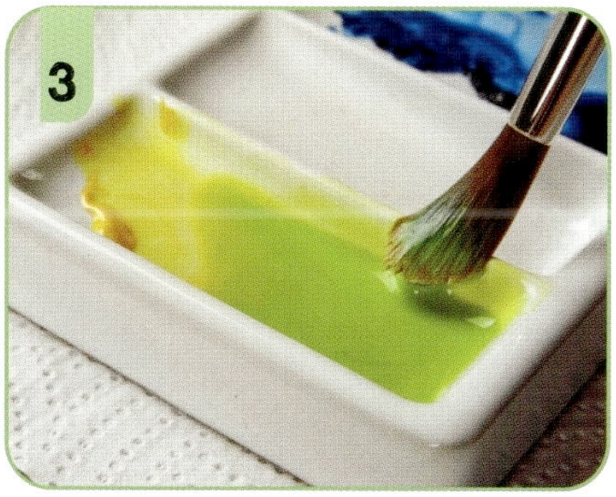

3 Mix well, then you can start to paint.

COLOUR CHART

Creating a simple chart like this will help you to practise mixing. Keep the brush well rinsed between mixes, and the paint on your palette clean. The colours used here are simply examples; you can substitute whatever colours you like.

1 Prepare small amounts of each colour in the wells on your palette. The first row and column headers say 'Winsor lemon' so paint pure Winsor lemon in the box (A).

2 The box below this in the Winsor lemon column has the Winsor yellow label, so combine the two colours in your palette and paint the resulting mix in this box (B).

3 Continue working down the Winsor lemon column in this way.

4 Working column by column, complete the remainder of the grid in this way to give a broad range of colours.

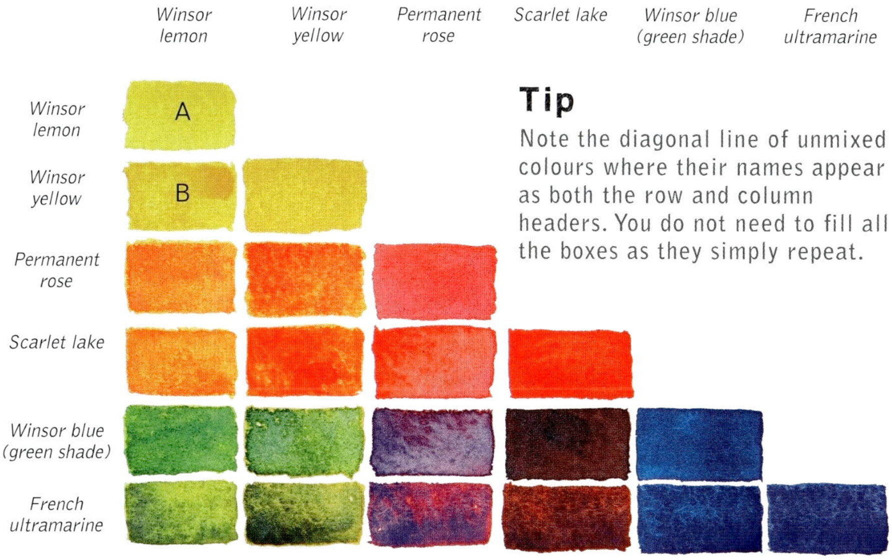

Tip

Note the diagonal line of unmixed colours where their names appear as both the row and column headers. You do not need to fill all the boxes as they simply repeat.

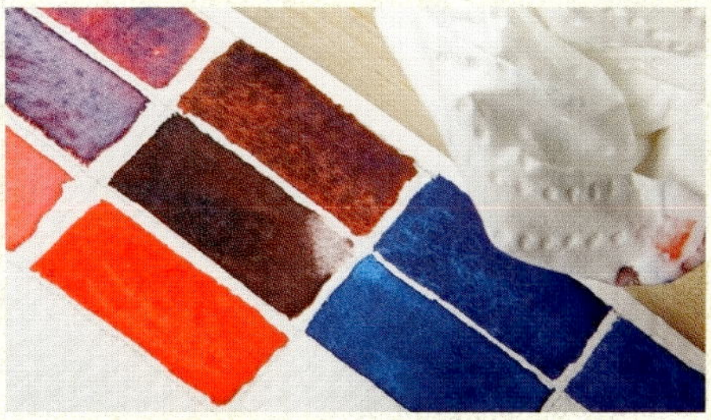

Staining colours

Allow the chart to dry, then use a damp brush to loosen colour then dab with kitchen paper to lift the colour away; you'll find out which colours will lift and which stain on that type of paper – useful to know as you get more adventurous in your work.

SKIES

Skies are a component of many landscape paintings. Although most of us enjoy a plain blue summer sky when we're outdoors, it lacks a certain dramatic appeal for a painting – though it may be enough where the focus is on spectacular mountains or a waterfall. If the sky is the focus of the painting, we may look for something more dramatic, and play down the mountains or landscape. In the examples here, the two colourful skies are quite powerful even if we cover up the hills, whereas the blue sky has little appeal by itself: each performs as required.

Painting skies offers perfect opportunities to practise techniques such as washes; lifting out; softening edges and negative painting to create clouds; glazing for transparent yet colourful skies; and wet-in-wet for soft blends into clean wet paper – or to allow colours to merge and create new colours. Granulating colours can be very effective in creating a stormy sky.

We often hear that we should use the same blue in our landscape or sea as we've used in the sky. With a limited palette (that is, with just a few colours) it is unlikely that you'll use colours that don't work together, but if you're unhappy with a painting where you've used two or more blues, try again using just one.

The sky often occupies quite a large area in a painting, so take this into account when preparing your colours. Mix plenty and remember that the colours will be paler once they dry.

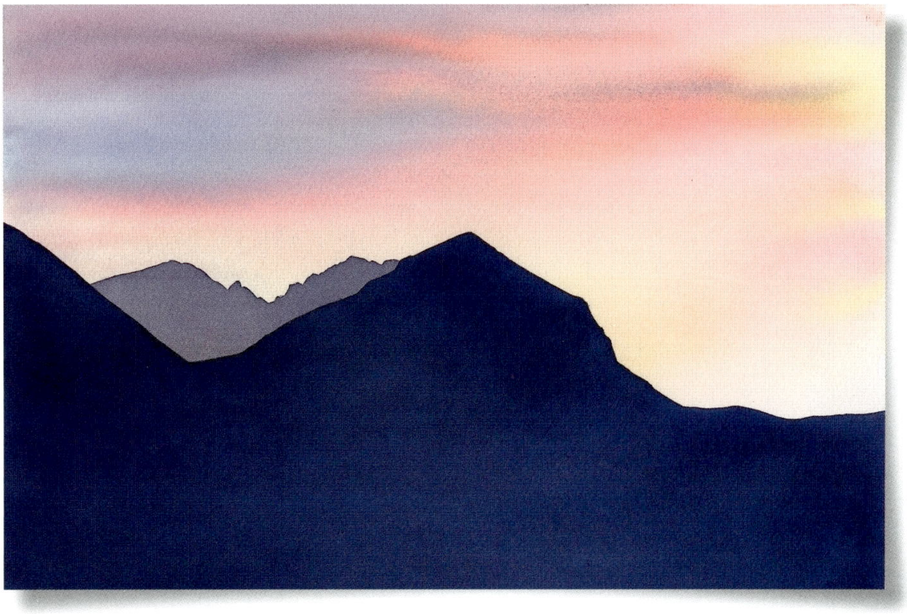

Moody Marsco

37 x 27cm (14½ x 10½in)

Evening skies can be quite colourful, sometimes dramatic, sometimes serene. I love the contrast of warm and cold colours and the simplicity of this one. The dark wash was painted over a thoroughly dry sky; a large pot of strong but fluid colour was prepared and the area was painted quickly.

GREEN SKIES

Occasionally beginners can find their sky turns green because they've used bright blue and bright yellow, which mix to make a bright green. Avoid green skies by:

- Making careful choices of the blue and yellow paints you use. Try using a subtle yellow, such as raw sienna, with a red-tinged blue like French ultramarine.
- Trying out the colours you plan to use on spare paper before beginning the painting itself.
- Separating the yellow and blue areas in your painting with an area of clean water, dry paper or another colour.
- Using glazing rather than working wet in wet.

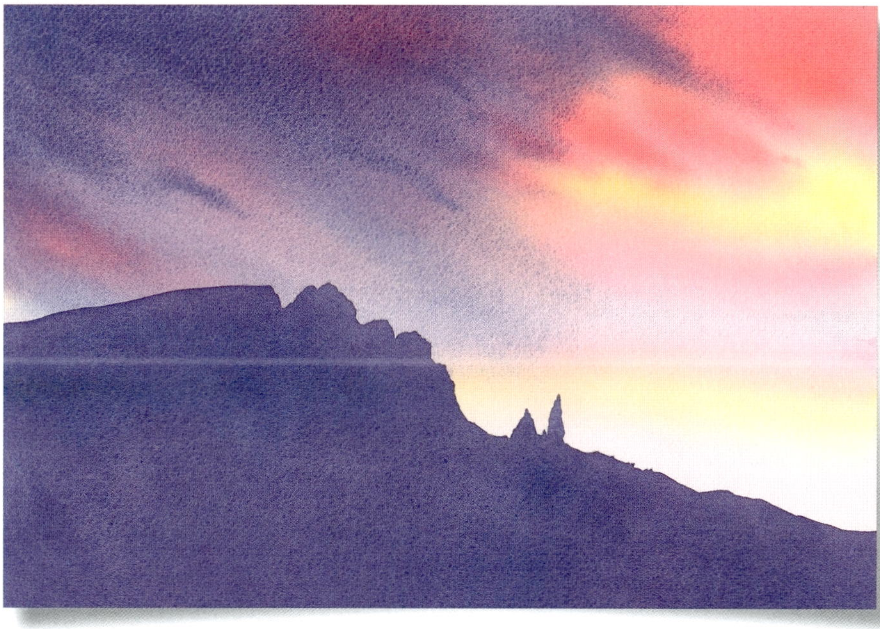

Storr Aurora

37 x 27 cm (14½ x 10½in)

Here colour was almost poured onto wet paper and allowed to drift diagonally all over the paper. The hills are painted wet on dry, but with weaker colour than used on *Moody Marsco* (see opposite), allowing a little of the wash beneath to shine through.

The Ben Deargs from Moll

37 x 27cm (14½ x 10½in)

I can almost feel the sun on my back as I remember this walk. It was early in the morning, the sun just beginning to warm an already bright day. The softest of clouds were gently lifted from the dry wash with a slightly damp brush and tissue; lifting from wet paint would have resulted in clouds that were too bright for this occasion.

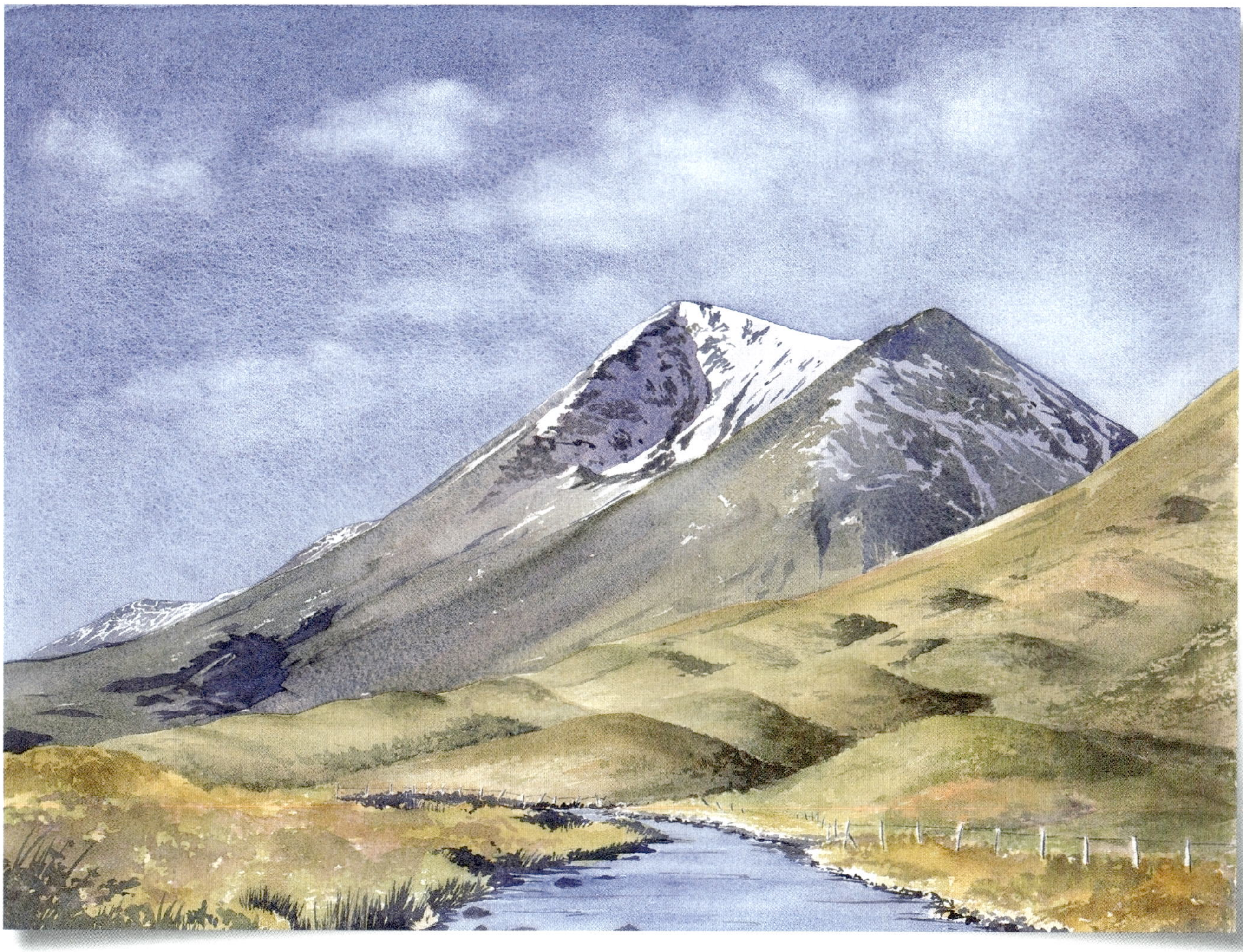

YOU WILL NEED

Paint colours: French ultramarine, raw sienna, burnt umber

Brushes: size 10 round

Other: tracing number 1, kitchen paper

Summer sky

A clear blue sky, with clouds lifted out from the wet wash, provides a simple but effective first step to painting skies like those shown in the reference photograph.

When mixing French ultramarine and burnt umber, add the burnt umber a little at a time: it's a strong colour that can quickly overpower the blue.

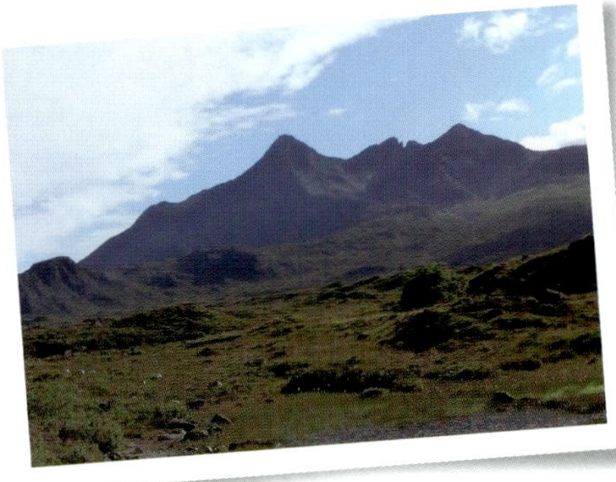

GRANULATION

This painting uses French ultramarine, a colour that gives a beautiful mottled effect called granulation. This is a characteristic of the paint, and caused by the particles of paint sinking into the textured surface of the paper.

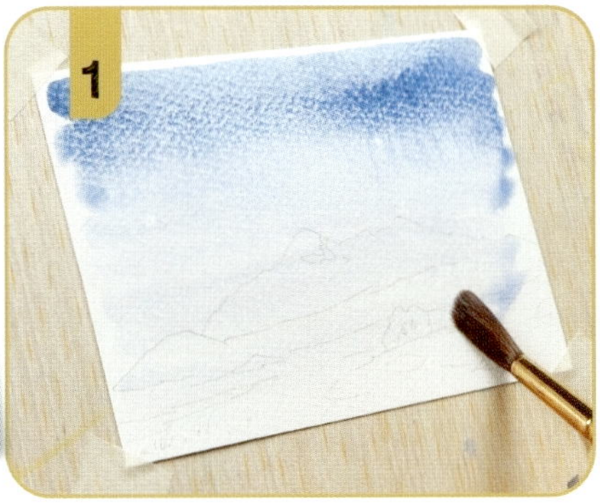

1 Have a piece of kitchen paper handy, crumpled into a ball. Secure your paper to the board, then paint the paper all over with a graduated wash of French ultramarine, introducing pure water instead of a second colour. This will result in the sky becoming gradually paler as it drops below the horizon.

WATCHING PAINT DRY

There are times when we really need to watch paint dry in order to avoid backruns, or to judge the degree of dampness for the effect we require. If you wish to work wet in wet, you need to learn how to judge this crucial stage by observation – watching paint dry – and experimenting with different colours and dilutions. A stronger mix will spread less than a very weak one of the same colour, while some colours spread more readily than others. Practise to see how they soften or spread into a wash.

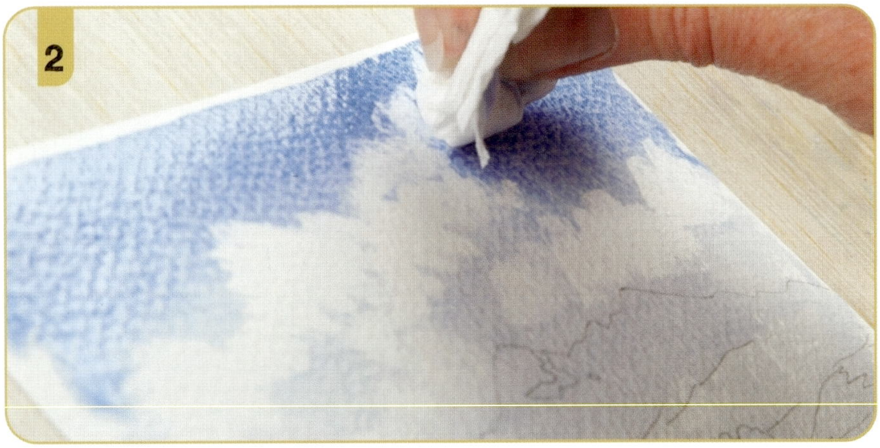

2 While it is still damp, lift out cloud shapes with the kitchen paper, making larger clouds at the top and smaller ones lower down. Work quickly and turn the kitchen paper frequently so that you don't put the paint back onto the painting. Allow to dry.

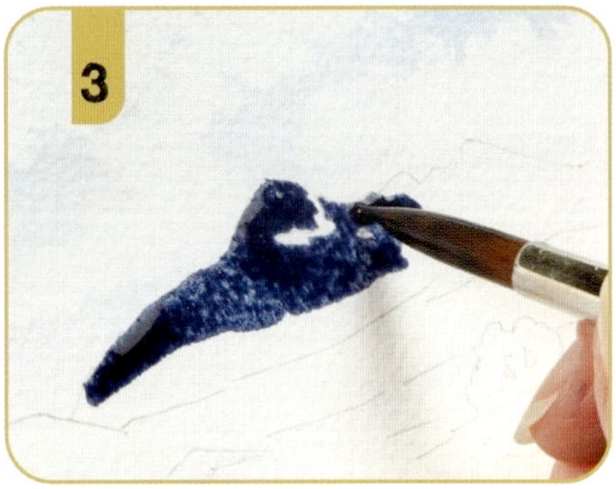

3 Paint the hills with a mix of French ultramarine and burnt umber, omitting the white area.

Technique: Lifting out

Lifting out is the controlled removal of wet paint using kitchen paper, as shown here. You can also lift out dry paint using a combination of brush and kitchen paper (see page 55). The degree of success – that is, how much paint is removed – will depend on the colour and paper used.

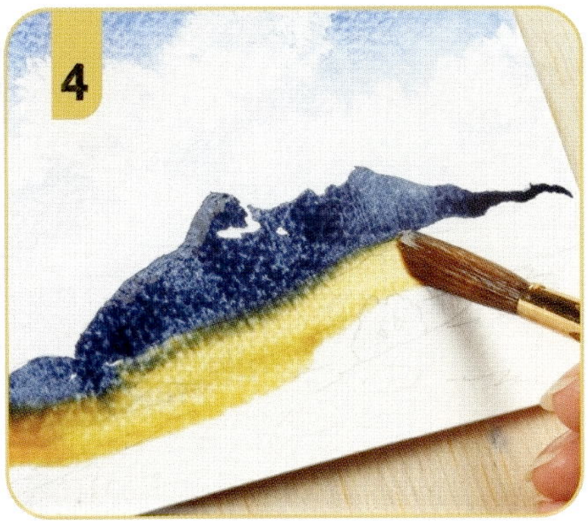

4 While the hills are still wet, paint the moorland below with pale raw sienna, allowing the two colours to blend on the paper.

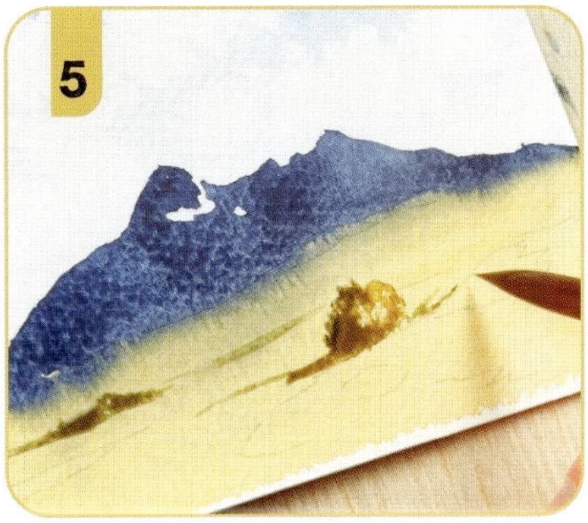

5 Using a raw sienna and French ultramarine mix, paint the shadow side of the mounds. For the shrub, use raw sienna and then a little French ultramarine, placing the colour in tiny dots – see stippling, below – and allow them to touch so that the colours can merge.

Technique: Stippling

Stippling is simply making lots of tiny dots of colour near to one another. It is useful for creating variation of colour in foliage, or to suggest small rocks and pebbles.

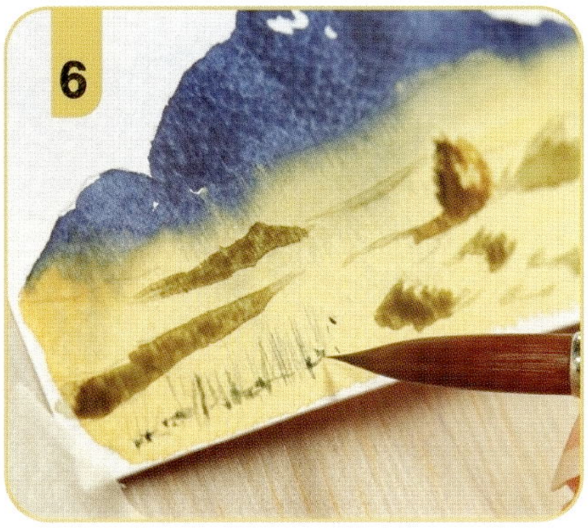

6 Add a few grass/stone details using a French ultramarine and burnt umber mix.

Technique: Fine grasses

Simply paint numerous fine lines, starting at the base of the grasses and flicking the brush towards the top – that is, in the direction of growth. For a solid 'base', finish with a horizontal line.

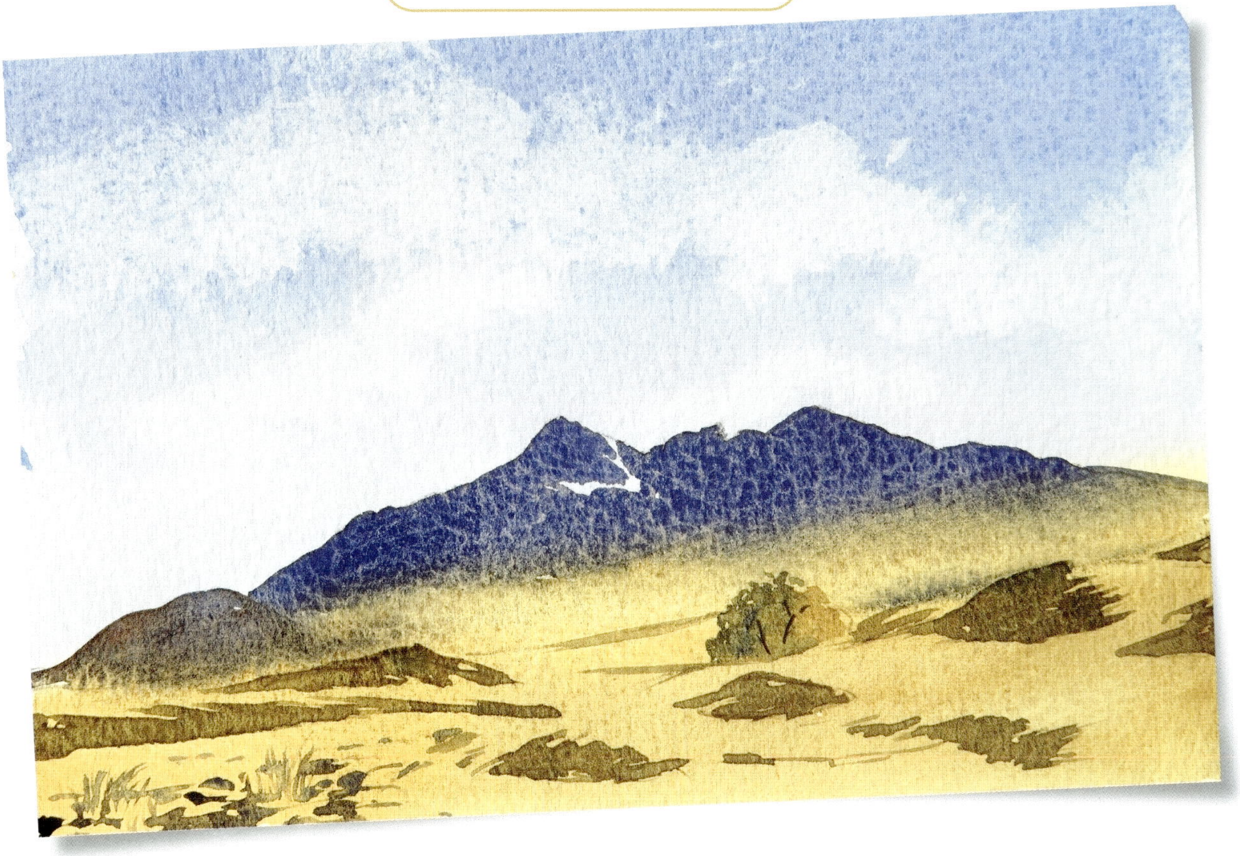

YOU WILL NEED

Paint colours: French ultramarine, raw sienna, burnt umber

Brushes: size 10 round

Other: tracing number 2

Rainy days

Blue skies are generally enjoyed by all, but they don't necessarily provide the mood you require in your painting. To creating a feeling of very wet weather, here's a simple method which allows the rain to fall in front of the hills; rather than confining it to the sky above and in the distance. It can be a little messy, just like a very wet day.

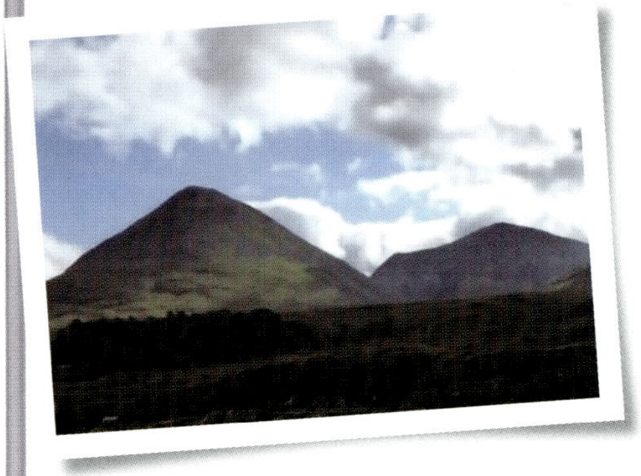

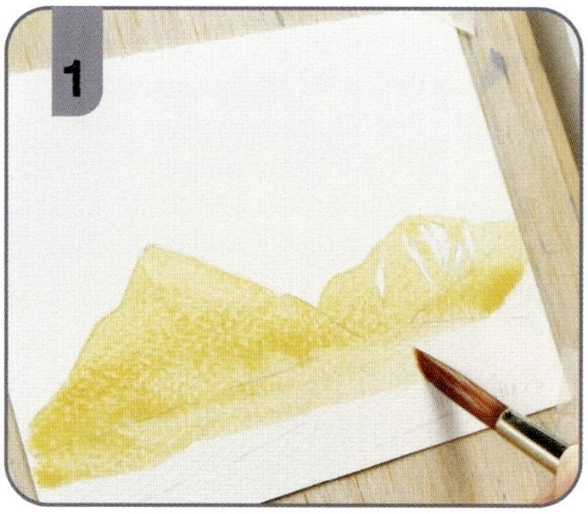

1 Paint the hills (omitting the snow areas) and moorland with raw sienna.

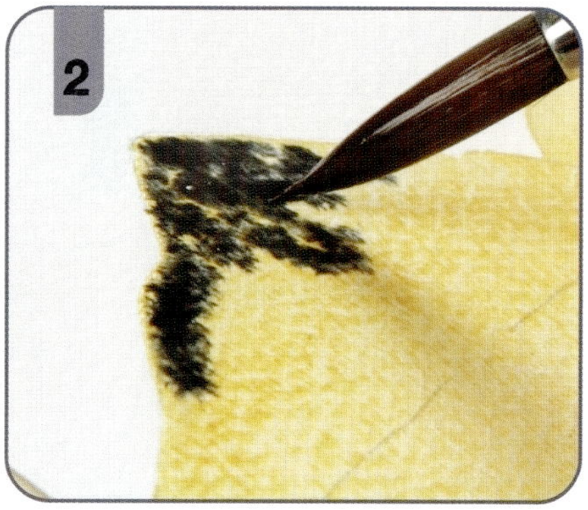

2 While wet, drop a French ultramarine and burnt umber mix in to the hills. Touch in the paint with the tip of the brush, allowing the colours to move around and blend.

Technique: Dropping in

Dropping in involves putting a loaded brush to the paper and allowing the colour to spread onto the paper naturally. If left alone, the paint diffuses into the wet surface to give a wonderful soft result.

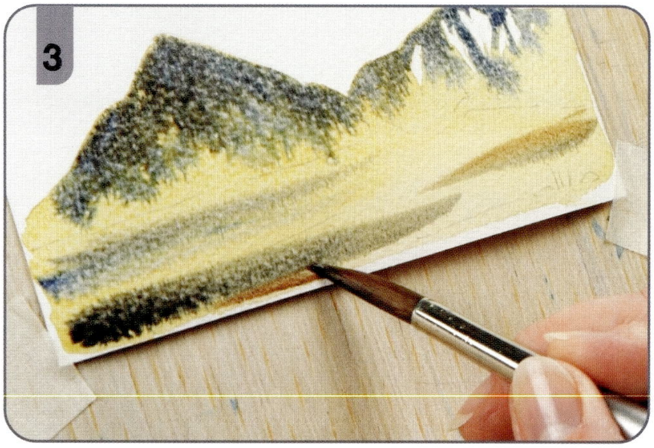

3 Add a few strokes to the moorland using a stronger mix of burnt umber and French ultramarine, plus a stroke or two of pure burnt umber in the foreground.

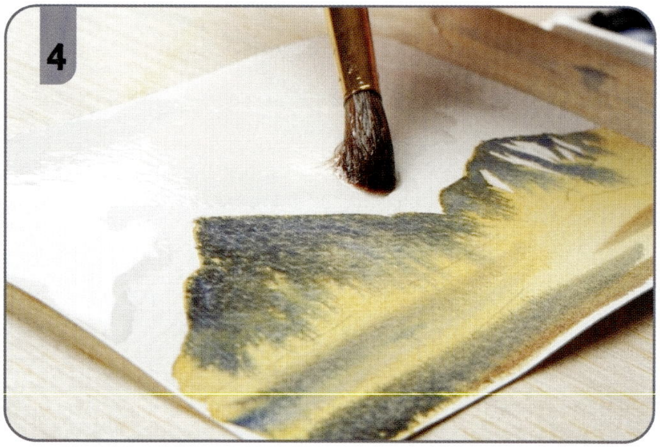

4 When sure that the painting is thoroughly dry, re-wet the whole surface quickly with clean water and minimal brushstrokes (you don't want the paint to soften and loosen from the paper).

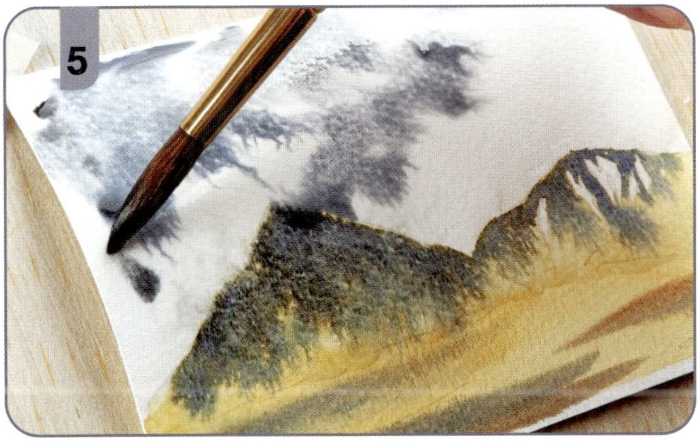

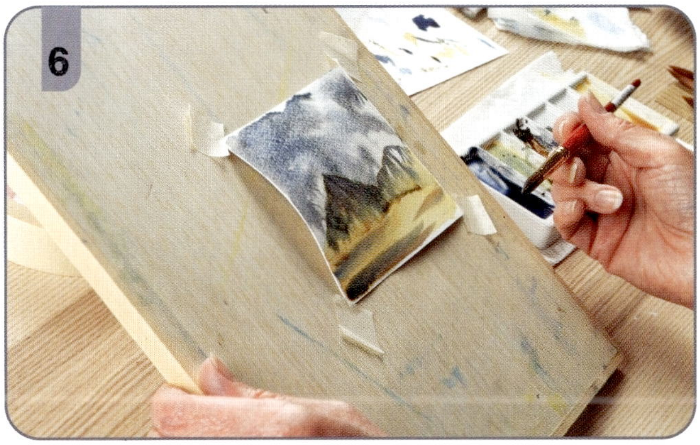

5 Drop a mix of French ultramarine and burnt umber into the sky.

6 While the paint remains wet, pick up your board and tilt the paper slightly to encourage the rain to move diagonally across the paper.

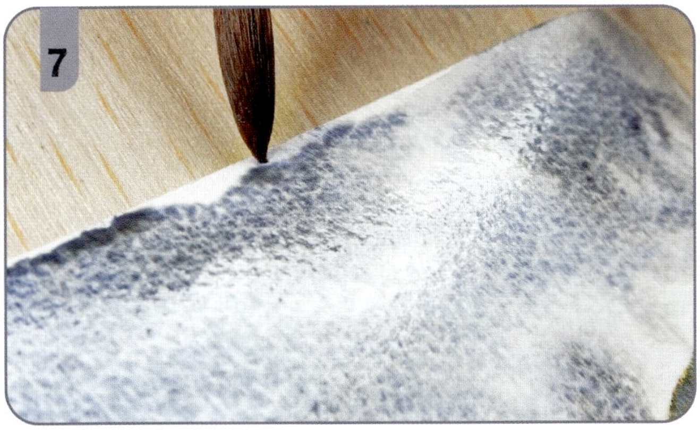

7 If necessary, mop up any drips that collect at the edges to avoid backruns. You can do this by touching the drips with kitchen paper or the tip of a 'thirsty brush'. Once dry, add a few foreground details with the colours used already to finish.

Technique: **Thirsty brush**

A thirsty brush is one that is damp but has been blotted on kitchen paper to ensure that is is dry enough to 'drink up' moisture. Touched to wet paint, it will draw liquid into it, which allows you to lift out wet paint in a very controlled way. Be careful to use just the tip, or you risk removing too much paint. Sable or sable/synthetic mix brushes tend to be better for this than synthetic hair brushes.

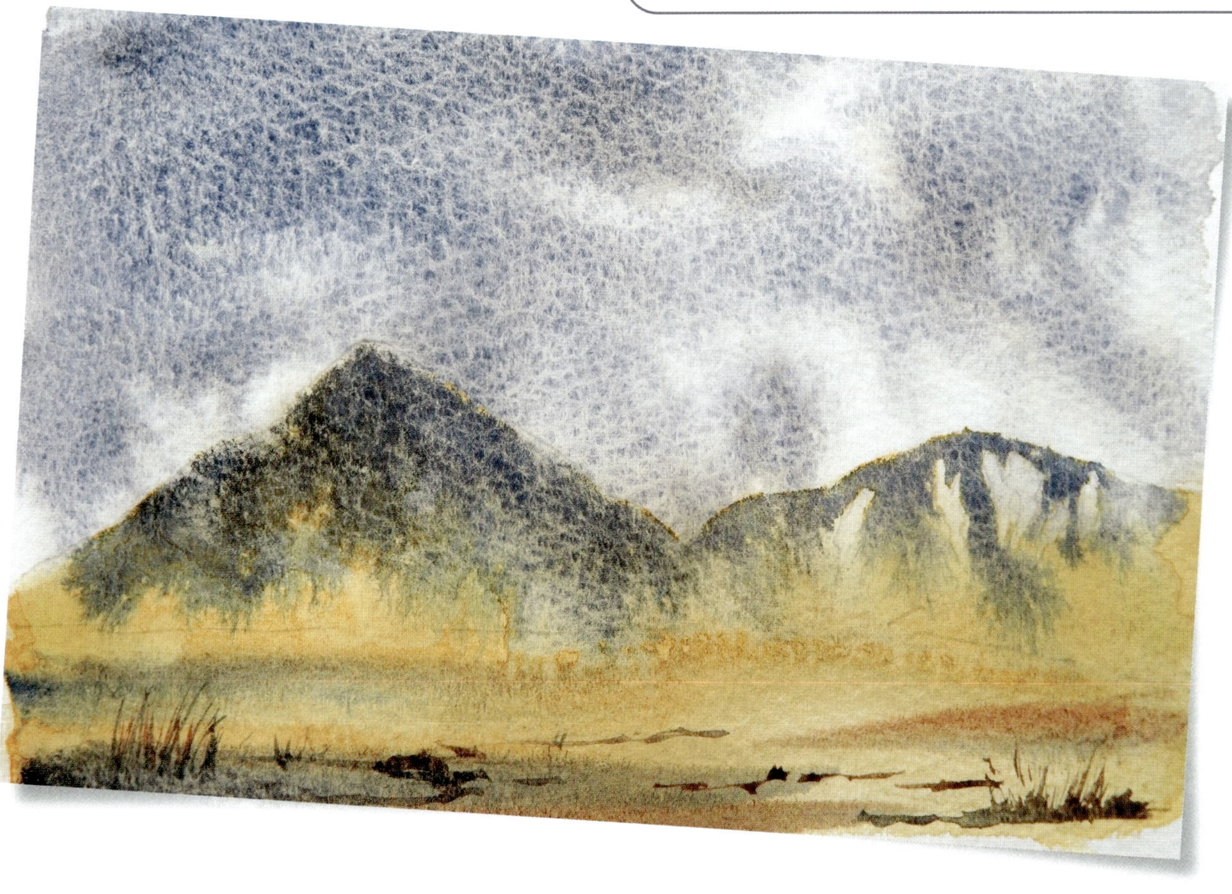

Colourful clouds

YOU WILL NEED

Paint colours: French ultramarine, raw sienna, permanent rose

Brushes: size 10 round

Other: tracing number 3, putty eraser

Capturing the effect of sunlight and shadows on billowing clouds may seem daunting, but it can be quite simple if you plan your work. The clouds are painted 'negatively', that is, created by the blue painting around them; and the colours within them placed carefully to avoid the likelihood of unfortunate colour blends. Here, placing the pink clouds next to the yellow keeps the blue separate from the yellow, reducing the chance of green clouds occurring.

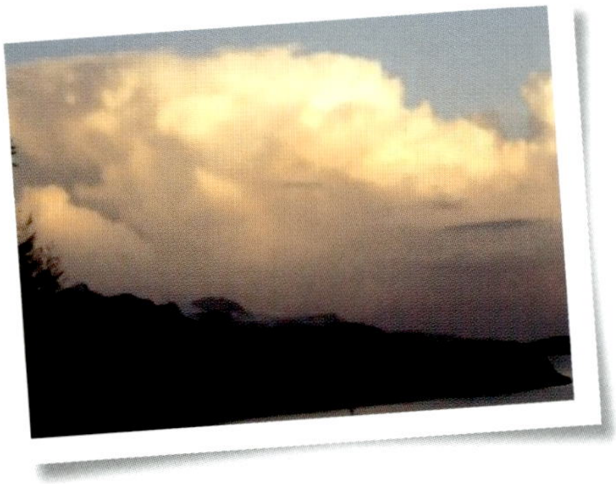

NEGATIVE AND POSITIVE PAINTING

Positive painting is simply picking out features directly – painting a cloud itself, for example – while negative painting is suggesting the shape of an object by painting the area around it. Here, we suggest the cloud by painting the sky behind it – an example of negative painting.

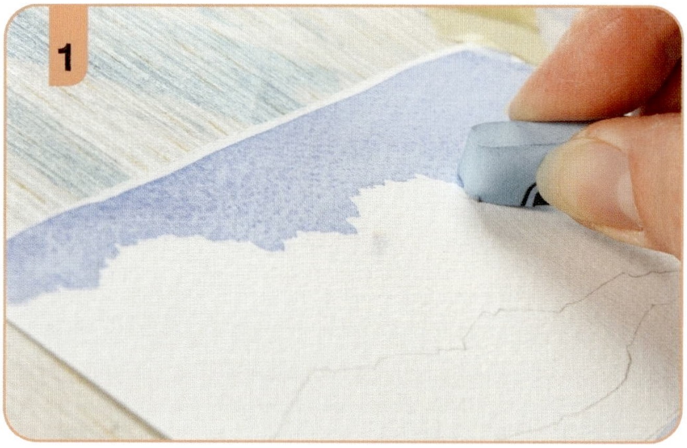

1 Paint the sky with French ultramarine, quickly creating a ragged edge for the clouds before the paint dries. Soften the cloud edge on the right with a clean damp brush. Aim to paint up to, but not over, the pencil lines. Once dry, use a soft eraser to remove the pencil line. It isn't always necessary or desirable to remove pencil, but there are some occasions when it is best removed, particularly when the surrounding areas are very light in tone.

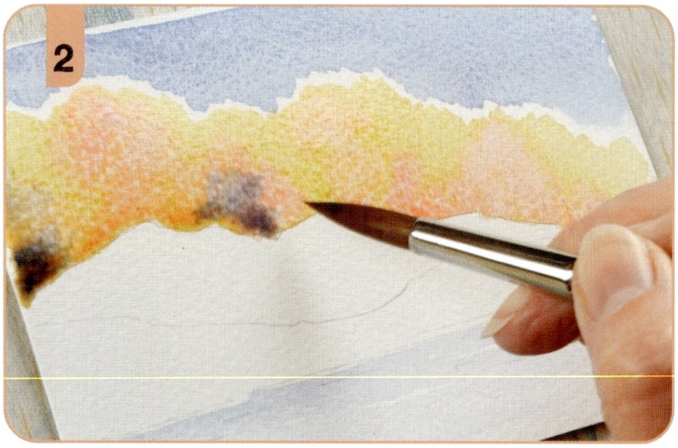

2 Paint the sea with very pale French ultramarine, leaving a few thin horizontal lines of clean, dry paper. Paint the cloud with pale raw sienna, leaving a ragged white line at the top edge, then drop in permanent rose, and add French ultramarine to the pink area for the darker areas of the cloud.

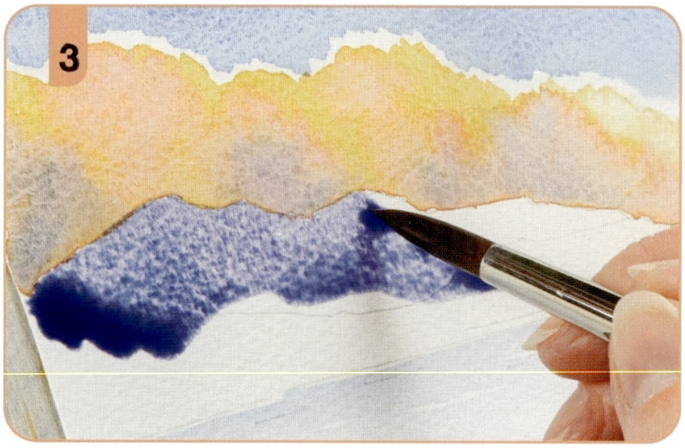

3 With a mix of French ultramarine and a little permanent rose, paint in the land mass.

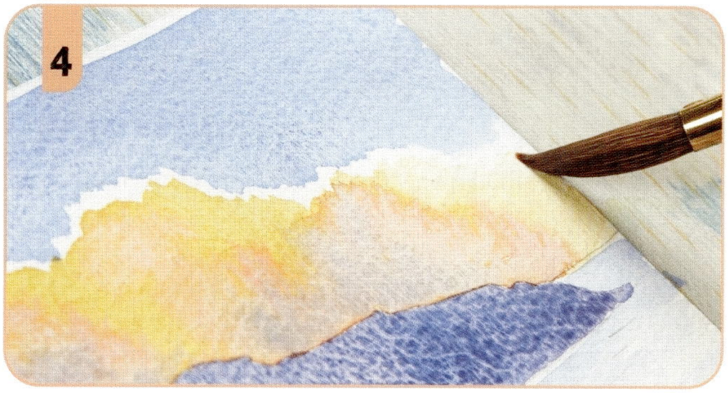

4 Lift the top right-hand edge of the cloud using a clean, damp brush.

Technique: Softening

To soften an edge, use a clean, damp brush to draw the colour away from the edge of the wash. The amount of water is critical: if your brush is damp, you will gently encourage the paint to move; but if your brush is very wet and you push it into the wash, you're likely to create a backrun as the pigment is lifted and pushed out of the way.

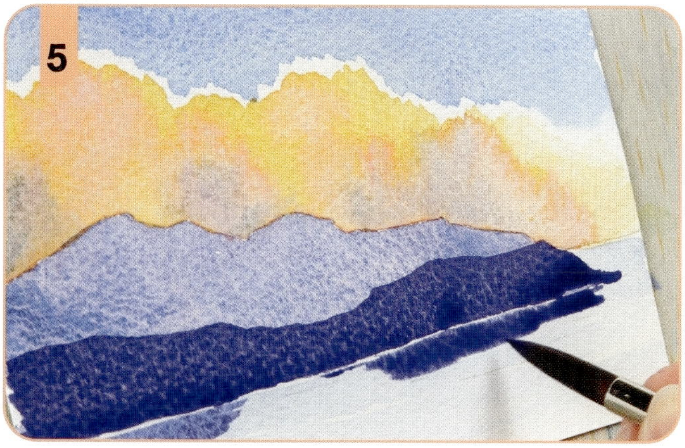

5 Paint the nearer land mass again, with a stronger mix. Add a few horizontal lines to suggest reflections in the sea, leaving a thin white line at the shore.

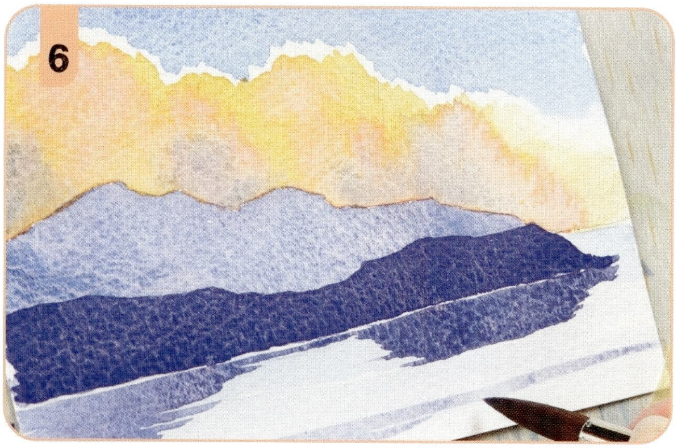

6 Add a few lines of French ultramarine to the lower part of the sea to reflect the blue area of the sky. Add a touch of pale permanent rose here and there, but leave some areas unpainted on the sea to reveal the pale wash underneath.

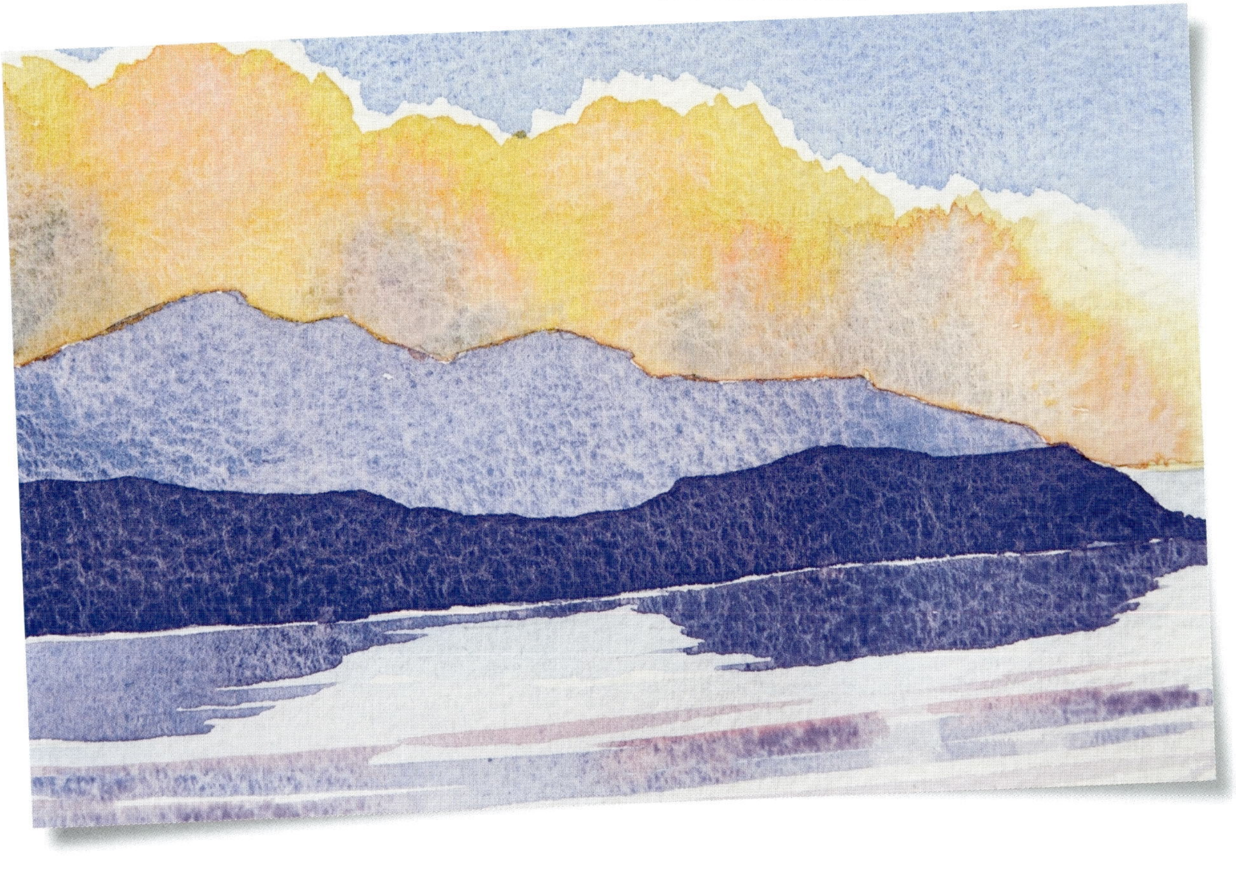

Sunrise and sunset

YOU WILL NEED

Paint colours: raw sienna, permanent rose, French ultramarine

Brushes: size 10 round

Other: tracing number 4

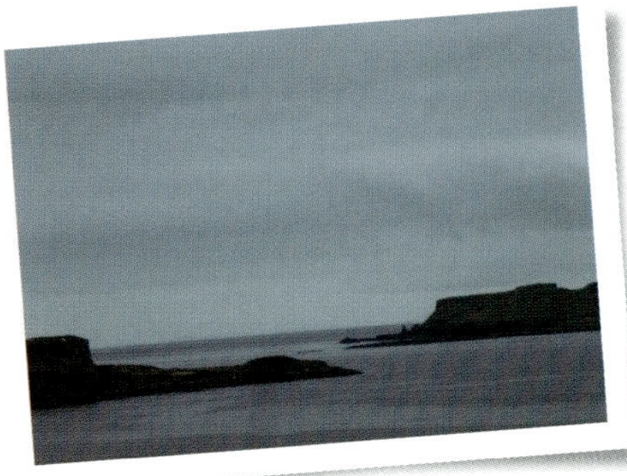

People often paint sunrises and sunsets with thickly applied oranges and reds that dry dull and have none of the beauty that is possible with watercolour. The technique of glazing will allow you to build colour that has a luminous look. It is useful for building colours and tones – and if, after two or three washes, you don't have quite the overall colour you require, you can add another wash. In this example, you would do so before adding clouds or land.

1 Using raw sienna, paint a graduated wash over the whole paper. Allow to dry completely.

2 Now paint a graduated wash of permanent rose over the whole paper. Again, allow to dry completely.

3 Paint a graduated wash of raw sienna, then immediately prepare a medium-tone mix of permanent rose and French ultramarine.

4 While the paint is still wet, 'drop in' clouds with this mix, allowing the cloud colour to spread into the damp paint. Begin cautiously; if the first cloud spreads too far, allow the wash to dry a little more before continuing.

5 Once the raw sienna wash has dried, Dilute some of the cloud mix to make a paler version. Use this to paint the most distant islands. Add a few horizontal lines to the sea, suggesting ripples.

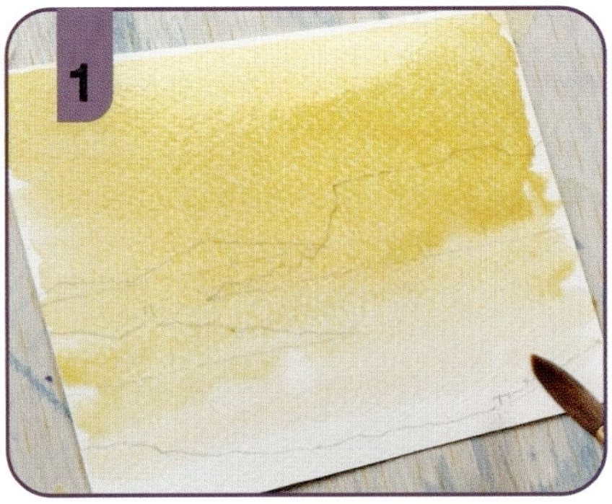
1

Technique: Glazing

Glazing is simply painting one or more thin layers of transparent colour over dry washes. Each layer is a glaze.

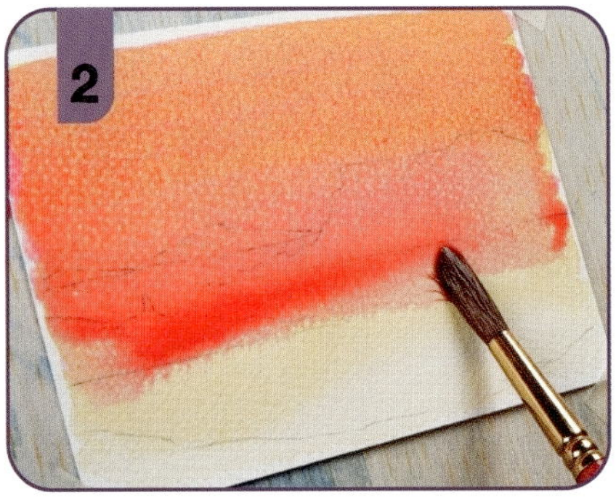
2

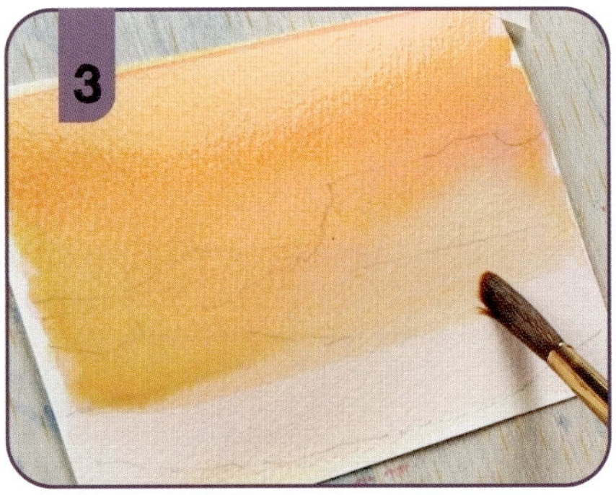
3

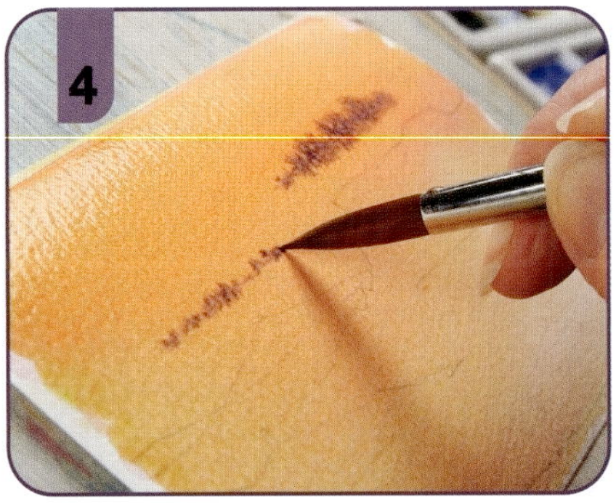
4

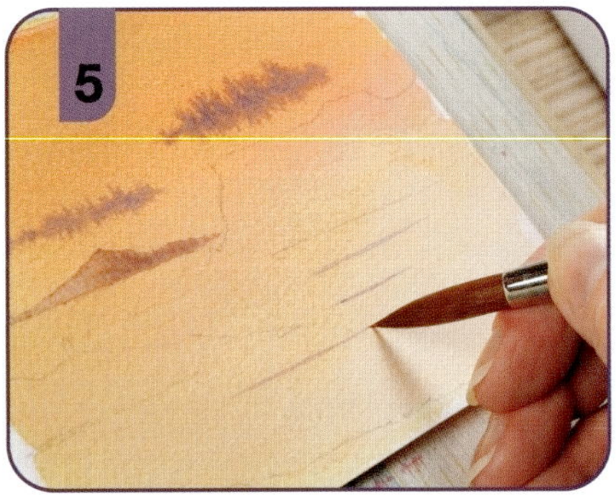
5

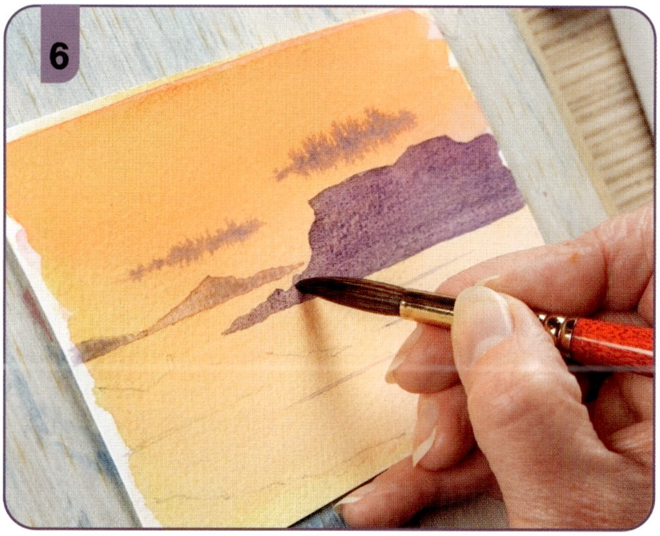

6 Paint the land mass in the middle distance using a medium tone of the cloud colour – you can strengthen a mix simply by adding more paint to it.

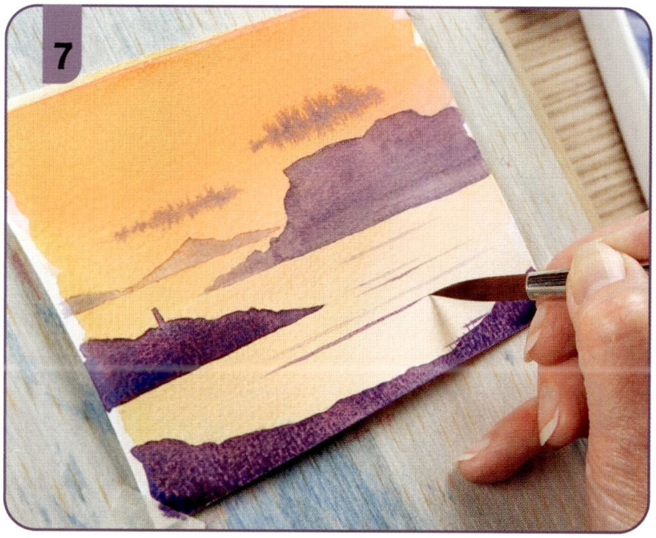

7 Use a stronger mix to paint the nearest land mass and foreground, and add a few horizontal lines to the sea.

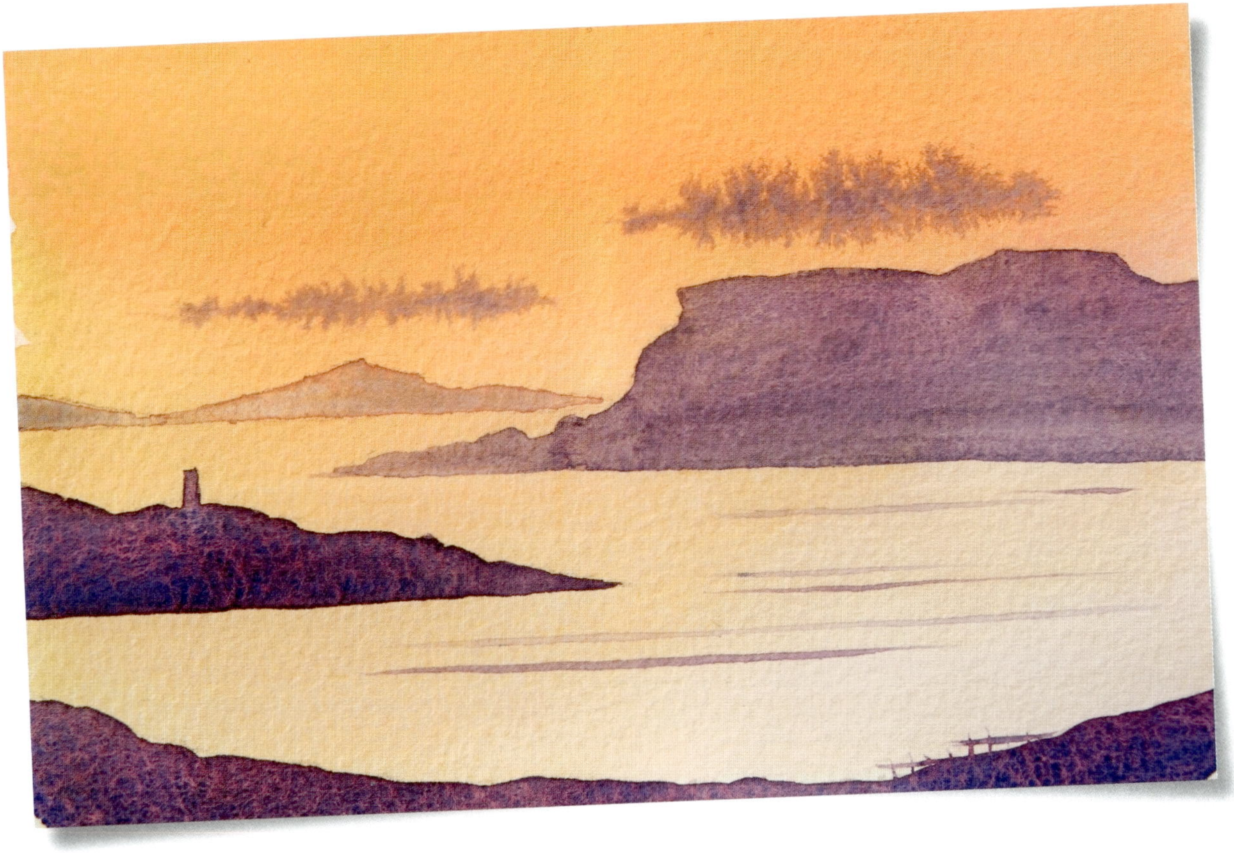

MOORLAND, FOLIAGE & TREES

You'll notice that there is no green paint in my selection of colours on page 9. I find that green paints that are used as purchased can be quite unnatural, and I prefer mixing my own. Nature rarely (if ever) gives us a large expanse of the same colour and tone of green, and we can be very lazy in assuming that 'grass is green' rather than observing the true colours and tones. Consider the moorland and mountain landscape. In summer, heather and bracken can be strong deep greens, but there may also be browns and russets left from last season. Heather blooms are only purple when at their best – they soon fade to pale pink-orange. Rushes and sedges can be quite strong dark green; bog myrtle anything from gold to green and brown. Mosses can be almost white when dry, through bright greens to orange/pink/red. In winter browns and golds and pale straw colours may dominate. Even grasses can be greens, bright golds and reds.

A good range of greens is achievable by mixing my blues with yellows, or browns. If a blue and yellow give me a green that is a little too bright, I may add a touch of red. If you have greens in your palette, try mixing them with other colours for a greater variety of colours.

Wet-in-wet techniques can give soft initial washes with a range of colour and tonal variations, as shown in the examples here. Drybrush can add texture, and combining positive and negative shapes creates detail.

Use of softer colours and foliage that is more blue than green can suggest distance, particularly when combined with stronger, warmer colours and more detail in the foreground. In *Five Sisters from Ratagan*, for example, vegetation in the shadows of the slopes of distant hills is suggested by the blue/greens, while nearer trees are painted in warmer tones. The tiny, distant, mature trees dropping down the foreground slope towards the shore merely hint at species, while the young birch trees in the foreground have been given more detailed treatment to show lighter, negatively-painted trunks and fine branches. All this adds up to a convincing, living landscape for mountains to inhabit.

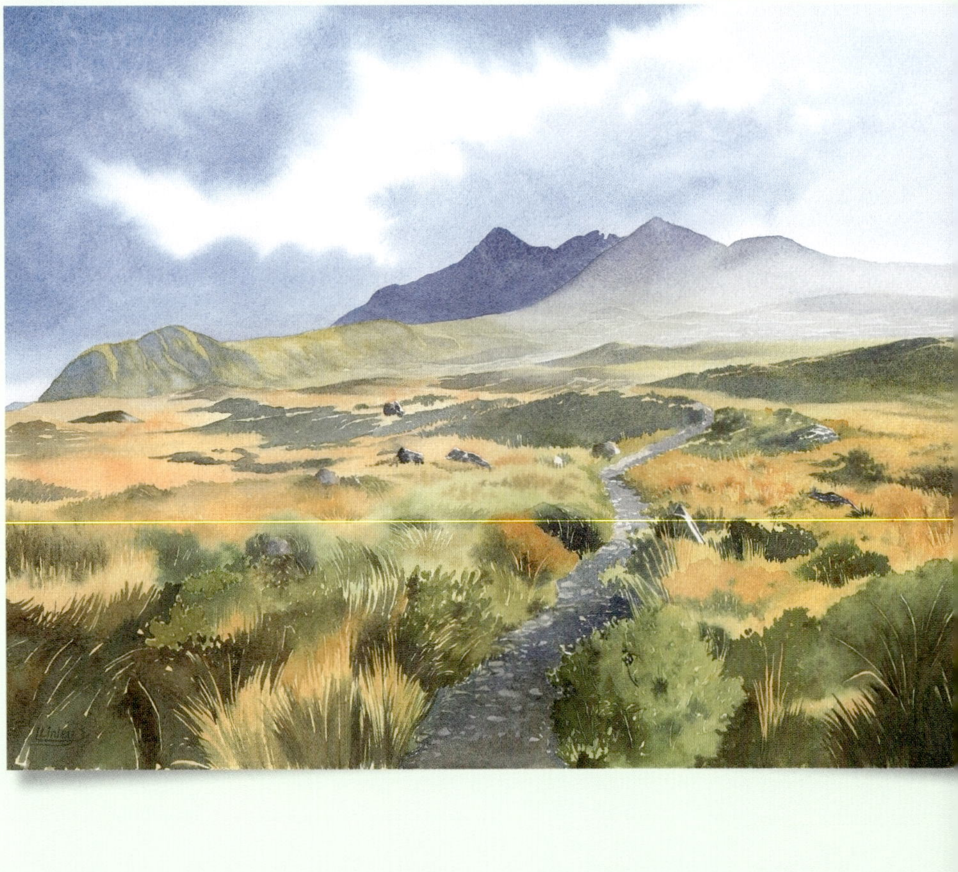

Cuillin Greens and Gold

37 x 27cm (14½ x 10½in)

Late afternoon/early evening on a summer day (the lightest part of the sky, on the right, tells me the time of day as I know this area well). The greens are bright but strewn amongst bright golds are not monotonous. Detail in the foreground gives way to hints of distant moorland.

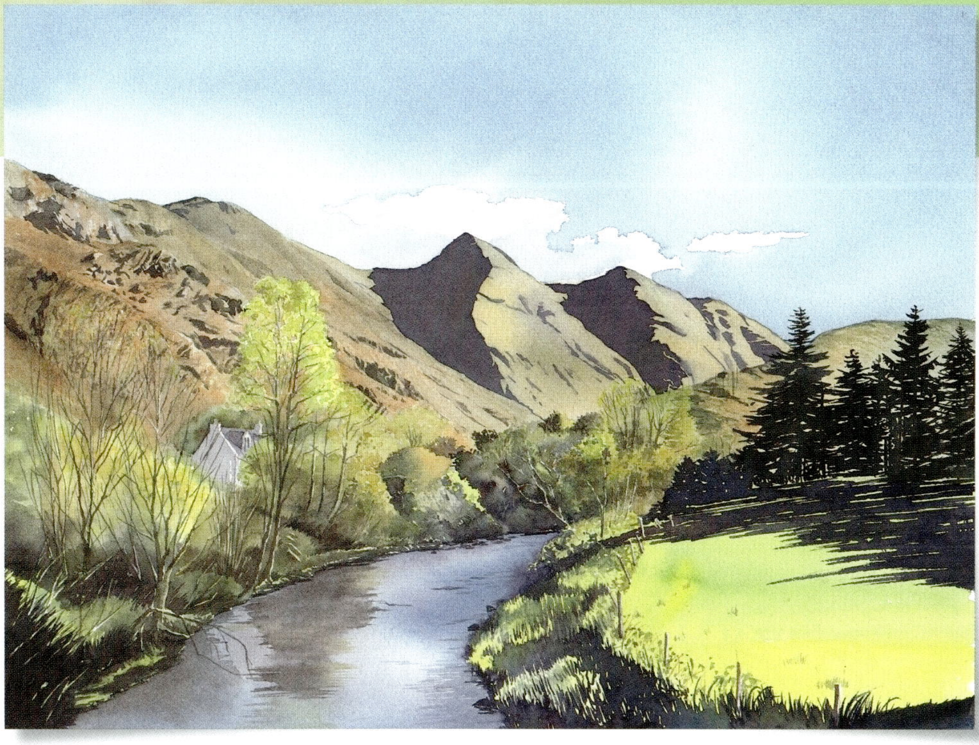

Sgurr Fhuaran from Shiel Bridge

37 x 27cm (14½ x 10½in)

An usually green mountain scene; these hills are clothed in grass and, seen here in spring colours, the foreground colours are at their brightest. Shadows are important in describing contours and adding contrast.

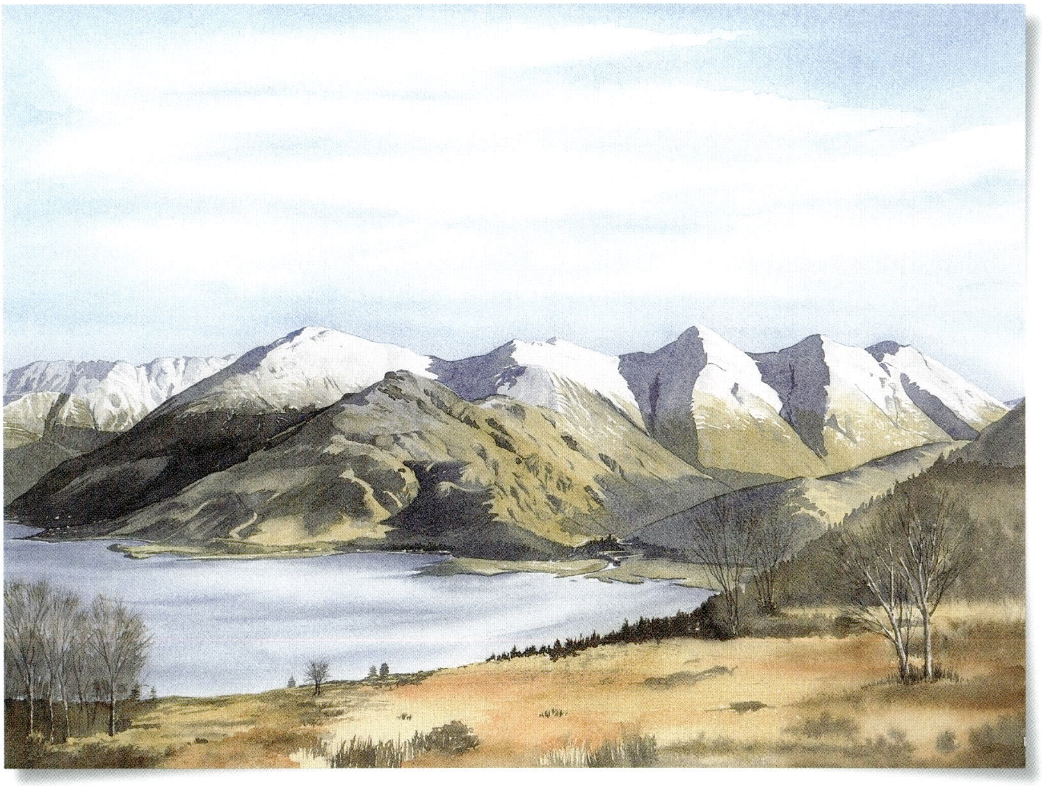

Five Sisters from Ratagan

37 x 27cm (14½ x 10½in)

This winter scene shows mountains capped in snow, yet there's a little warmth in the scene from their golden lower slopes and the warmer colours in the foreground; a very still day with only the subtlest of clouds in the sky.

YOU WILL NEED

Paint colours: French ultramarine, raw sienna, scarlet lake

Brushes: size 10 round

Other: tracing number 5

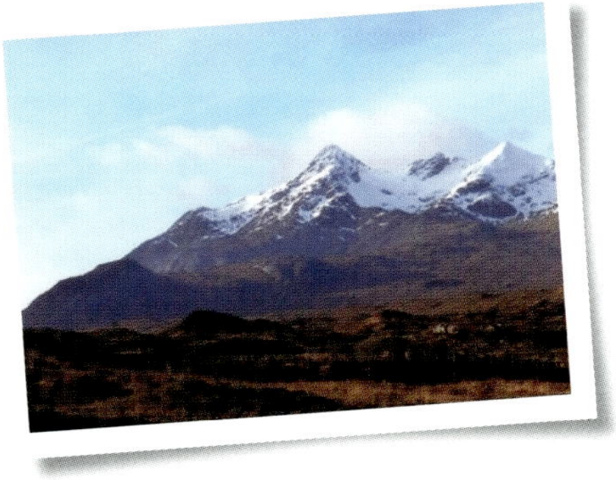

Winter moorland

Over winter, moorland colours become more muted as heather turns dark brown and grasses are bleached to pale straw colours. With a blue sky and the sun illuminating the pale golds, this limited palette can be very pleasing.

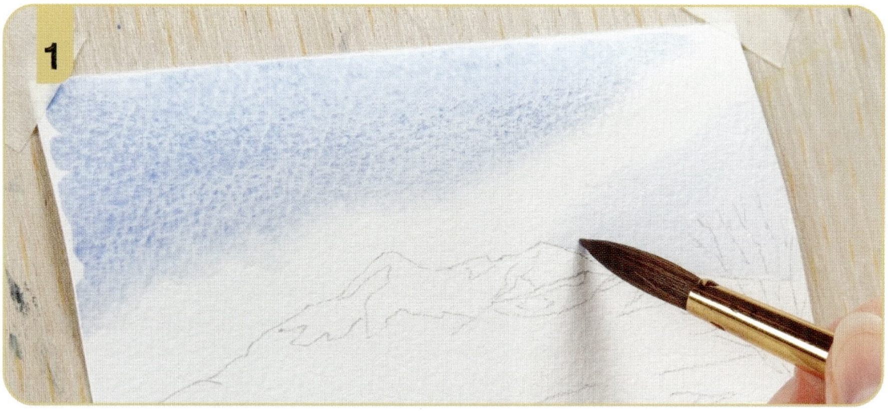

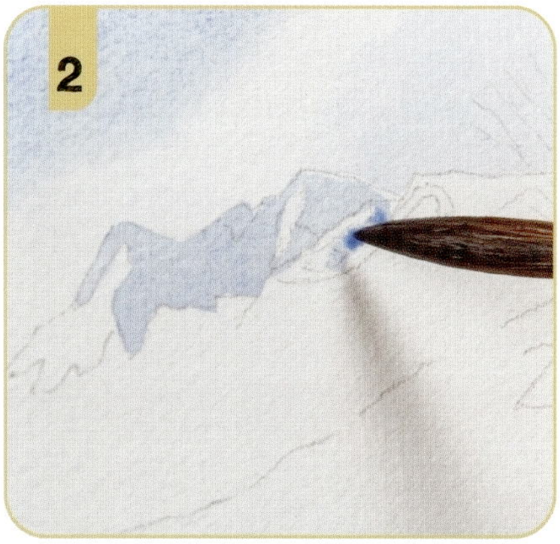

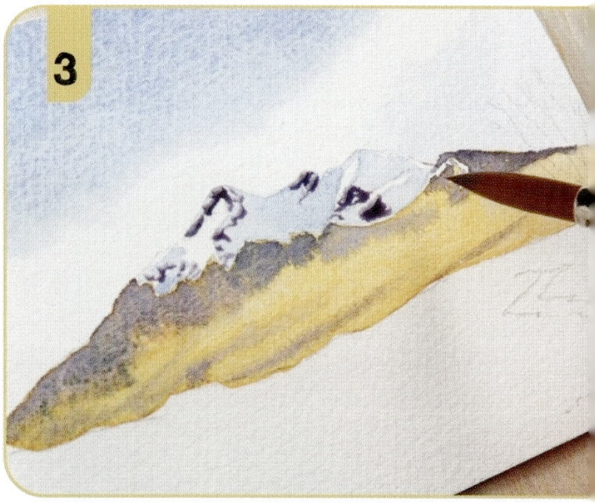

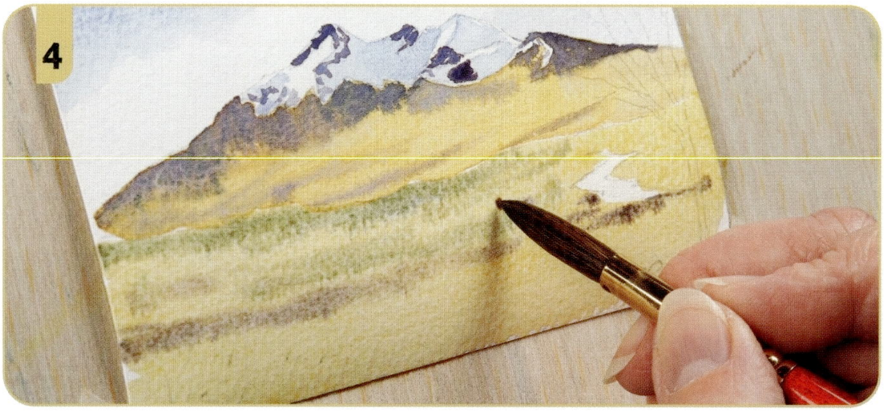

1 Paint the top of the sky with French ultramarine, then soften the edge with a clean damp brush touched gently to the edge to encourage the paint to move downwards. Paint pale blue below the softened edge, working over the top of the moorland.

2 Paint the distant hill with mid-blue, omitting areas that are to remain white.

3 Using raw sienna, paint the lower part of these hills. Drop in a mix of French ultramarine and scarlet lake on the left-hand and upper parts of the area while damp. Use the same mix to add rock detail to the snowy areas.

4 Paint the moorland with raw sienna, avoiding the stream. While the wash is damp, add French ultramarine to create a dull green; and use a French ultramarine and scarlet lake mix for the shadow areas. Don't overwork them; allow them to bleed.

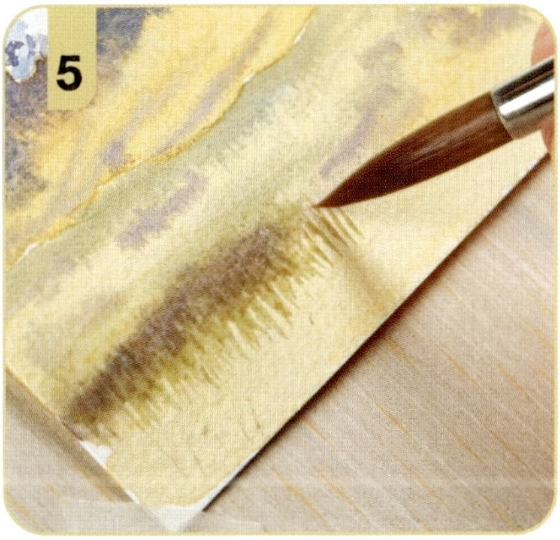

5 Negative paint (see page 24) a few foreground grasses with a French ultramarine and raw sienna mix, then paint a few positively below.

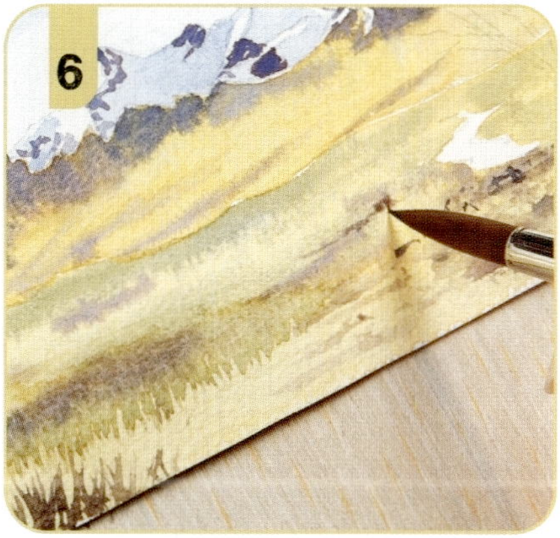

6 Drybrush (see page 13) a French ultramarine and scarlet lake mix on the foreground to suggest stones, then add a few dots of this colour for larger stones.

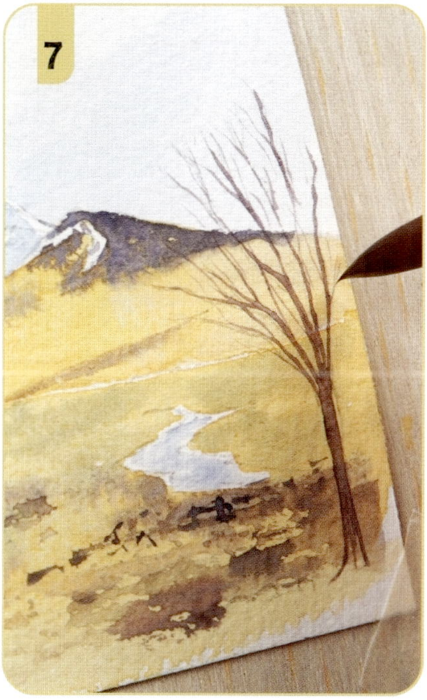

7 Paint the stream with pale blue and suggest a stunted sapling with a mix of French ultramarine and scarlet lake.

Technique:
Splitting the brush

For grasses, instead of using a fan-shaped brush, you can load a little paint on your round brush. Gently press the hairs between your fingers to form a rough fan shape as shown. Put brush to paper, and flick the brush in the direction of growth for the grass. Move the hairs around to avoid a stencil/repeat pattern effect.

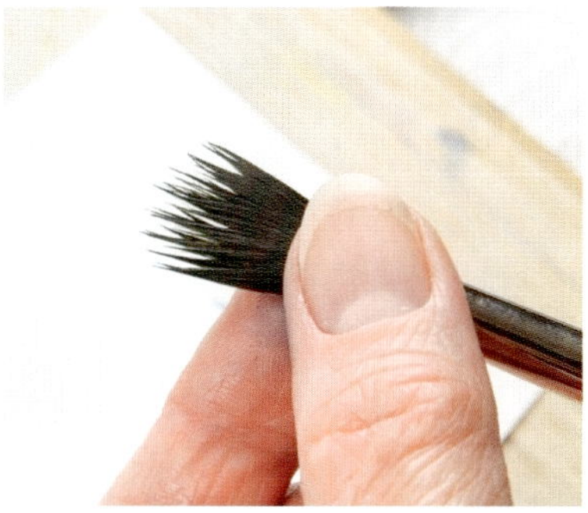

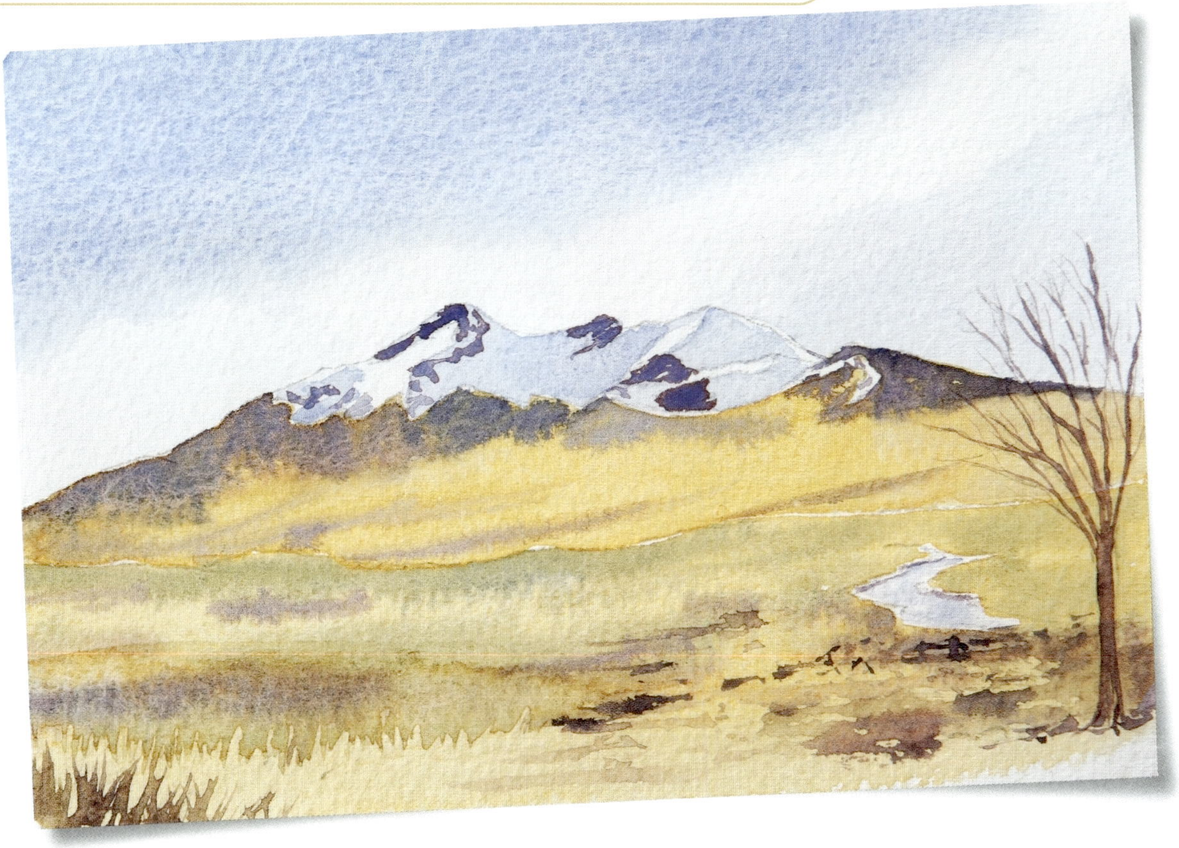

Summer moorland

YOU WILL NEED

Paint colours: cobalt blue, raw sienna, Winsor yellow, Prussian blue, permanent rose, burnt umber

Brushes: size 10 round

Other: tracing number 6

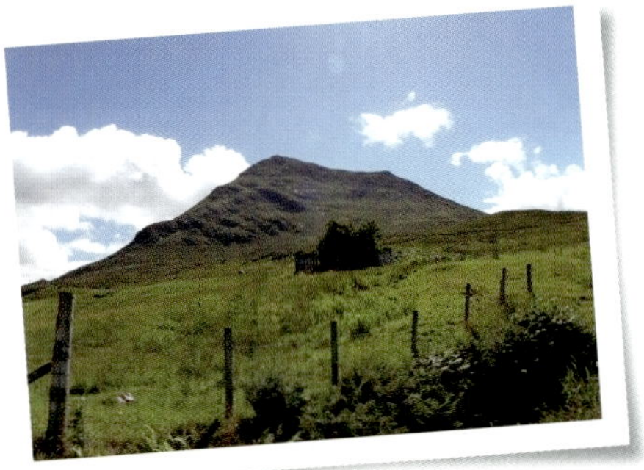

Even in summer, mountain greens will rarely be as strong as in a rural scene where verdant crops/fields are common. Here, grazing cattle have left areas of grass very short, and fresh growth is bright in the sunshine; darker older foliage contrasts and the foxglove gives a reminder of the time of year.

Look and see for yourself. Whenever you are outdoors, make written or painted notes about what you see. Skills in observation will improve your painting.

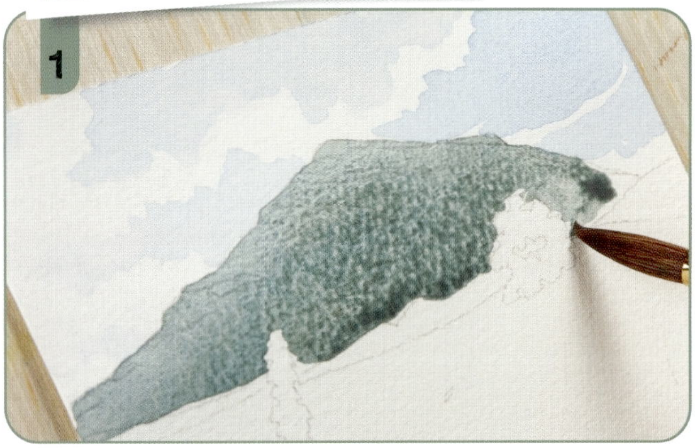

1 Paint the sky with cobalt blue, working around the clouds, and allowing the blue to be lighter at the left-hand side of your painting than the right in order to make it a little more interesting, and to suggest the direction of light. Use a damp brush to soften some clouds on the left. Once dry, paint the hill using a green-tinged blue, mixed from cobalt blue and raw sienna.

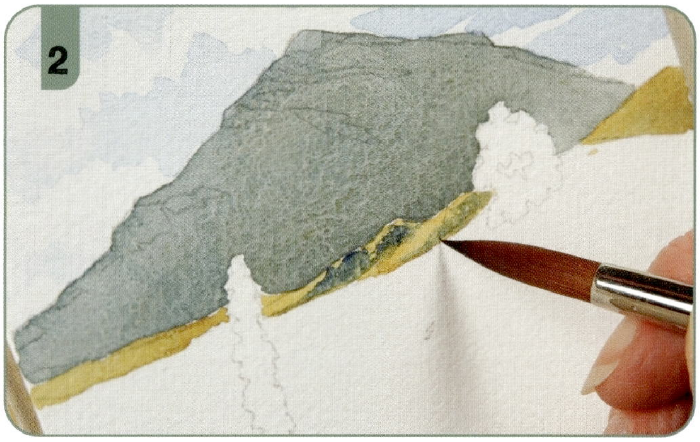

2 Paint the band of distant moorland with cobalt blue mixed with more raw sienna; this time creating a slightly green-tinged yellow. Add detail to the area between the trees with touches of a Prussian blue and permanent rose mix.

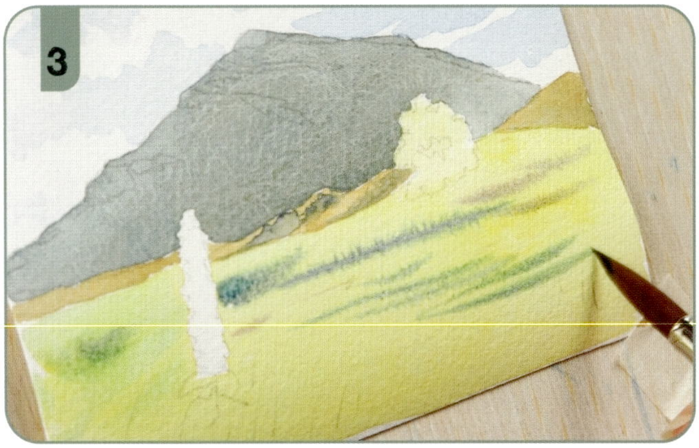

3 Paint the foreground moorland/field and the tree with Winsor yellow. Working wet in wet, use a little Prussian blue and permanent rose mix to create darks across the moorland.

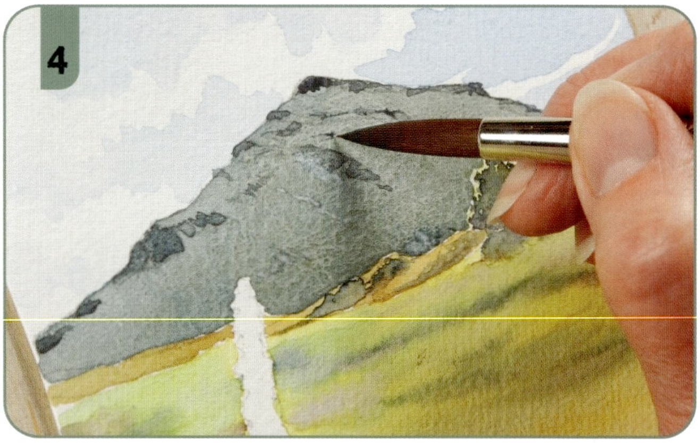

4 Paint the shadow areas of the distant hill with a cobalt blue and burnt umber mix, soften a few edges with a clean damp brush. Use a little Prussian blue and permanent rose mix to create darks on the tree, leaving some of the yellow showing through.

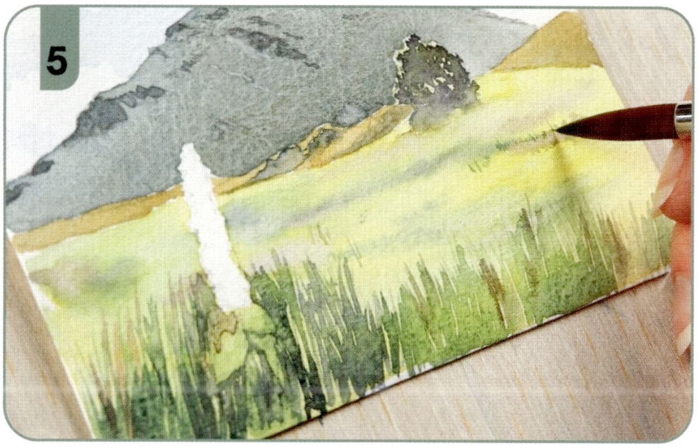

5 Using variable mixes of Winsor yellow/Prussian blue/permanent rose, paint the foreground leaving some areas of the previous wash untouched so that the yellow shows through, painting some grasses negatively, some positively.

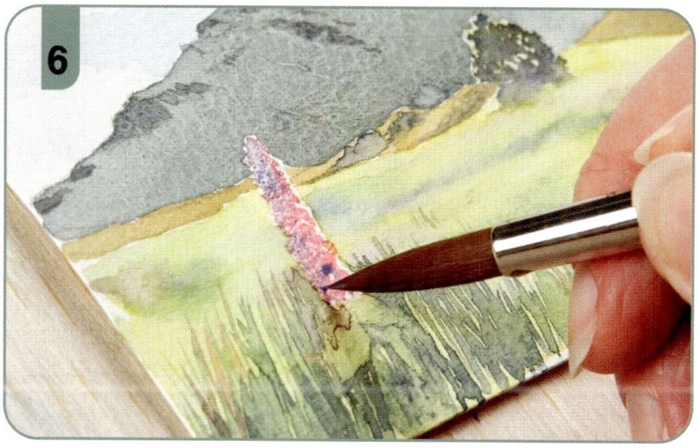

6 For the foxglove, use dots of permanent rose, leaving a white edge here and there and adding a little cobalt to the damp paint for shadow areas.

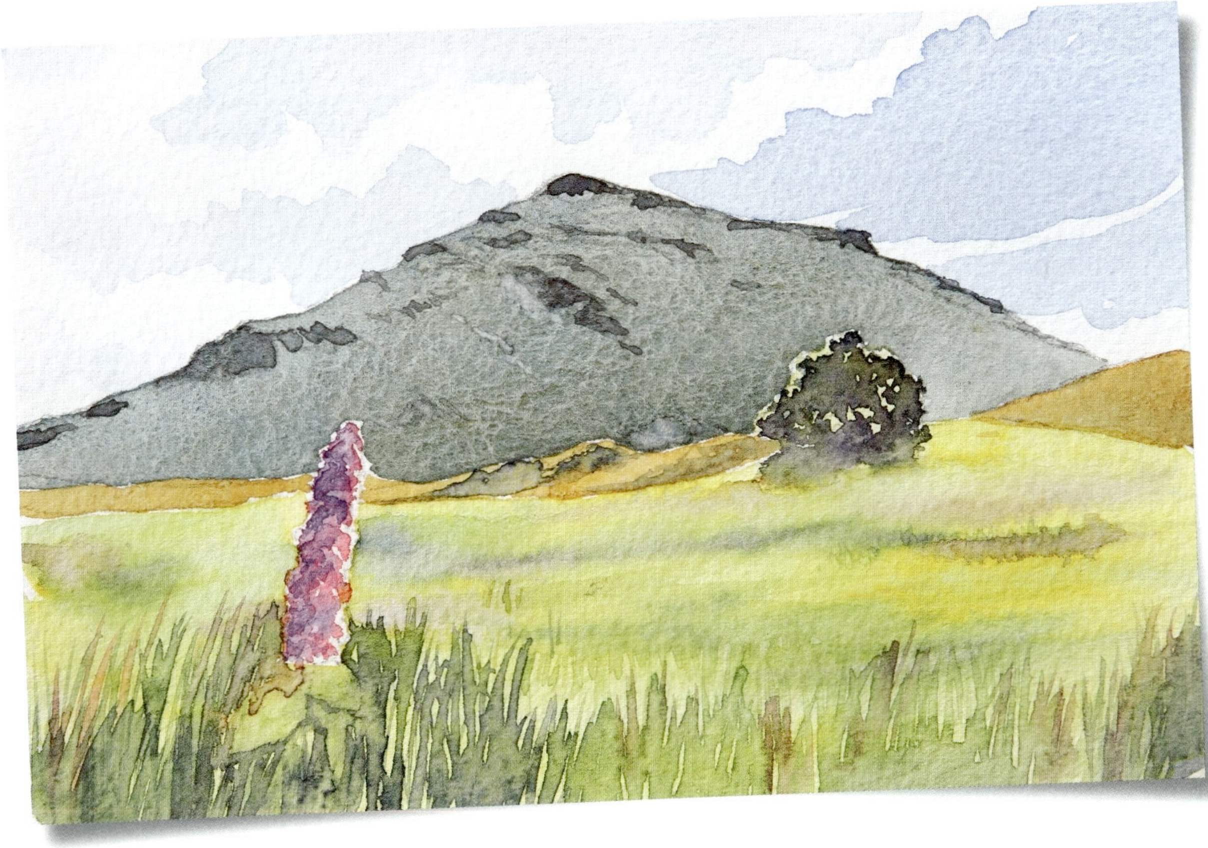

Distant trees

YOU WILL NEED

Paint colours: French ultramarine, burnt umber, Winsor yellow, Prussian blue

Brushes: size 10 round

Other: tracing number 7

Foliage seen at a distance will be influenced by atmospheric perspective (see page 38), and will therefore be painted using softer, bluer tones than if we were viewing the same subject at close range; in the middle distance we can still differentiate between the various tones and colours.

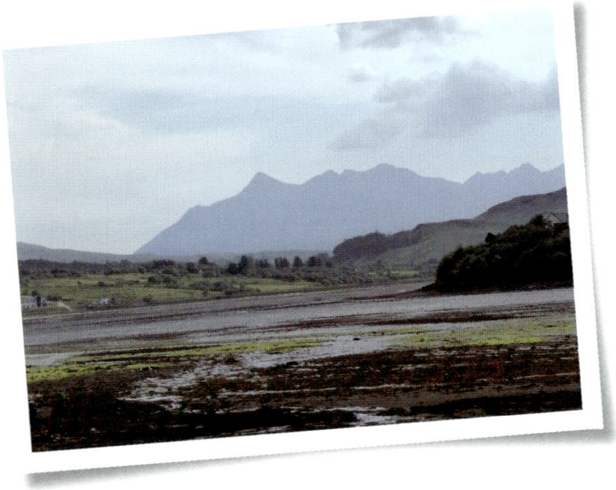

STRENGTH AND DISTANCE

Bear in mind that watercolour dries to a paler tone than it appears when wet. This is particularly important to remember when working wet in wet, as the already-wet surface increases the dilution of the paint, making the result paler than you might expect.

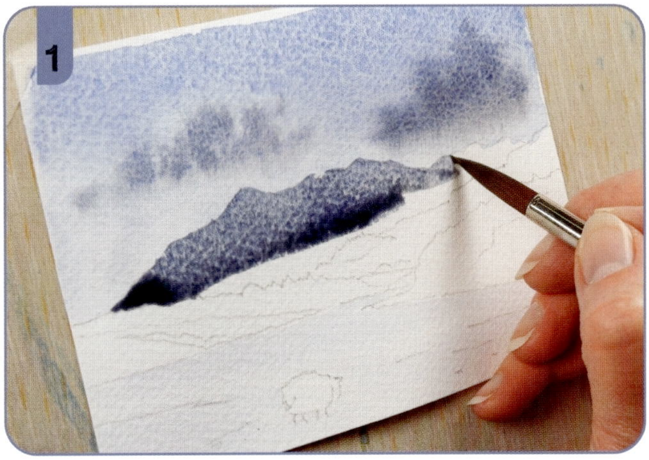

1 Paint a graduated wash of French ultramarine over the sky. While this is still damp, drop in clouds (see page 22) with a strong mix of French ultramarine and burnt umber. Paint the sea and shore with a pale wash of French ultramarine, painting around the sheep. Once dry, add the distant mountains with the French ultramarine and burnt umber mix.

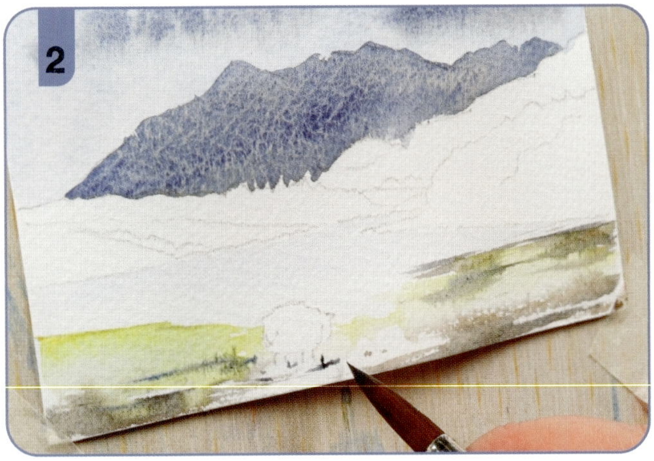

2 Once dry, make drybrush strokes of Winsor yellow and some of the French ultramarine and burnt umber mix over the sea and shore, to create bright citrus yellow-greens and warm and cold neutrals (brown-greys and blue-greys). Add a few dots of French ultramarine and burnt umber mix for the stones on the shore.

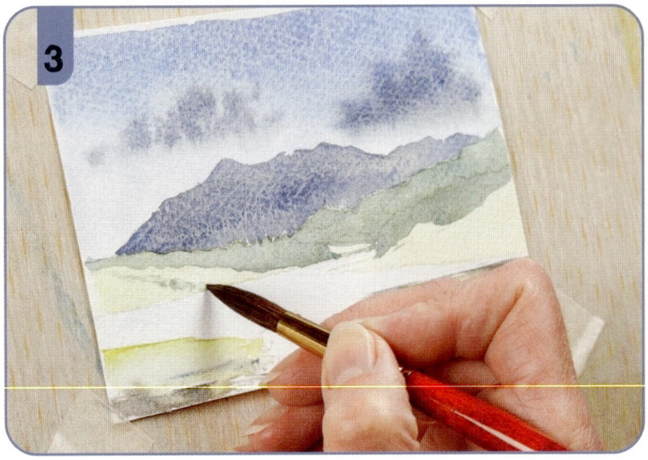

3 Paint the fields and forest with a pale wash of Winsor yellow and a tiny amount of French ultramarine to make a fresh pale yellow-green. Add more French ultramarine to make a bluer mix, then glaze the most distant fields once they have dried.

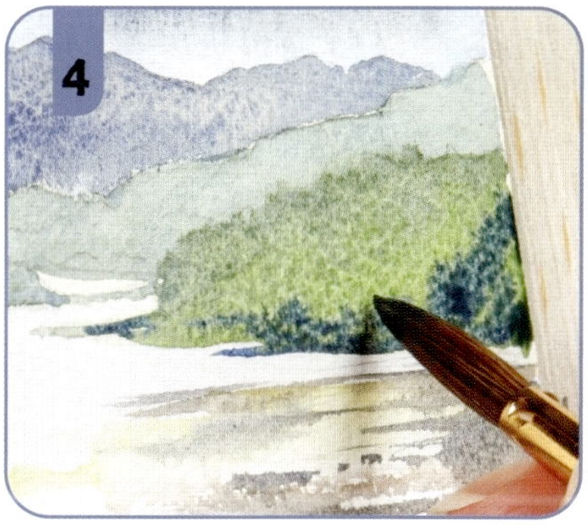

4 Paint the trees on the right with a stronger mix of Winsor yellow and French ultramarine (more blue). While this is still damp, add darks with French ultramarine and burnt umber to create the impression of larger rounded trees.

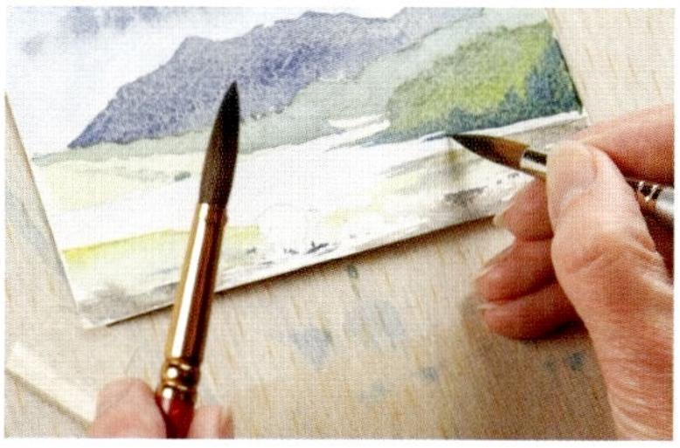

Technique:
Using two brushes

Using more than one brush saves time when switching between colours, or between applying washes and more detailed work, like drawing out fine lines from a wash. If you use the same brush for both tasks, you need to remove surplus paint from the brush each time you switch.

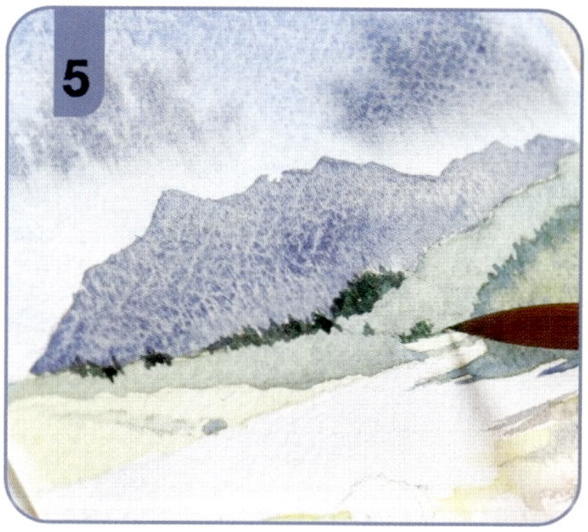

5 Using burnt umber and a tiny amount of Prussian blue, paint the darker conifers in the distance – be careful not to make them too dark.

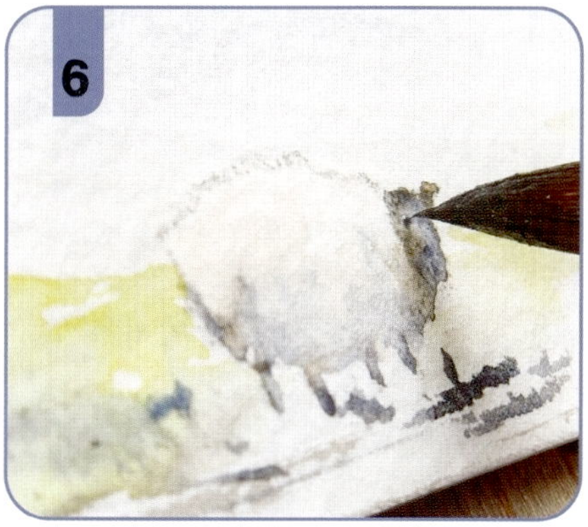

6 Paint the sheep's head, legs and underside with pale French ultramarine and burnt umber mix. Soften these into the upper part of the sheep's body. As optional finished touches, you can add shadows on the water with the French ultramarine and burnt umber mix, and glaze the foreground with Winsor yellow.

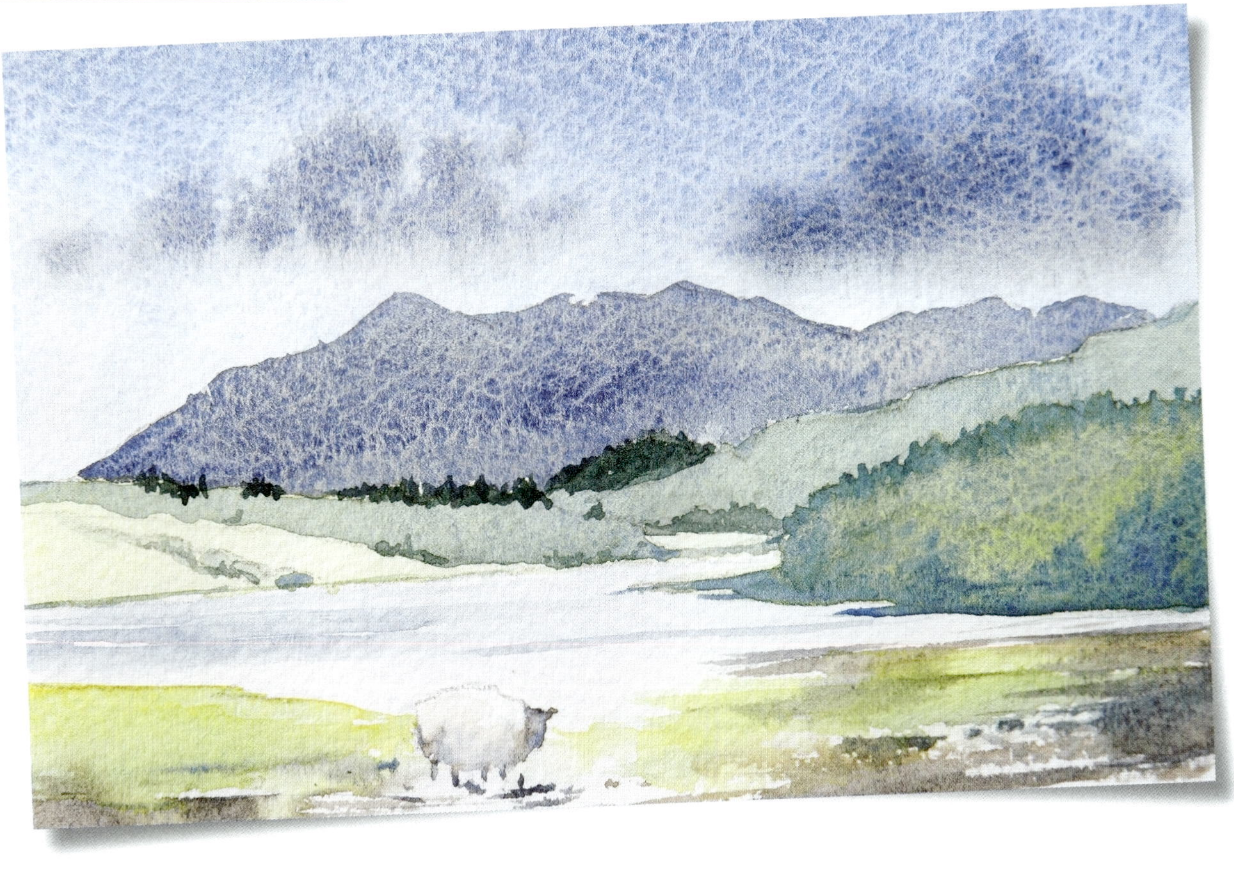

Trees up close

YOU WILL NEED

Paint colours: French ultramarine, burnt umber, Winsor yellow

Brushes: size 10 round

Other: tracing number 8

In general, landscape colours are very seasonal, but evergreens like holly, pines and spruce retain their colours throughout the year (and even these are brighter with fresh growth in the spring).

Forestry plantations can often present a dull dark mass so we need to break this up with colour, tone and textural differences. Nearness to the subject allows us to see the full range of colours and detail, but even so, we don't need to paint every leaf – just give an impression.

1 Using a mix of French ultramarine and burnt umber, paint the sky, leaving the clouds unpainted. Soften the effect on the right with a damp brush, then paint the distant moutain using the same colours, beginning with a very light tone.

2 Working wet in wet, introduce a pale green made from Winsor yellow and French ultramarine for the foothills, then add more paint to the mix to strengthen it. Use this to lay a wash over the rest of the foreground.

3 Paint the path with the French ultramarine and burnt umber mix, leaving some areas unpainted to suggest puddles.

4 Add detail/midtones to the rocks and to the mound on the left-hand side.

5 Start to paint the coniferous trees with a green made from Winsor yellow and French ultramarine. Use short strokes from the trunk outwards. Try to work quickly to keep the marks lively.

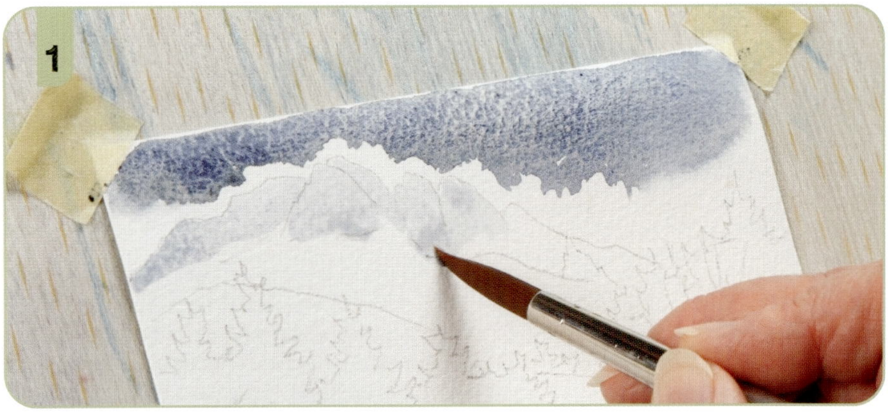

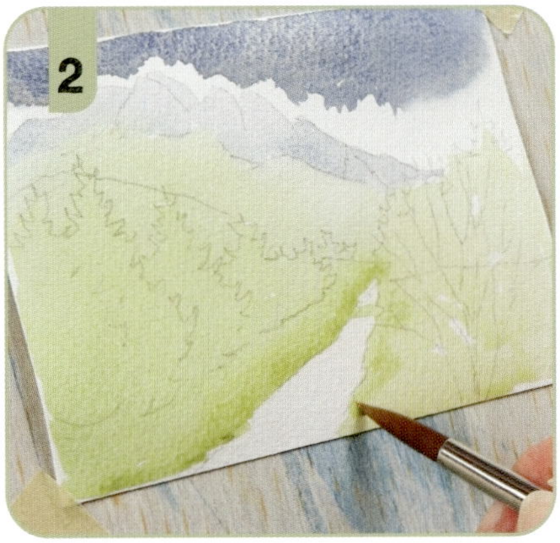

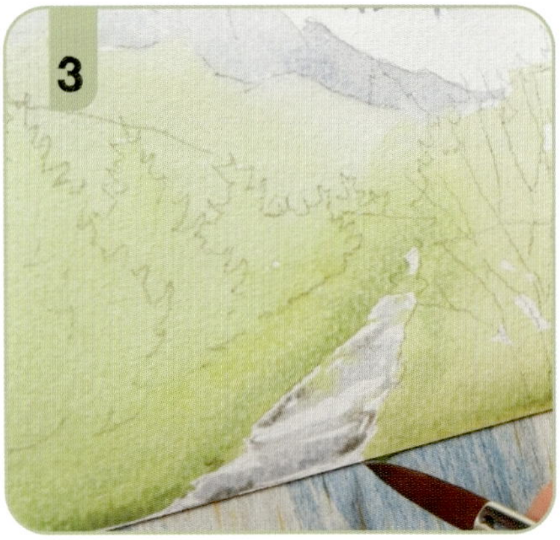

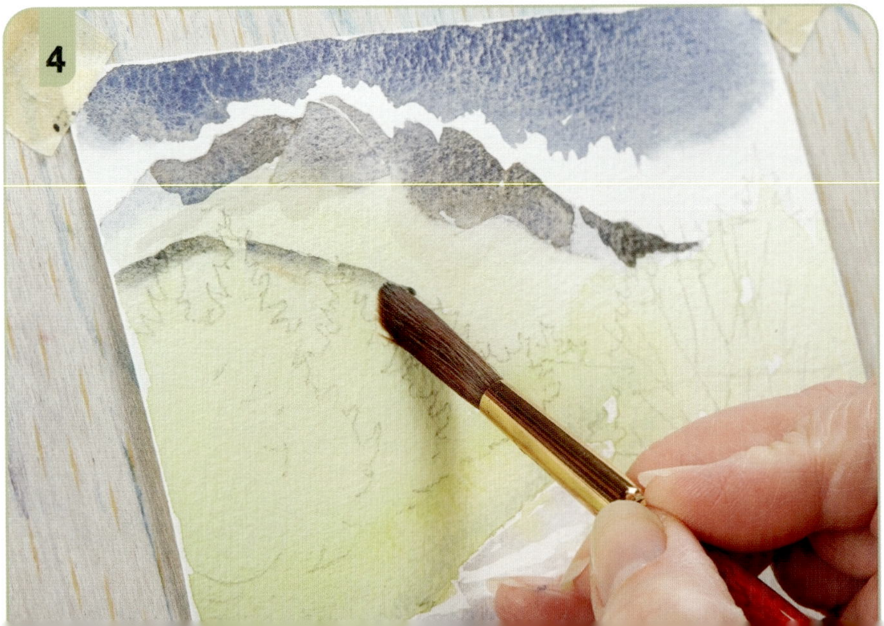

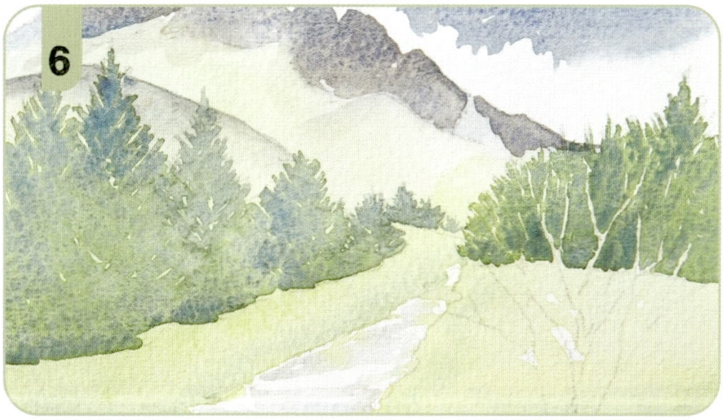

6 Develop the rest of the trees in the same way, leaving a gap for the foreground tree.

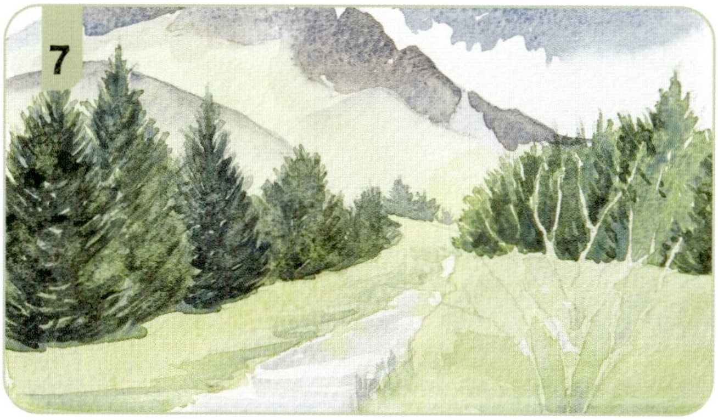

7 Use a diluted version of the same mix to add another wash to some areas of the foreground grass, painting around a few twigs on the tree and creating a few grasses at the path edge. Once dry, add some burnt umber to the mix and build detail and depth in the trees.

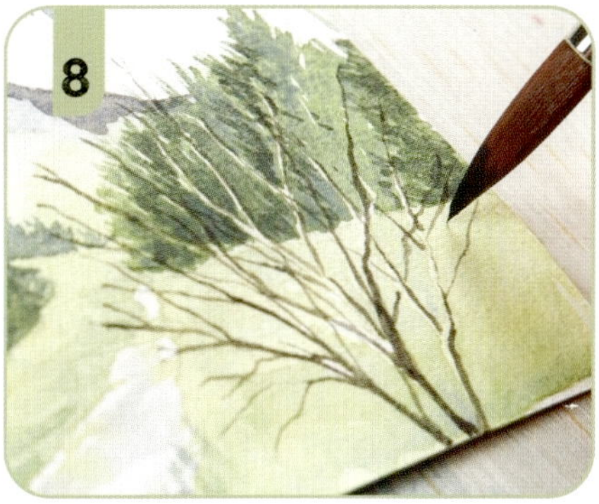

8 Add darks to the foreground tree, using French ultramarine and burnt umber mix to 'draw' branches out of the wet paint of the trunk.

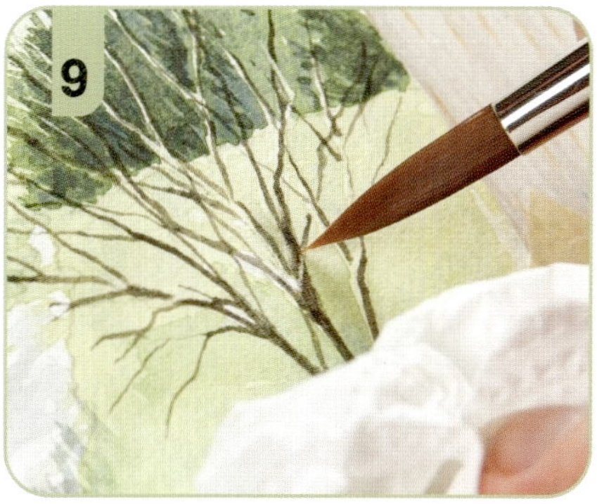

9 Lift a few highlights from foreground branches.

Technique: Reserving highlights

Be careful to leave your highlights – don't overpaint the gaps. This way, the white of the paper serves as a bright area. Don't worry if you do go slightly over the lines: if necessary, you can lift out additional highlights.

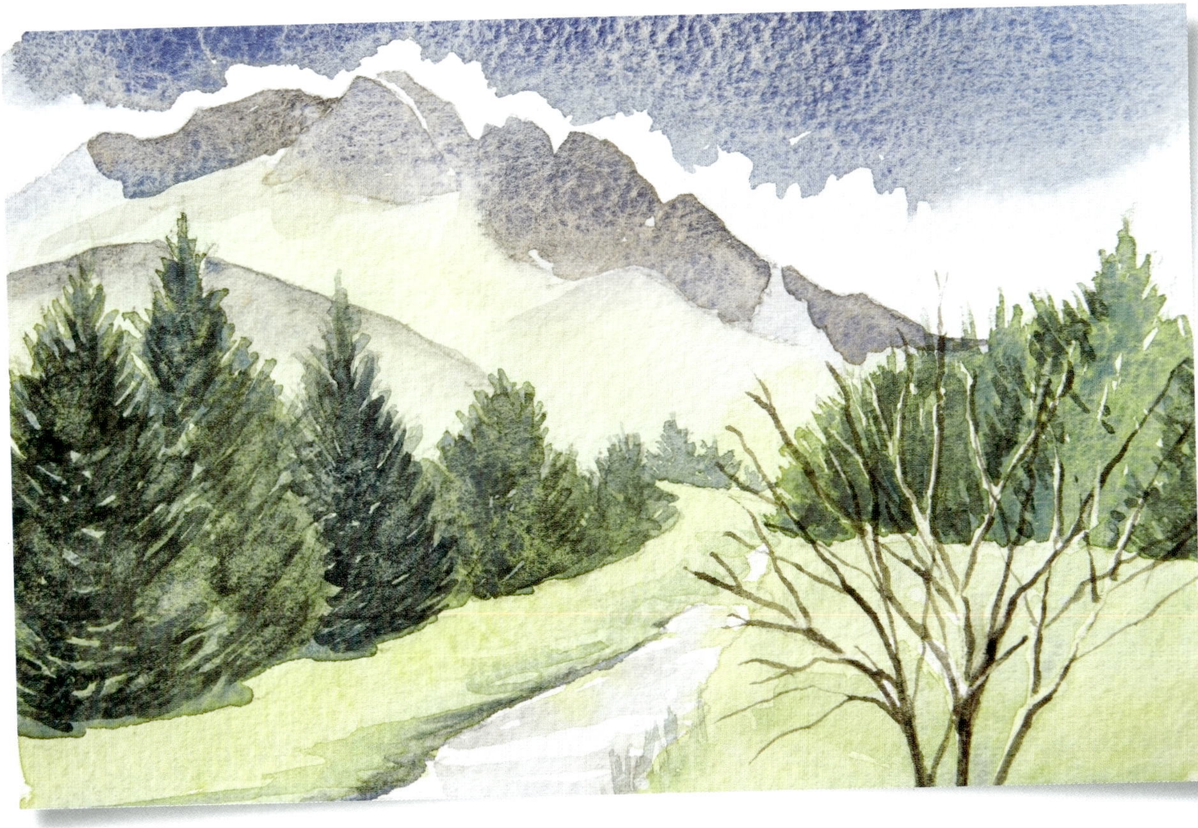

ATMOSPHERE & PERSPECTIVE

Perspective – this word strikes fear into the heart of many an artist, whether amateur or professional. Usually it is linear perspective that causes the worry, This is where converging lines and vanishing points are used to convey distance and a three-dimensional effect. This is most often encountered in a built environment where there are man-made elements that converge at a point in the distance, such as train tracks. It is possible to learn linear perspective – if you seek out a book that is aimed at artists rather than architects, you'll find it easier to follow.

Relax – the type of perspective more likely to be considered in a natural environment is atmospheric, or aerial, perspective: the natural reduction in the detail, tone and colour we can perceive when looking into the distance. Even in the most colourful scene, the effect of atmospheric perspective reduces the colours we can actually see.

We all know that if we were to travel to that distant place the colours would be just as vivid as we see them in the foreground, but we are unable to see all those colours over distance. In order to simulate the impression of distance we use receding colours (blues) in the distance and use warmer advancing colours (reds) in the foreground.

Change of scale can further the impression of distance, such as decreasing size of known/familiar objects, and placing one feature in front of another.

Skye Bridge from Balmacara

54 x 19cm (21½ x 7½in)

A sunny day, with haze reducing colour and detail; a palette of blue, a little warmer in the foreground. Artistic licence wasn't required here; the work was done for me.

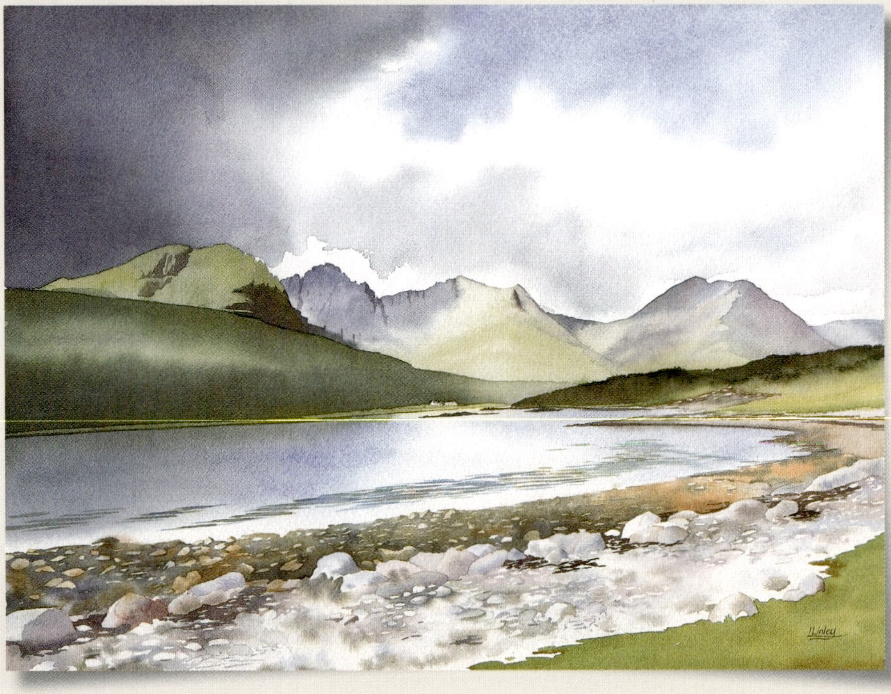

Blaven from Suisnish

37 x 27cm (14½ x 10½in)

This painting has only subtle warmth in the foreground. I considered whether to add a red buoy at the water's edge or a person in a red jacket on the shore, but I find the mood pleasing, and resisted the temptation to do more.

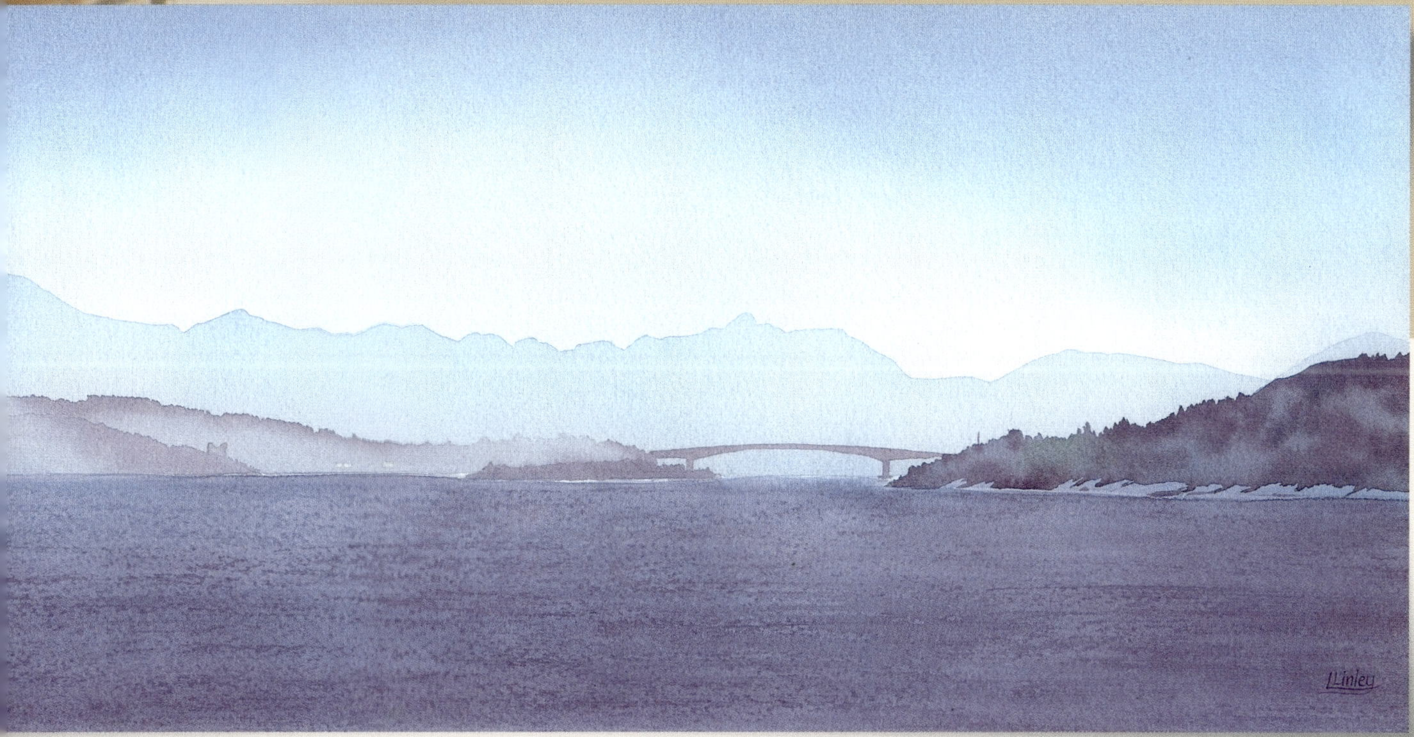

Autumn Colour Blaven

37 x 27cm (14½ x 10½in)

The hills, already seen as blue in the distance, are darkened by shadow, and contrast with the sunlit moorland. The autumnal colour of the moorland grasses warms the foreground and enhances the feeling of distance within the painting.

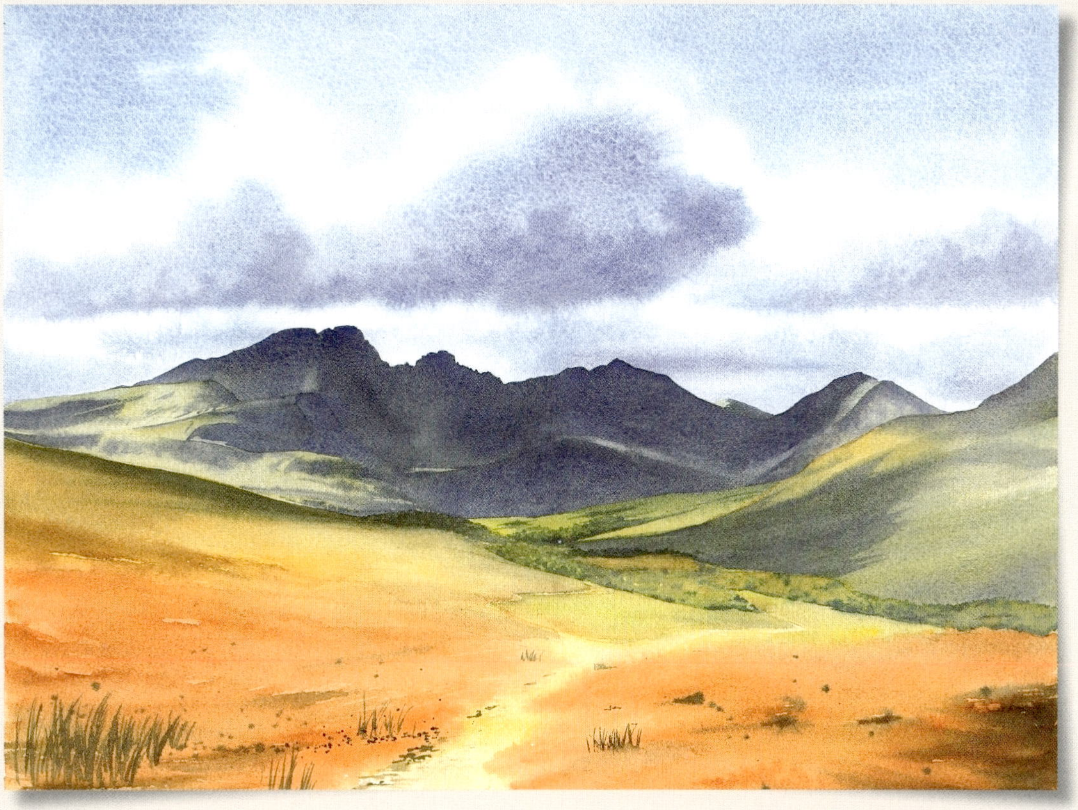

YOU WILL NEED

Paint colours: permanent rose, French ultramarine, Winsor yellow, scarlet lake

Brushes: size 10 round

Other: tracing number 9

Mountains and molehills

In order to indicate to the viewer that we've featured a large hill in a painting, we may need to give some indication of scale. Sometimes the viewer will be so familiar with a scene that this is self-explanatory, but at other times we may need to provide a clue.

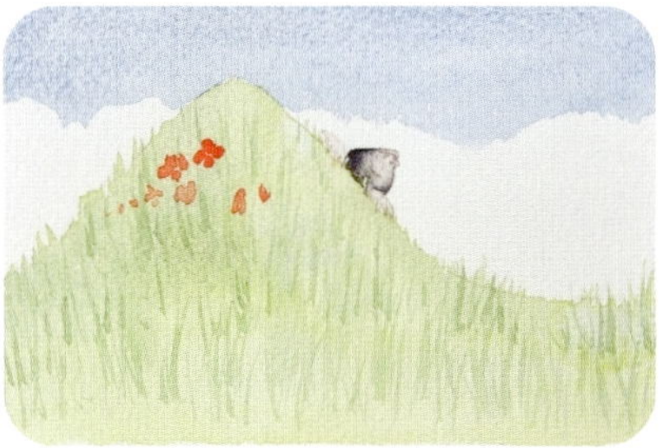

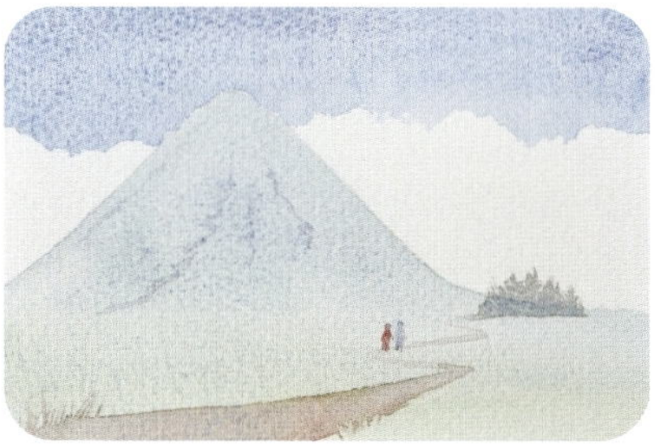

Technique: **Suggesting scale**

Both of the simple illustrations above use the same underlying tracing as the step-by-step project here but with changes to suggest different scales. On the left, there are clues that the shape represents a very small hill – a molehill, in fact. The colours are bright; the markings for the grass are the same size throughout; and the red flower makes it clearer (warm colours advance in the image, while cool colours recede). Finally, Mr Mole has been added to make things absolutely clear!

On the right, use of subdued, blue-green, receding colours tells much of the story in conveying distance through atmospheric perspective (see page 38), but a tapering path, along with contrast in size, tone and detail between the distant forest, figures, and foreground grasses all give more information. The people also give a familiar point of comparison to give us a sense of the hill's size.

REUSING TRACINGS

You can use the same tracing provided for the main project if you wish to try this exercise for yourself; add the mole (in dotted lines) for the close-up painting and the figures (in pale grey) for the distant version. Leave both out for the main project!

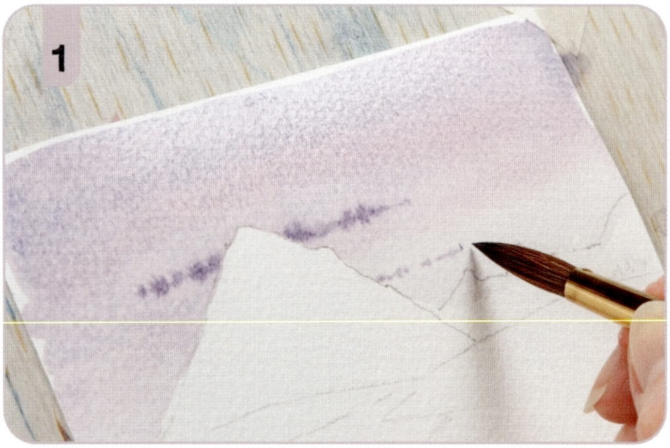

1 Paint a pink-purple sky using a wash of French ultramarine that fades into permanent rose. Add small clouds behind (rather than above) the mountain to help to suggest the scale.

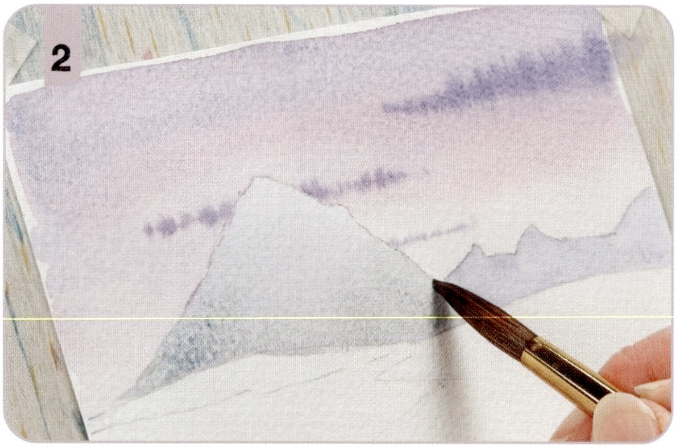

2 Add more French ultramarine to the original mix and paint the distant hill with a flat wash. Having no detail makes it look more distant. Add Winsor yellow to the mix and paint the main mountain.

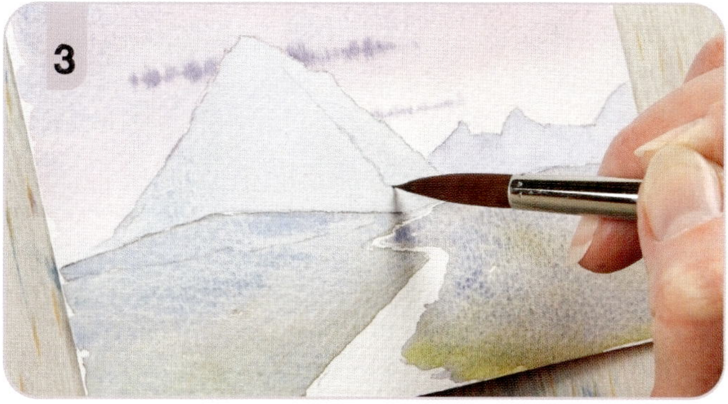

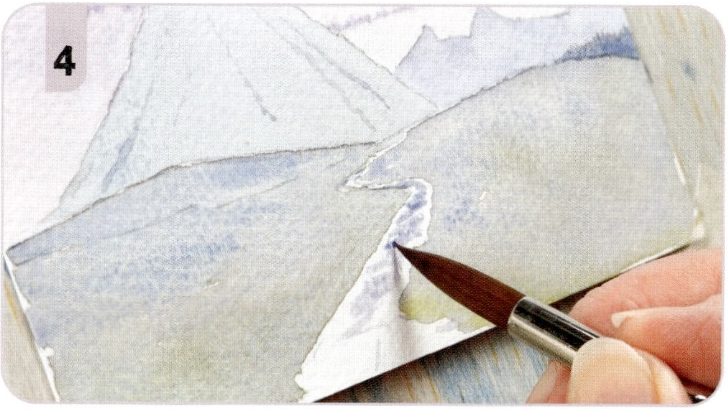

3 Strengthen the mix and paint the foreground, avoiding the stream; then detail the mountain with the same mix, touching the paint on with the tip of the brush to make fine marks.

4 Still using the same mix, add some tiny trees on the right-hand side of the horizon, then begin to paint the stream. As you advance, add gradually more permanent rose to the mix. This warm colour will advance, helping to give the impression that the stream is getting closer.

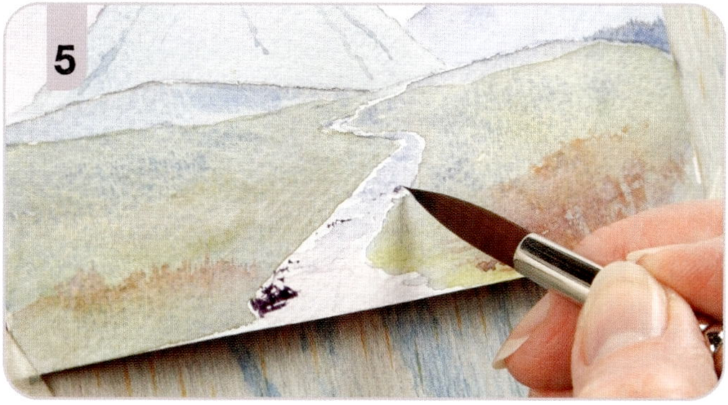

5 To finish, add another wash over some of the moorland and some touches of scarlet lake – another hot, advancing colour – and some dark touches of a French ultramarine and scarlet lake mix in the foreground to create detail on the stream.

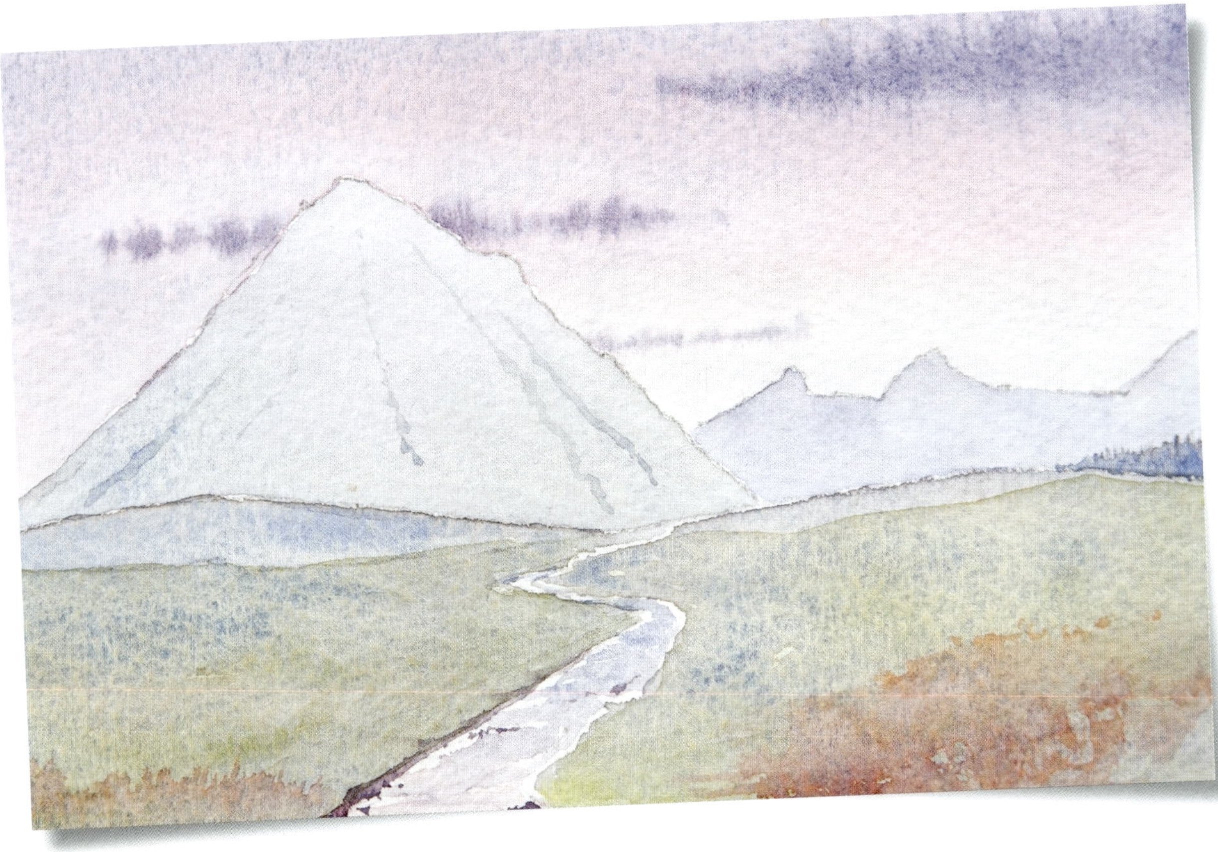

Placing features in the landscape

YOU WILL NEED

Paint colours: raw sienna, French ultramarine, burnt umber,

Brushes: size 10 round

Other: tracing number 10, kitchen paper

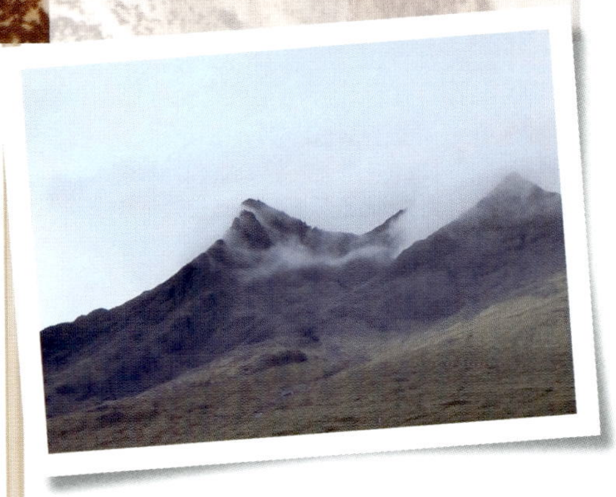

Often all we see of a mountain is a silhouette; distance, weather and lighting conditions may make it impossible to see more detail. Mist can reveal much about the contours of a mountain, showing peaks that are not revealed in good weather, and telling us which are closer and which are more distant. Look for these effects in the reference photograph.

1 Wet the paper all over and drop in very pale French ultramarine and burnt umber mix to the sky and hills and raw sienna below, allowing the colours to blend. Drop in stronger French ultramarine and burnt umber at top left.

2 Paint the peaks with a stronger mix of the sky colour. If you begin with the tallest pinnacle of the peak on the left and paint alternate pinnacles, you can save on drying time whilst avoiding the risk of one peak bleeding into another. As you paint each pinnacle soften the underside with a clean damp brush. Allow to dry.

3 To paint the remaining pinnacles on this peak, paint clean water carefully to each, and the area below it, add a little (more concentrated/stronger) colour to each and allow it to bleed.

4 Paint the peak on the right; see if you can deliberately create a backrun at the top by waiting for the peak to dry a little before adding a touch of water.

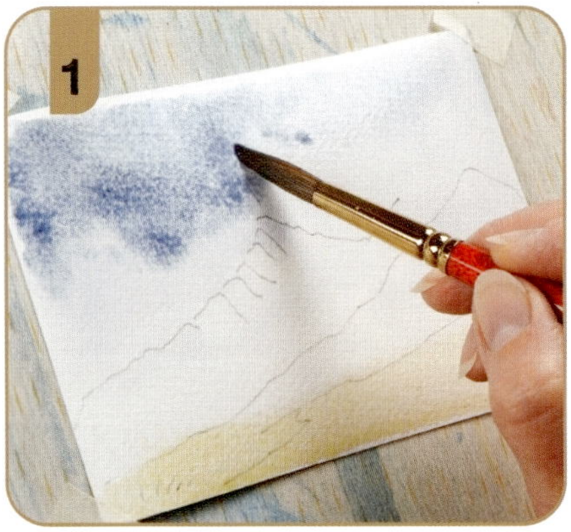

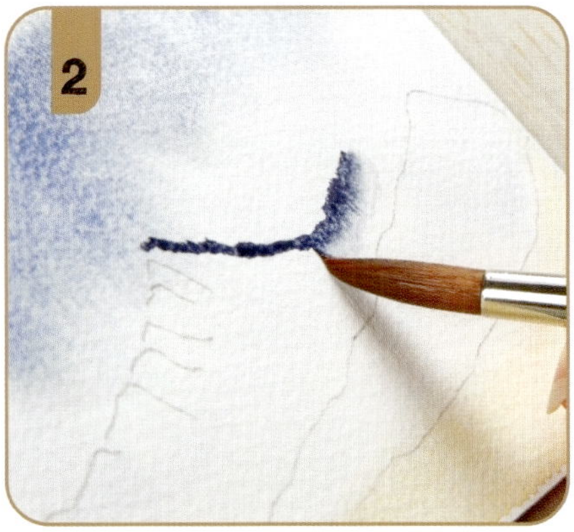

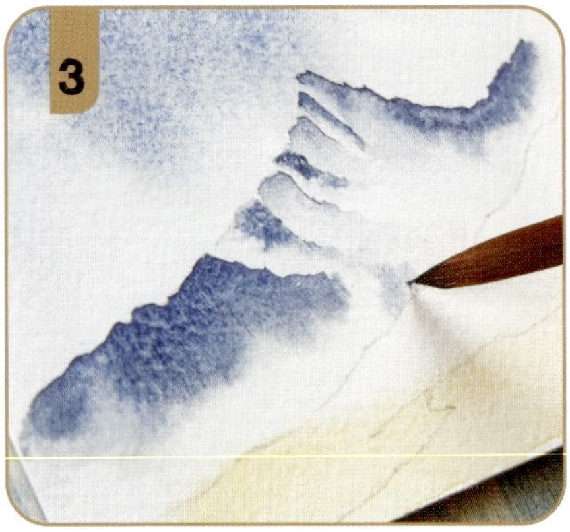

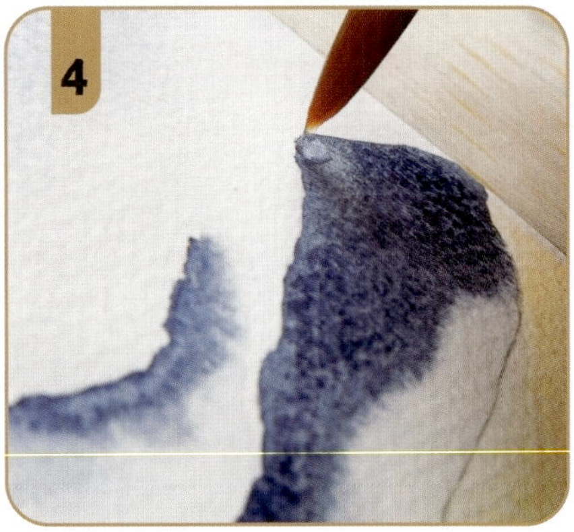

CREATING BACKRUNS

Don't be upset if you can't create a backrun. We usually try to avoid them (see page 14) so deliberately creating one can sometimes be a challenge.

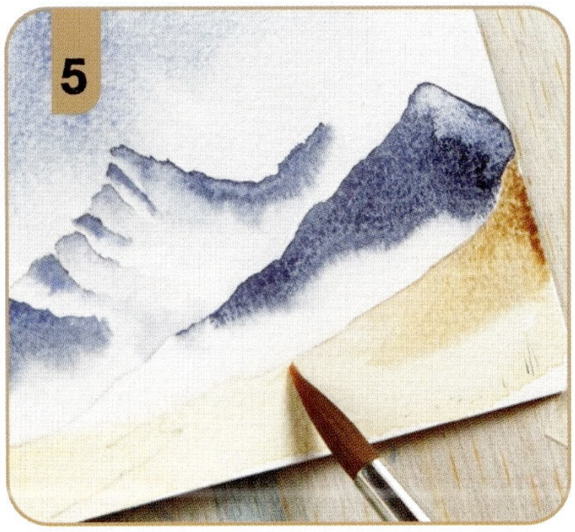

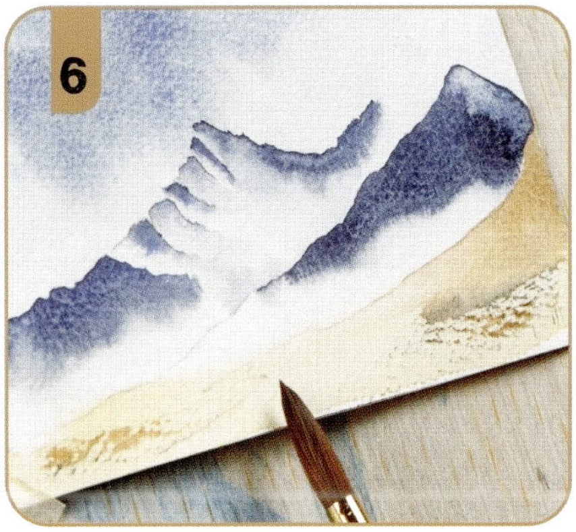

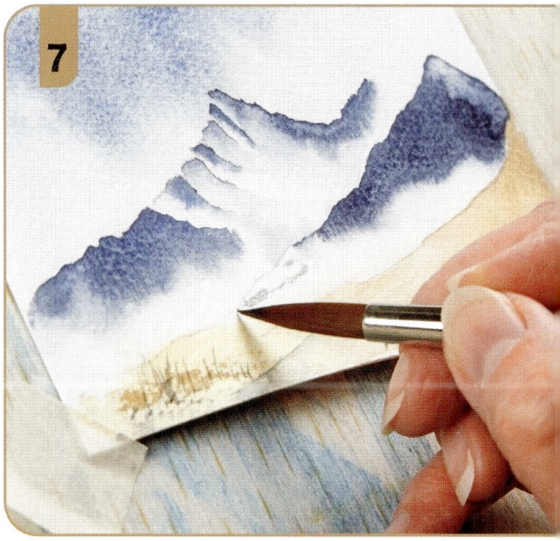

5 Add burnt umber to the small hill on the right to suggest proximity; soften the lower edge.

6 Drybrush a little texture onto the foreground, using French ultramarine and burnt umber. Wash your brush and make another stroke or two in drybrush style, to soften some of the drybrush paint.

7 Add a few details such as foreground grasses or stones, using more burnt umber in the French ultramarine and burnt umber mix to warm it a little. If any paint has spread too far, lift carefully by gently working with a slightly damp brush and dabbing with paper towel.

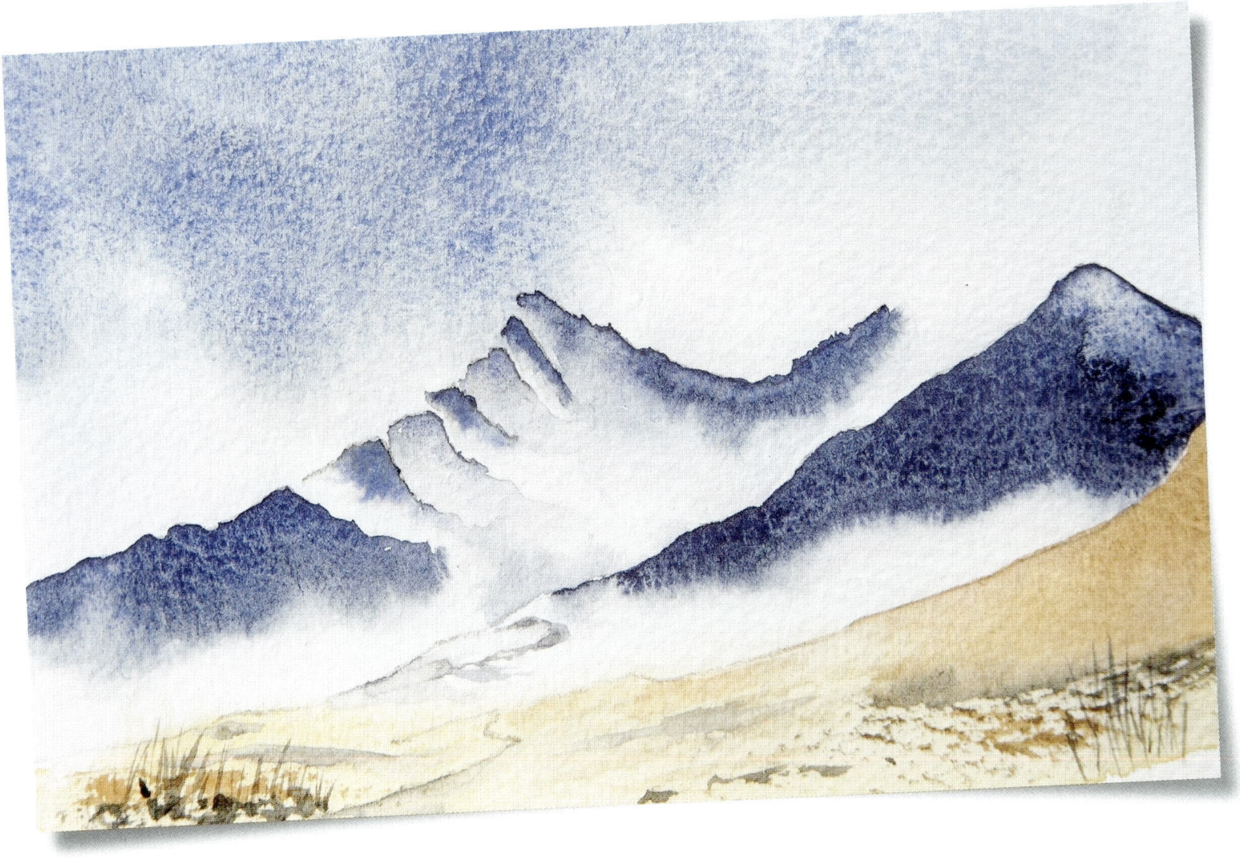

YOU WILL NEED

Paint colours: permanent rose, Prussian blue

Brushes: size 10 round

Other: tracing number 11, kitchen paper

Tone and distance

Building tone in layers, from light to dark, is useful for creating the illusion of distance through atmospheric perspective. It can be useful to practise this layering with one colour so that you learn to judge tones in isolation.

Once you have worked through this project as shown, you might like to try again. This time, vary the project by making one or both of the graduated washes darker at the foot of the paper instead of the top, or using a different colour, such as raw sienna for the first wash, and seeing how this influences the overall colour.

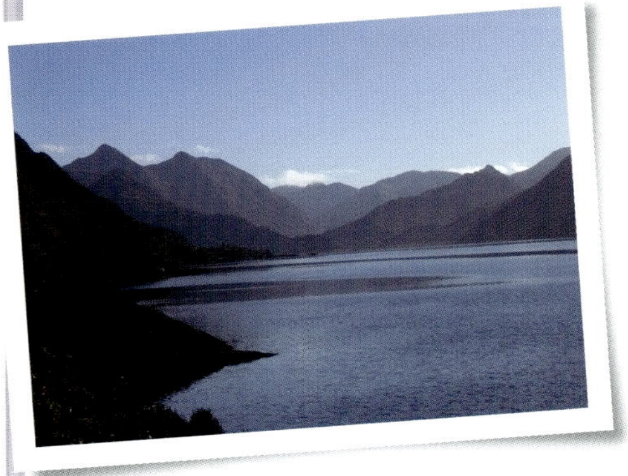

Technique: Lifted glazing

You can increase the interest in a sky, where you lift colour by using two washes, letting the first wash dry before painting a second and lifting out from that to reveal the first wash.

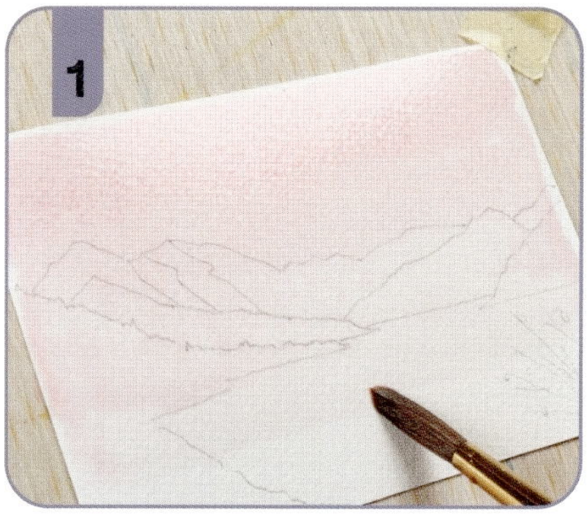

1 Apply a pale graduated wash of permanent rose over the whole paper. Next, make a mix of permanent rose and Prussian blue. Prepare plenty of the wash as we'll use the same well of colour for multiple glazes.

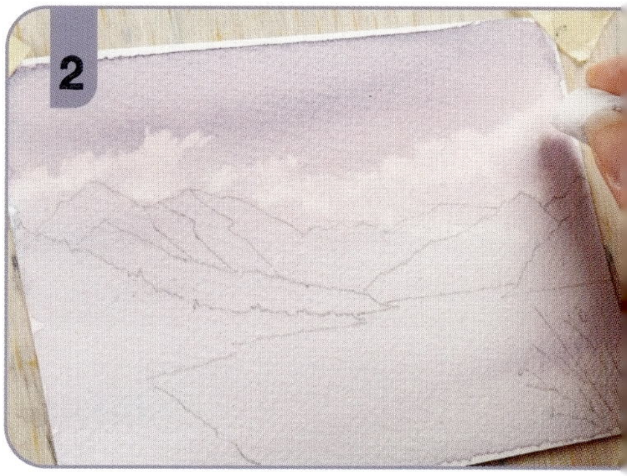

2 Paint a pale graduated wash of the mix over the whole page. Quickly lift out clouds with the kitchen paper, making larger clouds at the top of the paper and smaller ones below.

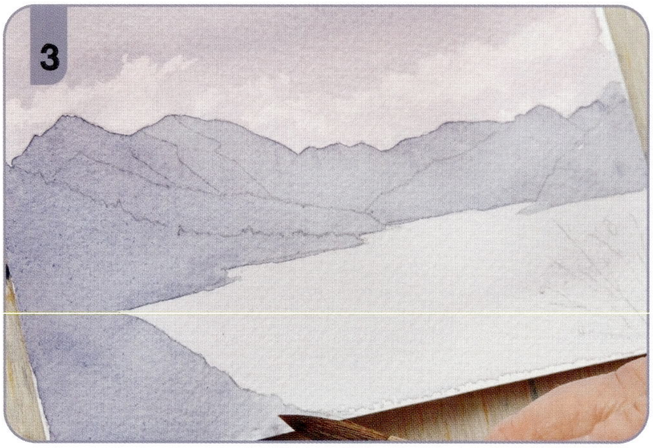

3 With a mix of Prussian blue and permanent rose, paint all the mountains and land with a flat wash. Allow to dry.

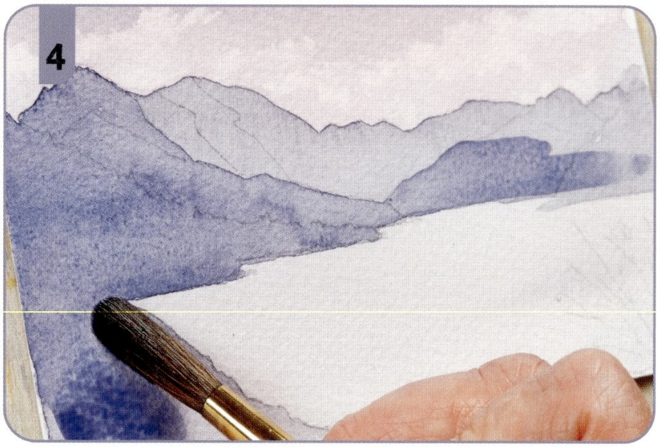

4 Glaze the mountains and land with two more washes, omitting the distant ones. Allow the first wash to dry before applying the second.

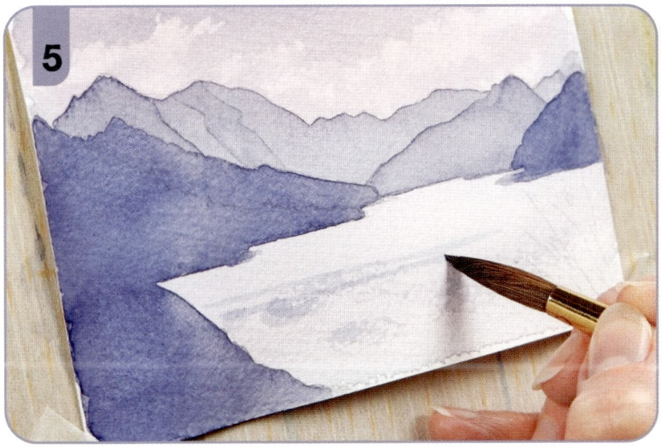

5 Paint the foreground – the mountains on the left and right, and the nearer land – once more, then use the same mix to add a few horizontal lines to the sea.

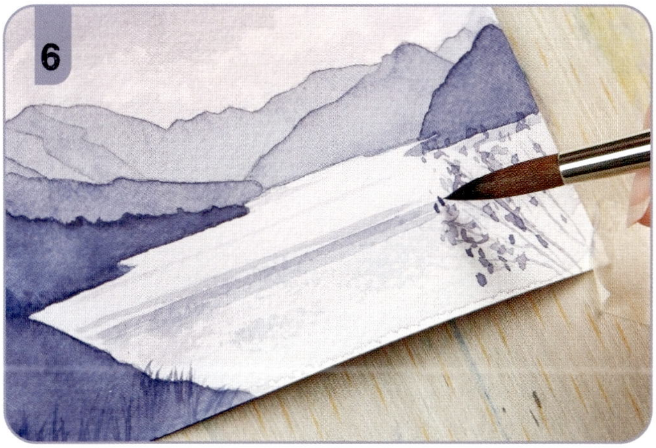

6 Once dry, paint the nearer hills again, dropping in some darker tones while damp. Use these to create the distant tree tops and foreground grasses, wet in wet and wet on dry. Add the tree in the lower left, allow to dry, then add a few more leaves, overlapping some of the original ones.

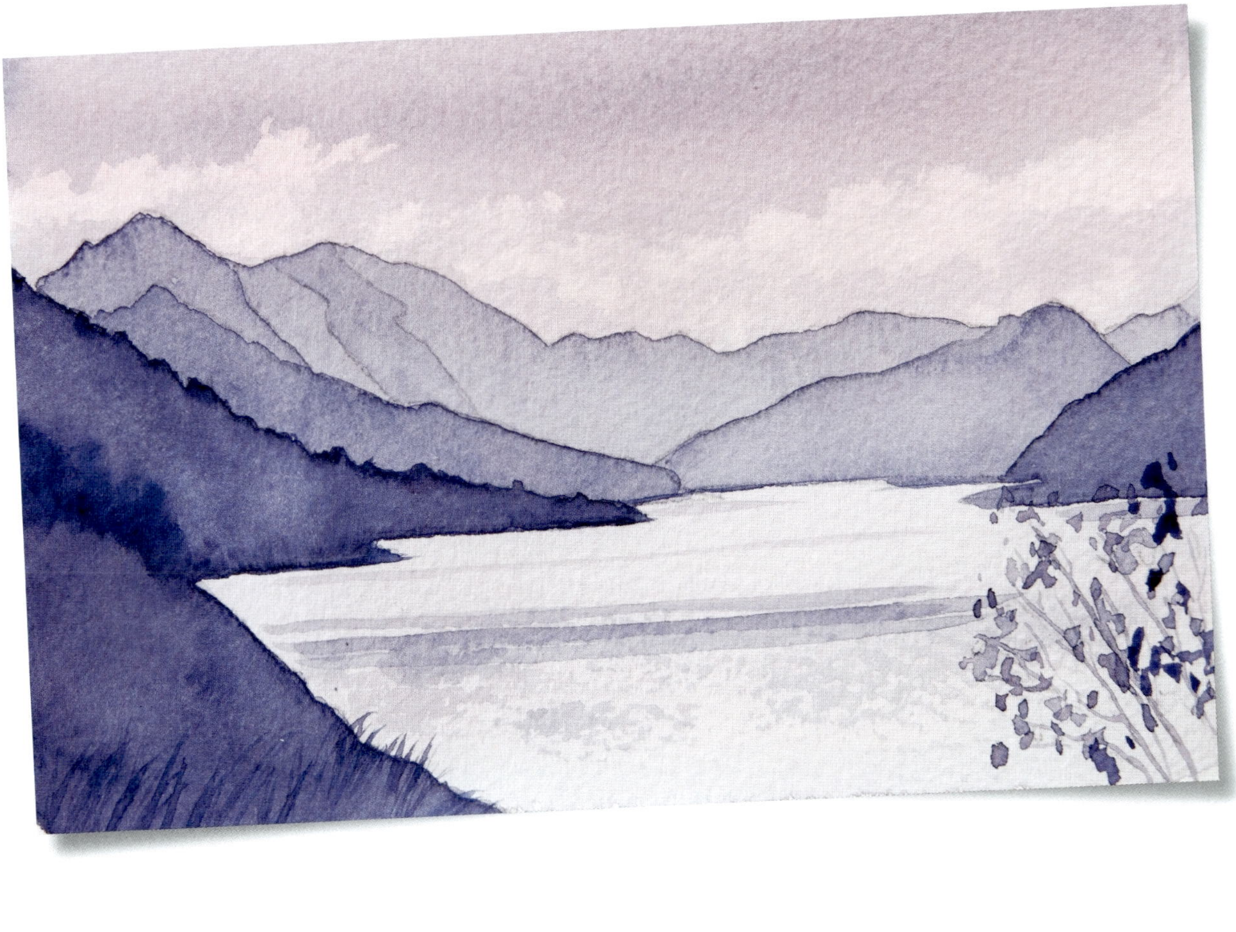

YOU WILL NEED

Paint colours: raw sienna, burnt sienna, permanent rose, burnt umber, French ultramarine.

Brushes: size 10 round

Other: tracing number 11

Technique: Gaps for speed

Leaving thin slivers of unpainted paper between adjacent washes means that one cannot run into another. This eliminates the need for the first wash to dry before moving on to the next, thus increasing speed.

Colour and distance

This scene uses the same reference photograph and tracing as the previous project; but here we are introducing colour to the painting. Advancing (warmer colours) and receding (cooler) colours are used here to create a feeling of distance.

Familiarity with the scene means you can push yourself to work more swiftly, so we introduce the technique of leaving gaps between areas to speed up your pace. Here the cloud band gives a natural gap.

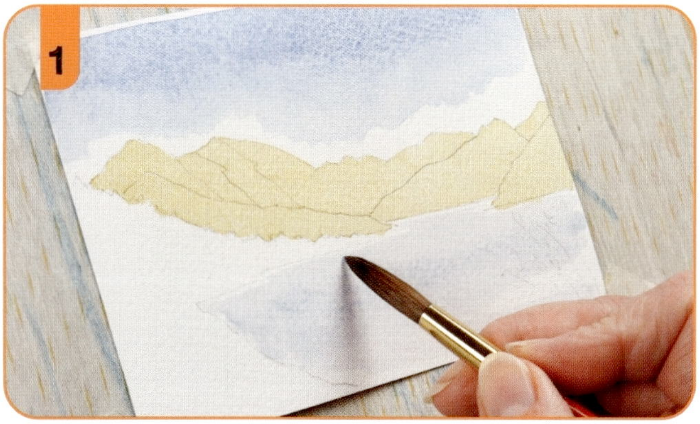

1 Using French ultramarine and a graduated wash, paint the sky above the cloud band; then with raw sienna, paint the mountains. (It should be safe to do this if you left a band of cloud above all the peaks.) With pale blue, paint the sea, leaving a thin line unpainted at the shoreline.

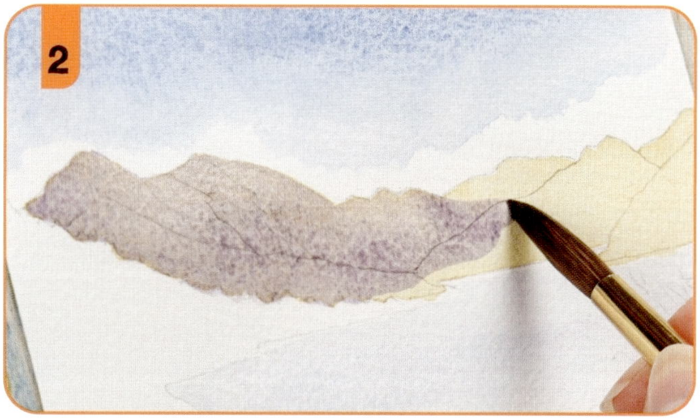

2 Paint the mountains again, this time using a pale mix of French ultramarine and permanent rose.

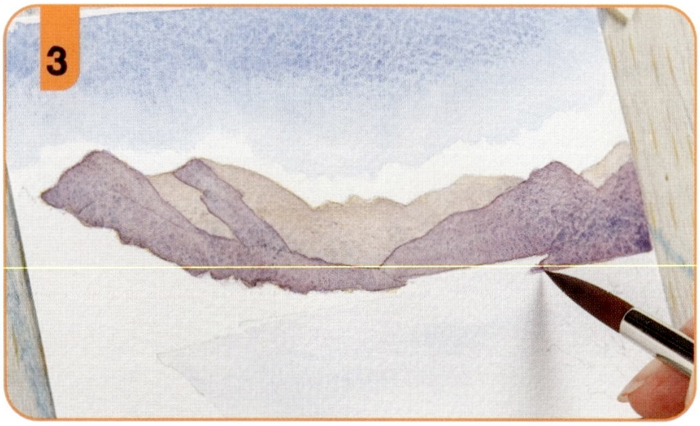

3 Once more, using the same colours, paint the mountains as shown.

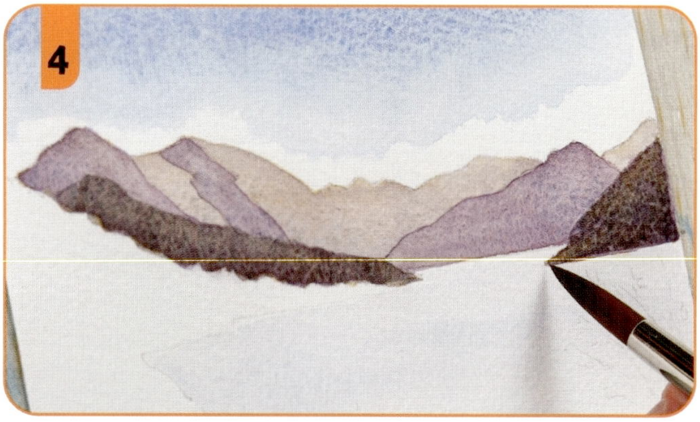

4 Once dry, paint the nearer mountains with a mix of raw sienna, permanent rose and French ultramarine.

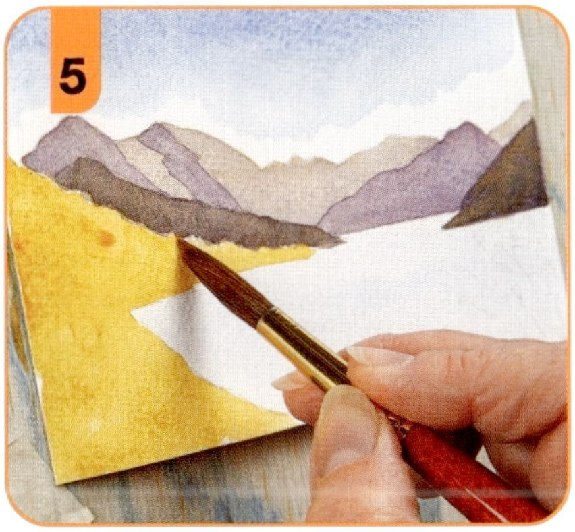

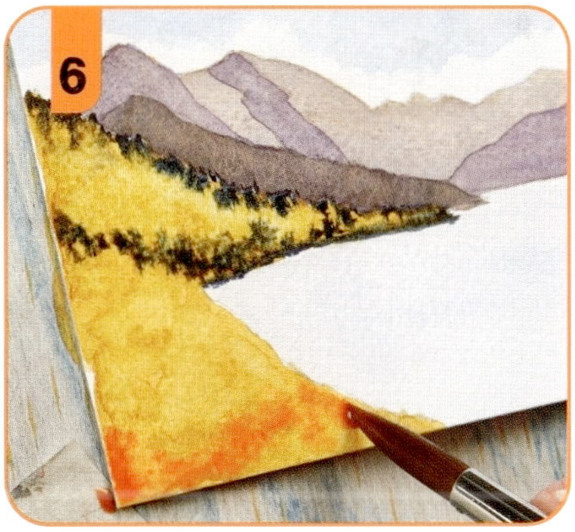

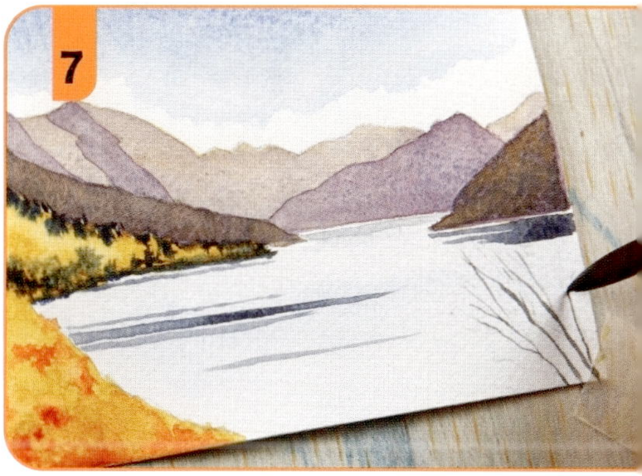

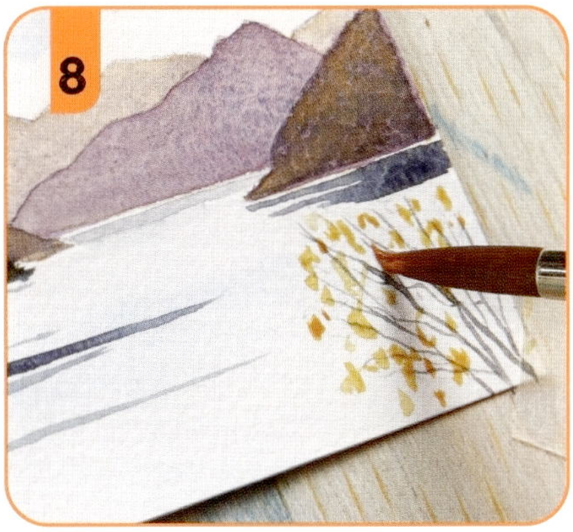

5 Beginning with raw sienna, paint the trees and bank on the left.

6 While the wash is damp, add burnt sienna and French ultramarine here and there, allowing the colours to blend. Add a mix of French ultramarine and burnt umber as the paint dries so that the colour will spread less.

7 Add some horizontal lines to the sea with a mix of French ultramarine and burnt umber, and paint the branches of the tree in the foreground with the same mix. Use just a little paint on the brush so that you get a good point, and paint the twigs in the direction of growth.

8 Create the leaves with dots and dabs of raw sienna and burnt sienna, allowing the colours to bleed into one another.

LET LIGHT THROUGH

Add more paint to the leaves to strengthen the colours, if you wish, but try to leave the sea colour showing through some of the leaves.

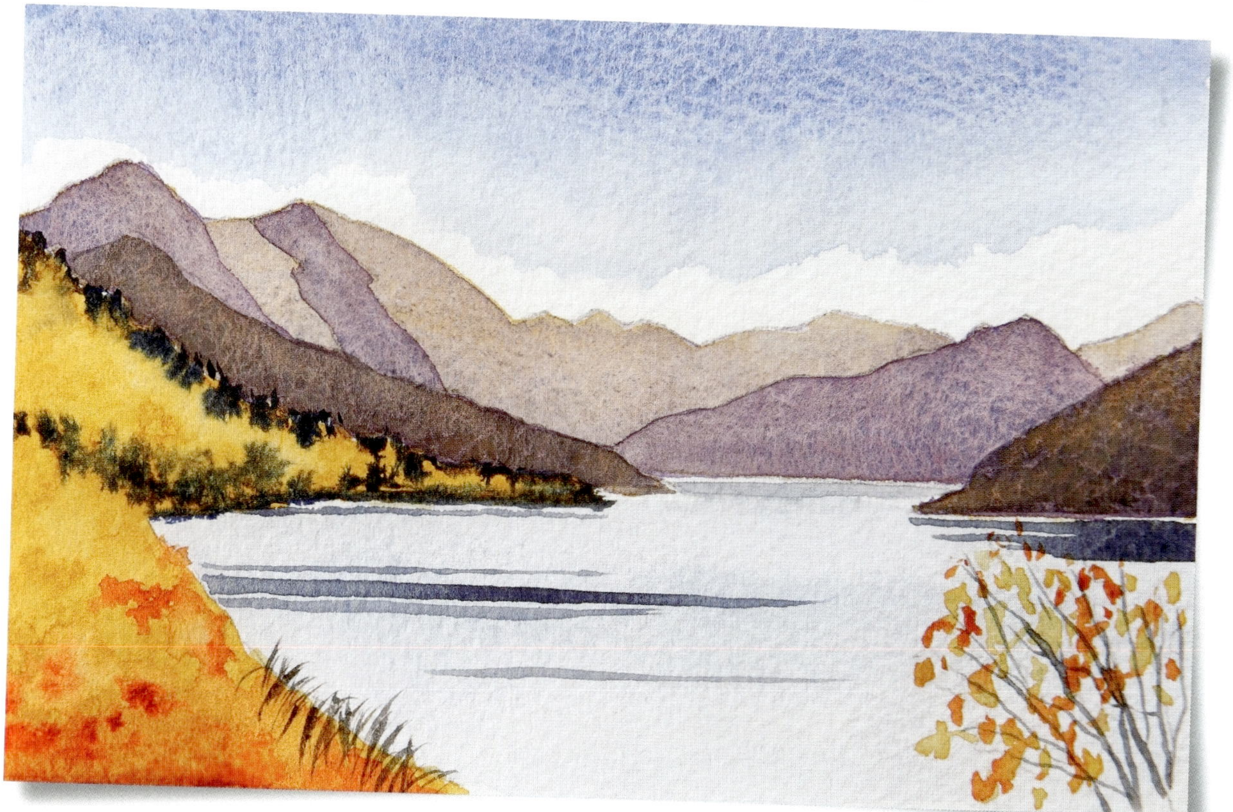

Mist

YOU WILL NEED

Paint colours: raw sienna, burnt umber, French ultramarine

Brushes: size 10 round

Other: tracing number 12

A damp day will often be quite dull because colours are subdued and features are generally made indistinct by the weather conditions. Working on wet or damp paper with limited colours helps us to portray a damp day while mixing colours gives warm and cool greys.

As you paint, look ahead. Bear in mind that the paint will spread on the wet surface and give a fuzzy/soft focus effect. Don't panic: this softness is the effect we're looking for here, rather than accuracy or detail. Secondly, prepare plenty of each mix; this project relies on timing, so you don't want to run out at a critical point.

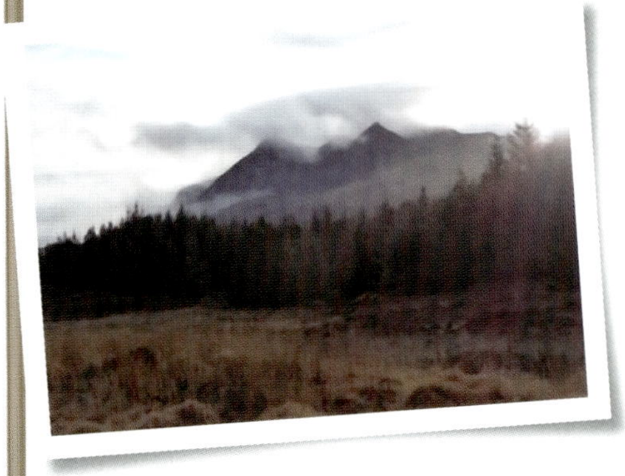

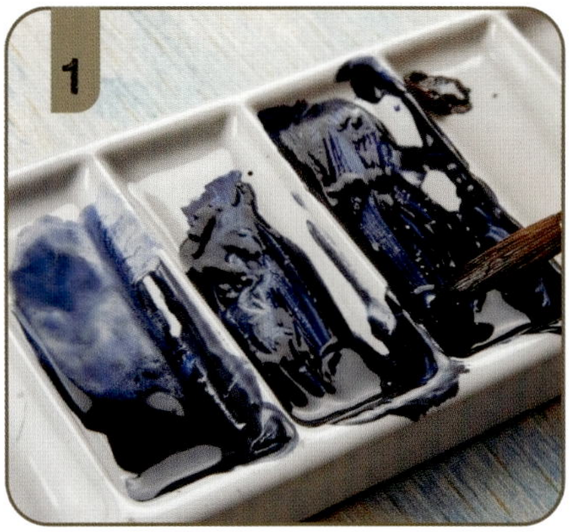

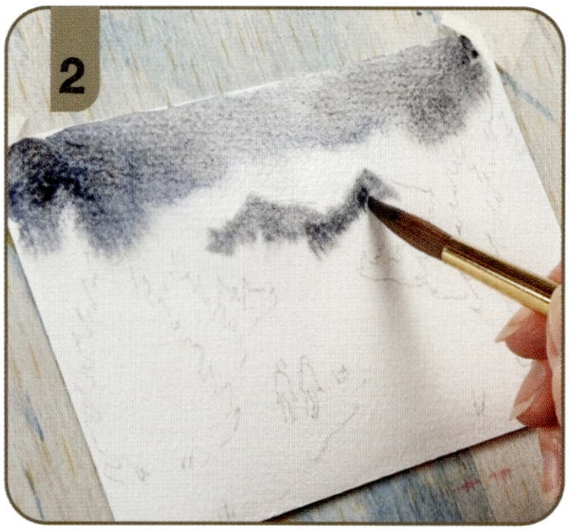

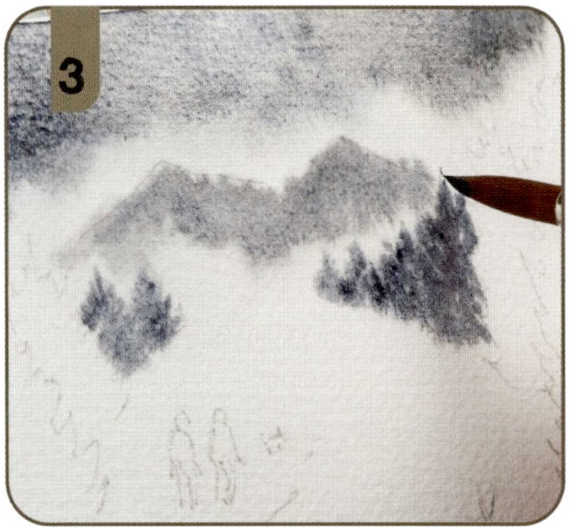

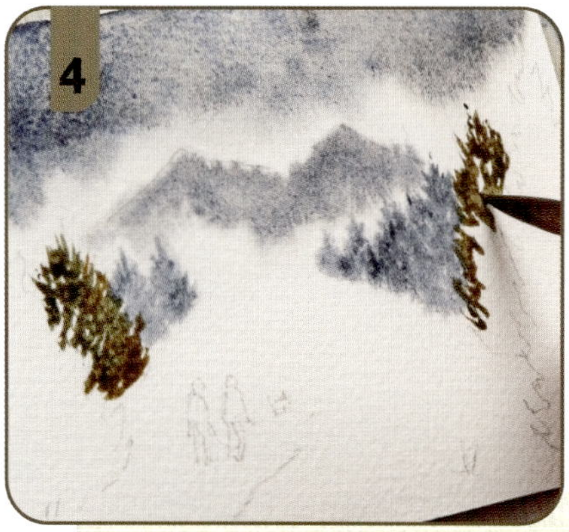

1 Prepare a French ultramarine and burnt umber mix in three different dilutions: one medium strength, one stronger, and another quite concentrated. Remember that watercolour will soften and lighten on damp paper, so it's important not to go too dilute, even for a pale effect.

2 Wet the paper all over. Wait a few seconds for the paper to begin to absorb the water, then quickly drop in clouds and paint the hills with the palest mix.

3 While the paper is still damp, paint the distant trees with the slightly stronger mix. Aim to leave a misty gap between the hills and tops of the trees.

4 Add nearer trees adding a little raw sienna to the French ultramarine and burnt umber mix.

DRYING TIMES

When working wet in wet, drying times will vary depending on temperature and humidity. If you find the paper is drying too quickly, you can sometimes create more favourable conditions for your work by wetting the paper once, allowing the paper to 'drink', then wetting the paper again; as the paper has already absorbed some water, it will take less out of the second application.

5 Paint the foreground trees with a stronger mix of French ultramarine and burnt umber, with a little raw sienna added.

6 Re-wet the foreground, then add touches of the most dilute well of the sky colour to suggest the path.

7 Once dry, add small indistinct figures – just a few simple lines. Keep the colour pale to begin with, and if you're happy with the shapes you can drop in darker tones.

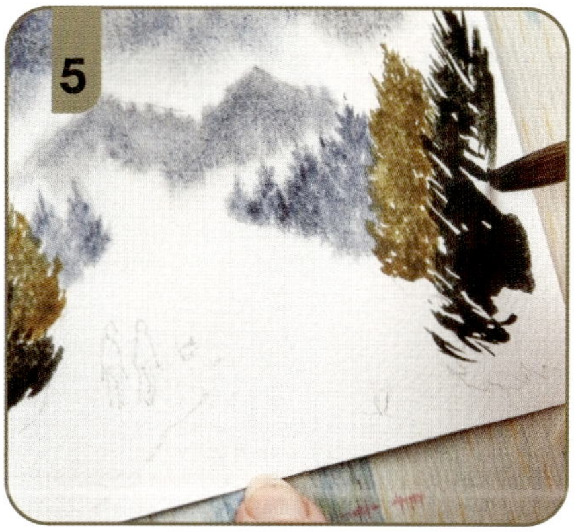

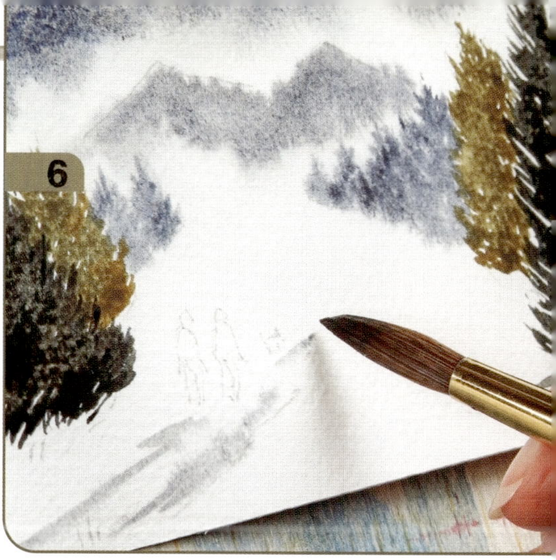

REMOVING PALE PAINT

If you aren't happy with the result, it's easier to remove pale colours. Allow the paper to dry, then try again.

8 Using the tree mix, add foreground details – shrubs and grass – to the dry paper. These help to take away the stark whiteness in the centre.

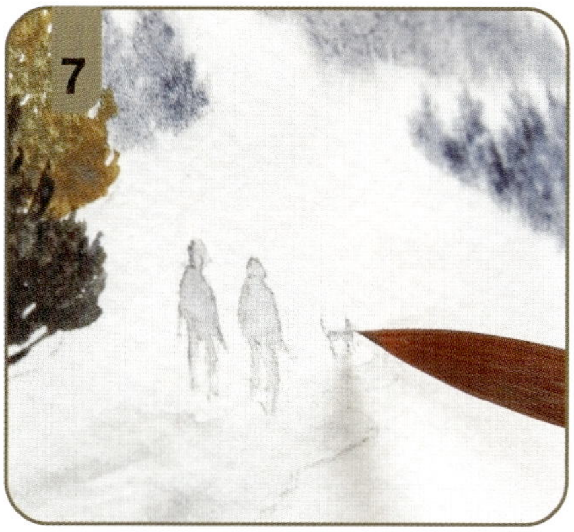

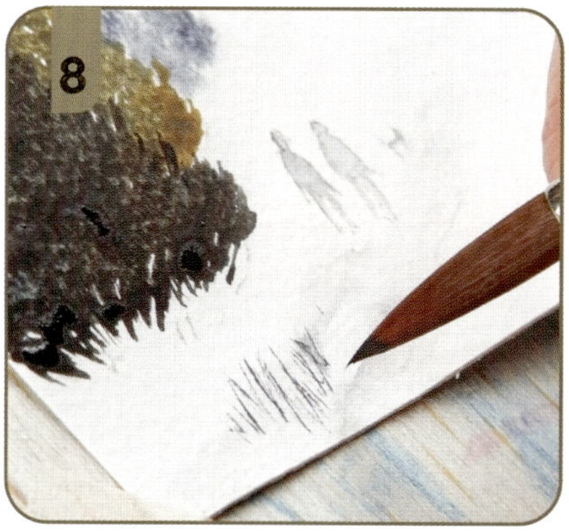

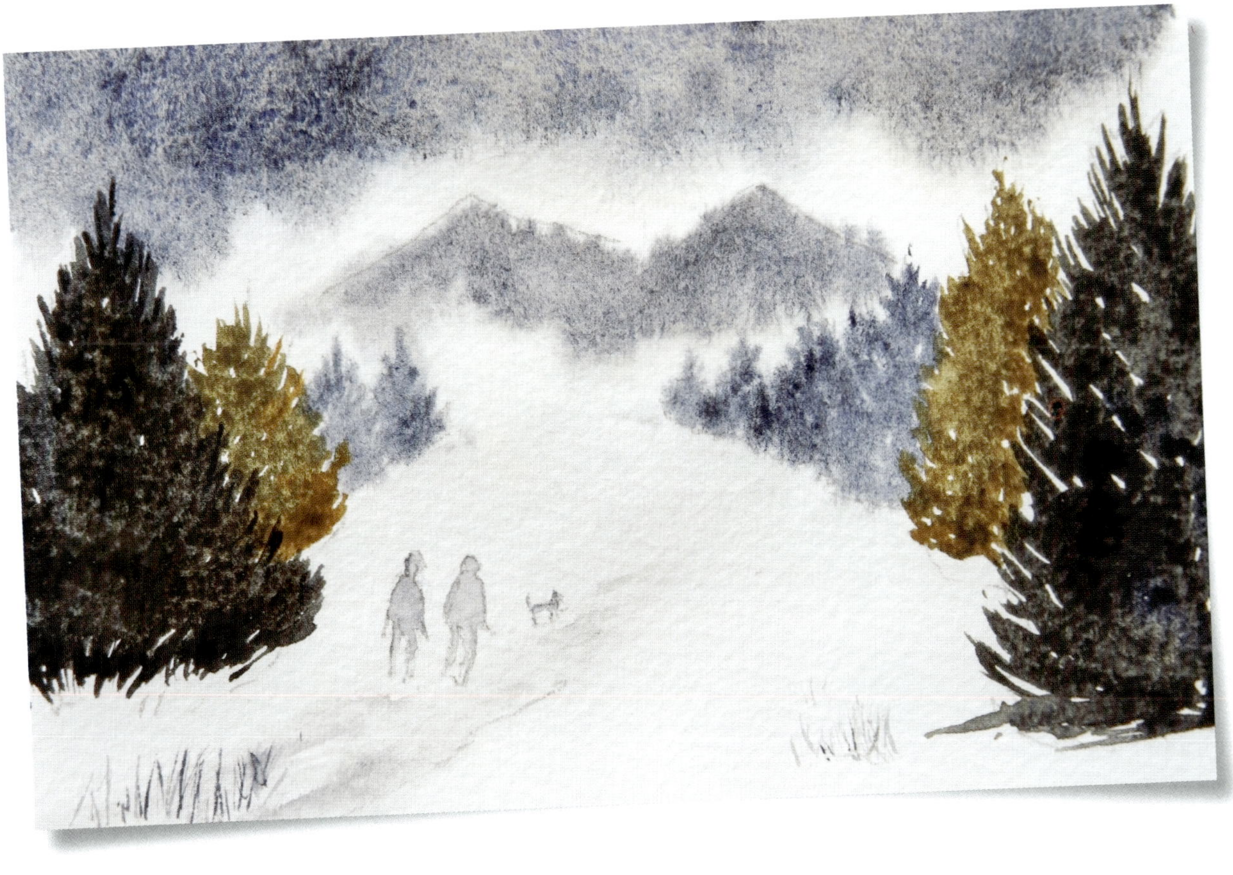

ROCK & STONE

We tend to think of mountains, rocks and stones as being 'grey' or 'brown' but even if that were true, we don't have to paint them as seen; different light and weather conditions can affect the colours we see, and our imaginations can change them too.

I like to collect reference material such as the outline of hills in good visibility when mountains are free of cloud. Clear days can also be dull days, uninspiring for painting purposes, but we use the information we've gathered to create a particular mood. We are free, as painters, to change things as we wish.

In painting rocks and stones, we can paint them more effectively by looking at them as areas of light and darks, tones, instead of trying to define individual rocks. Distant hills will not reveal their details to us; suggesting the odd gully or pinnacle may be all that's needed.

In portraying rocks both in the distance and close up we can use tones and advancing colours (warm colours that we use for foreground) and receding colours (cooler colours that we use to 'push back' parts of our painting into the distance), and detail (or lack of it) to create an impression of distance.

Cuillin from Carbost

54.5 x 22cm (21½ x 8½in)

The rugged shape of ridgelines make wonderful silhouettes. I made numerous visits to this location before I found the whole ridge free of cloud and then I used the outline in this scene depicting soft early evening lighting.

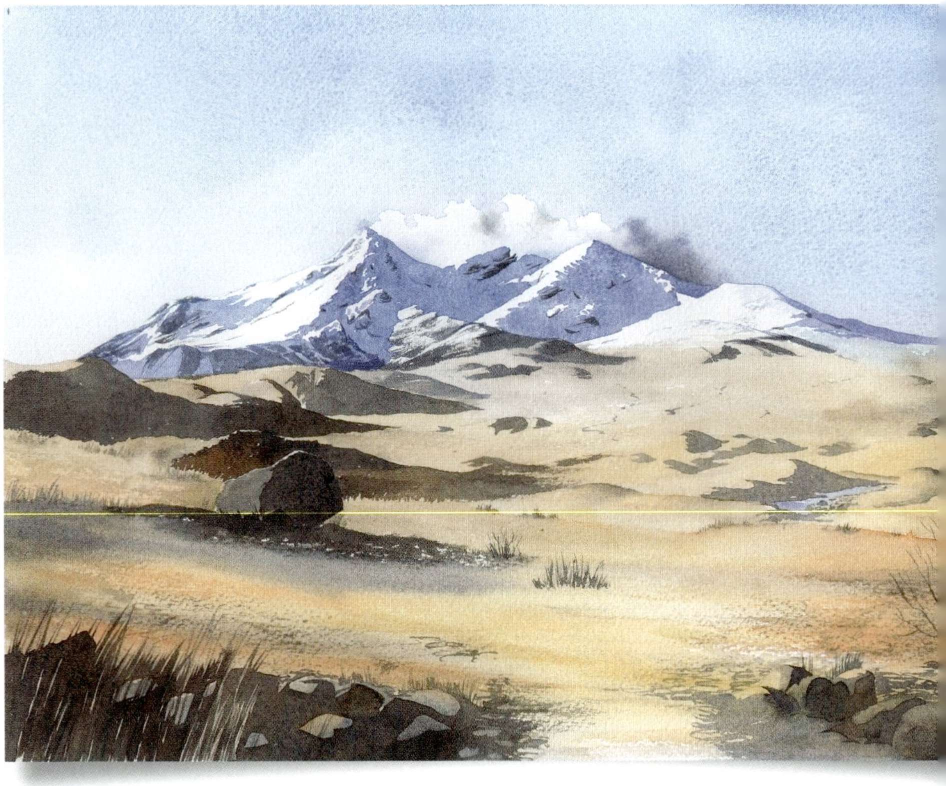

Cuillin Snows, Sligachan

37 x 27cm (14½ x 10½in)

A still, calm, dry day in the Cuillin as seen from a popular car park. I omitted the car park, road and signage which would have marred the wilderness effect. I've used only a few colours for the cool snows and a little more warmth in the foreground. The focus is very much on the snowy hills, where the blues enhance the whiteness of the paper.

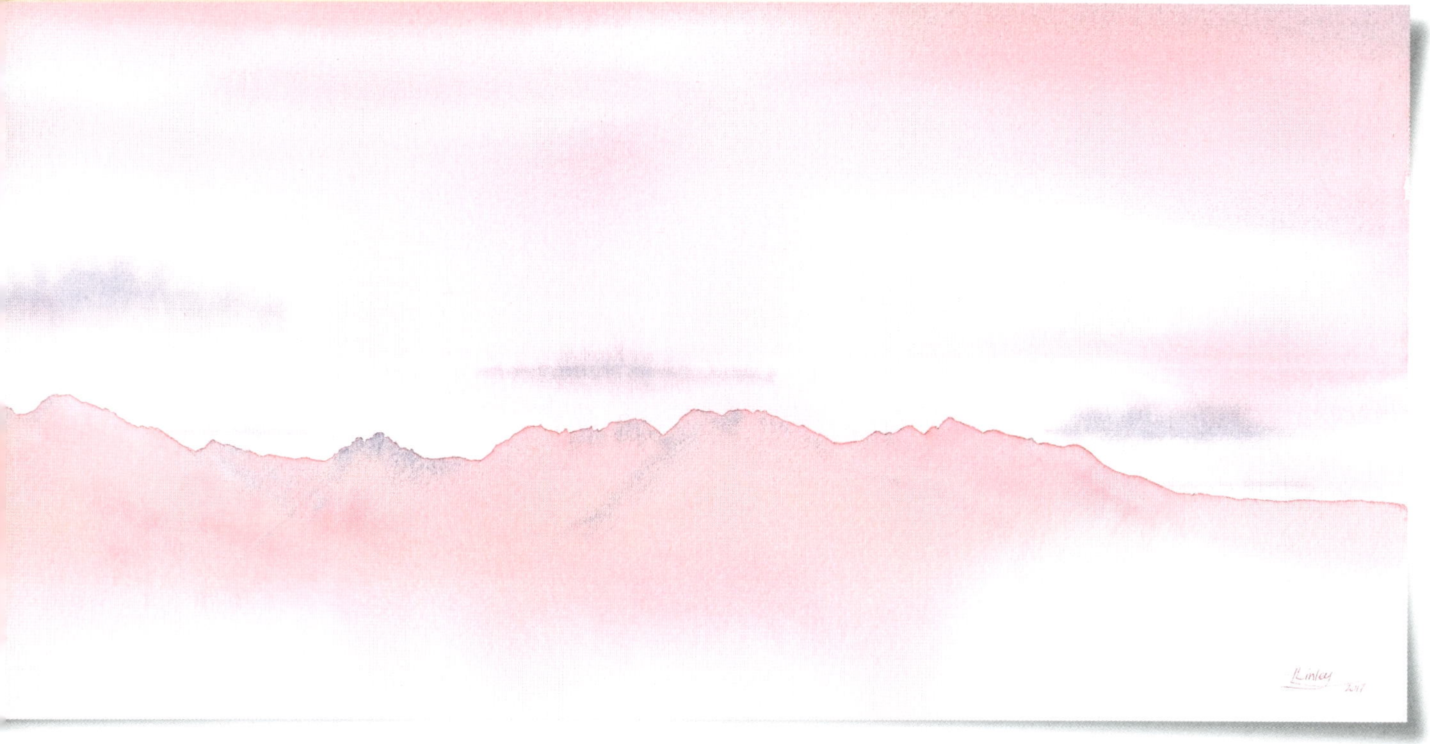

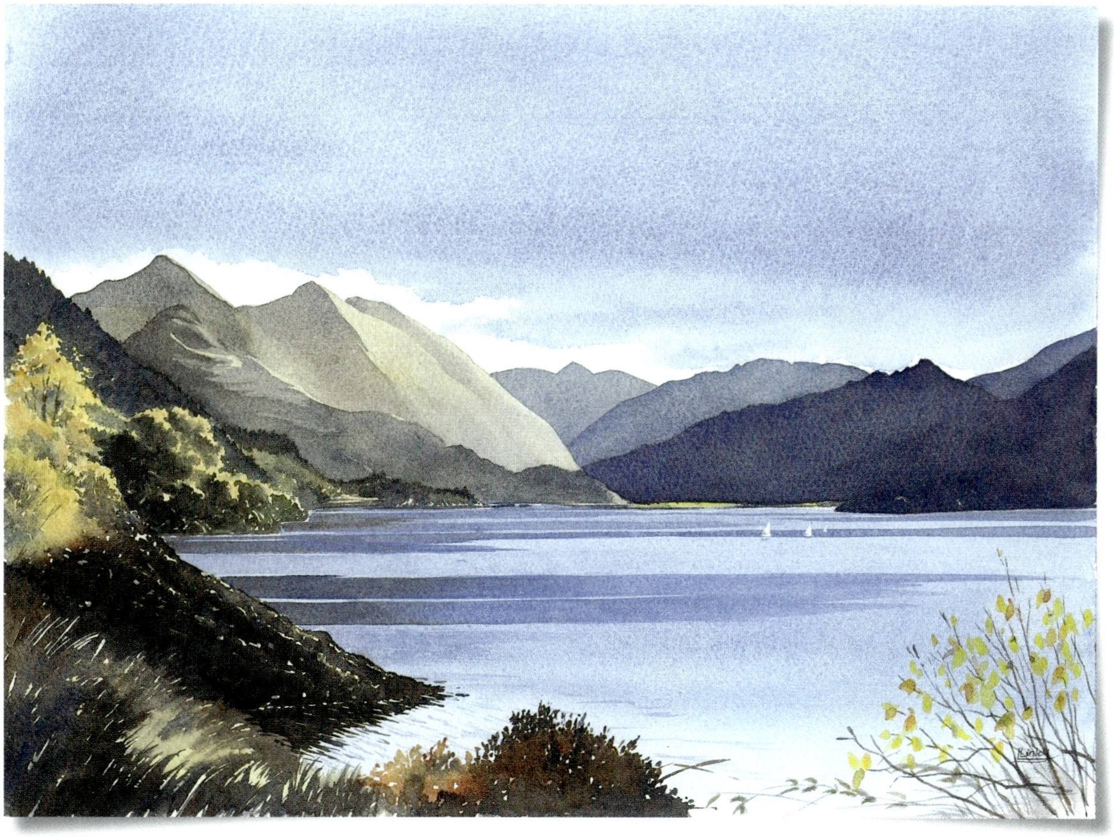

Five Sisters from Loch Duich

37 x 27cm (14½ x 10½in)

Another calm, still day. One side of the glen is in deep shadow while the other side is in strong sunlight so darker, cooler tones have been used on the right, with the left in brighter, warmer colours. Highlights on trees have been created by negative painting around the golds. This painting was the inspiration for the projects on pages 44 and 46.

Rock textures

Here we have rocks of all sizes; a huge mountain in the distance, the cliff, then rocks and pebbles and foreground; colours and detail are used to create that feeling of distance. This project is all about creating rocky effects, rather than attempting to paint every pebble.

YOU WILL NEED

Paint colours: raw sienna, burnt sienna, burnt umber, French ultramarine

Brushes: size 10 round

Other: tracing number 13

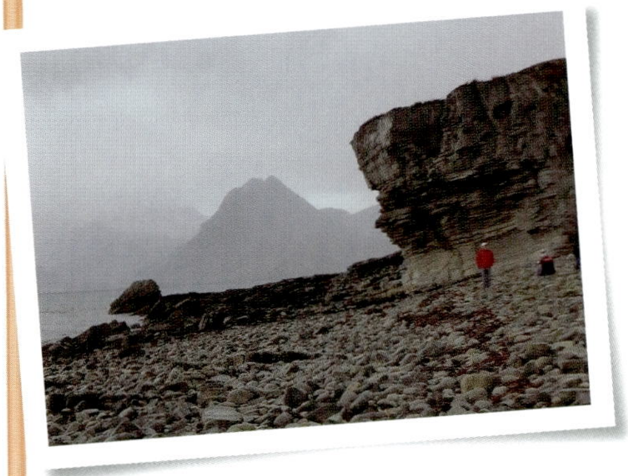

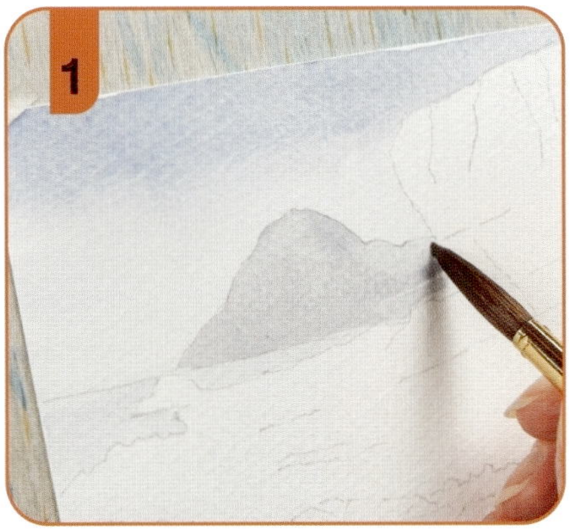

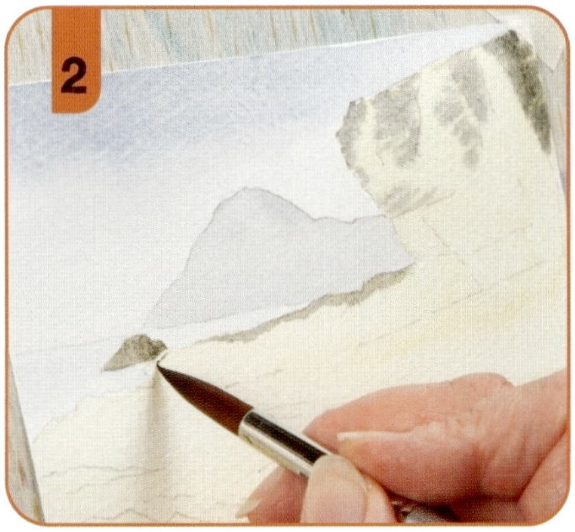

1 Using a pale grey-blue mixture of French ultramarine and burnt umber, paint the sky, distant hill, and sea. When dry, paint the hill again with a similar mix.

2 Wash over all the rocks, cliff and beach with very pale raw sienna. Drop in French ultramarine and burnt umber mix over the darker areas of the cliff and the rocks across the centre of the painting.

3 Paint the distant rocks on the beach, then shadows and strata lines in the cliff face (using the point of your brush and a little paint in order to retain the point on your brush). Soften a few edges, and vary the proportions of the colours you use.

4 Drybrush French ultramarine and burnt umber over the middle-distance area of the beach to suggest a few pebbles.

5 Paint the foreground rocks with French ultramarine and burnt umber mix, beginning with loose dots and squiggles.

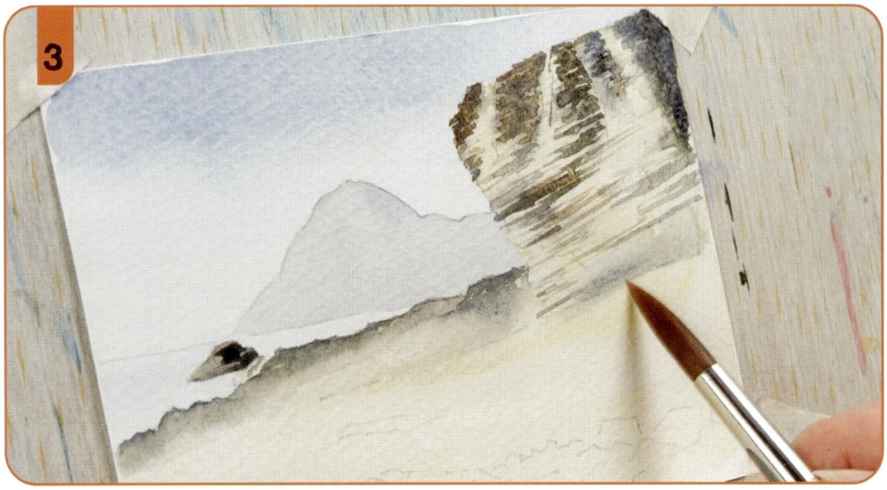

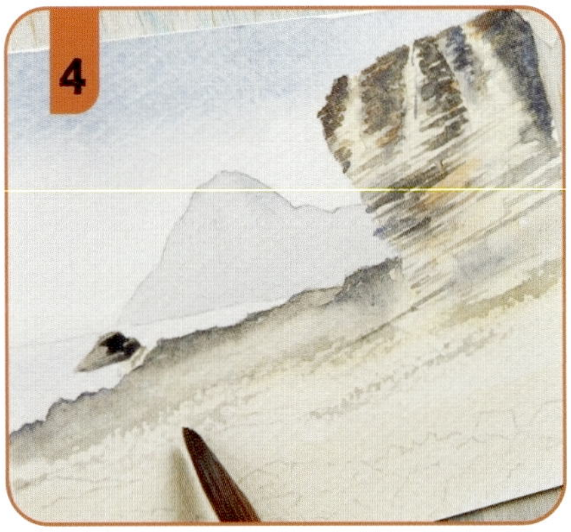

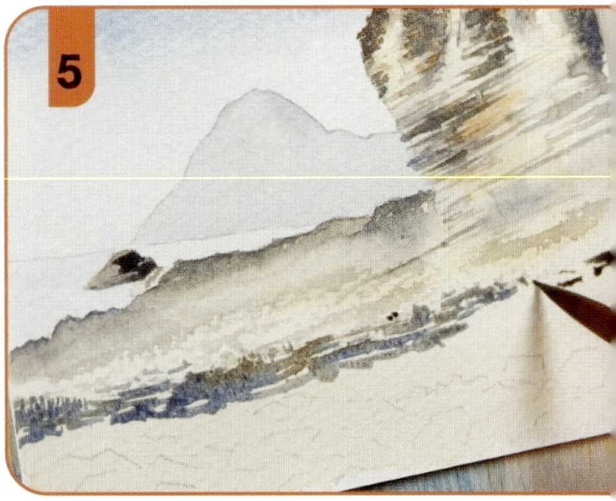

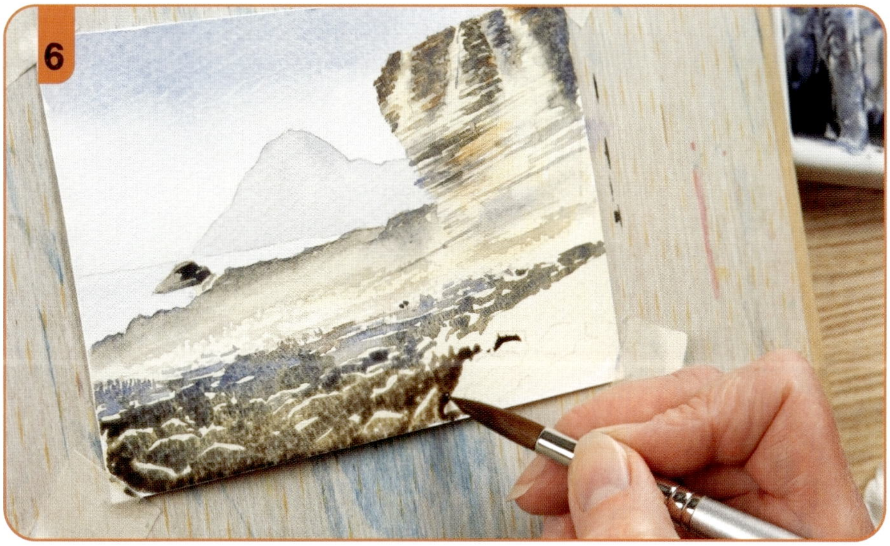

6 Make the colour a little stronger and more biased towards brown as you come forward into the larger rocks; keep the paint wet so that each rock merges with the next. Leave highlights unpainted to define the tops of the rocks.

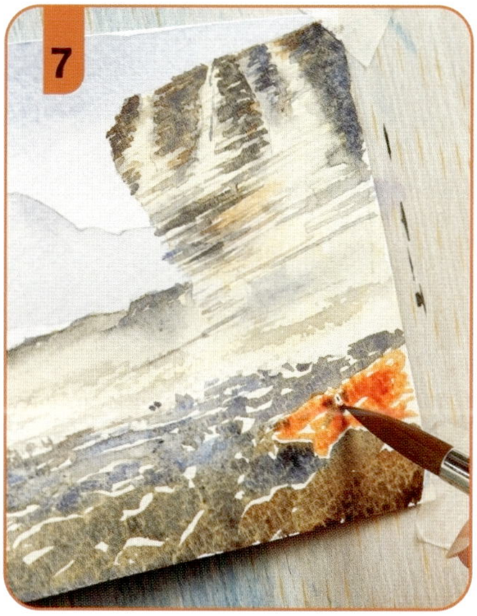

7 Using a little burnt sienna paint the seaweed on the beach.

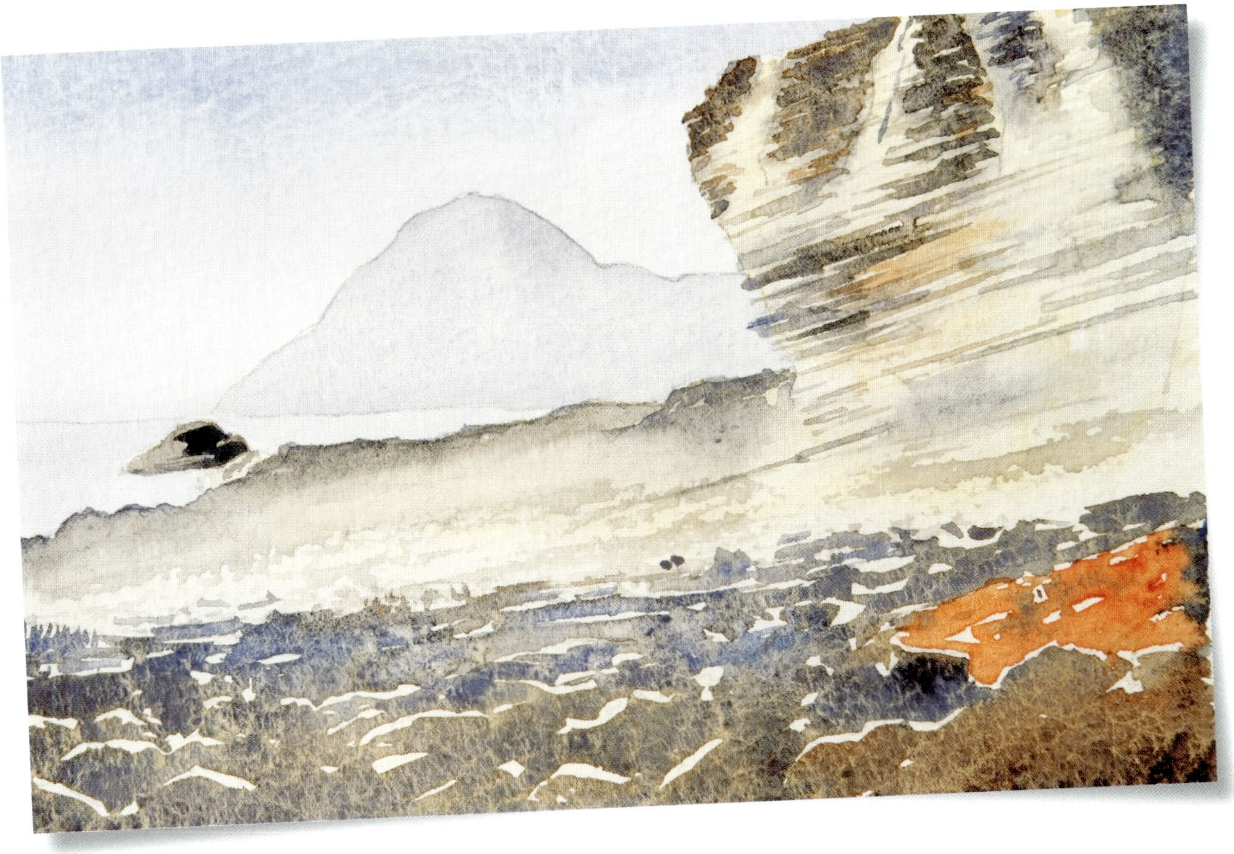

Waterfall

YOU WILL NEED

Paint colours: burnt umber, French ultramarine

Brushes: size 10 round

Other: tracing number 14

Creating texture on rock need not be complicated. By using the natural granulation that occurs with this mix, putting washes on and leaving the colours to 'do their magic', the textures are created for us. Tones are built with more layers of the same mix. The colours will separate a little in your palette; it can be pleasing to allow this (by not stirring up the colours too often), rather than have flat colour throughout.

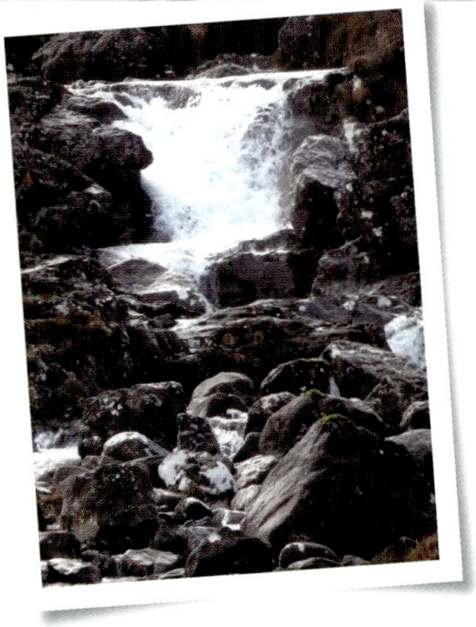

1 Make a pale mix of the colours and paint everything except the waterfall.

2 Stipple a few dots of pale French ultramarine on the waterfall, allow some of these to join up. Add a few dots of stronger French ultramarine and burnt umber.

3 Use a stronger tone of the mix to paint the rocks. Starting from the top with a blue-biased mix, work down while gradually changing to a brown-biased mix. Leave the lightest areas of the rocks unpainted: keep the paint wet so that one area flows into another. This also allows the paint to granulate.

RE-TRACING

If your lines have been lost under the first wash, you can allow the painting to dry and re-trace, but as this is an exercise and there's no 'correct' shape for a rock, you could just do your best without the lines.

4 Once the rocks are dry, use a darker mix to overpaint the darker areas of all the rocks, again keeping the paint very fluid on the page. Drop in stronger darks here and there to further vary the tone.

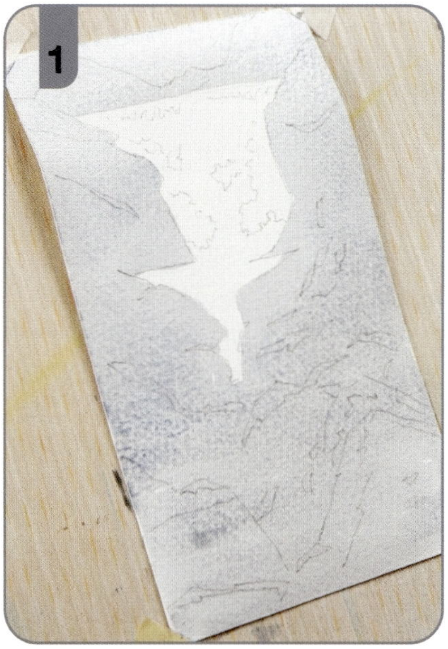

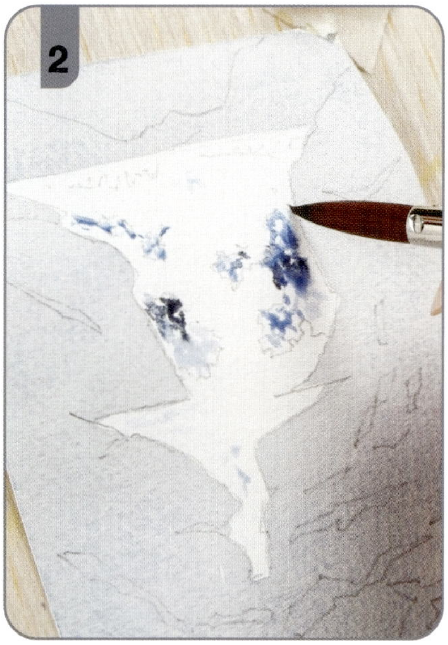

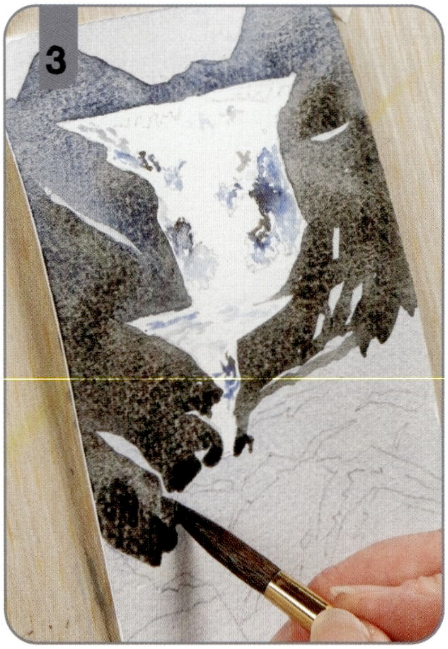

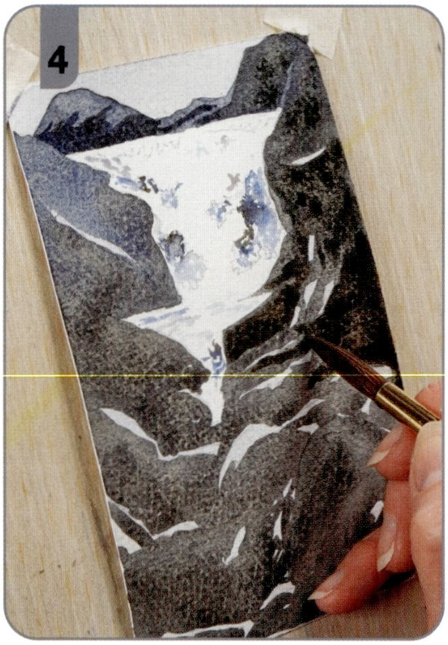

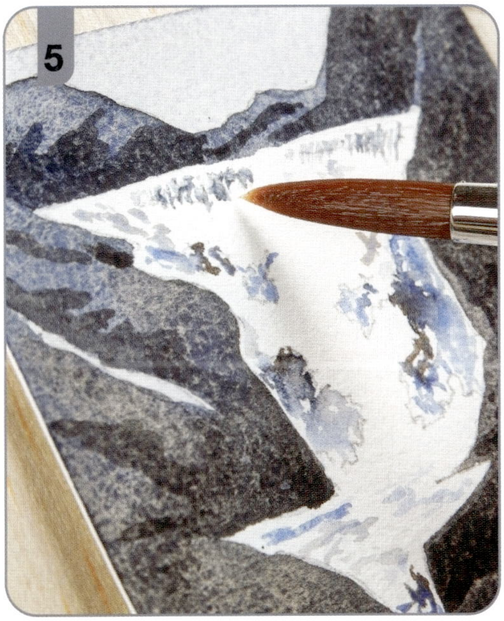

5 Add the darker details to the top of the waterfall with short marks that follow the curve of the waterfall. Use the same mix as the rocks, but slightly diluted. This helps to give the illusion that parts of the rocks are visible through bright, clear, foaming water.

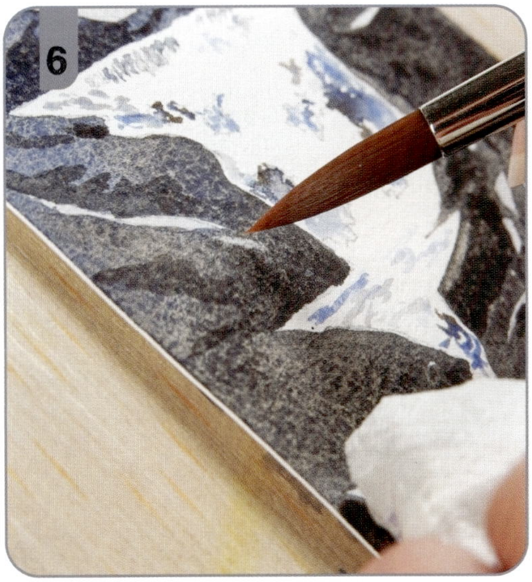

6 Lift out a few highlights from the dry paint of the rocks using a damp brush to loosen the paint and kitchen paper to blot. Avoid creating soft, fuzzy edges – use the point of your brush to create sharp, angular highlights.

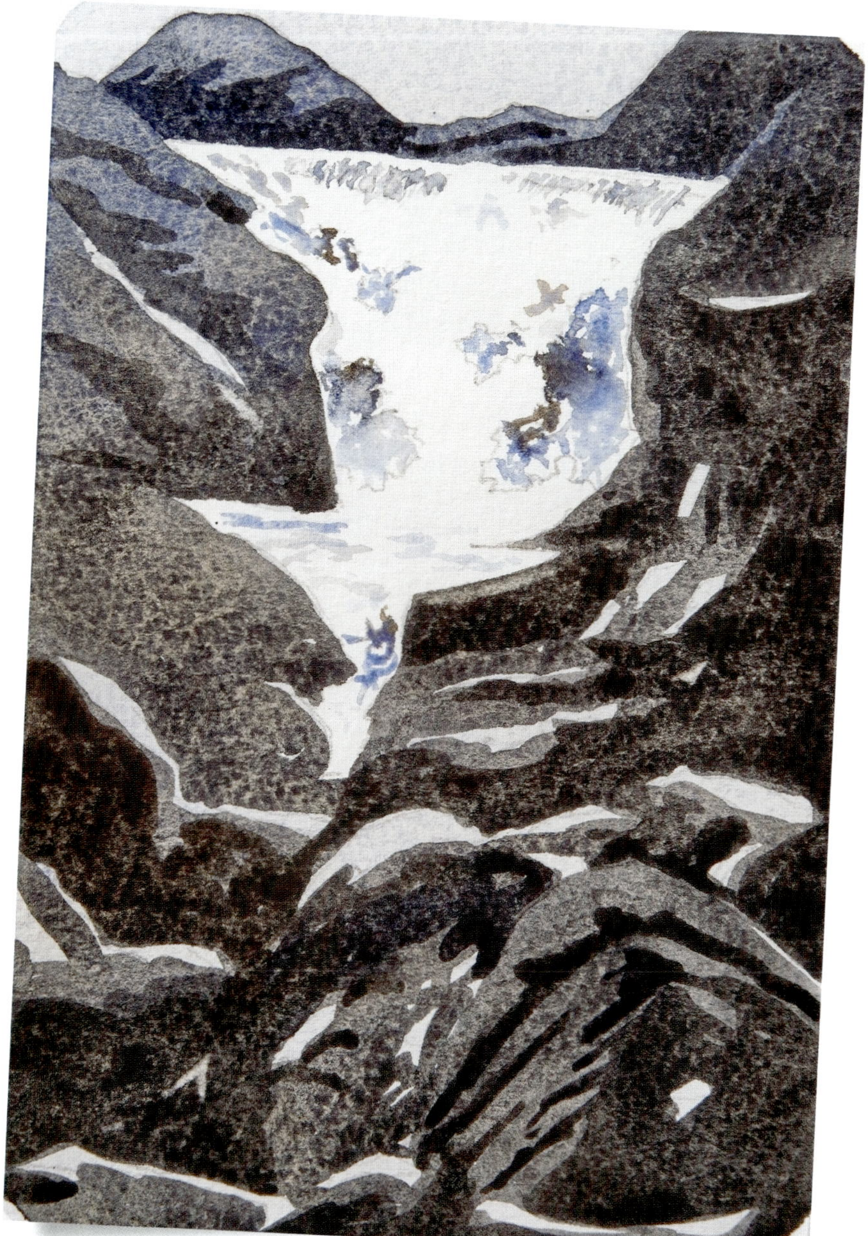

YOU WILL NEED

Paint colours: Winsor yellow, permanent rose, burnt sienna, burnt umber, French ultramarine, cobalt blue

Brushes: size 10 round

Other: tracing number 15

Sunlight and shadows

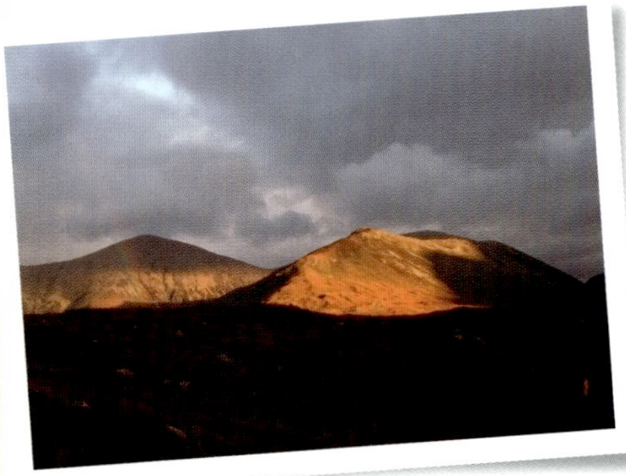

Shadows are created when something blocks a light source; they always fall away from that light. Their length, shape and sharpness changes according to the distance between the light and the object, and the angle of the light. Low winter sun creates long shadows, for example, while noon on a summer's day will be almost free of shadow. Shadows reveal contours and add tonal interest to a scene. Here, clouds and mountains interrupt light from the sun.

The hills are part of the Red Cuillin, a ridge of granite rock on the Isle of Skye, which can appear red-tinged in certain light. Here it's the late evening autumn sun illuminating the vegetation on the nearer hill that gives the strong colour. Seen from the start of the Loch Coruisk walk at Sligachan, the scene is a stark contrast of warm oranges and cool shadows cast by the low sun and tall hills.

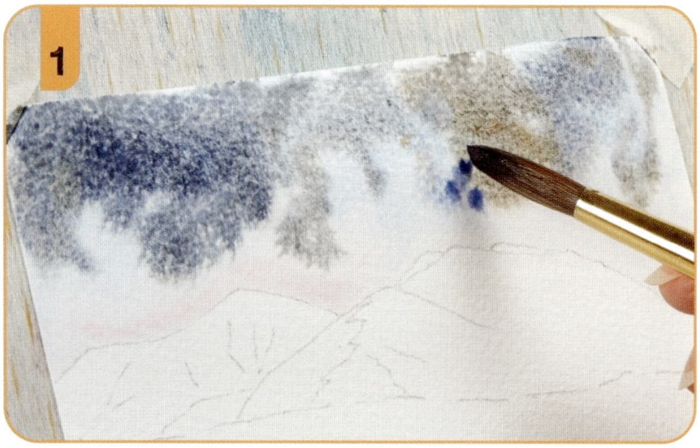

1 Wet the sky area, drop in pale cobalt blue for most of the sky with very pale permanent rose below. While this is still damp, drop in clouds of French ultramarine and burnt umber mix.

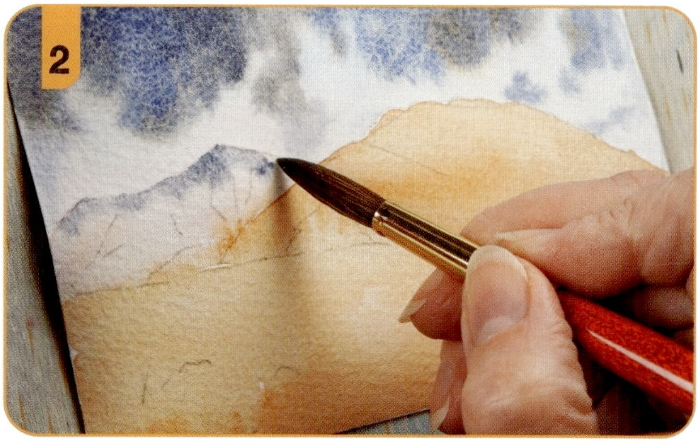

2 Paint the hills – pale permanent rose and a little burnt sienna to the hill on the left and burnt sienna to the hill on the right; allow the two hills to merge together. Continue with burnt sienna for the moorland, then drop in a French ultramarine and burnt umber mix to the top of hill on the left for the cloud shadow.

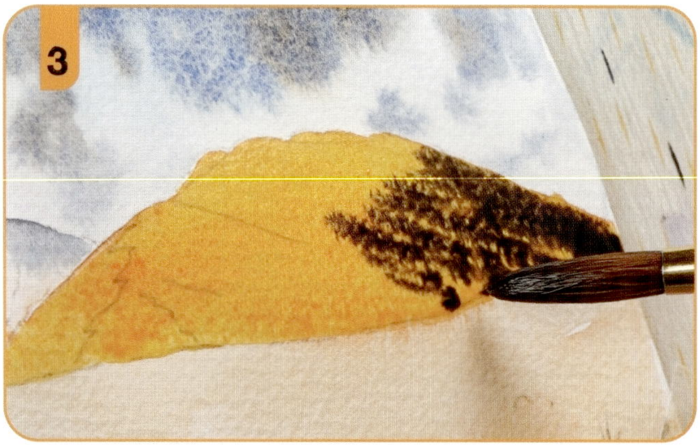

3 Re-wet the hill on the right and drop in burnt sienna and Winsor yellow. When this is damp, paint the cloud shadow with a stronger mix of French ultramarine and burnt umber, making diagonal movements with the brush. The dampness of the paper should give you slightly blurred, soft edges.

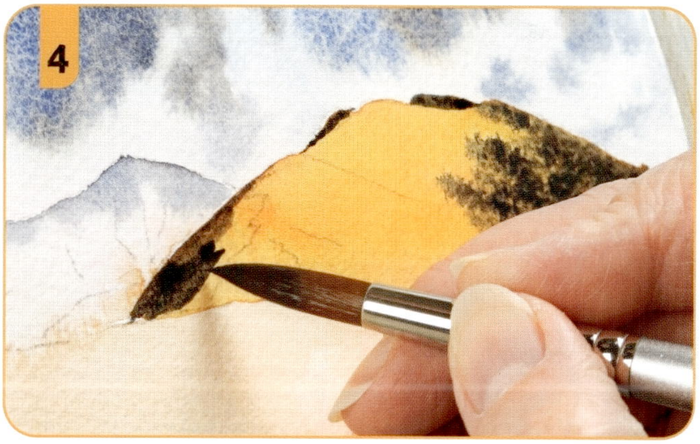

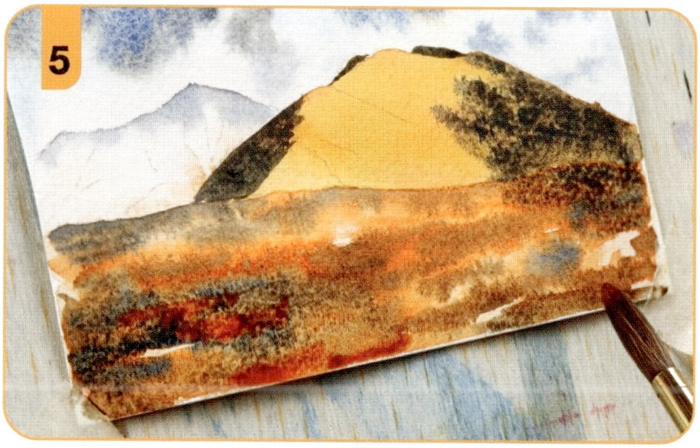

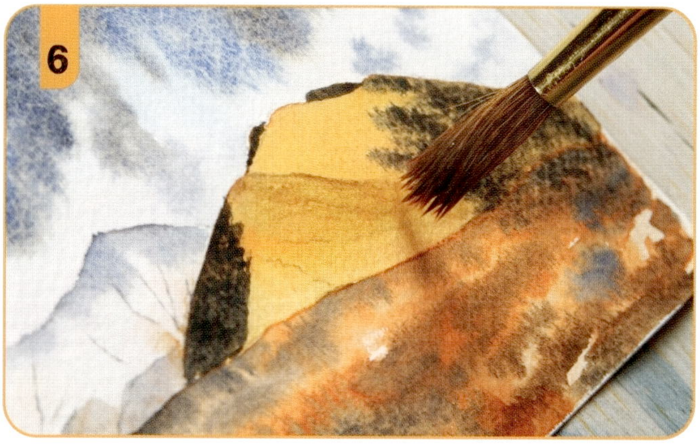

4 Paint the top of the hill on the right and the shadow to the left of this hill using the French ultramarine and burnt umber mix. Aim to create crisp edges by using the point of the brush.

5 Re-wet, roughly, the moorland (it does not matter if some areas remain dry). Paint some stronger darks to add a little texture to the foreground, using burnt sienna and the French ultramarine and burnt umber mix added wet in wet.

6 Add detail to hills and foreground with a dilute mix of burnt umber and French ultramarine, applying the paint with a split brush (see page 31).

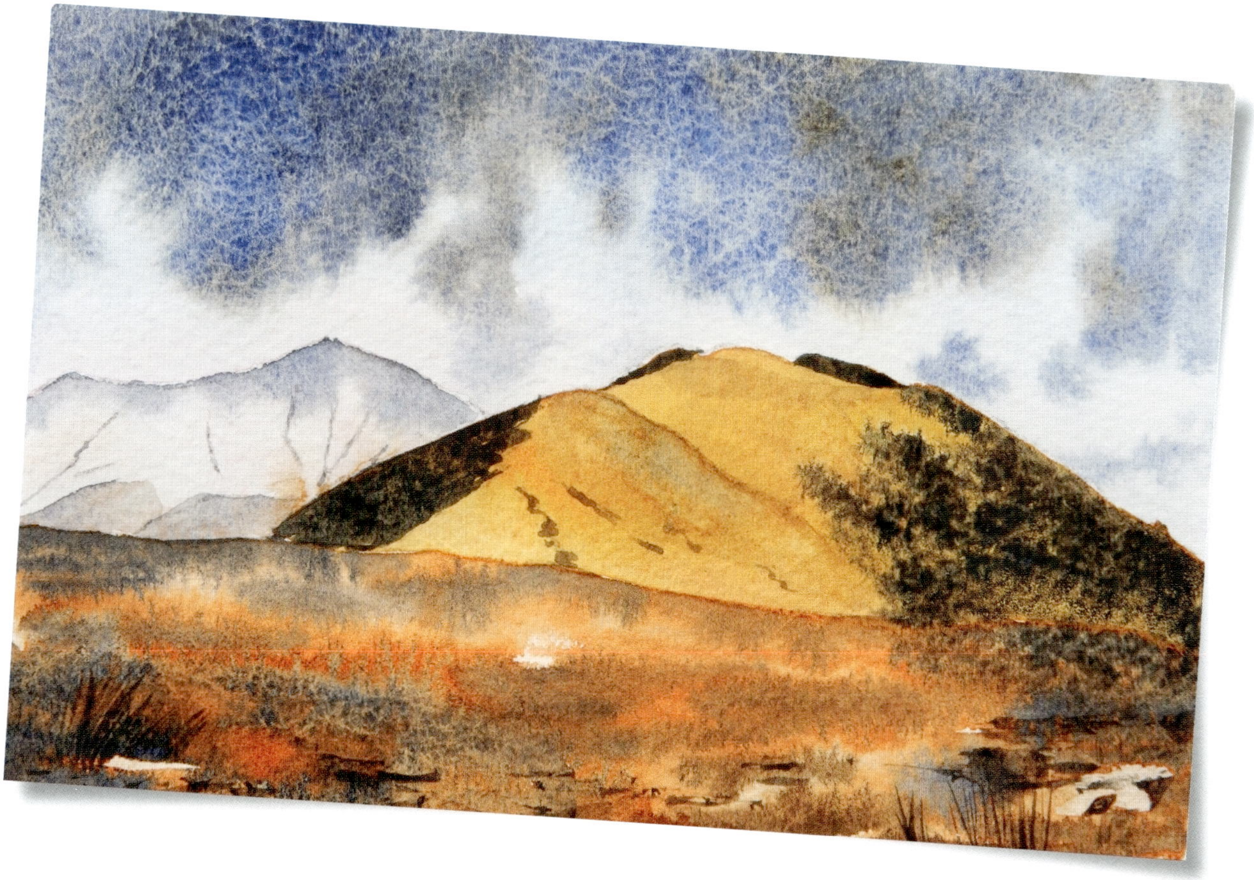

Mountain ridge

YOU WILL NEED

Paint colours: cobalt blue, raw sienna, burnt umber, French ultramarine

Brushes: size 10 round

Other: tracing number 16

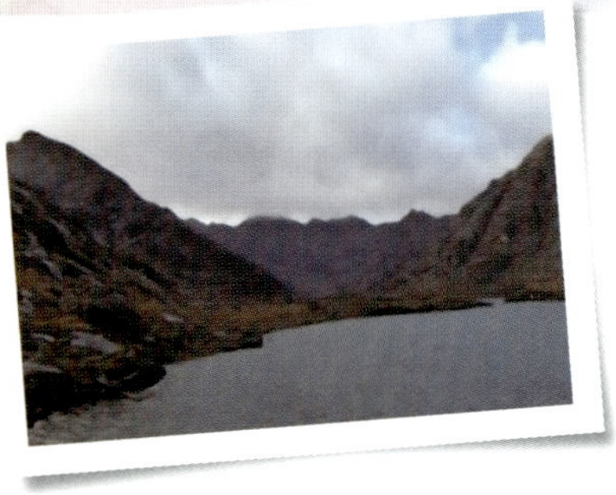

When working with complex shapes such as a mountain ridge you may find that you get a dark outline or streaky result if you paint the outline very carefully and then 'fill in' with colour, because the outline will have dried and show through the wash. You need to keep your leading edge wet as you work (just as when painting any wash), but this can be a challenge when you wish to portray the ridge line accurately.

To avoid this, you could turn your paper so that you can paint the ridge more easily (the orientation will depend on whether you are right- or left-handed), and the 'leading edge' is shorter. Whichever method you choose, put plenty of paint on, keeping it wet and keeping it moving to reduce the chances of streaks and backruns.

1 Using cobalt blue, paint the sky as shown, working around the clouds. Soften the edge in one or two places. Next, wet the pool area and drop in cobalt blue to the left.

2 Paint the mountains using a mix of French ultramarine and burnt umber.

3 Using a pale version of the French ultramarine and burnt umber mix, paint the shadow on the clouds, just above the ridge. As with the clouds, soften the edges.

4 Using raw sienna, paint the hill on the right and the moorland. While this is damp, drop in a little cobalt blue to the bottom, where the moorland comes down to the water. Drybrush a little texture to the pool, using any remaining cobalt blue in the palette well.

5 Paint the large hill on the left with a flat wash of French ultramarine and burnt umber. The underlying colour can lift easily, so work confidently and swiftly to avoid this. Don't fiddle!

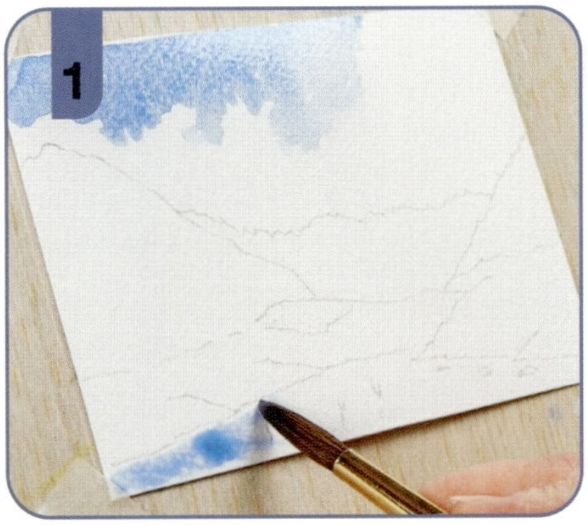

1

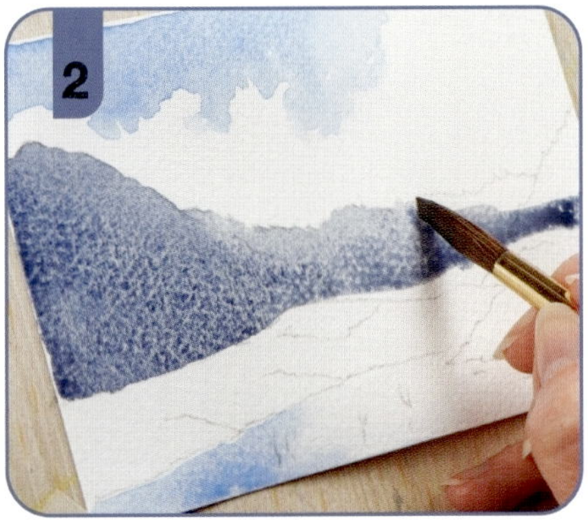

2

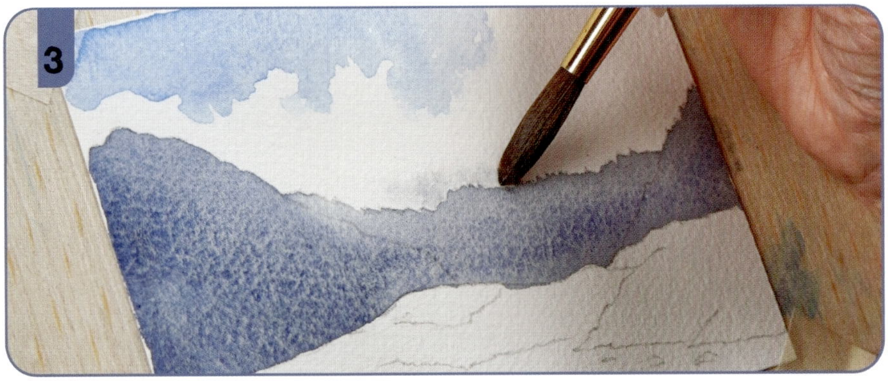

3

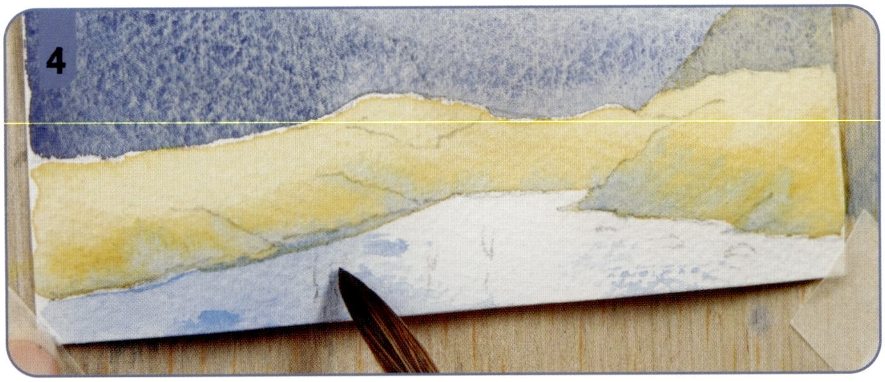

4

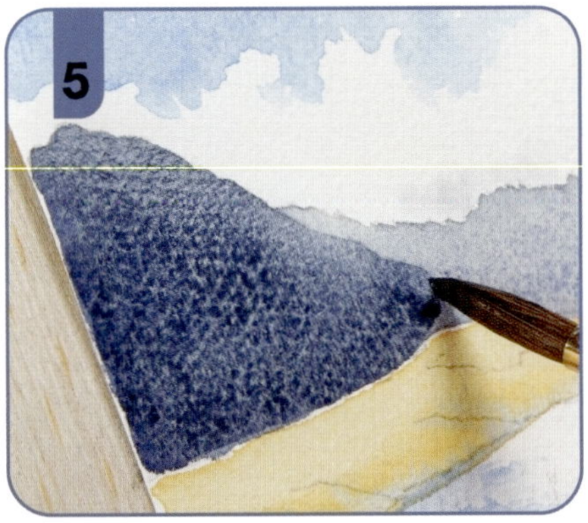

5

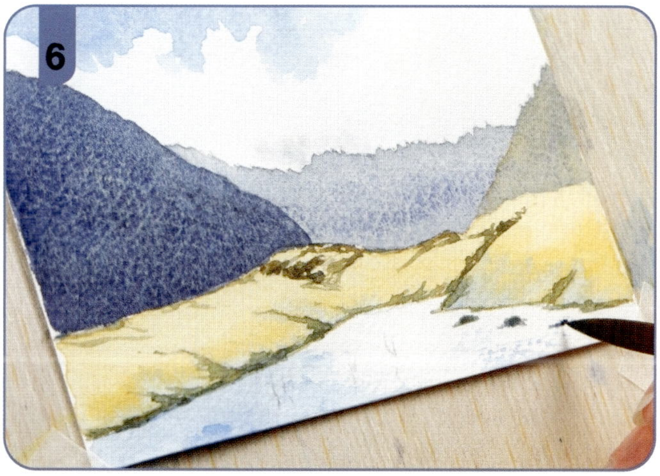

6 Using a mix of French ultramarine and raw sienna, add detail to the moorland and rocks and grasses to the pool.

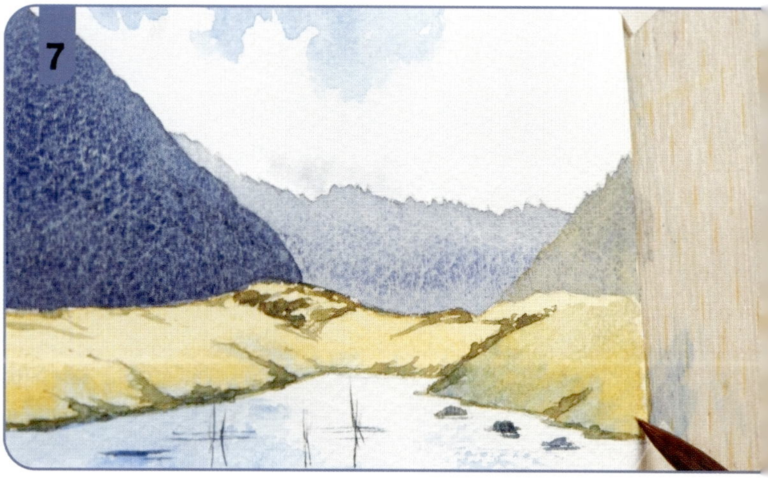

7 Develop the moorland by overlaying a little dilute mix of French ultramarine and raw sienna.

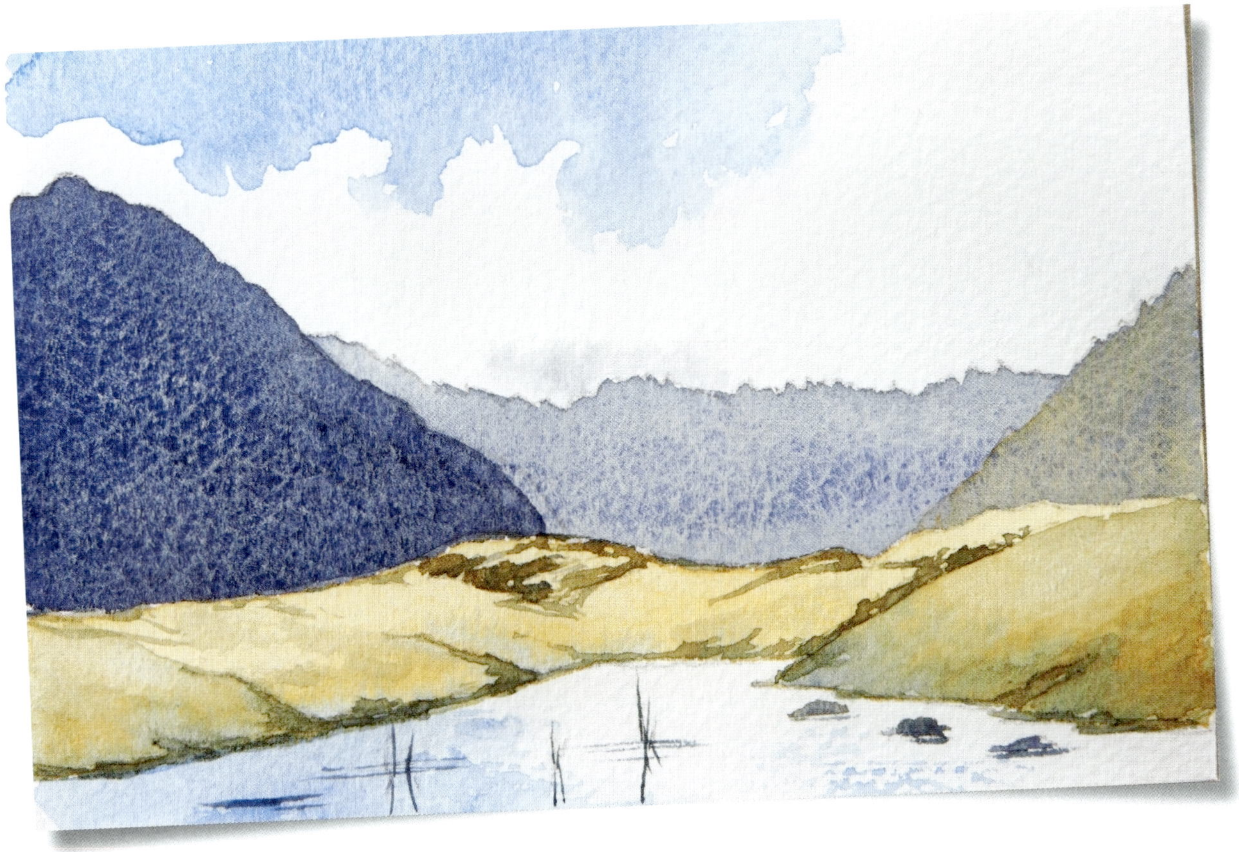

WATER

You were probably taught that water has no colour, but recent research has revealed that it does indeed have an inherent hint of blue. Whatever the science, there are many possibilities when it comes to painting it. Both observation and imagination are hugely useful. We're often told that the colour of the sky should be reflected in the water, but looking hard will often reveal situations where this is not so. Whether you choose to stick to 'the rules' or paint what you see is up to you.

Rivers in spate can be reddened by soil or peat churned up by the force of water or washed down from fields and moorland. Seas can be many colours – often several at once – as shallow water over sand gives way to shallows over weed and rocks and then deeper waters which may show the colours of disturbance of the sea bed. Puddles can reflect small areas of sky that we may not have noticed otherwise.

Reflections always come towards the viewer and change according to how far away the reflected object is from the water; whether the surface of the water is still or moving; and the direction in which the object leans. Reflections falling on still water are crisp mirror images; but a reflection of a light on a distant shore may travel a great distance across choppy water. Again, observe; see for yourself.

Apart from problems with reflections, beginners' mistakes often include having too little water on the paper when painting water. To avoid this, allow the paint to flow – just as water does!

Cuillin from Waterfall

37 x 27cm (14½ x 10½in)

In this scene the mountains play a supporting role in setting the scene, so that I could make more of the waterfall running down nearby. The light is quite flat, which helps to keep the focus on the pattern created by the water breaking over the rocks.

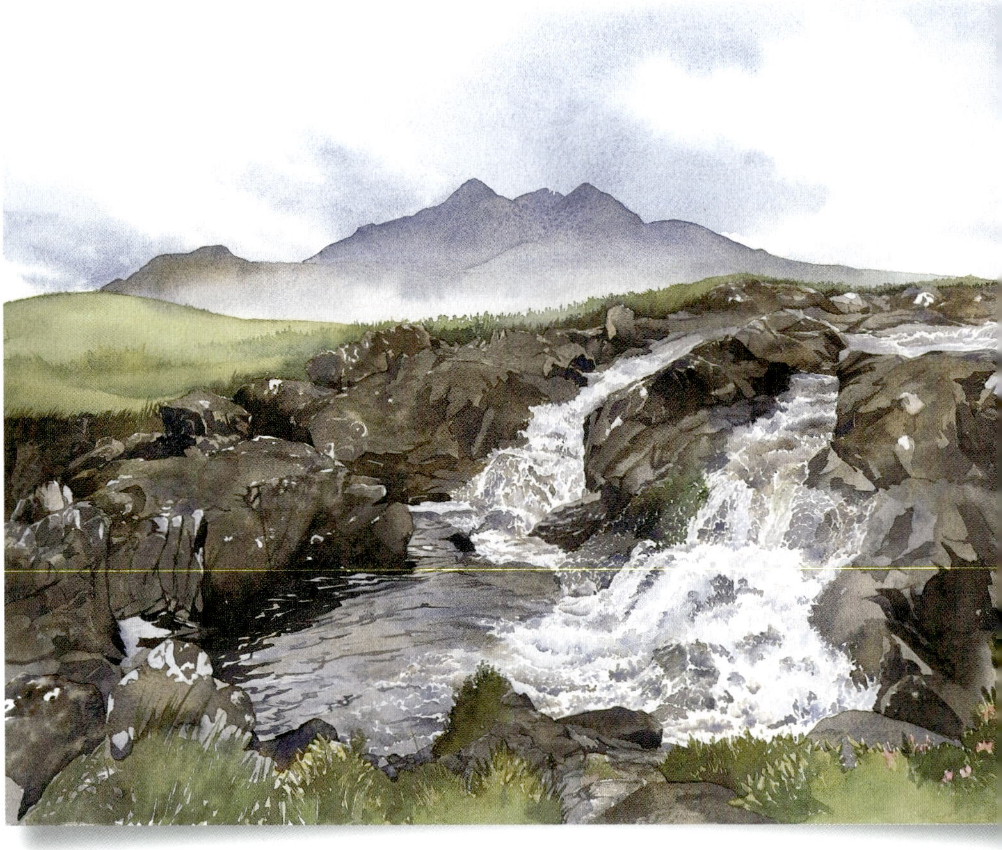

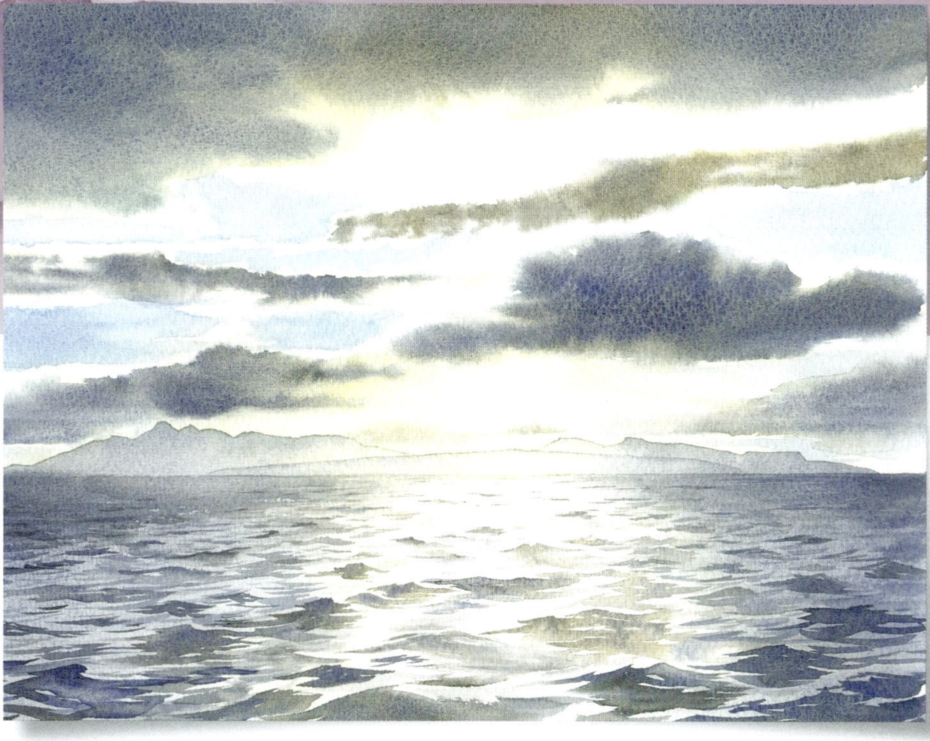

Eigg and Rum from the Boat

37 x 27 cm (14½ x 10½in)

One late October day I took the boat trip to Loch Coruisk. It was a dull day with rain looming as we set off from Elgol, but as we returned the low evening sun shone beautifully over the distant islands of Eigg and Rum. This is a limited palette, French ultramarine and burnt umber with a little raw sienna.

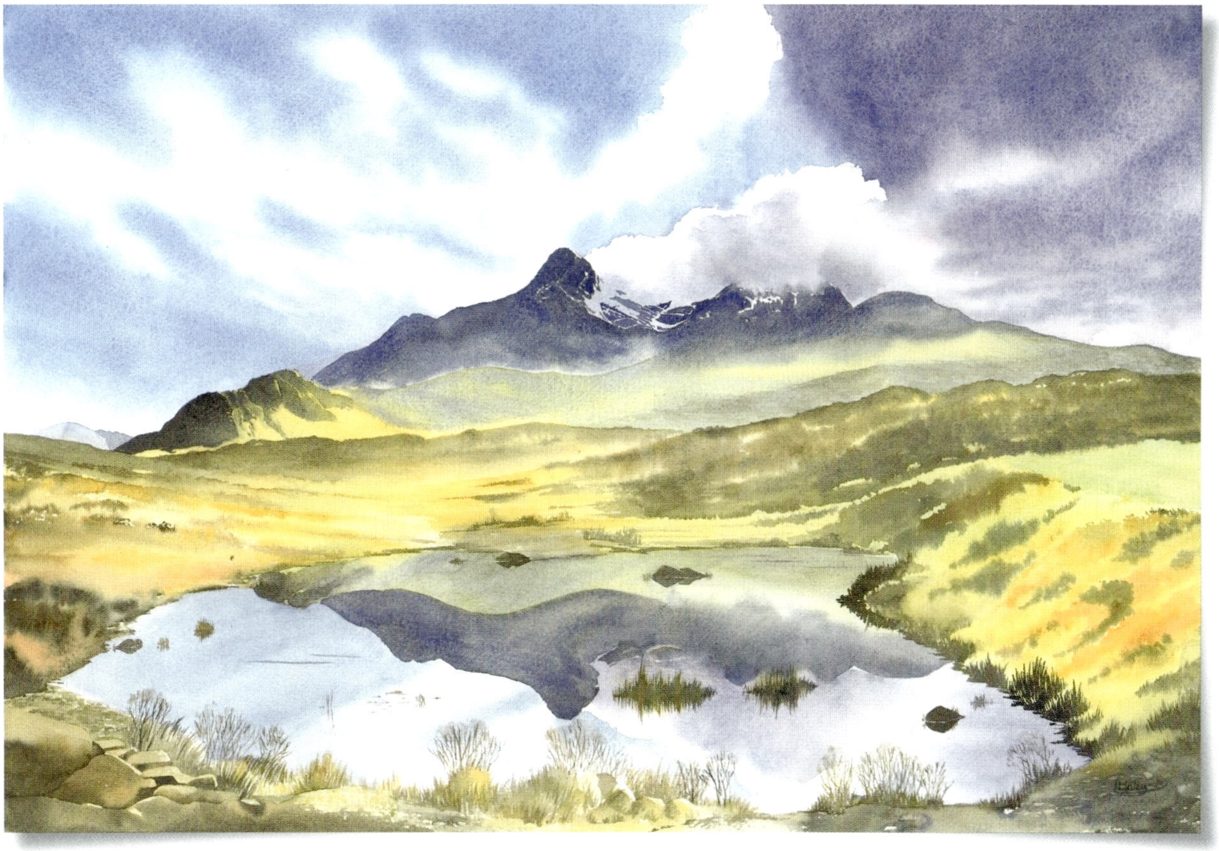

Cuillin Reflections, Winter

55 x 37cm (22 x 14½in)

A very still cold winter's day provided sharp reflections in the shallow pool and the blue sky is complemented by the subtle golds of the moorland. The edges of the mountain peaks have been lost into the clouds, hard edges beside soft ones. The moorland has been left indistinct in the distance, and more detailed in the foreground. The snow states this is a winter scene, and the almost leafless shrubs reinforce the idea.

Reflections

Still water is occasionally seen as 'still as a millpond' and this gives crisp mirrored reflections, but it often has a slight shimmer when ruffled by a gentle breeze; that's what we'll look at here.

While getting used to the wet-in-wet technique you might find it useful to paint reflections before the subject that's actually making them; that way if your reflection goes a little astray you can adjust the position of the subject to match it.

YOU WILL NEED

Paint colours: French ultramarine, burnt umber, raw sienna, permanent rose

Brushes: size 10 round

Other: tracing number 17

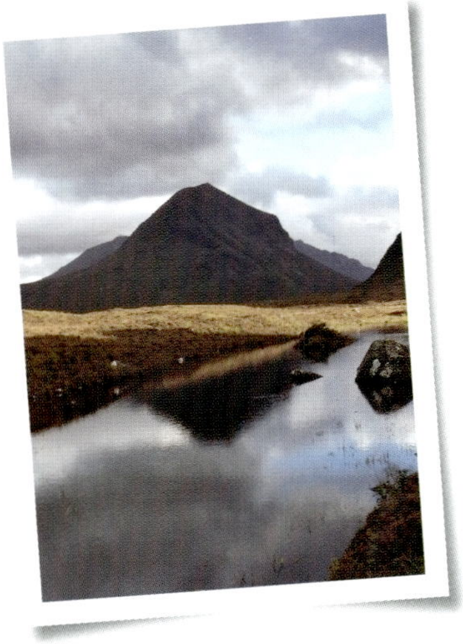

1 Wet the sky area and drop in clouds with a French ultramarine and burnt umber mix. Dampen the pool area and drop in reflections to loosely mirror the clouds, hill and the rocks as shown. Allow to dry.

2 Use the French ultramarine and burnt umber mix to paint the main hill. Paint the golds of the moorland below the pool with raw sienna. While wet, drop in permanent rose, then French ultramarine and burnt umber mix to darken.

3 Paint the golden moorland between the pool and the hills using raw sienna.

4 Using a French ultramarine and raw sienna mix, paint over the gold areas to create a soft green.

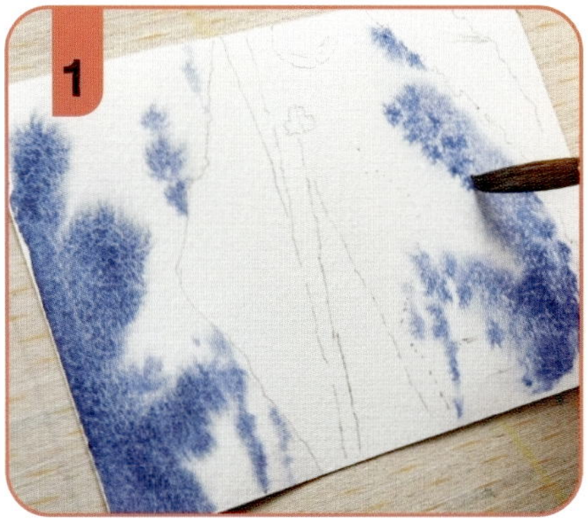

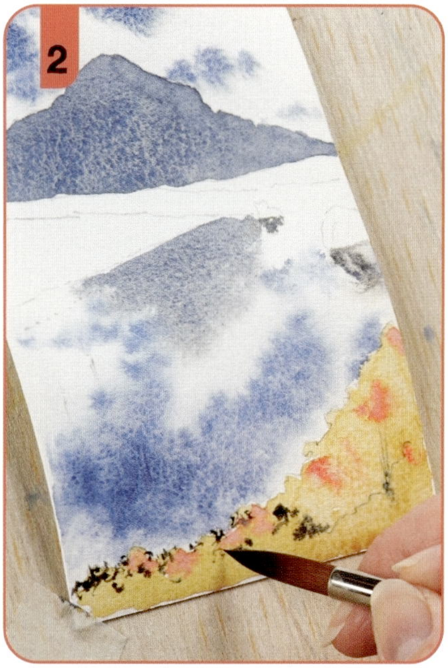

PAINTING REFLECTIONS

When painting reflections, you may find it helpful to turn your painting on its side, as shown here. This makes it easier to check the symmetry.

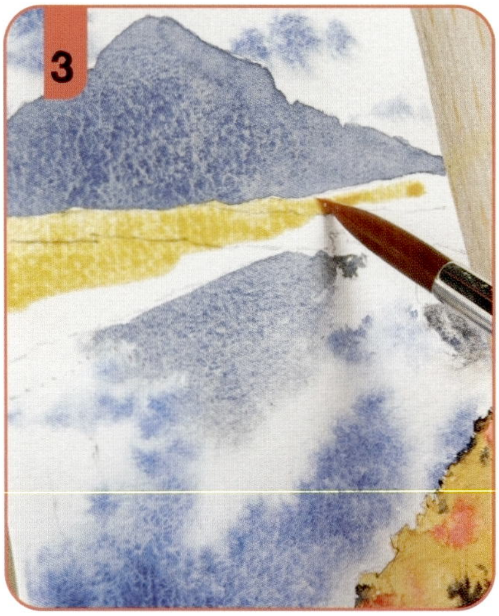

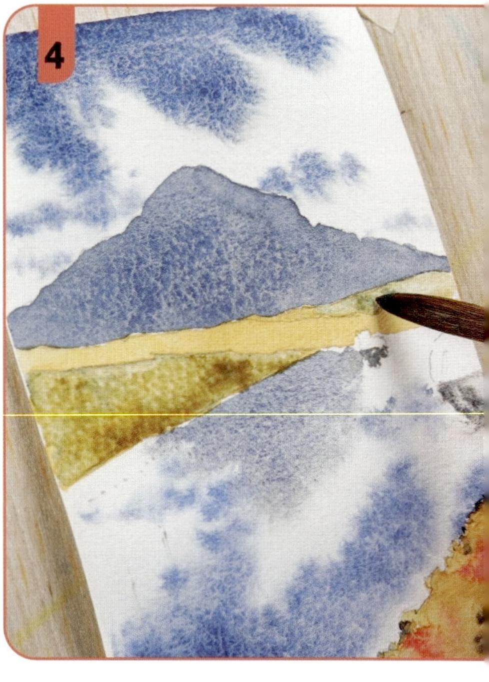

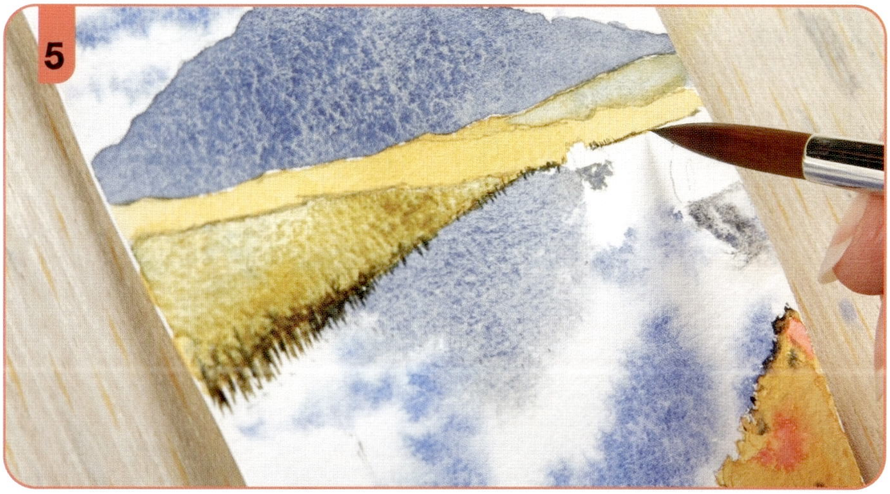

5 Drop in a darker mix of the same colours near the water's edge and paint the reflections of the grass, then paint the water's edge to the right of the rock.

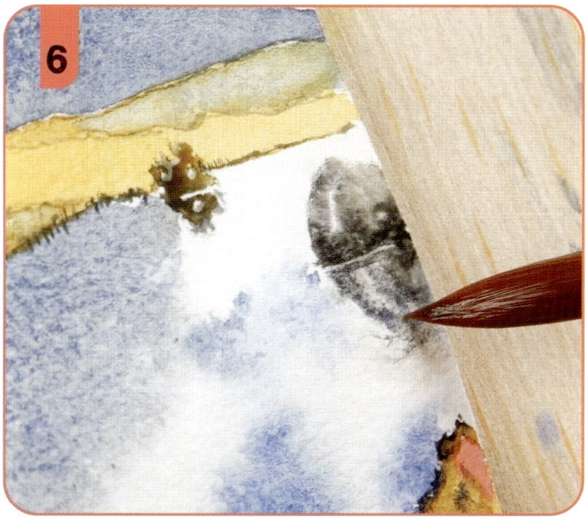

6 Paint the rocks in the pool with a combination of two mixes: French ultramarine and burnt umber, and French ultramarine and raw sienna.

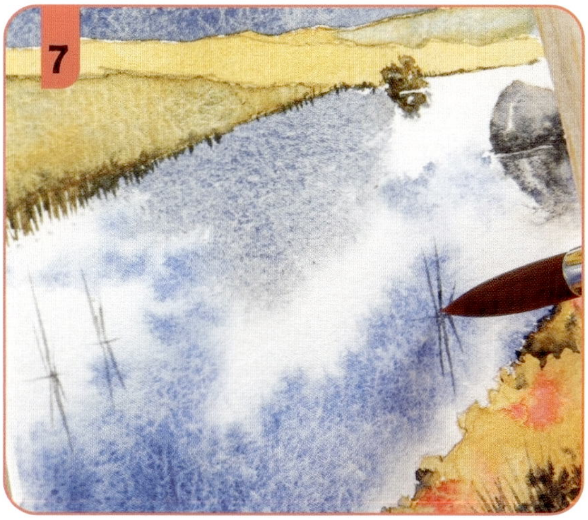

7 Paint a few grasses in the foreground and in the pool. If necessary, slightly sharpen the reflection of the hill with a pale mix of the hill colours to finish.

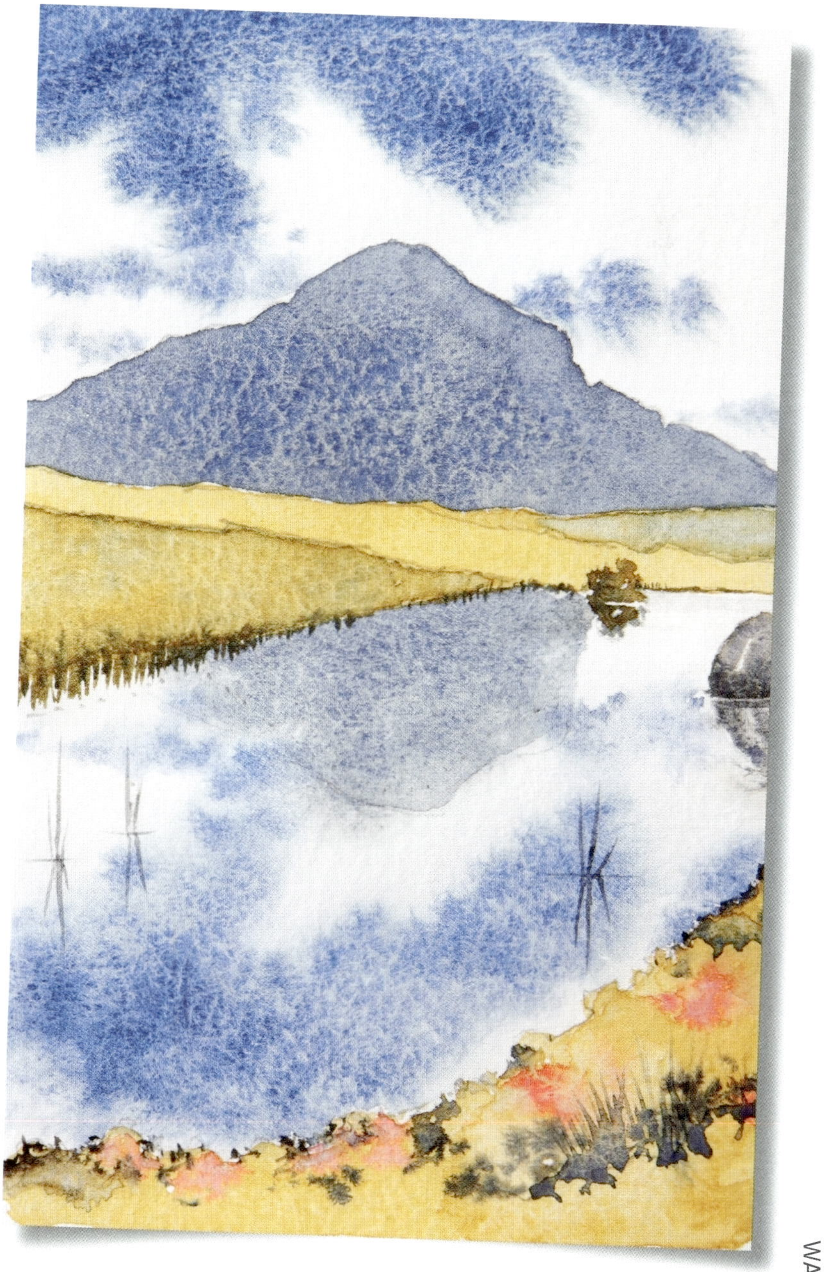

Mountain and sea

YOU WILL NEED

Paint colours: raw sienna, burnt umber, French ultramarine

Brushes: size 10 round

Other: tracing number 18

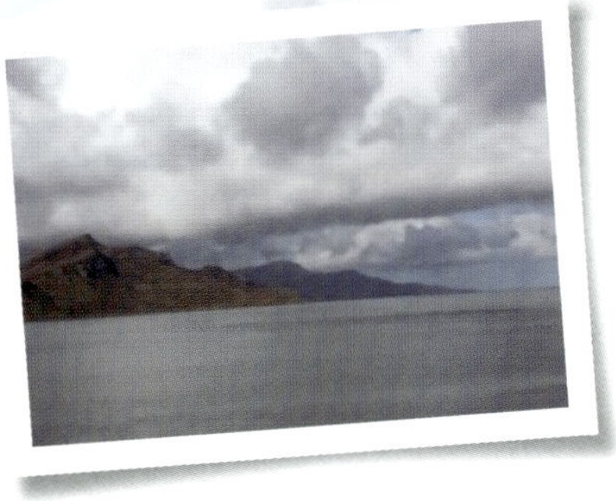

Making water look wet: sometimes 'less' really is 'more' – the less you do to create an effect, the more effective the result. This project shows you how to create the impression of a thin layer of water over the beach. We paint the wash that represents the water over a dry wash that represents the beach; the sand then naturally shows through the water, just as in life.

The tracing includes some fine details of wave crests and distant sails. Don't despair if you accidentally paint over these at step 3; carry on, then try again with a new tracing when you have time. Alternatively, you could cut slivers of masking tape for the sails, removing them when the painting is completely dry.

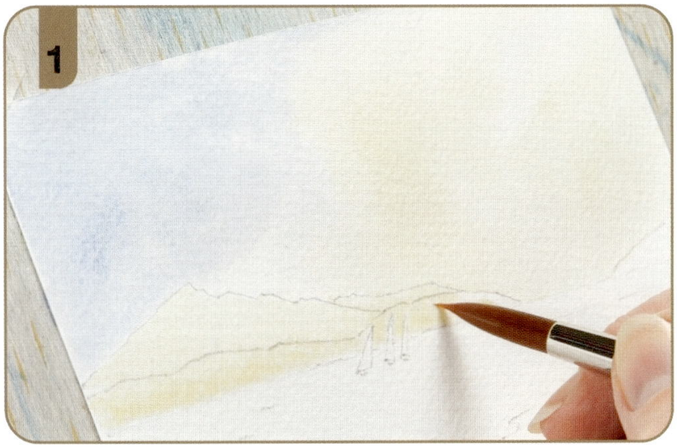

1 Wet the sky. Drop in very pale raw sienna to the centre and right, French ultramarine to the left. Paint the distant hills (on the left) with the same pale raw sienna.

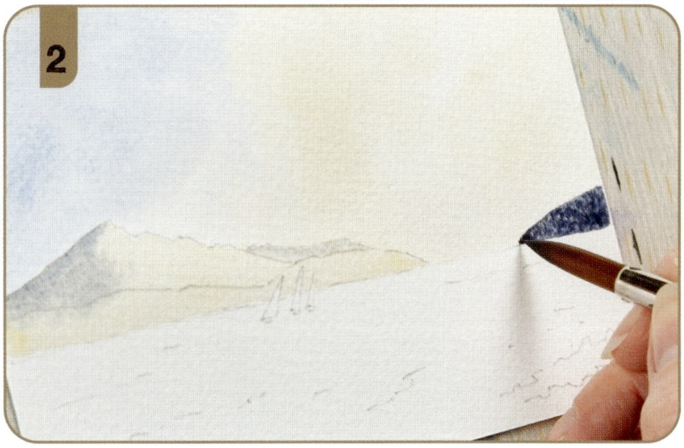

2 While the distant hills are wet, drop in a pale mix of French ultramarine and burnt umber. Paint the hills on right with a stronger mix of the same colours.

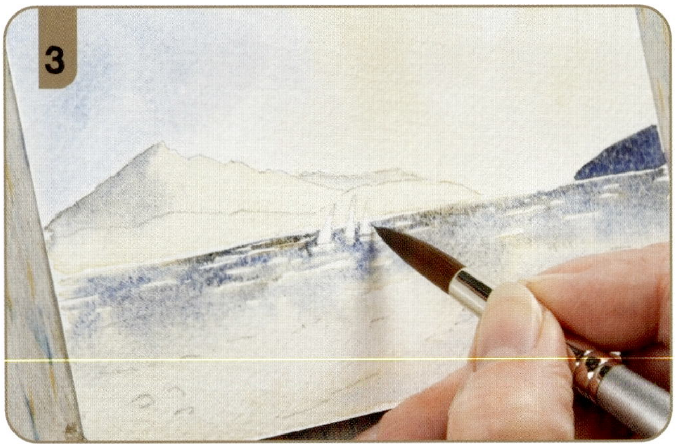

3 Paint the sea and beach with pale raw sienna, leaving the sail shapes and a few small horizontal bands of paper – for waves – unpainted. Drop in the French ultramarine and burnt umber mix to the sea, particularly further away, towards the horizon.

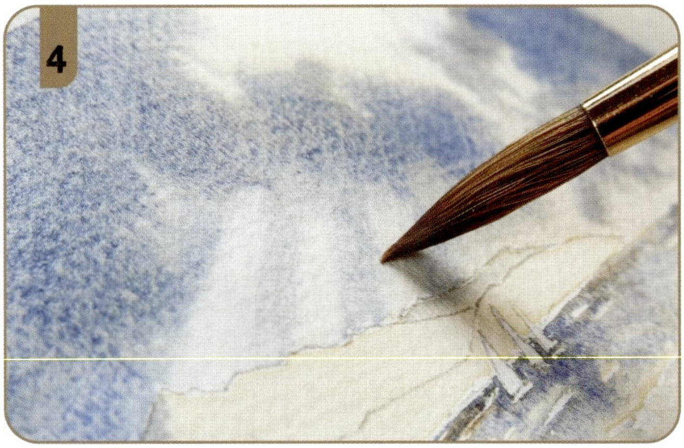

4 Rewet the sky and paint the storm cloud with a stronger mix of French ultramarine and burnt umber. Create a few sunbeams while the paper is still damp (these should radiate from the light area of sky); lift out and add colour as necessary while the paint is still damp. Try not to overwork these, we need only a 'suggestion'.

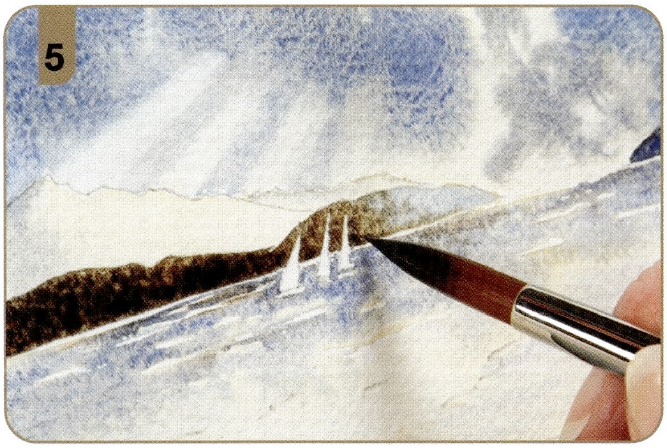

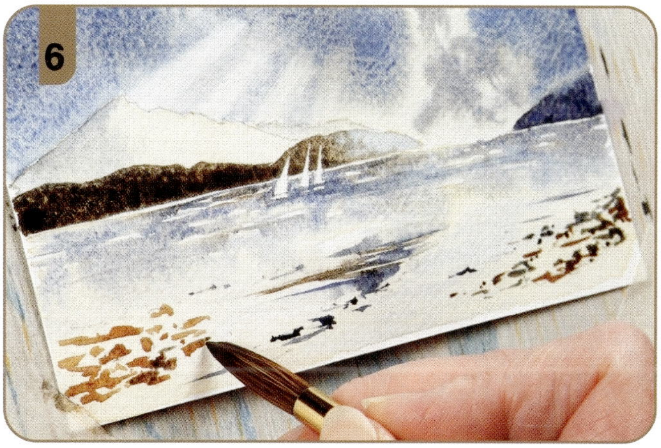

5 Add a little more burnt umber to the French ultramarine and burnt umber mix for the foremost land mass. Use a pale blue mix where it is more distant.

6 Mix various combinations of French ultramarine and burnt umber, making some more blue, some more brown, and in varied strengths (i.e. with more or less water), paint dots and broken strokes/drybrush for the stones and detail on the beach.

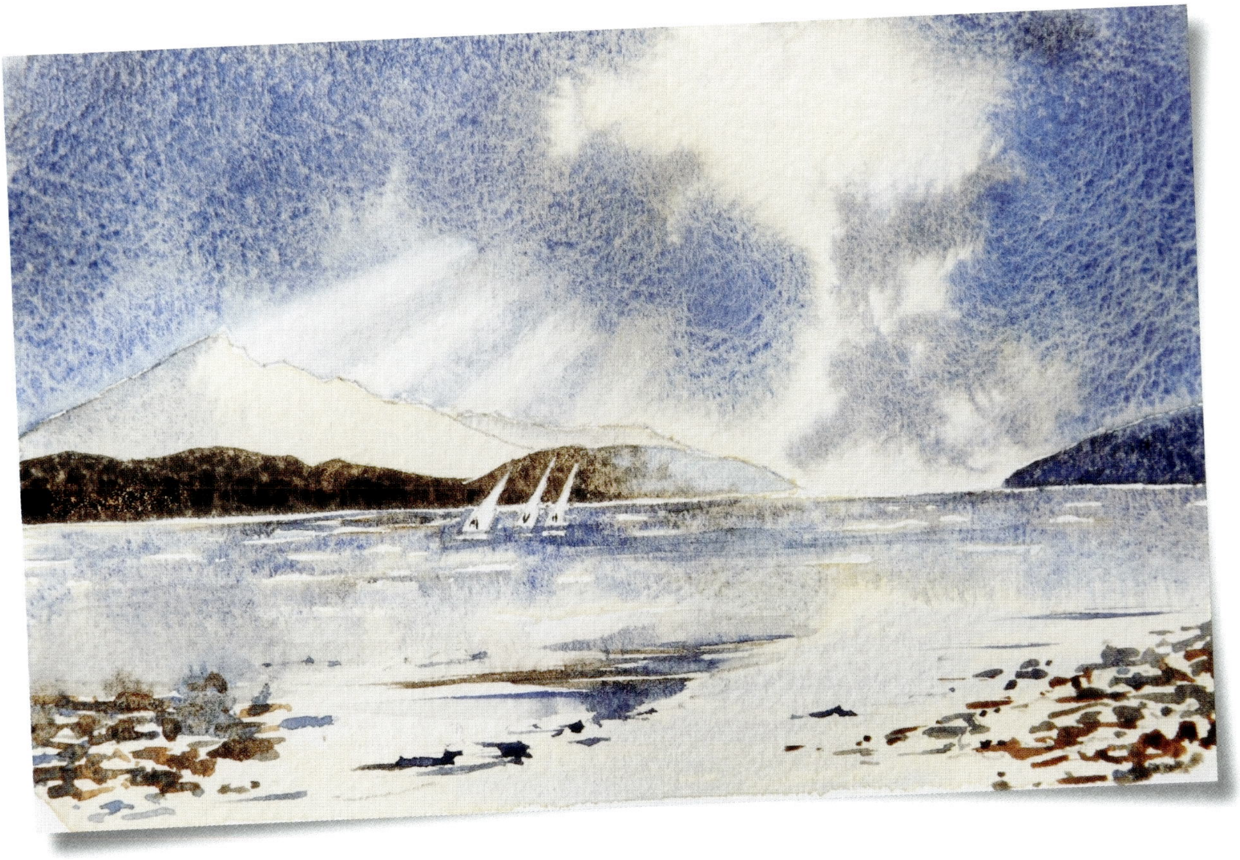

YOU WILL NEED

Paint colours: French ultramarine, burnt umber, raw sienna, burnt sienna

Brushes: size 10 round

Other: tracing number 19

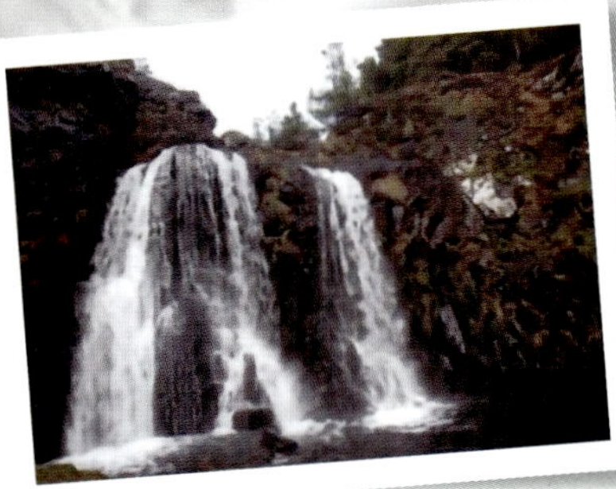

Waterfall – white water

The subject is a waterfall. We tend to think of these as 'white', although much depends on how much water there is, the point of origin and whether it falls uninterrupted or hits rocks on the descent. Here a combination of wet on dry, wet in wet and drybrush is used to portray the waterfall, with colour and tones used to enhance the whites.

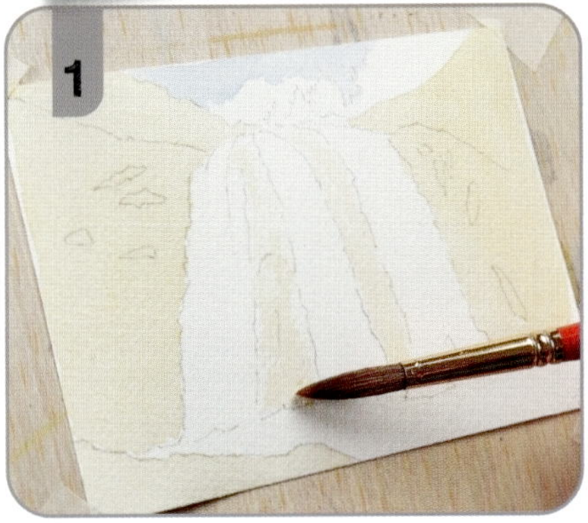

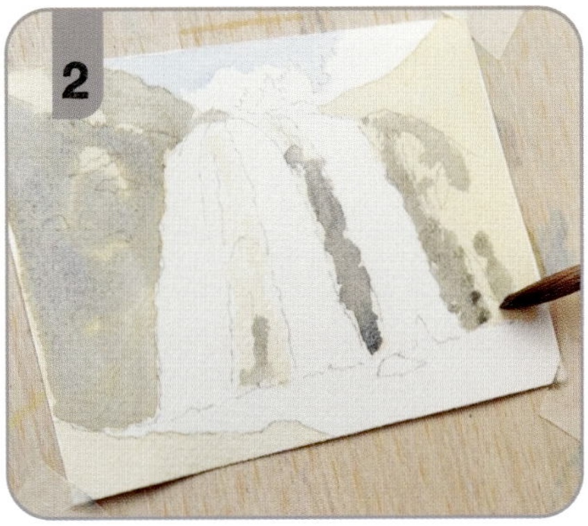

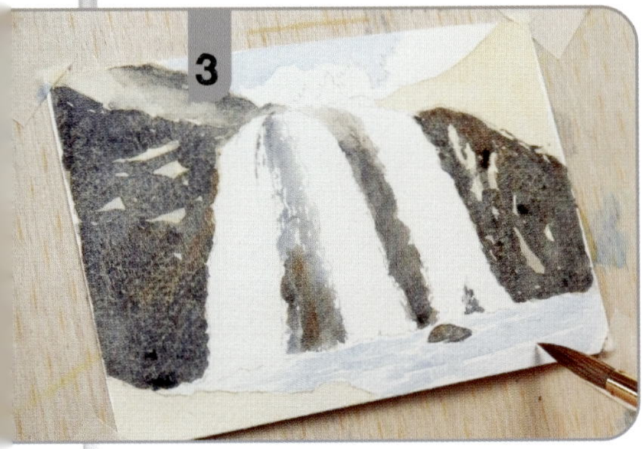

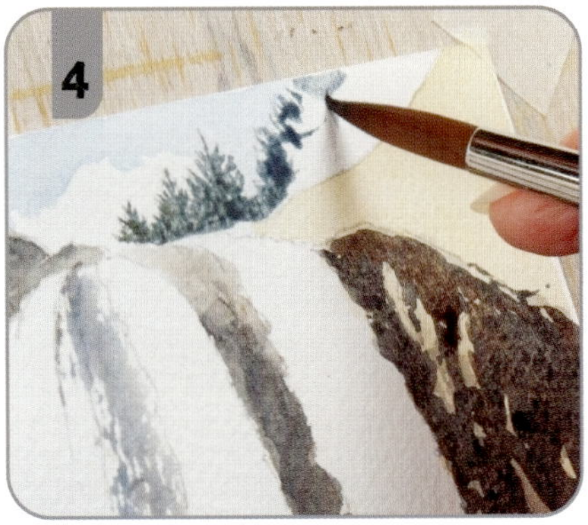

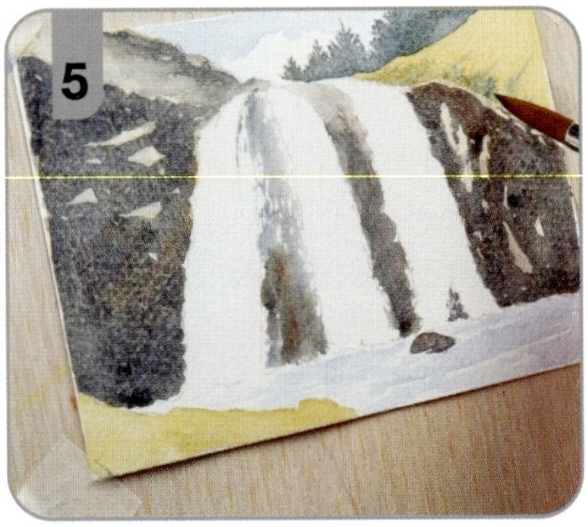

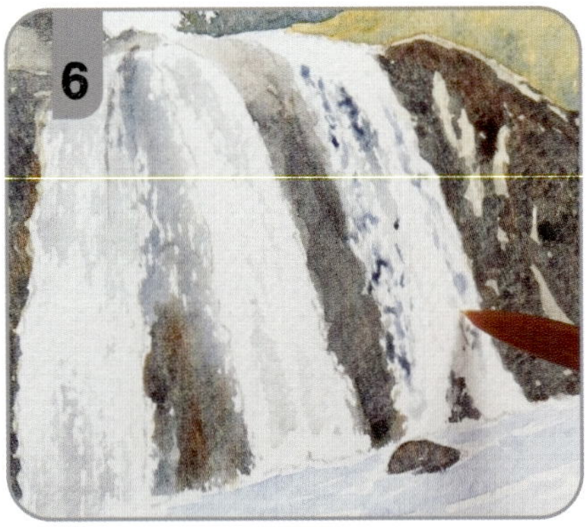

1 Paint the sky with pale French ultramarine, painting around the cloud, then paint raw sienna over all the rocks and land.

2 Use drybrush technique for the rocks at the sides of the waterfall to create a broken edge. Drop in midtone French ultramarine and burnt umber here and there.

3 Paint a midtone French ultramarine and burnt umber mix over the rocks leaving a few areas of the previous wash unpainted for highlights on the rocks. Paint some areas of the waterfall with French ultramarine and burnt umber, and the pool with French ultramarine, leaving some areas unpainted to suggest ripples.

4 For the trees use French ultramarine and raw sienna – load just a little paint on the brush at a time, in order to retain a fine point on it.

5 Wash over the grassy areas again with raw sienna, dropping in dilute French ultramarine for variation.

6 Begin to develop the darks of the waterfall and rocks using French ultramarine and burnt umber mix. Aim for a variety of soft and hard edges by using a combination of wet on dry, wet in wet, and drybrush techniques. Soften edges further here and there for further variety.

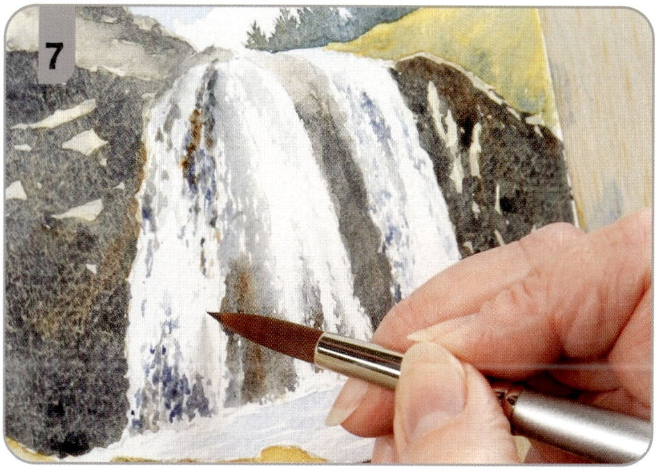

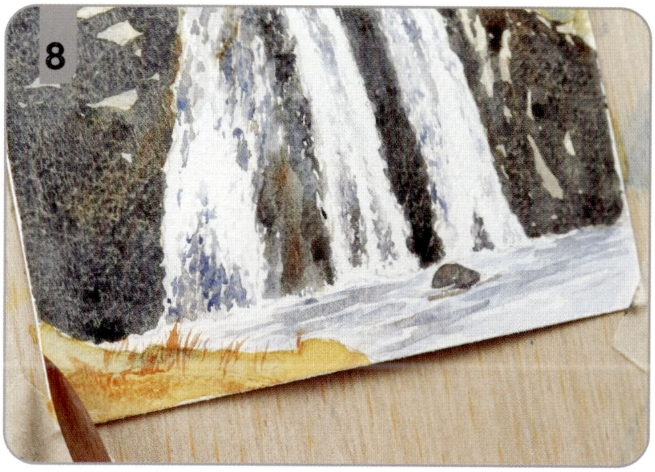

7 Continue to build up detail and interest in the waterfall itself. Keep an eye on how much clean paper remains as you work – it's important to leave enough white spaces for the contrast to work, and the effect to be fresh.

8 Create more of a sense of depth in the pool with the addition of a little burnt umber, then add foreground grasses with burnt sienna.

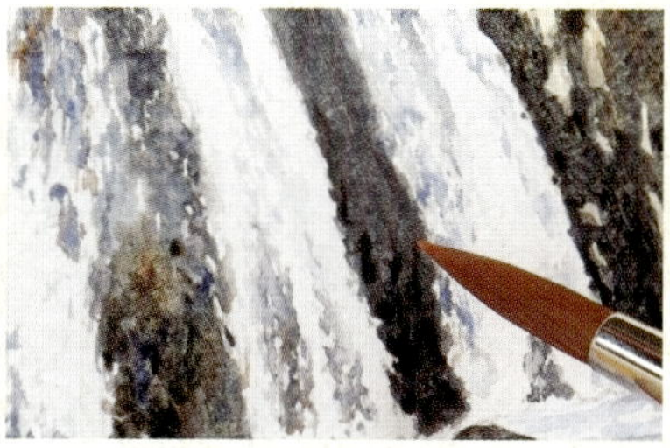

IRREGULAR SOFTENING

If any areas of the waterfall look too harsh, or the rocks are too dark or dense, use a clean damp brush to soften them, then dab with kitchen paper to lift small areas of colour. Don't overdo it, and try to keep the shapes and sizes irregular.

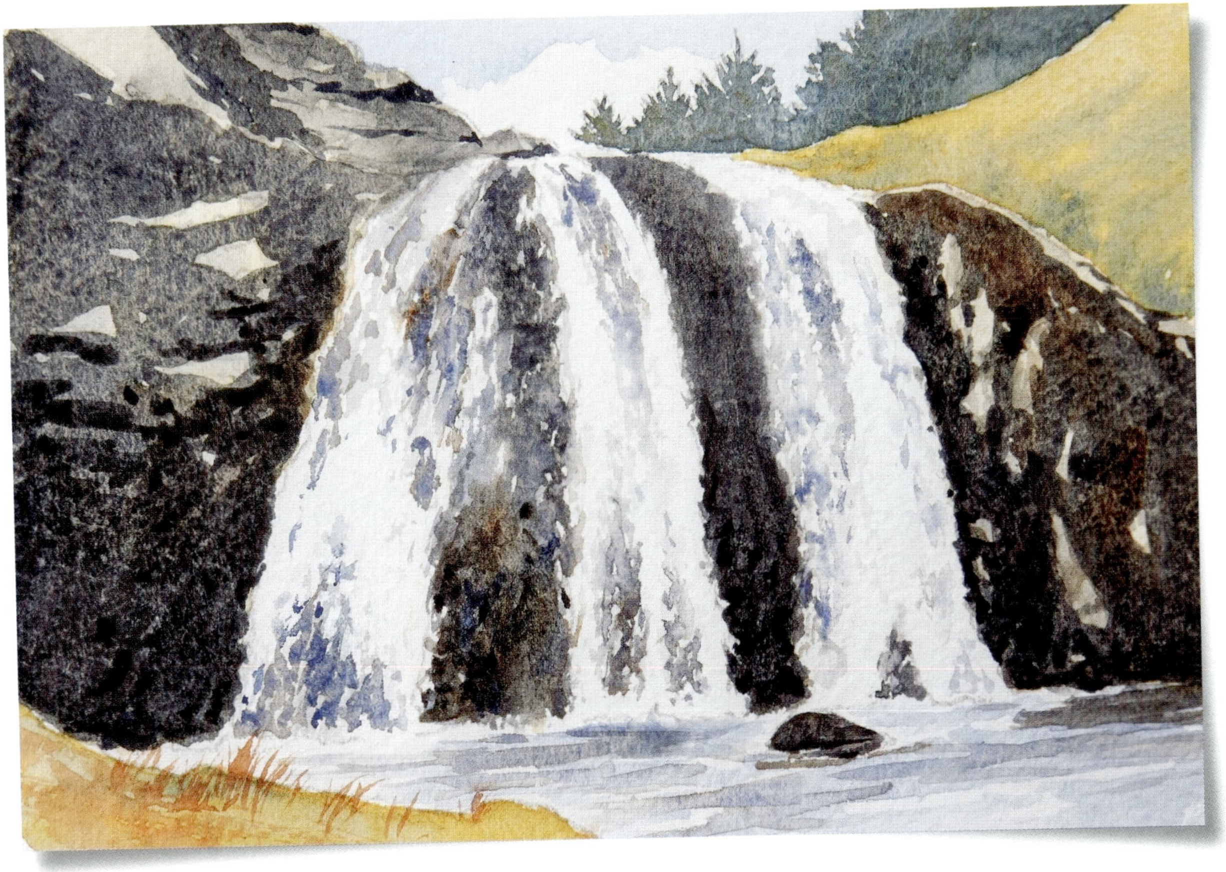

YOU WILL NEED

Paint colours: French ultramarine, raw sienna, burnt sienna, permanent rose

Brushes: size 10 round

Other: tracing number 20

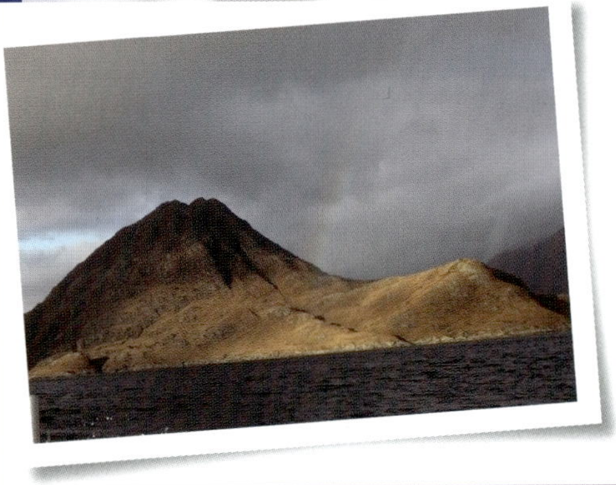

Wavelets and ripples

When painting wavelets and ripples it's important to look at the shapes that actually occur rather than guessing or rushing to complete the work and painting a sea of worms or small fish. Wavelets and ripples need to be fluid and smooth: a combination of hard and soft edges may make them more convincing. Try to convey perspective in the size of the waves you paint; larger in the foreground, smaller in the distance.

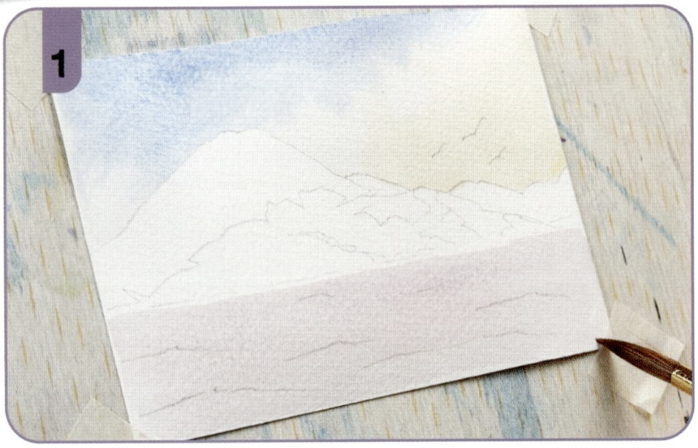

1 Wet the sky area. Drop in French ultramarine to the top, and raw sienna to the lower right sky. Use a light, dull purple mix of French ultramarine, burnt sienna and permanent rose to paint the sea, leaving a fine line of clean dry paper below the land mass.

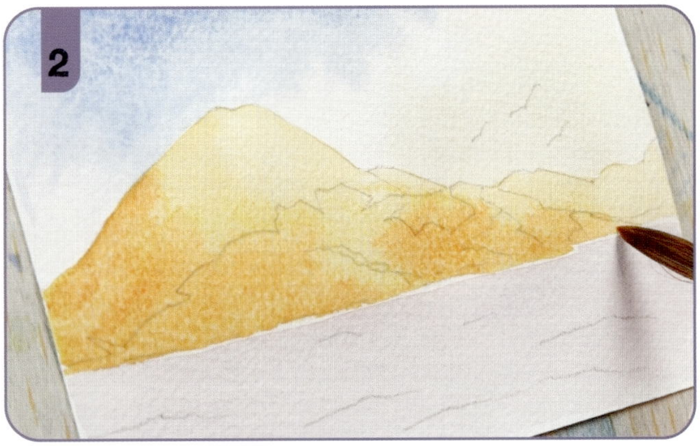

2 Paint raw sienna on to the hills, adding a little burnt sienna to the mix for the lower slopes.

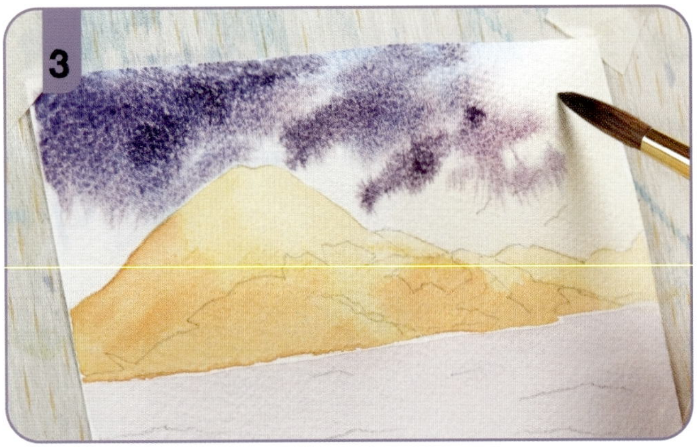

3 Rewet the sky and add storm clouds of a French ultramarine, burnt sienna and permanent rose mix.

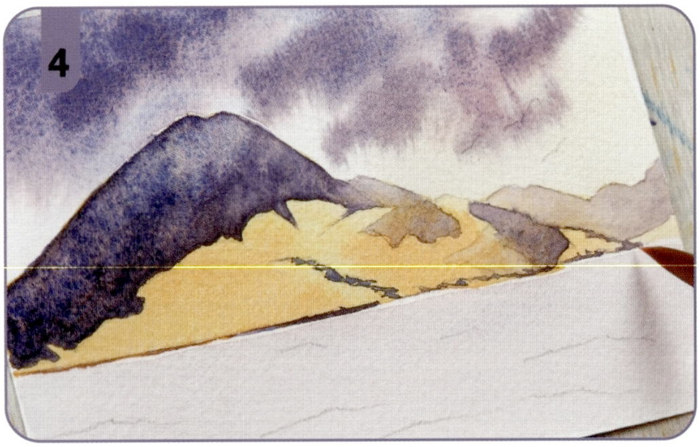

4 Paint a French ultramarine and permanent rose mix over the darker areas of the hill and the details at the shoreline.

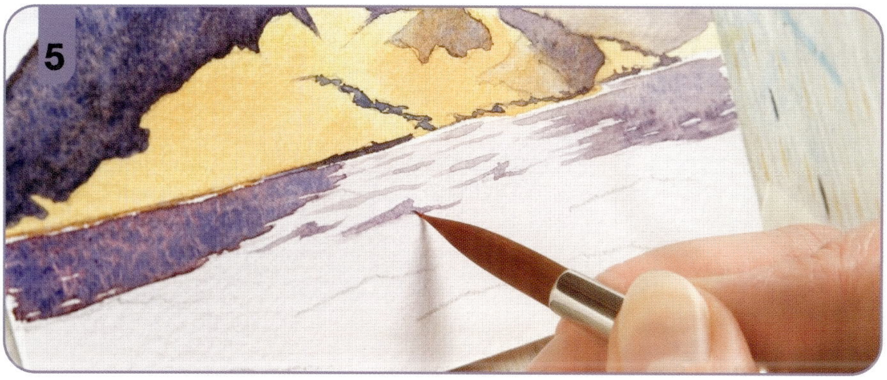

5 Strengthen the tones on the sea; darkest on the left where the hill is dark, and paint waves – starting with small pale fine lines in the distance.

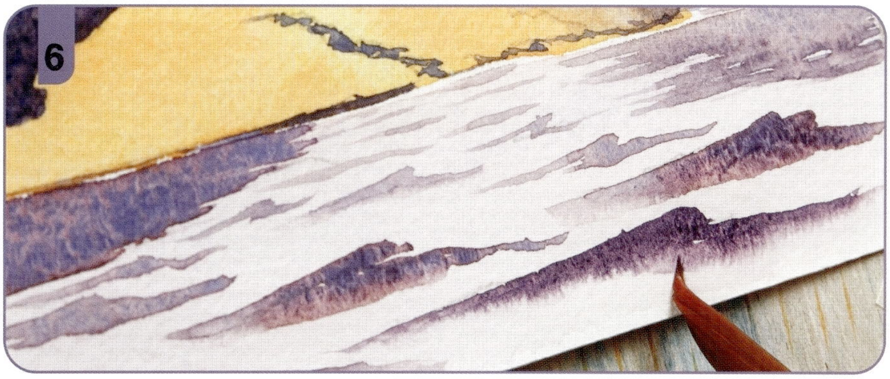

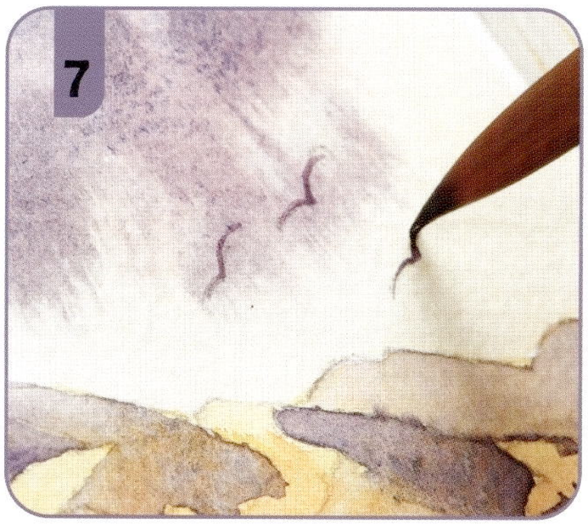

6 Add larger, darker, more widely spaced waves in the foreground, using a fluid ripple stroke. Soften the lower edge of a few of the larger ripples with a clean damp brush.

7 With a little paint on the point of your brush, add a few simple birds to finish.

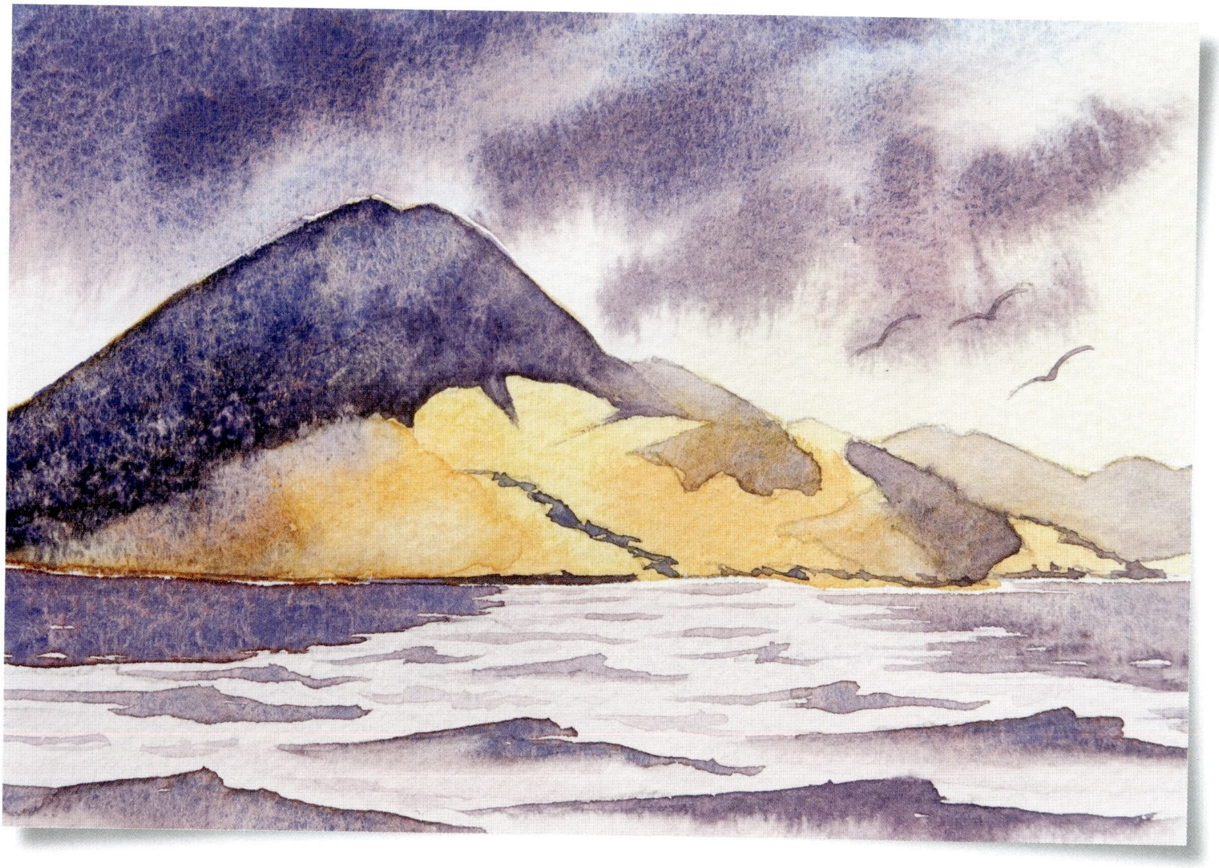

SNOW

Snow scenes are often popular and painting them can be most effective if done simply.

Look at the scene. Really look at the scene: is the snow really white? If seen at sunrise or sunset it may well be slightly pink; if sunlit it may appear slightly golden; on a dull day it may look grey. Is the snow a smooth thick blanket or thin windblown snow over moorland?

Consider whether you can use counterchange (light against dark) and lost and found edges to good effect.

Decide what you want to achieve; try to reduce the number of tones to three or four to keep the painting fresh. Remember shadows aren't black; keep them colourful and not too dark. Use the white of your paper for the lightest tones, put the washes on boldly, and try to resist the temptation to do too much. The paintings here were mainly achieved with three colours.

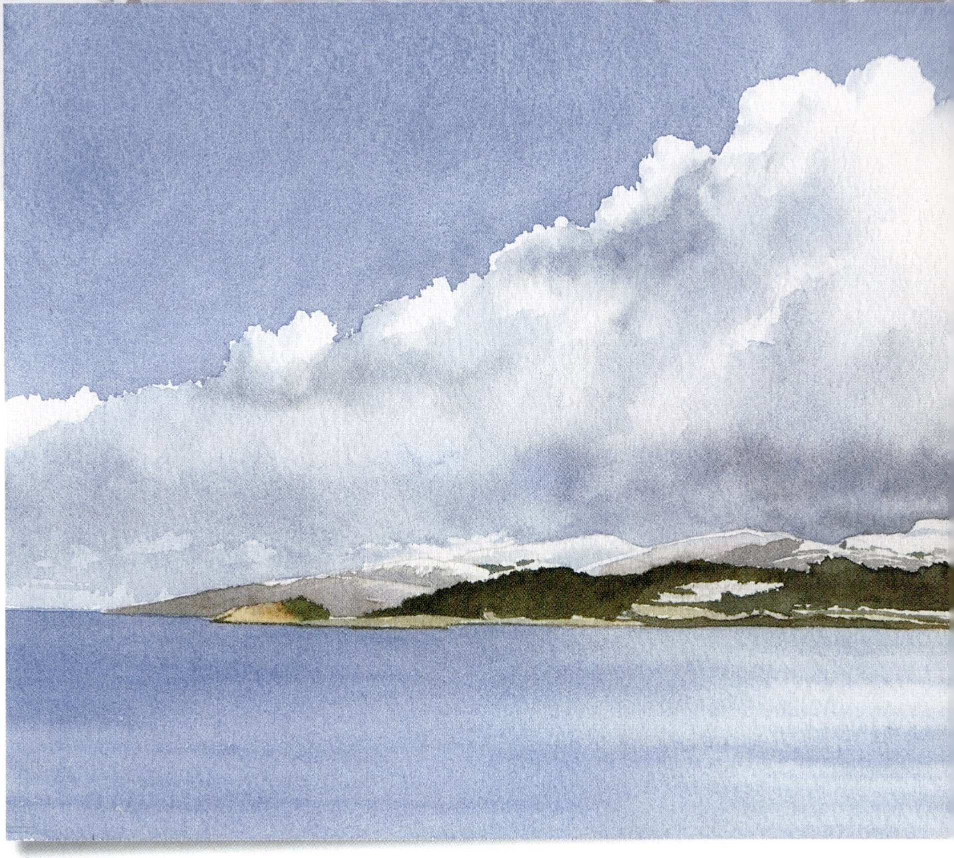

Raasay in Sunshine and Snow

54 x 18cm (21¼ x 7in)

This painting aimed to capture the island as seen under snow on a beautifully sunny day.

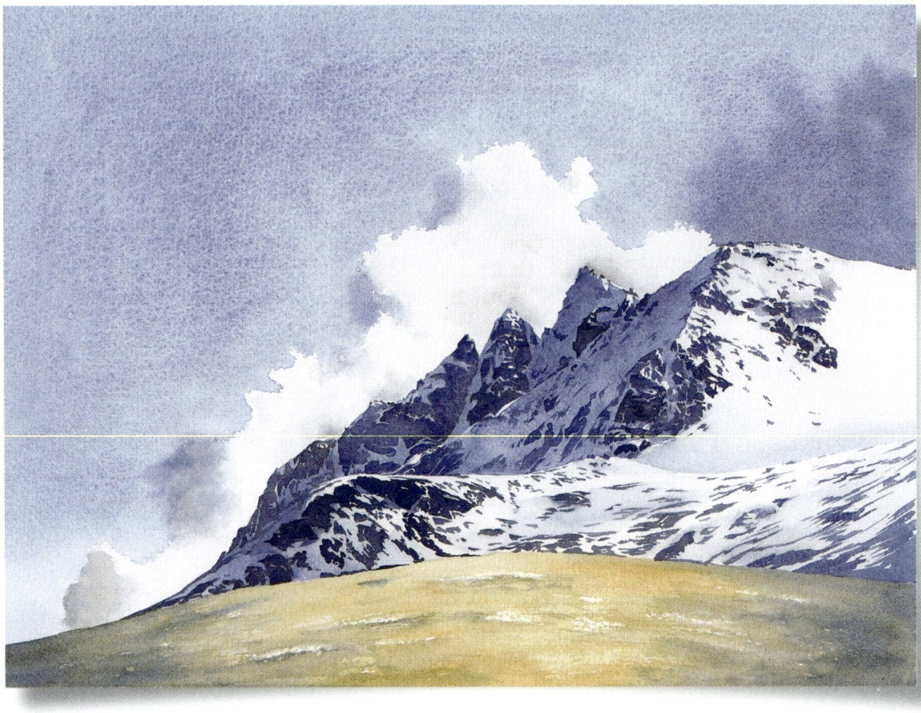

Pinnacle Ridge in Snow

37 x 27cm (14½ x 10½in)

Another very simple scene, largely as seen, however I used lighter tones on the foreground in order to maximize the effects of the darks in the snow, and used counterchange in the clouds (light against dark areas of hill and dark against light areas of hill).

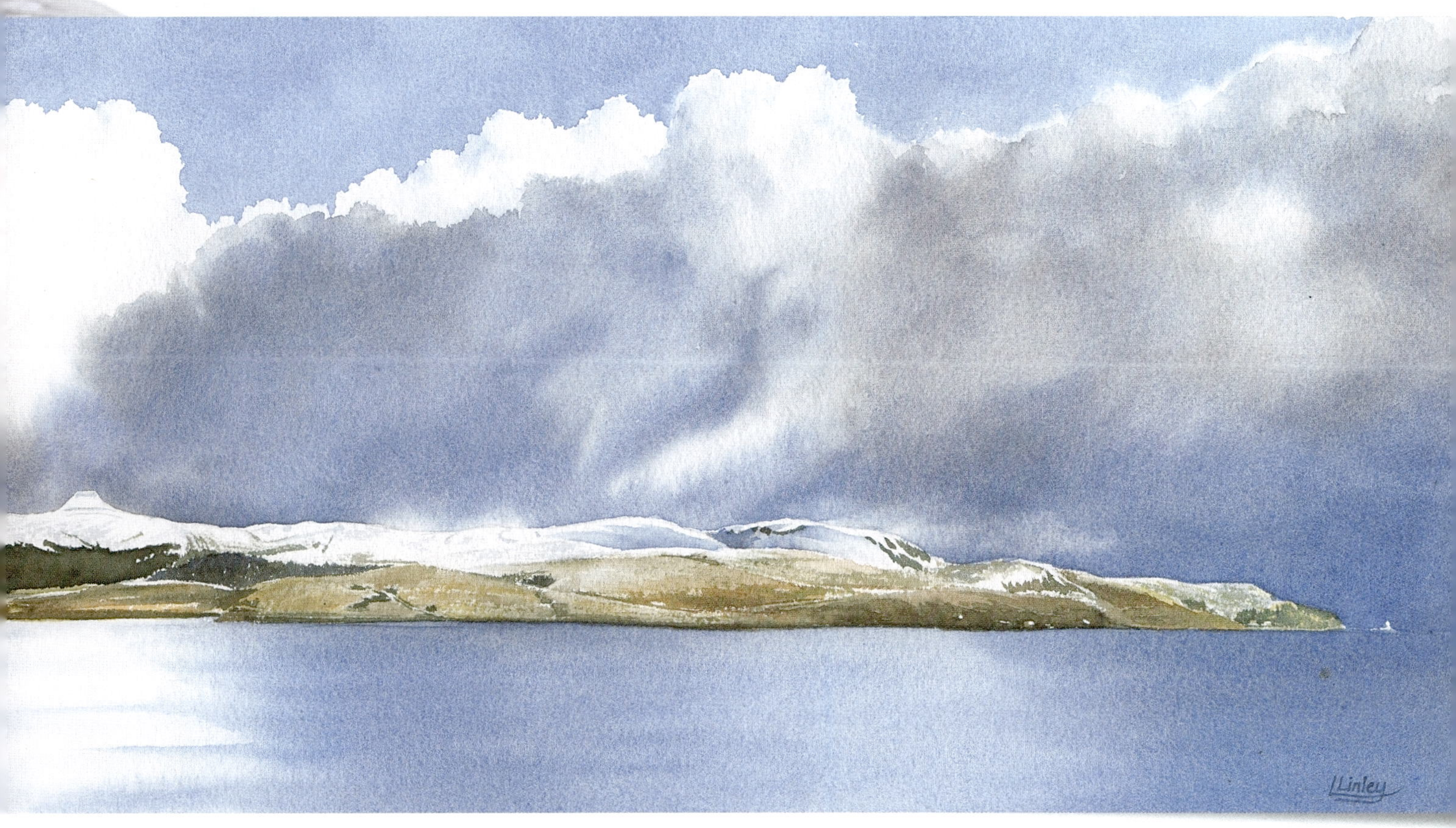

'The Whelk' in Snow and Sunshine

37 x 27cm (14½ x 10½in)

This painting is fairly true to the view that I saw on a January day in Glen Shiel; a crisp clear day with sun lighting up the snow in some parts while elsewhere valleys were in deep shadow. After making some thumbnail paintings (small rough sketches) to try out colours, composition and mood, I lightened the tones of the shadows a little and varied the textures within them. See page 81 for how the mood can be changed.

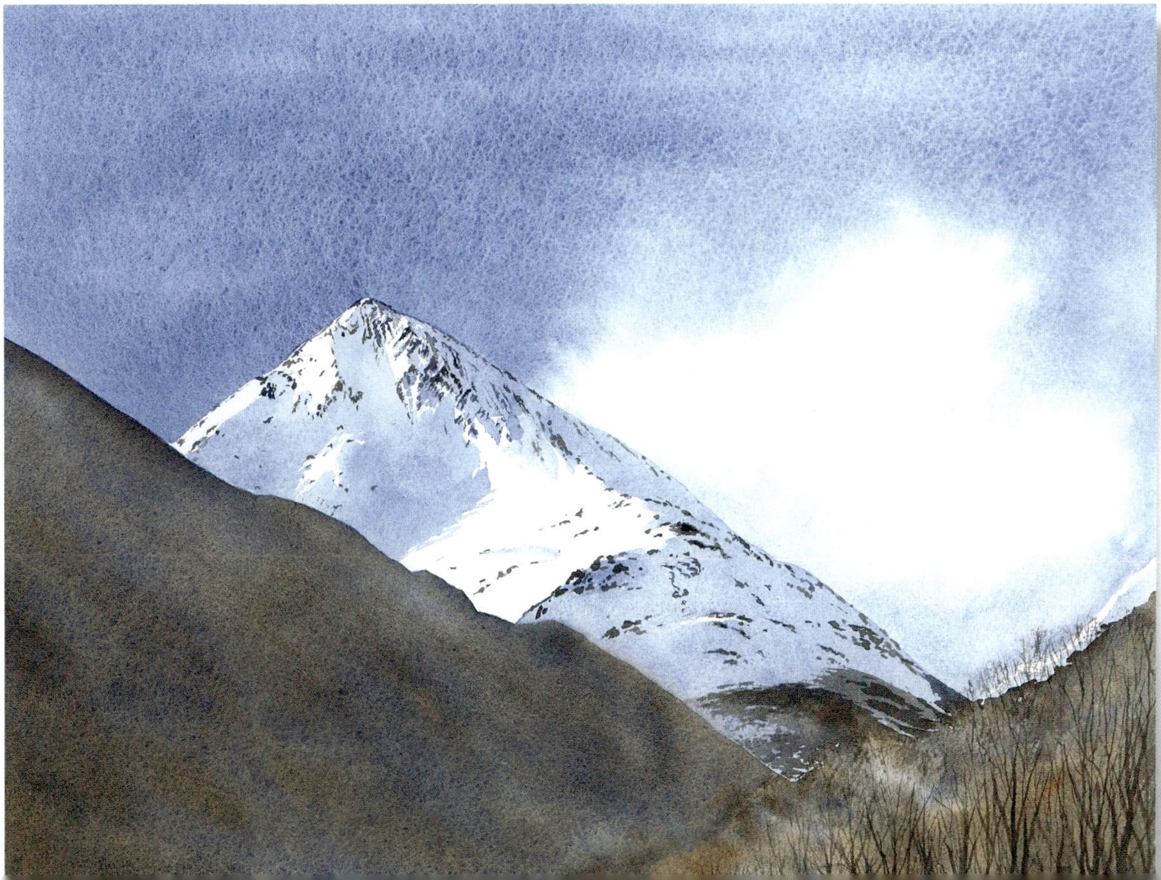

YOU WILL NEED

Paint colours: scarlet lake, burnt sienna, French ultramarine

Brushes: size 10 round

Other: tracing number 21

Snowfall – portraying white

Sometimes a potential painting simply pops up in front of you. As I drove beside the pictured loch, this sunlit peak appeared, a bright highlight on a dull day. I parked in a layby and walked back for a photograph. This simple scene uses strong tonal contrasts. The sky and foreground hill define the snow with its negative painted whites.

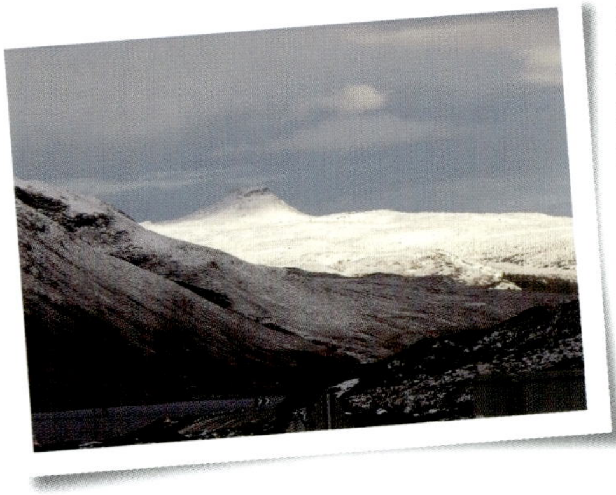

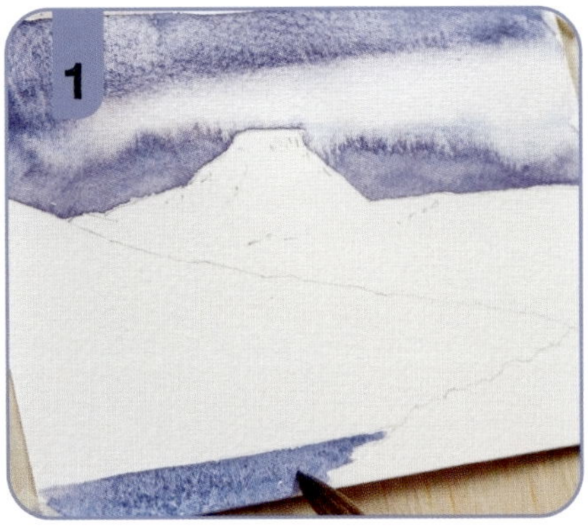

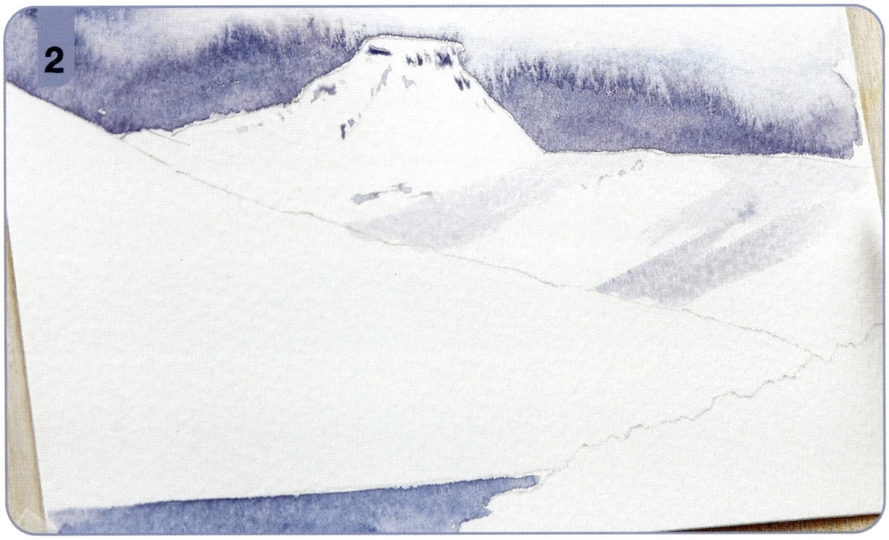

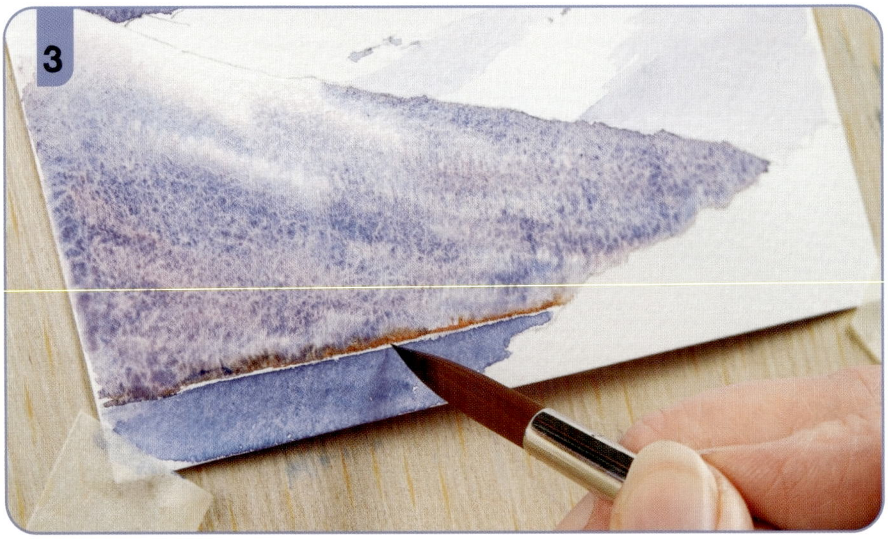

1 Wet the sky where it is to stay white. Quickly paint the rest of the sky with a mix of French ultramarine and scarlet lake, then allow the colour to blend into the clean wet area. Paint the loch with a slightly bluer mix of the sky colours.

2 Using the sky mix (French ultramarine and scarlet lake) paint the detail on the snowy peak. Next use broad strokes to paint the sweeping shadows on its lower slopes, with a slightly more dilute sky mix.

3 Wet the hill on the left, leaving a thin line of clean paper at the shoreline. Drop in sky colour down to the shore. While this is still damp, paint a thin line of burnt sienna to define the shoreline. It will soften into the hill but leave a crisp line on the dry paper near the sea.

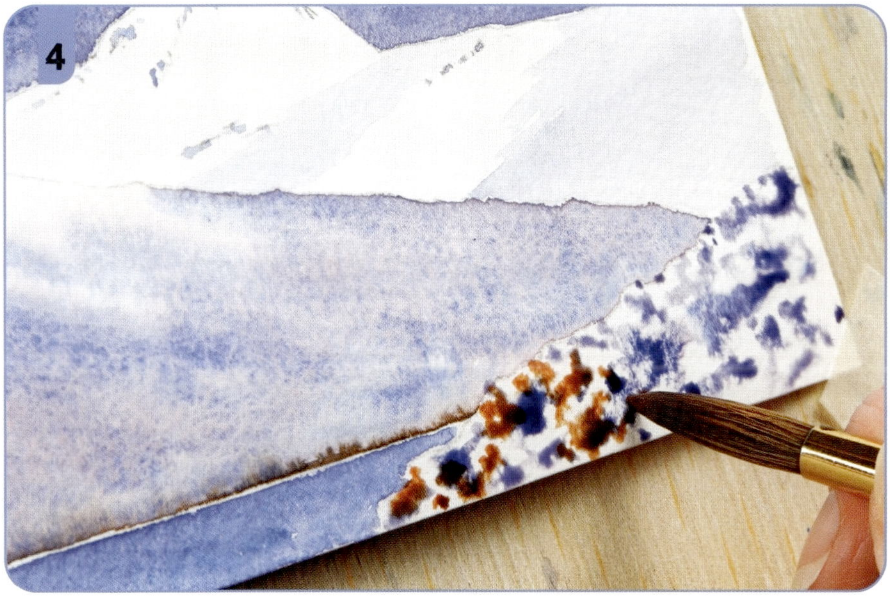

4 Dampen the foreground hill, leaving small areas of dry paper. Using burnt sienna and the sky mix, drop in colours, allowing them to spread and blend to create colour and texture.

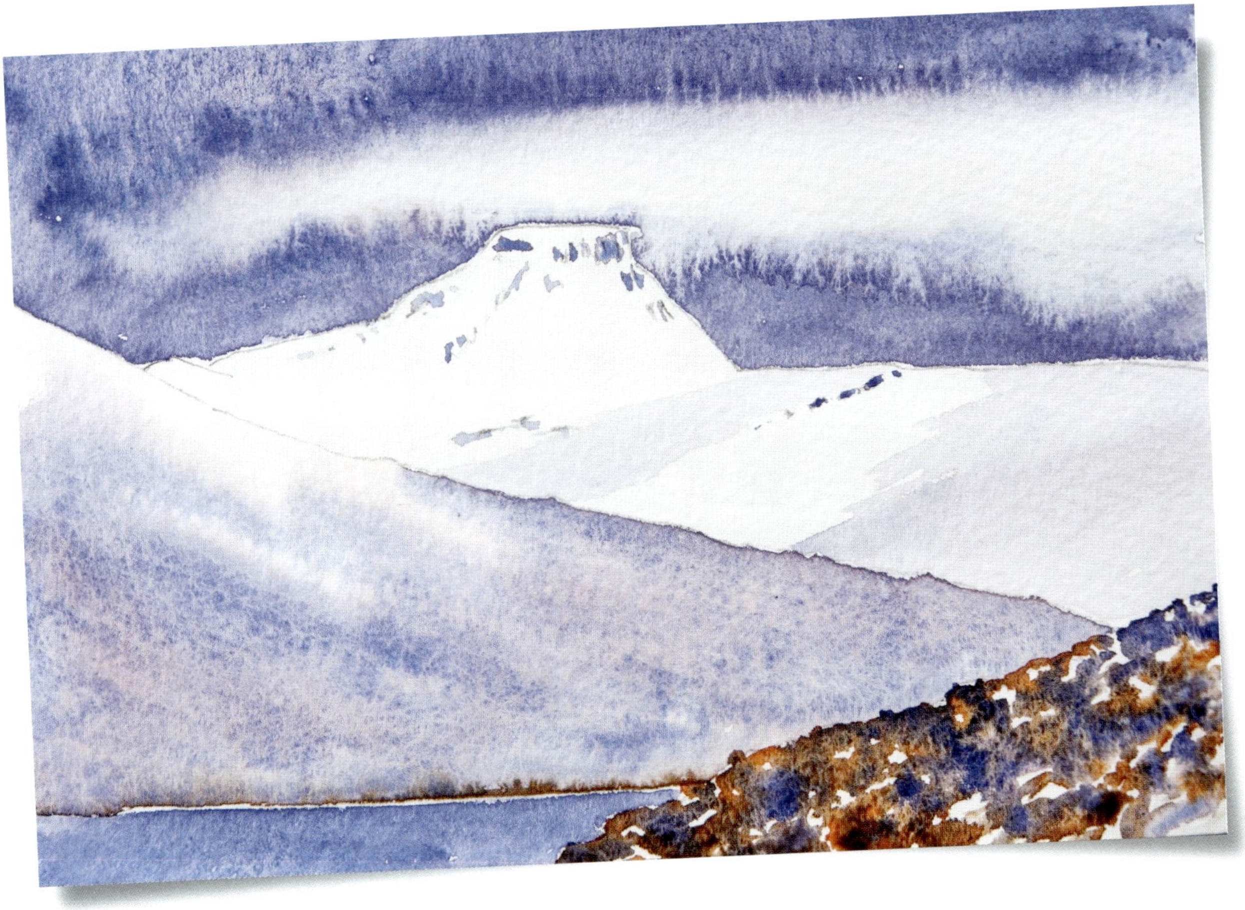

YOU WILL NEED

Paint colours: burnt umber, French ultramarine, burnt sienna

Brushes: size 10 round

Other: tracing number 22

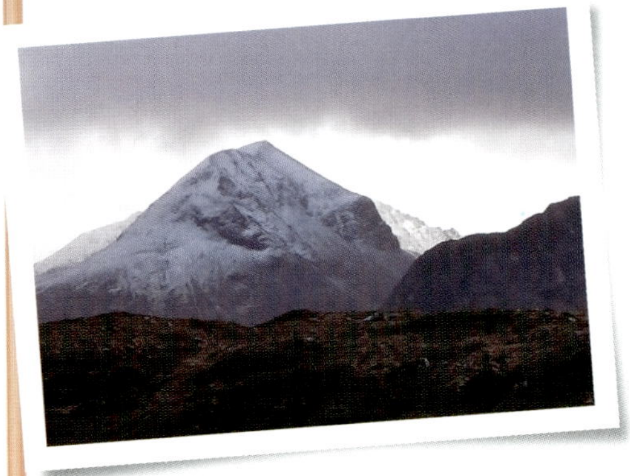

Making it look cold

Although the use of cool colours will give a chilly feel, it can also be unattractively cold; your painting can often be enhanced by introducing a little warm colour. By adding a little warmth to contrast with and bring out the cold, you can often make a more successful painting.

Try making paintings with and without warm colours and find out which approach gives you the result you wish for.

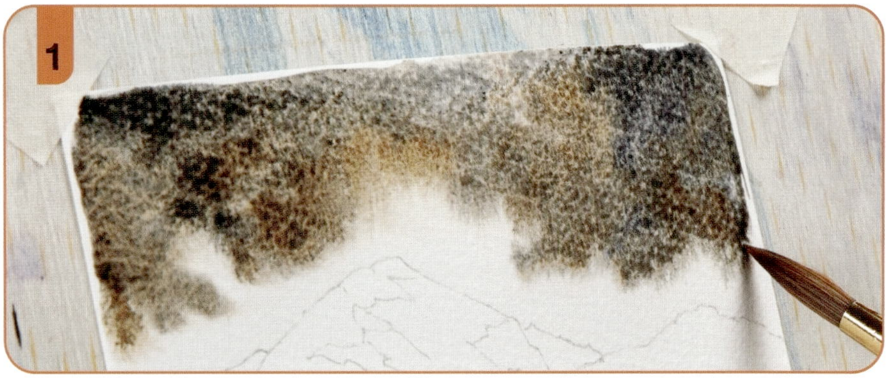

1 Wet the sky area and drop in a mix of French ultramarine and burnt umber to represent clouds.

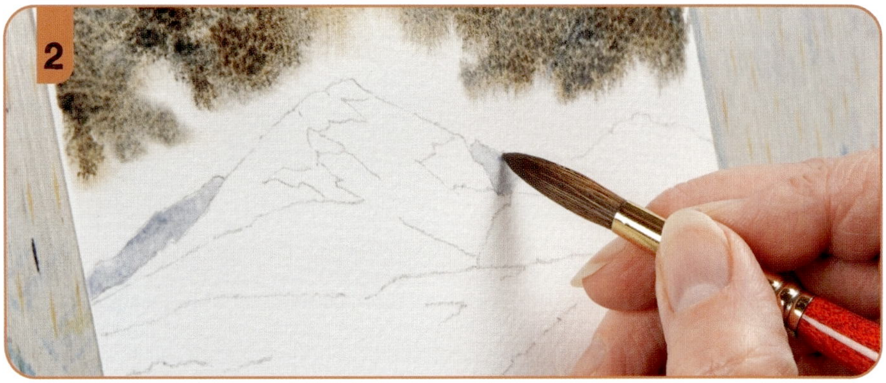

2 Paint the small areas of background hills (on either side of the main peak) with a grey-blue mix of French ultramarine and burnt umber.

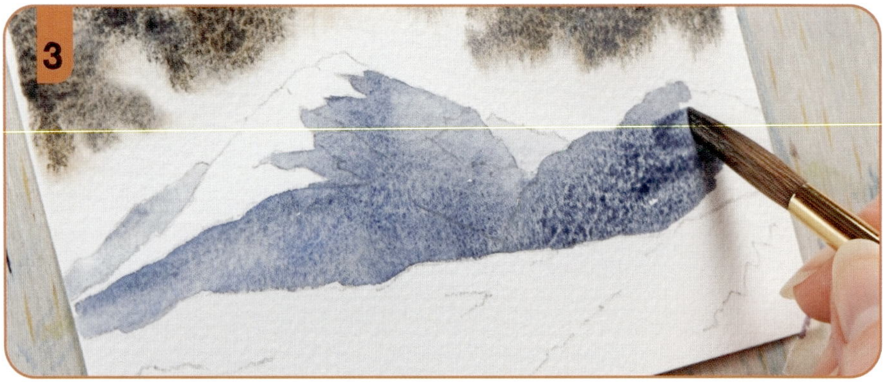

3 With a stronger mix, more biased to blue, paint the main hill and the hill to the right.

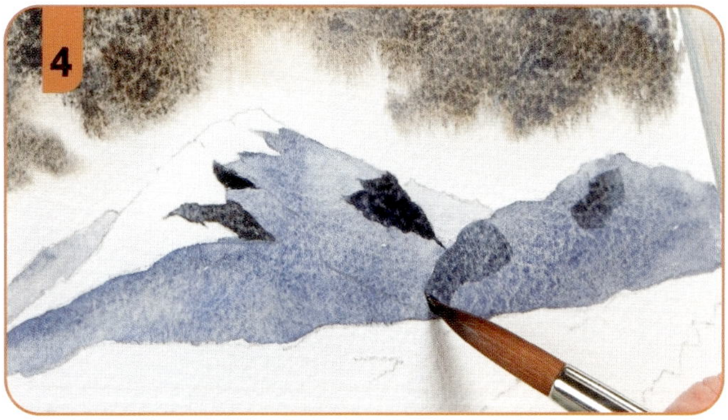

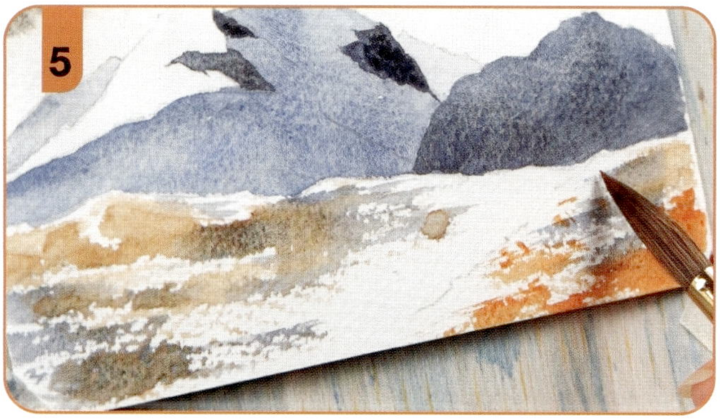

4 Add darker tones to the hills with glazes of the blue-biased mix.

5 Drybrush burnt umber over the foreground. While damp, paint strokes of burnt sienna and French ultramarine and burnt umber through it to soften here and there.

6 Further strengthen the hill in shadow with the blue-biased French ultramarine and burnt umber mix.

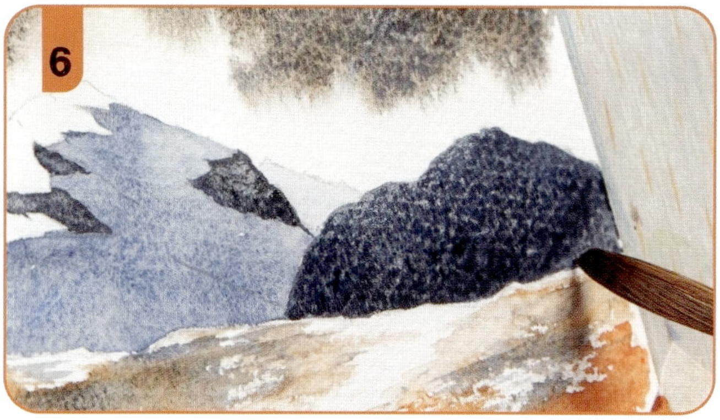

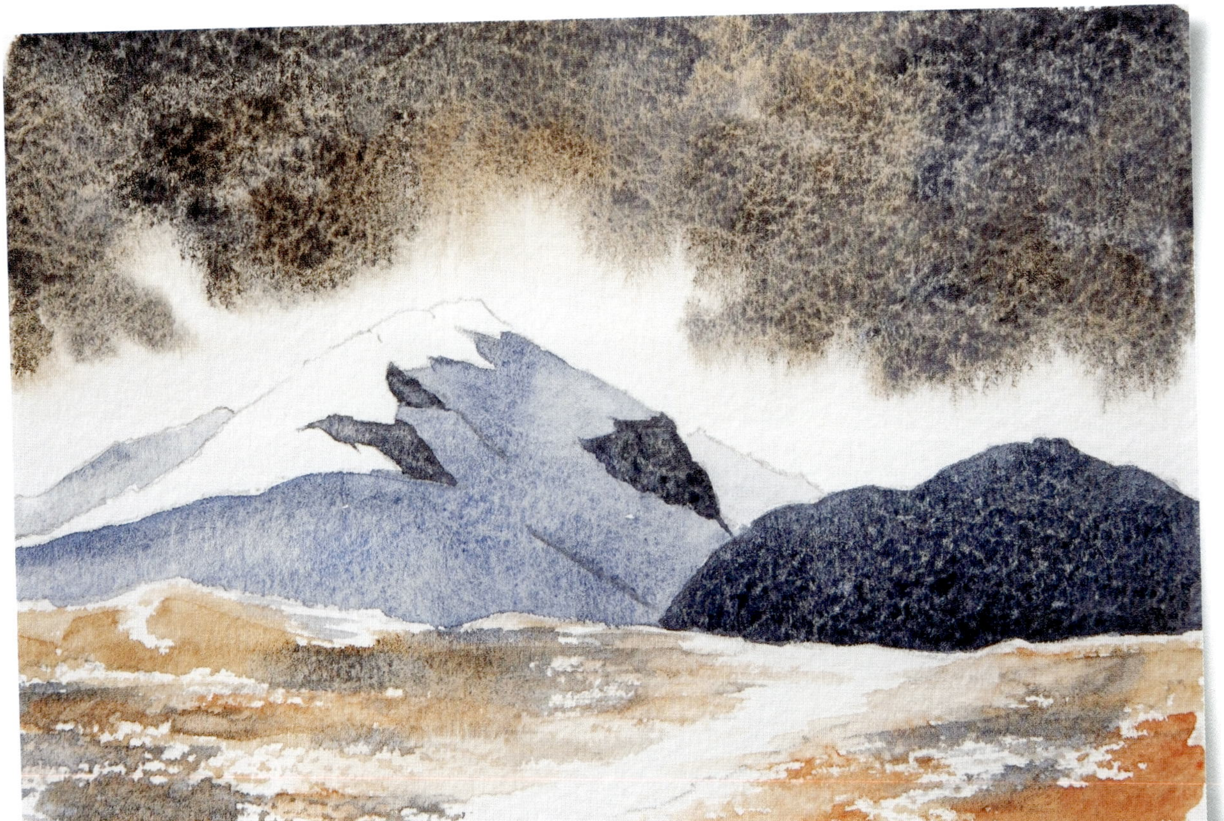

Warmth and coolness

YOU WILL NEED

Paint colours: French ultramarine, burnt umber, raw sienna, Winsor yellow

Brushes: size 10 round

Other: tracing number 23

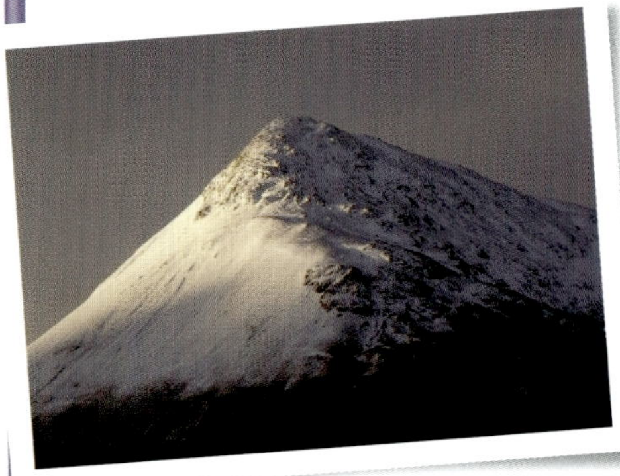

Sometimes it isn't enough to leave the paper showing through to give the white of snow, because the snow we need to portray appears softly golden in sunlight, greyed by shadow, or rosy in sunrise or sunset conditions. Contrasts of warm and cold will generally make a more interesting painting.

The main challenge here is painting the pattern of light and shadow on the central area of the mountain. Painting complex shapes can be time-consuming and, if you're not careful, you can end up with areas drying at different rates, resulting in backruns and a patchy finish. To avoid this, we work from one edge and keep a bead of paint moving.

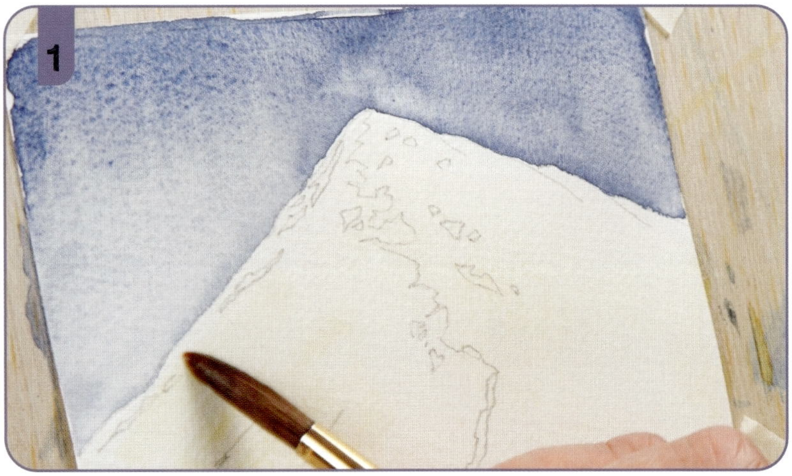

1

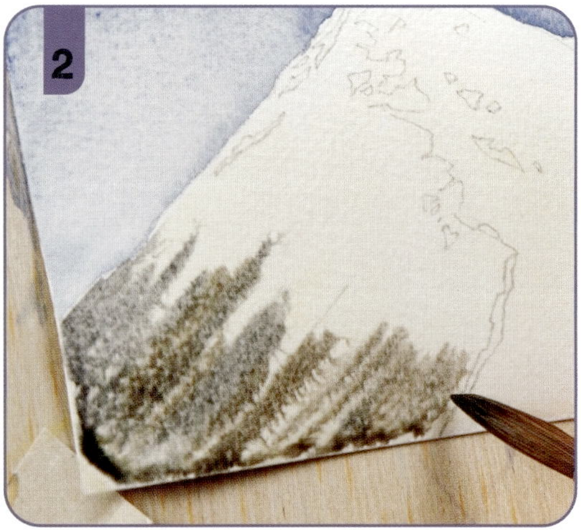

2

1 Wash French ultramarine and burnt umber mix to the sky, graduating it a little around the hill. Once dry, paint a very pale wash of raw sienna and a tiny amount of Winsor yellow all over the hill.

2 While the hill is still damp, paint a French ultramarine and burnt umber mix into the lower left-hand part of the slope.

3 Add more French ultramarine to the sky mix to darken it, then turn your paper and block in the shadow area on the right-hand side of the mountain. Draw the paint back and forth evenly to ensure the area is covered smoothly, trying to keep a 'bead' of paint as shown.

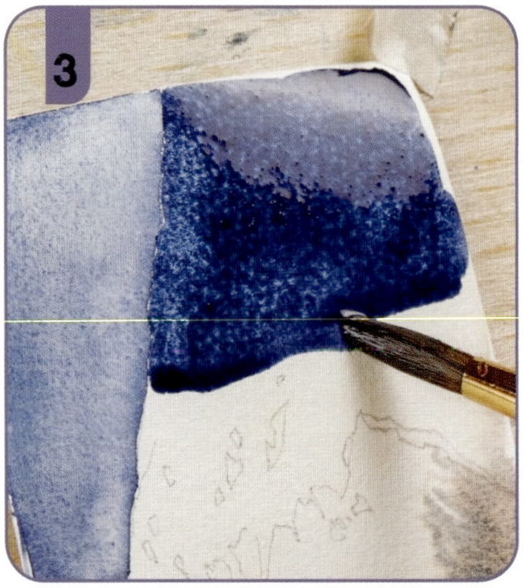

3

HANDLING COMPLEX SHAPES

Physically turning the painting lets us work from the shortest edge, which allows us to quickly and evenly block in the large area before we reach the small, detailed areas that need to remain as clean white paper. This gives us as much time as possible to work round the details, so there's no need to rush.

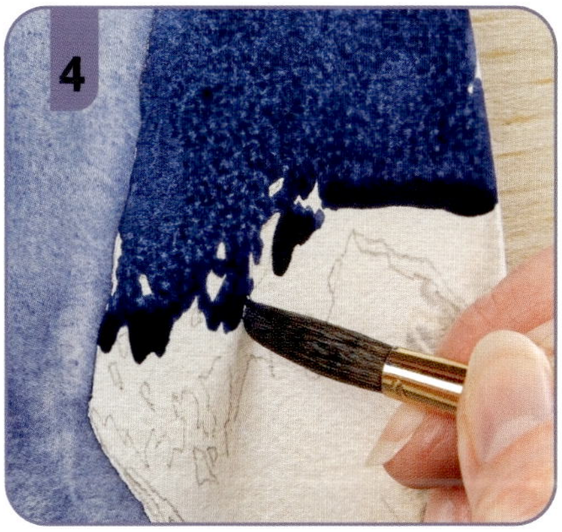

4 Using the point of your brush, draw the bead of paint around the areas of highlight. Continue to paint from side to side, around the shapes, so that the bead remains fluid – this is what will ensure the paint dries evenly for a clean finish.

KEEP GOING

If you accidentally paint over an area that's meant to be left white, don't stop. Carry on, and simply create another nearby.

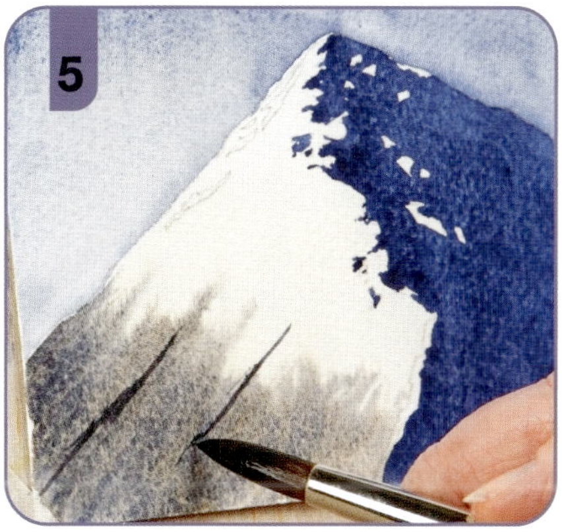

5 Continue to paint down to the line that makes the end of the shadow area. While you wait for the paint in the main shadow area to dry, use any remaining paint to add the small areas of shadow on the light side of the mountain, then use a strong mix of French ultramarine and burnt umber to indicate the gullies on the slope with diagonal strokes.

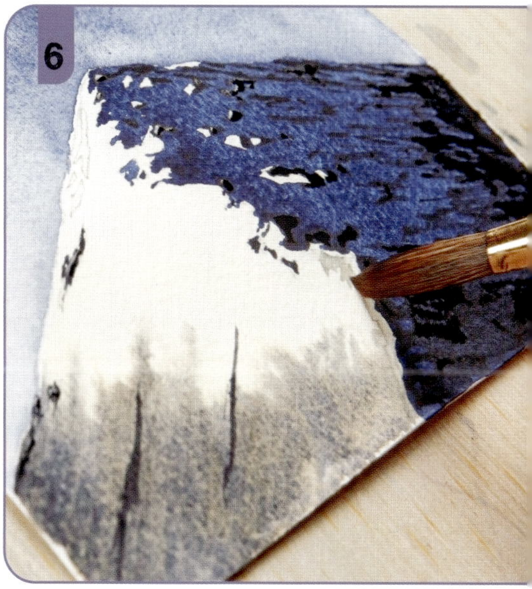

6 Using a strong mix of French ultramarine and burnt umber paint in the rocks on both the shadow and sunny sides of the hill. To highlight the sunny side of the hill, paint the small yellowish rocks on the top left with raw sienna and a tiny amount of French ultramarine.

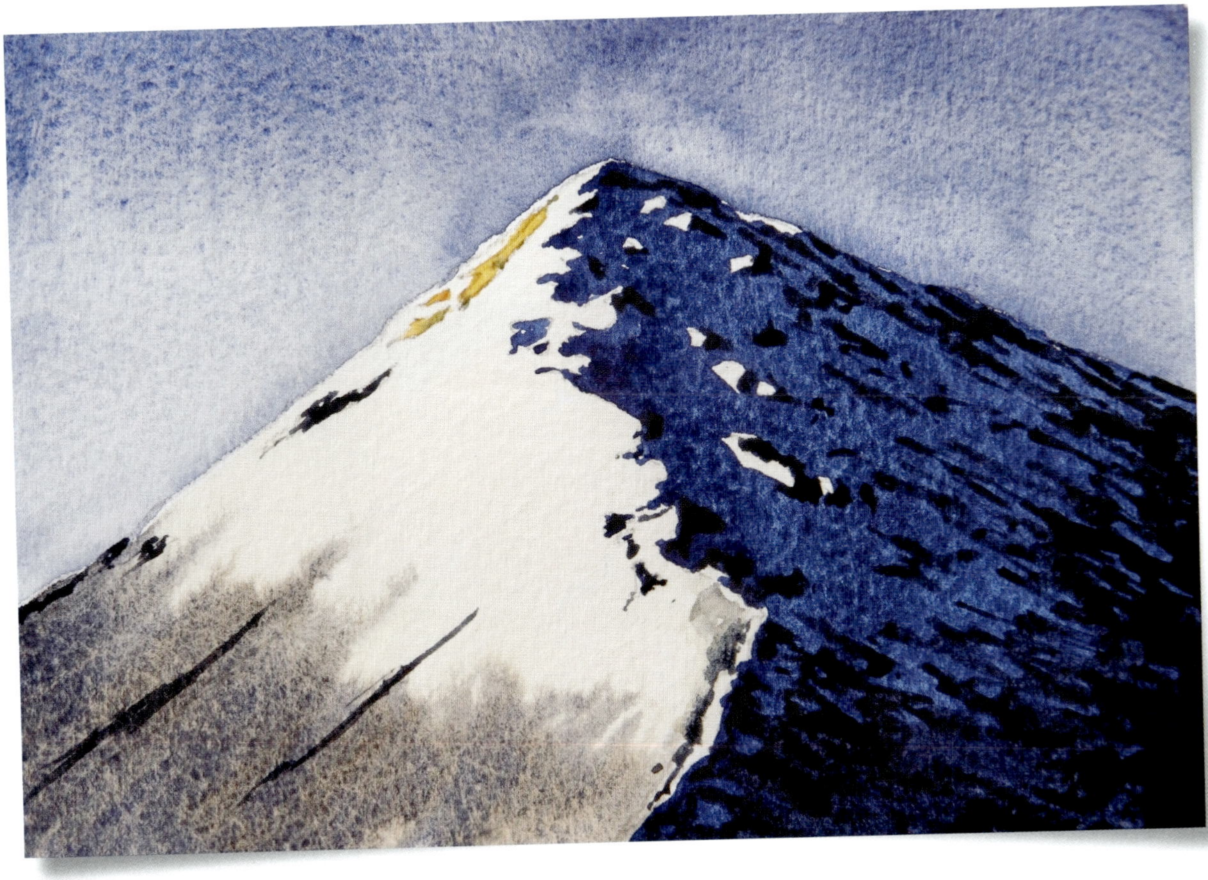

YOU WILL NEED

Paint colours: French ultramarine, cobalt blue, burnt umber, raw sienna

Brushes: size 10 round

Other: tracing number 24

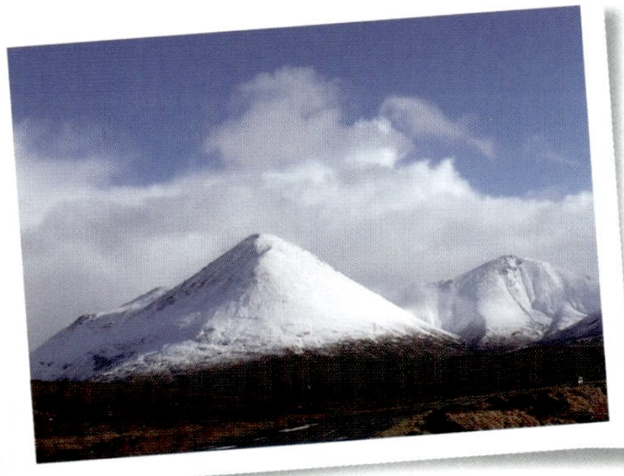

Adding interest

A tendency among beginner artists is to give everything an edge even when it's impossible to see one; we feel a compulsion to depict what we know is there. It's often better to trust your eyes and paint what you see, or to change what you see in order to create more interest. An edge you can see is known as a found edge; an edge you can't see is a lost edge.

For dramatic effect in your work it can also be useful to use an effect called counterchange. This is the contrasting of light with dark and dark with light. If it doesn't occur naturally in your subject, you can create it by moving objects around, or by introducing lights and darks as necessary. Here the clouds create subtle counterchange. If the shadow side of the hill had been placed beside a similar tone of sky, instead of a light sky, the effect would be lost. For a more dramatic example of counterchange, see *Pinnacle Ridge in Snow* on page 70.

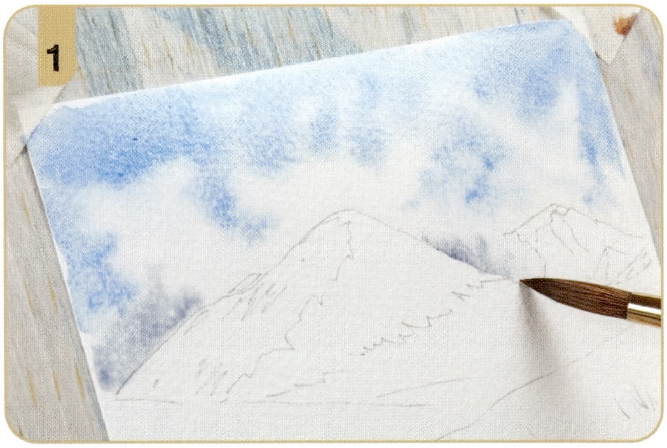

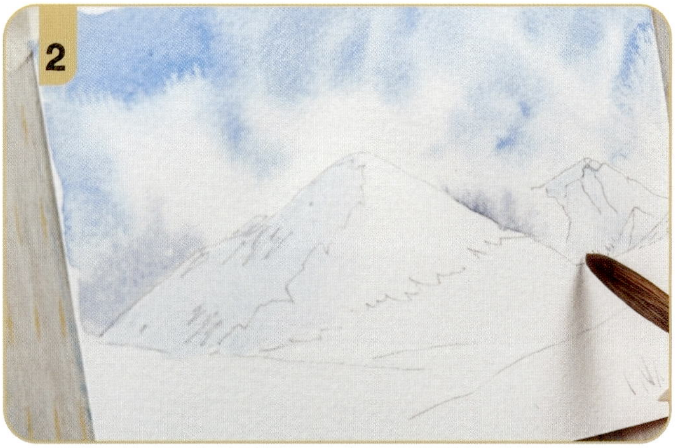

1 Wet the sky, including the valley between the hills. Drop in cobalt blue to the top, French ultramarine and burnt umber mix for the grey clouds; allow this to come into the valley.

2 Paint the hills with pale cobalt blue, omitting the right-hand side of the large hill; soften the edge towards the unpainted side but leave plenty of white.

3 Using a midtone mix of French ultramarine and burnt umber, paint the shadow areas of the snow.

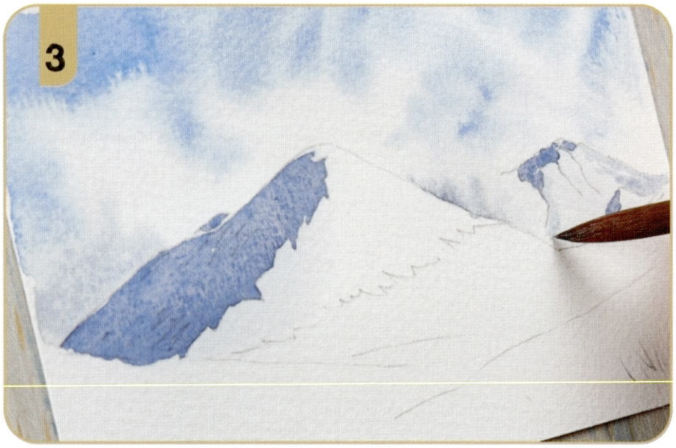

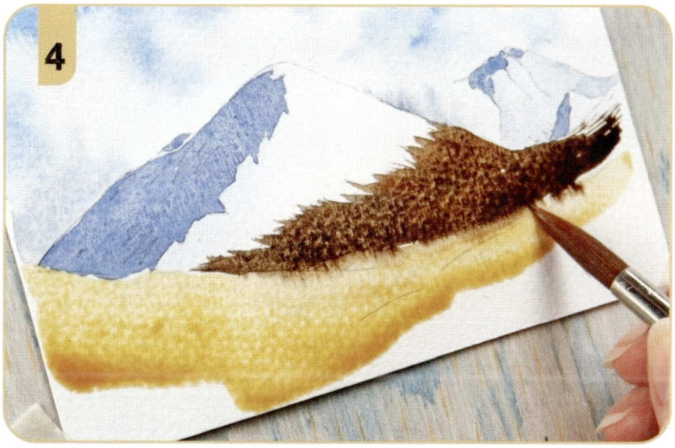

4 Using a French ultramarine and burnt umber mix, paint the lower slopes of the hills, changing to raw sienna for the foreground. To create interest here and there, drop in a little French ultramarine and burnt umber to the raw sienna.

5 Add darker detail with French ultramarine and burnt umber for the rocks in the snow on the left-hand hill.

6 Drybrush the French ultramarine and burnt umber mix onto the foreground on the left. Using positive and negative painting, create some grasses on the right.

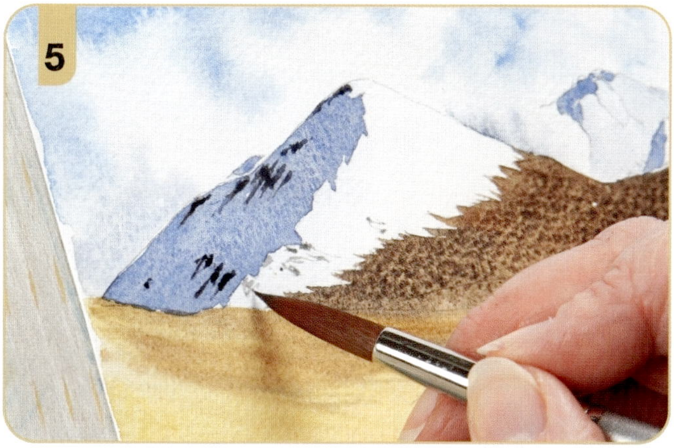

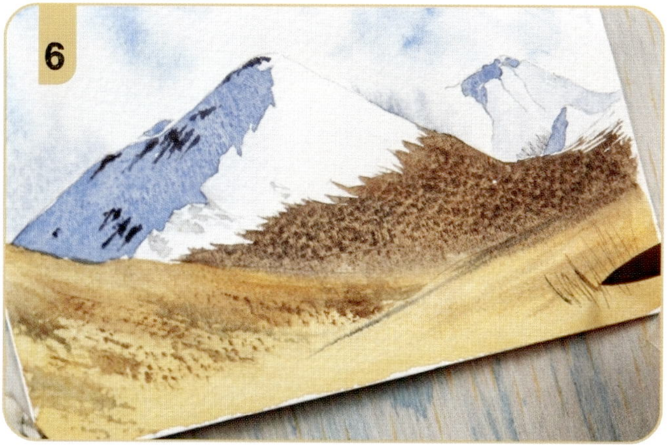

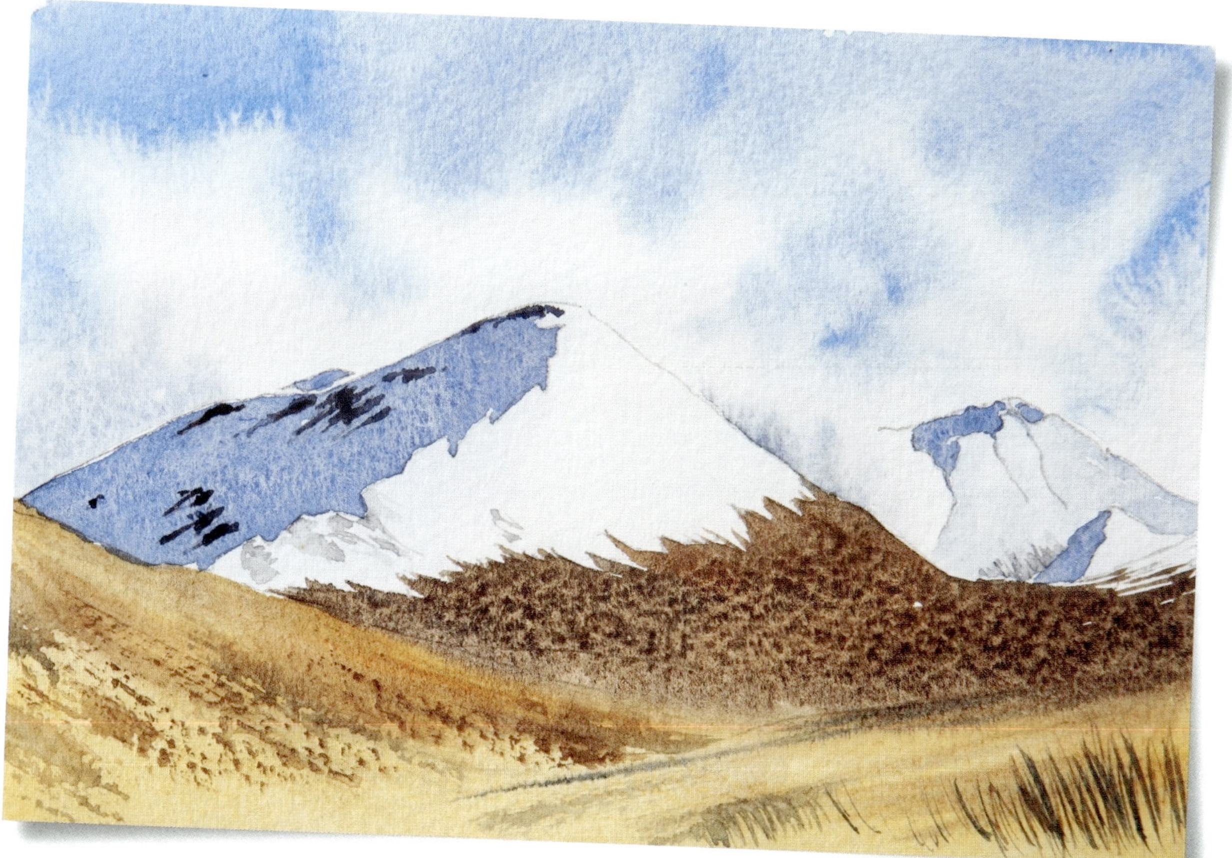

WEATHER, LIGHT & MOOD

What appeals to one person might not appeal to another, but many of us do respond in a similar way to certain 'moods', colours or weather conditions. We usually respond positively towards things that make us feel good; but a painting might also evoke memories of a holiday or an outdoor experience that was enjoyed despite poor weather or other challenges.

Creating a painting is not always about replicating what we see; a certain amount of drama or mystery in a work is likely to make it more appealing. I tend to select what I like before I begin to paint, but there are occasions when painting 'like it is', or as I'd planned to paint it, fails to produce a satisfactory result, and that pushes me to try something a little looser, using my reference material to create a mood. Living in a mountainous area for some years gave me plenty of reference material; and an awareness of just how many types of lighting, cloud and weather there can be.

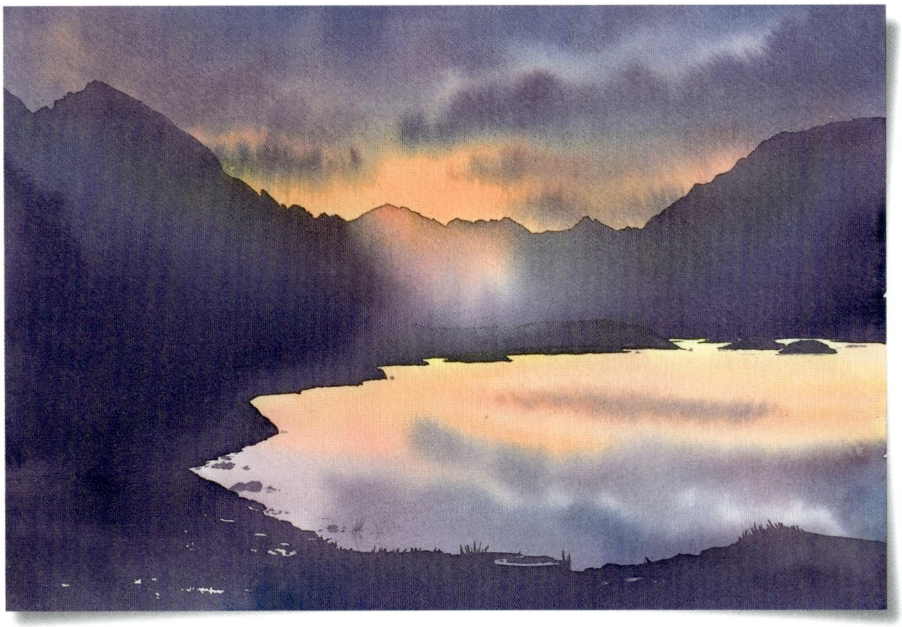

Loch Coruisk, Evening Light

37 x 27cm (14½ x 10½in)

On a cold, dull day and with limited time I was only able to get photographs. I attempted to paint the scene, failing on several occasions to brighten the mood with subtle changes of lighting. I went for a dramatic change and was very happy with the result.

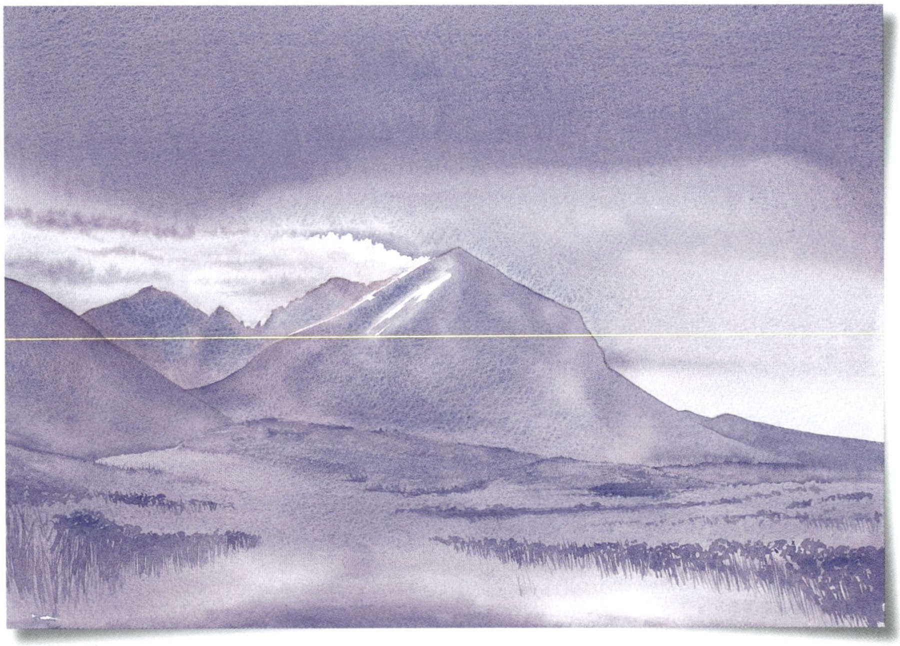

Moonlight on Marsco

37 x 27cm (14½ x 10½in)

Moonlight falling on wet/icy slopes created a glint of brightness on the mountain and the smoking chimney effect of the cloud appealed to me. Low light had reduced colour and detail, but added atmosphere. I changed the natural greys for soft purples.

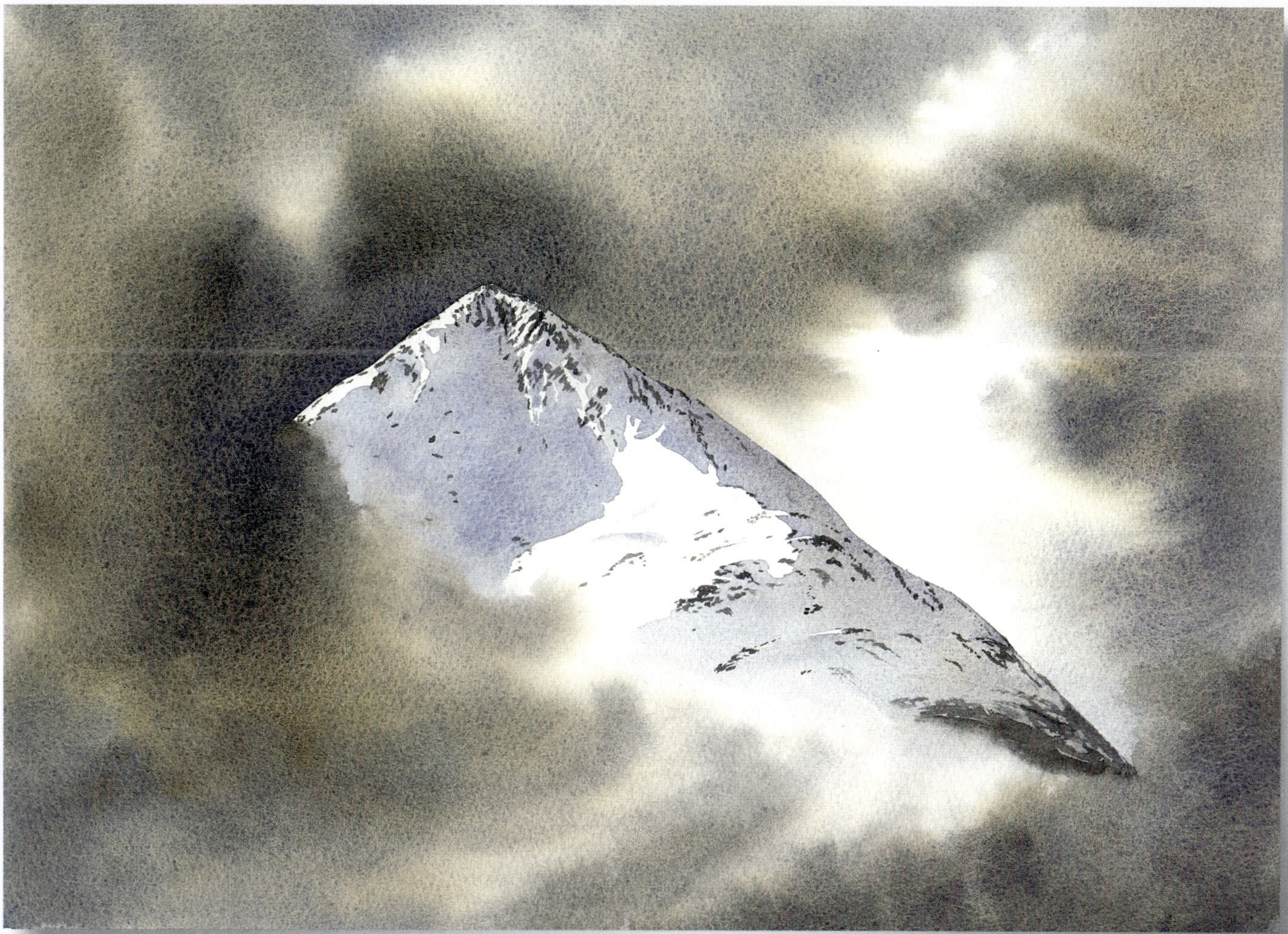

Encircled in Cloud

37 x 27cm (14½ x 10½in)

Here I have created clouds swirling around the snow-clad peak. Since we have no indication of how far away the ground may be, this painting introduces mystery to the subject and gives the possibility that the hill is taller than we might at first suspect.

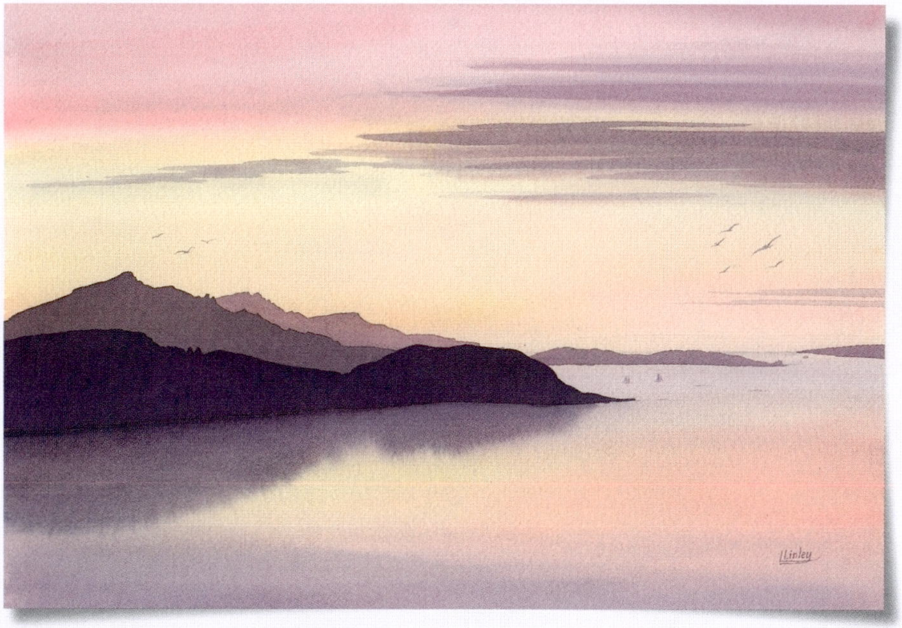

Evening Calm

37 x 27cm (14½ x 10½in)

A summer evening, warm yellows, pinks and purples for hills and sky, a calm sea. Glazes are useful for a sky like this where you may wish to overlay colours in a more controlled way than if you painted the sky as one wash. It's important not to use thick colour or work it until it lifts or becomes muddy.

Stormy sky

YOU WILL NEED

Paint colours: raw sienna, burnt umber, French ultramarine

Brushes: size 10 round

Other: tracing number 25

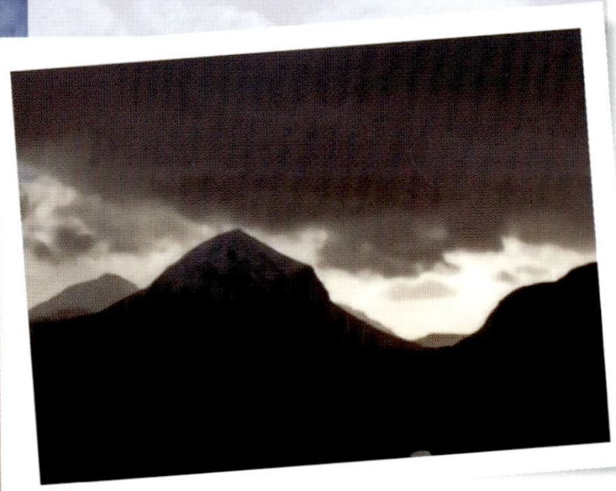

Dark skies often fascinate us, even when we know they mean 'bad weather'. Darks need to be handled carefully. You can't just use less water in the mix, as the paint must still be fluid. The key is to understand that the mix doesn't necessarily need to be extremely dark, just dark in comparison to other parts of the painting. Working wet in wet allows colour to flow and is likely to create pleasing effects with dark and lighter areas that work better than a flat area of colour.

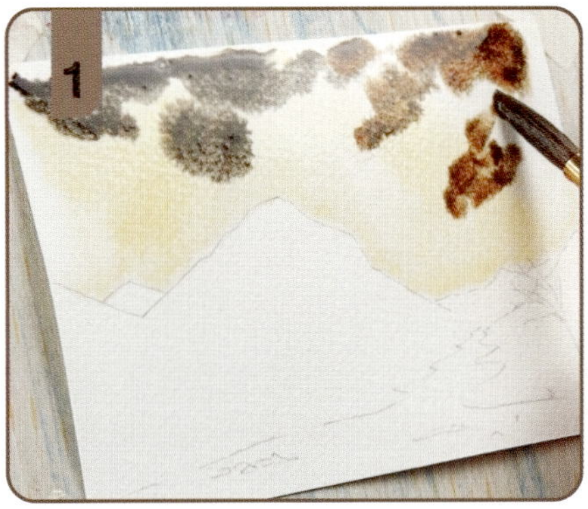

1 Prepare a French ultramarine and burnt umber mix. Don't over-mix this in your palette; allow it to be a little more blue in some areas and more brown in others. Wet the sky area and drop in pale raw sienna. While wet, drop in the French ultramarine and burnt umber mix, starting from the top corners.

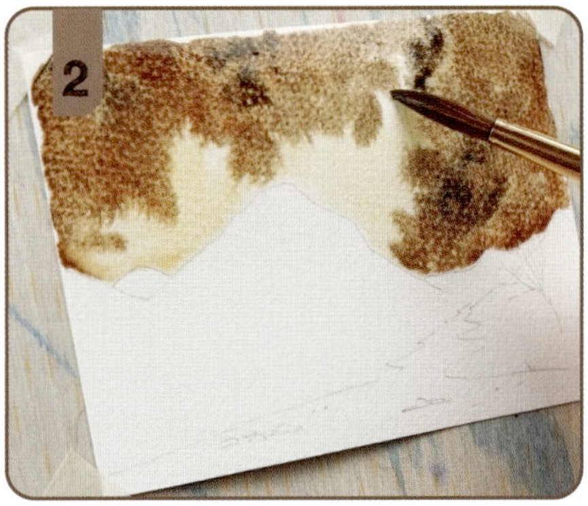

2 Work down towards the ridgeline, but leave a light area around the centre.

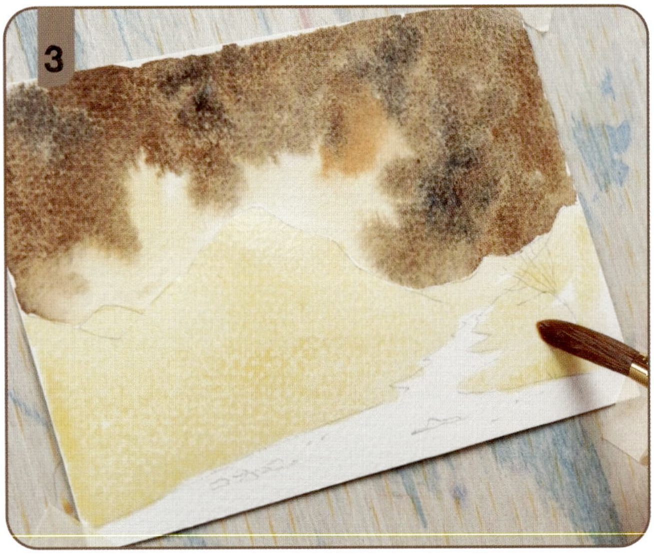

3 Avoiding the stream, paint the hills and land with raw sienna.

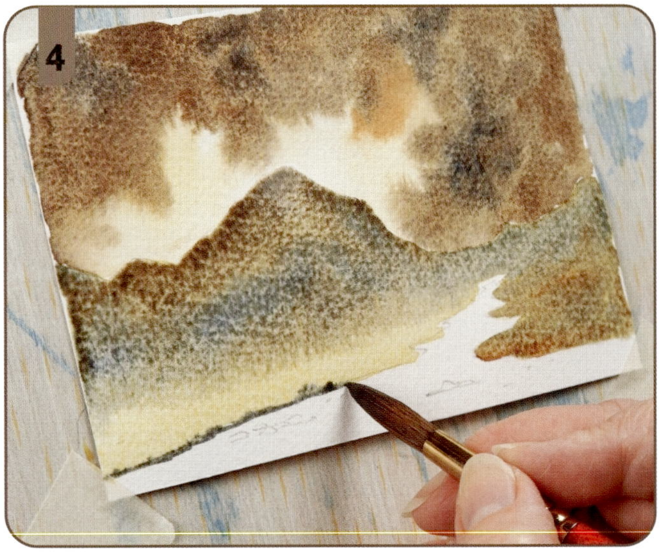

4 While the paper is still damp, drop in the hills and banks of the stream with the sky mix.

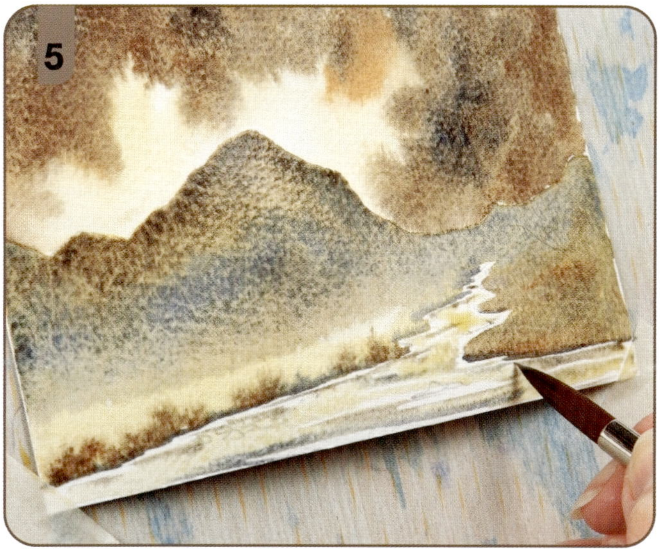

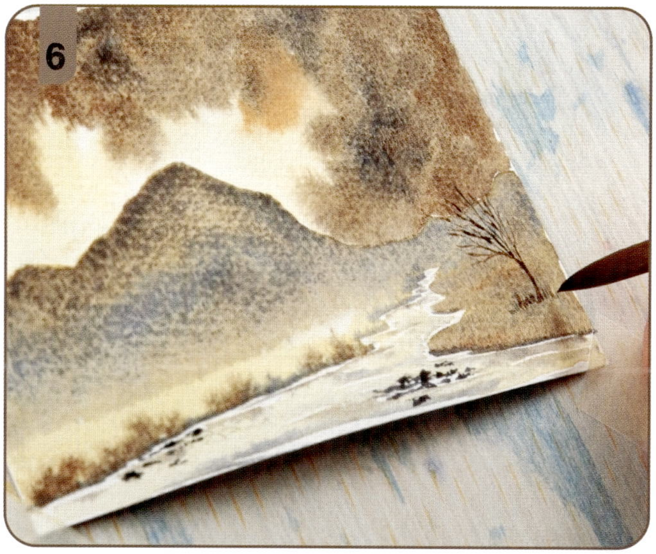

5 Paint the stream with raw sienna, leaving horizontal slivers of clean paper here and there (i.e. negative painting the highlights on the water) and dropping in French ultramarine and burnt umber.

6 Add a few foreground rocks, grasses etc. Remember to paint grasses and trees in the direction of growth, and with just a little paint on your brush so that it will form a fine point.

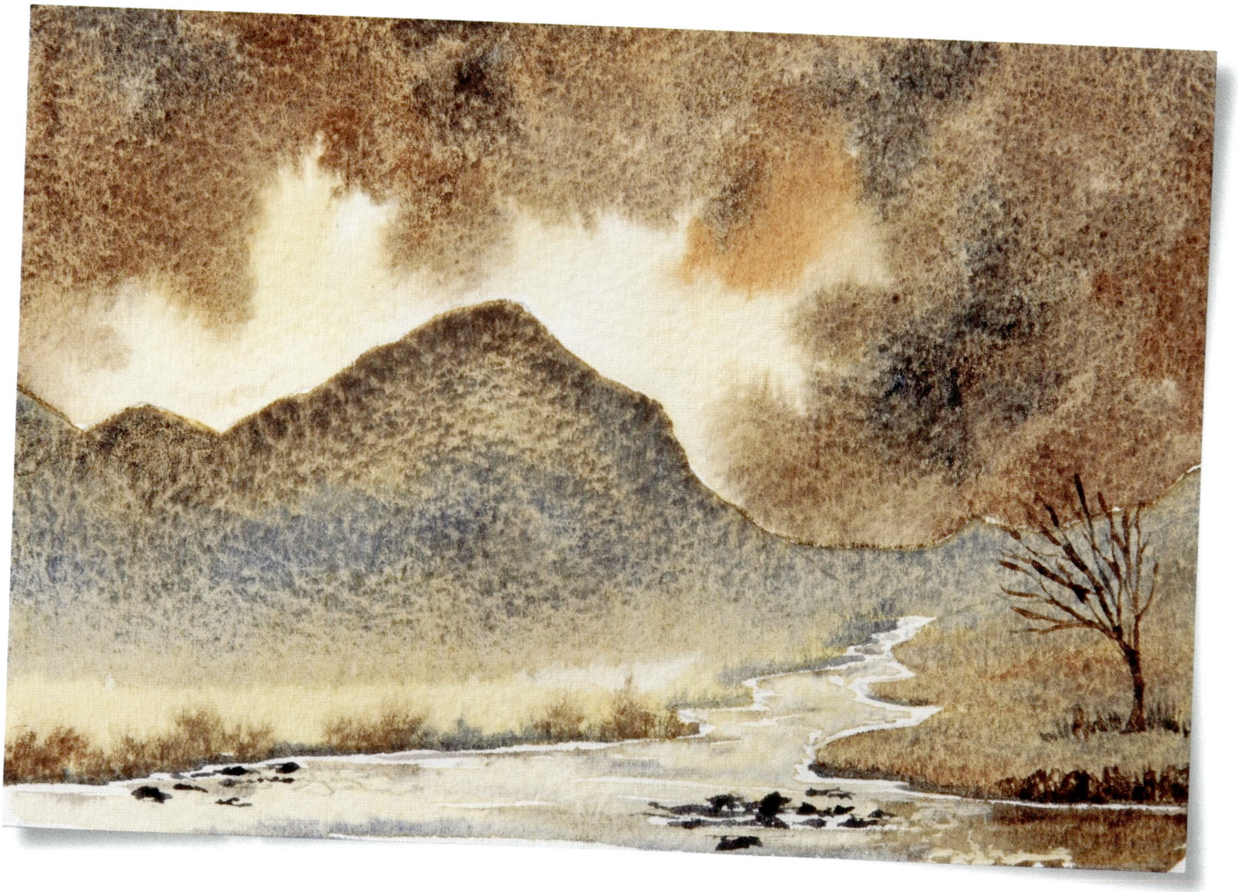

Wreath of mist

YOU WILL NEED

Paint colours: raw sienna, burnt umber, French ultramarine, cobalt blue

Brushes: size 10 round

Other: tracing number 26

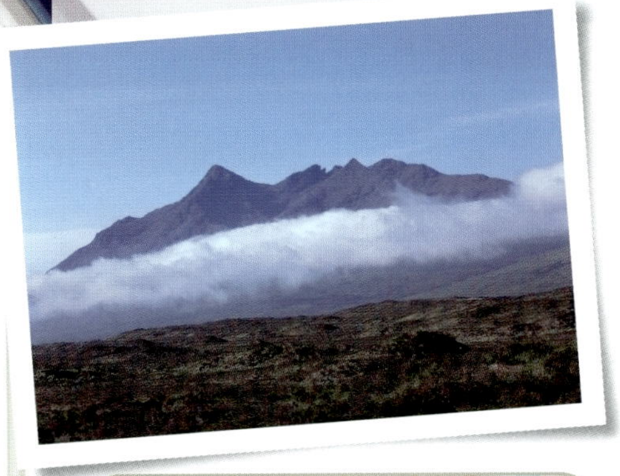

The beauty of living close to the hills is that you're more likely to catch a magic moment like that shown in the source photograph here – a mountain wearing a wreath of mist or cloud. Sometimes this effect lasts for hours, sometimes for moments. A photograph can be invaluable for capturing such effects, as there might not be time for a sketch.

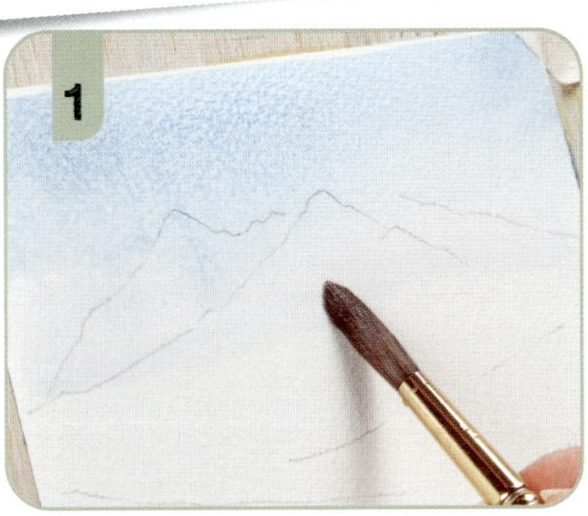

1 Paint a graduated cobalt blue wash to the sky, bringing the palest tones down over the tops of the hills.

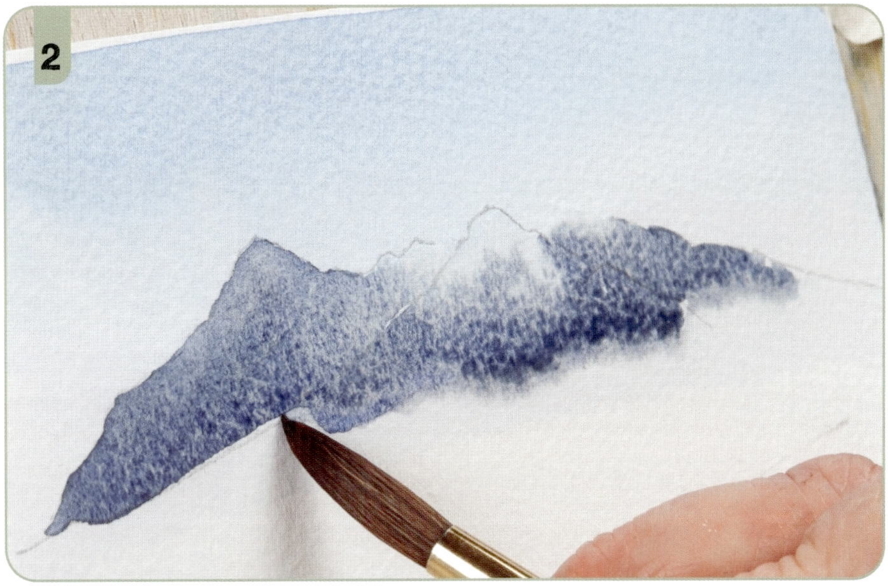

2 Apply water to the peaks that are to stay white, then paint the hills with a French ultramarine and burnt umber mix, softening the edges below as shown.

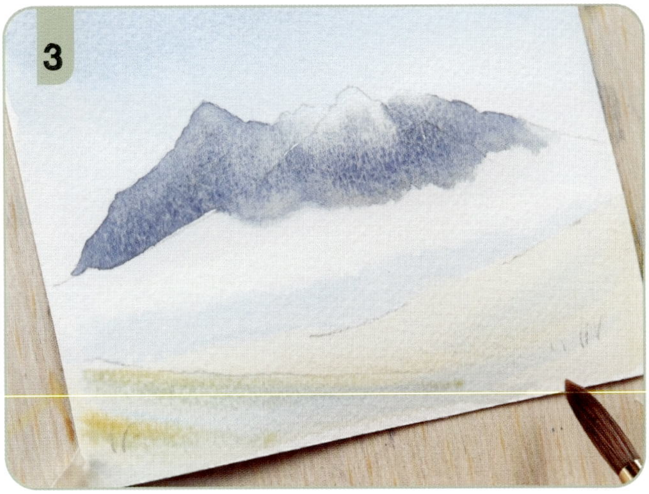

3 Using very pale cobalt blue, create the lower edge of the mist band, and soften the upper edge of this. Paint the land below with a pale wash of raw sienna, adding a few strokes of pale cobalt blue while this is still damp.

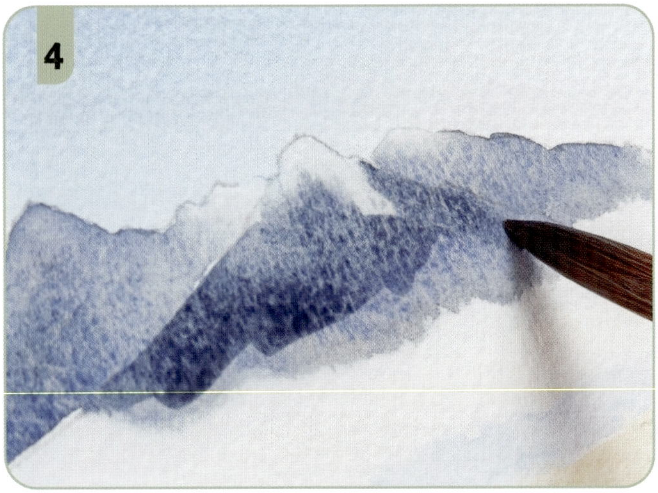

4 Paint the middle peak again, softening as before.

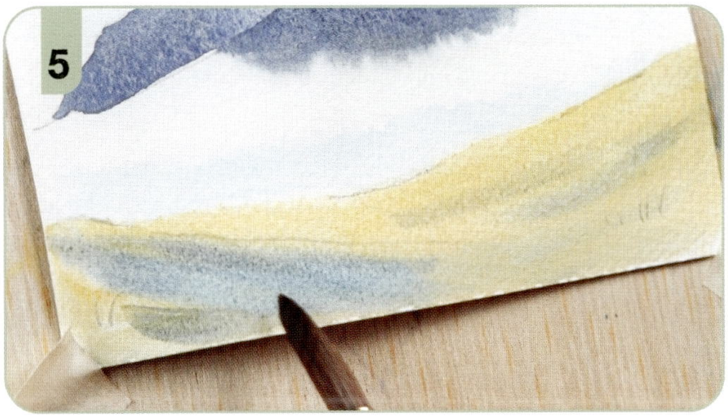

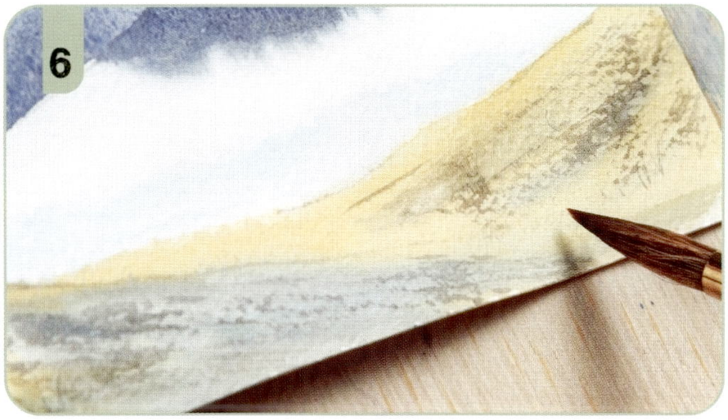

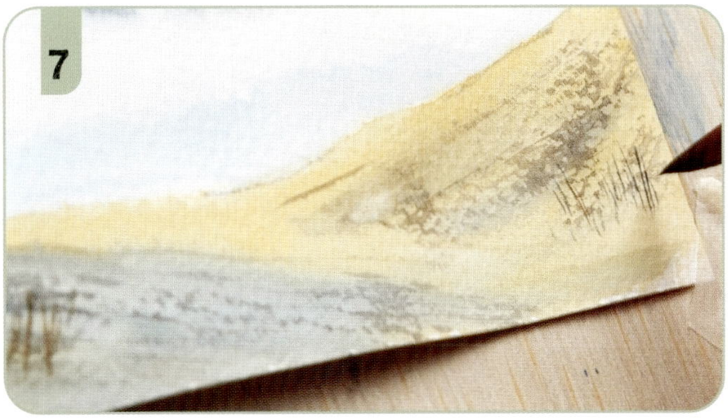

5 Wash the foreground with raw sienna, then add a few touches of cobalt blue.

6 Using a little burnt umber, drybrush texture over the moorland, then drybrush a little clean water through some of this to soften some areas.

7 With a little French ultramarine and burnt umber mix on your brush, create a few grasses to give scale to the foreground.

STRAY COLOUR

If any colour has strayed beyond where you wished it to go, lift out a little using a damp brush and kitchen paper.

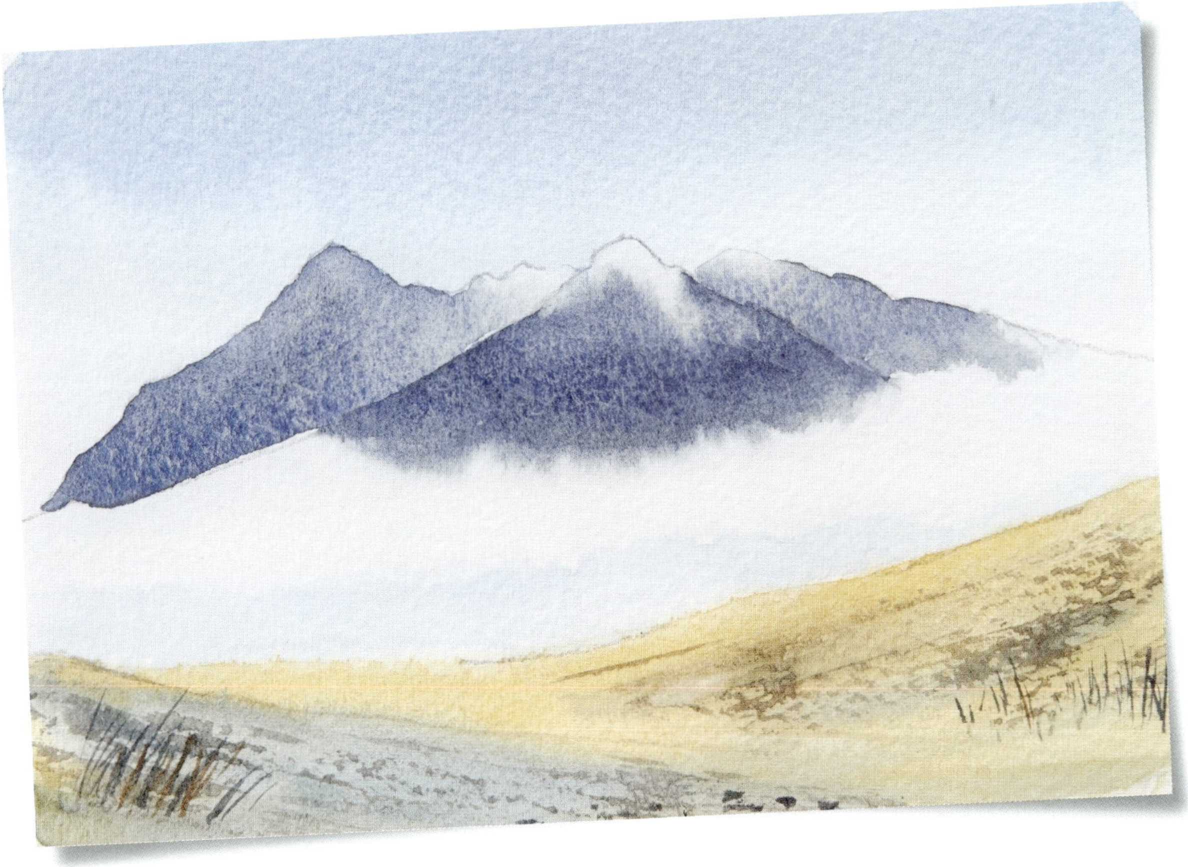

Bright water

YOU WILL NEED

Paint colours: French ultramarine, raw sienna, burnt umber, permanent rose, cobalt blue

Brushes: size 10 round

Other: tracing number 27

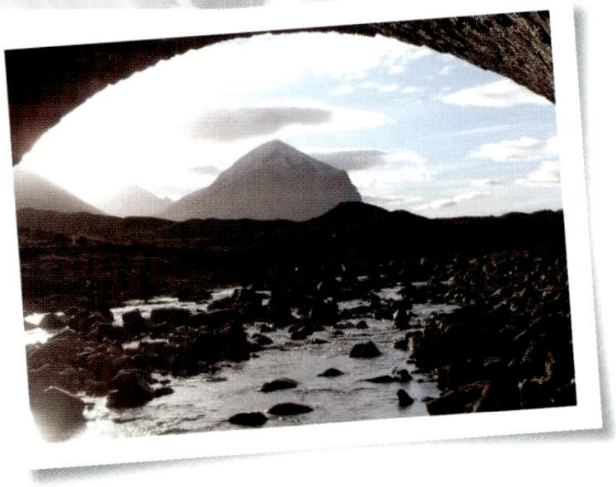

Light coming from behind or the side of an object creates lovely effects as little haloes of light contrast with shadows; it can turn a dark mass into an interesting arrangement of shapes.

When you come to the foreground in this project, it's important to allow the colour to flow from one rock to the next so that the rocks become a mass instead of individual shapes. Leave the light tops of some rocks unpainted for impact – though if you accidentally paint over one or two it won't matter too much.

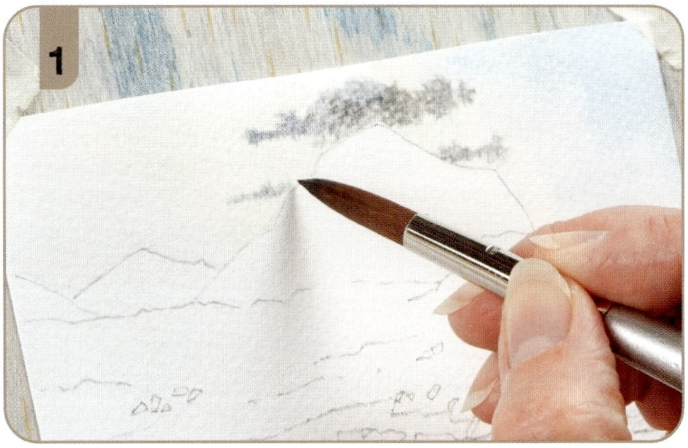

1 Dampen the sky area and drop in very pale raw sienna to the left and very pale cobalt blue to the right. Add a mix of French ultramarine and burnt umber for the clouds, keeping them light and subtle.

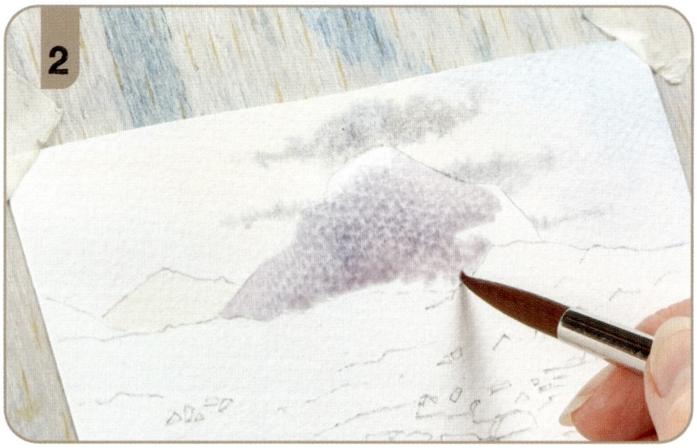

2 Using raw sienna, paint the distant hill and allow to dry. Wet the peak of the central hill with a damp brush, then paint the whole hill with the French ultramarine and burnt umber mix, adding a touch of permanent rose. The wet peak will create a highlight as shown.

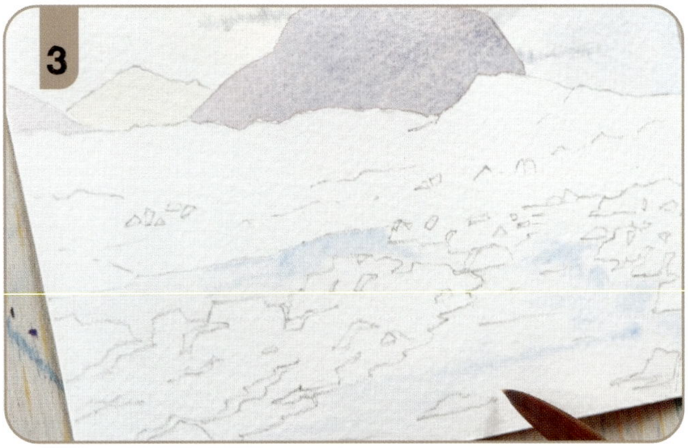

3 Paint the small hill on the far left of the painting. Next, dampen the water area and drop in pale cobalt blue. This helps to establish the area and make the complex tracing easier to 'read'.

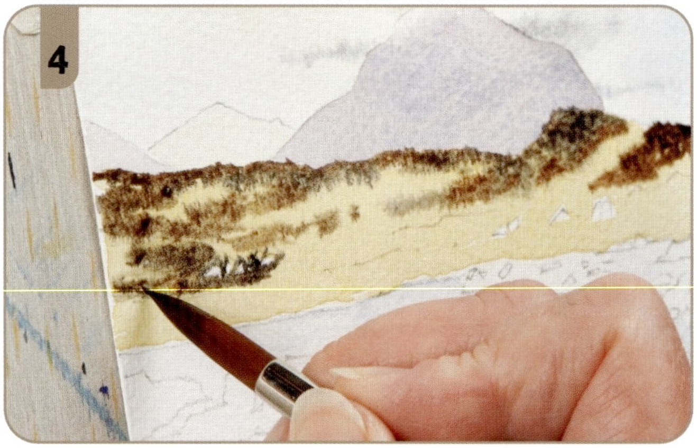

4 Cover the moorland with pale raw sienna, then use a French ultramarine and burnt umber mix for both the lower edge of the river bank and to touch in the heather.

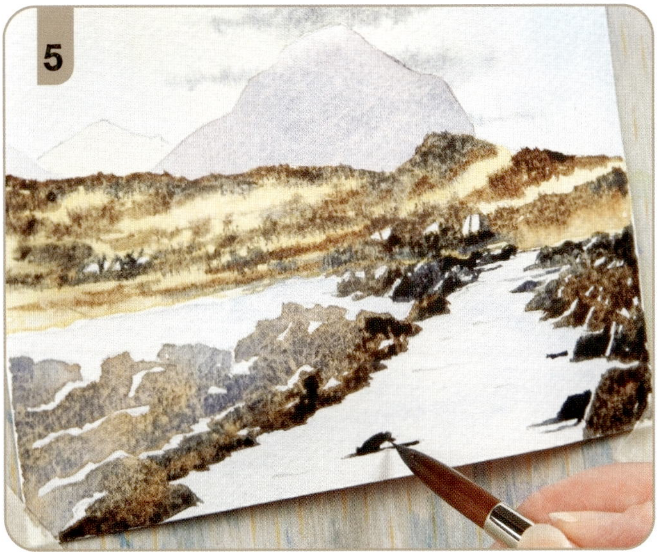

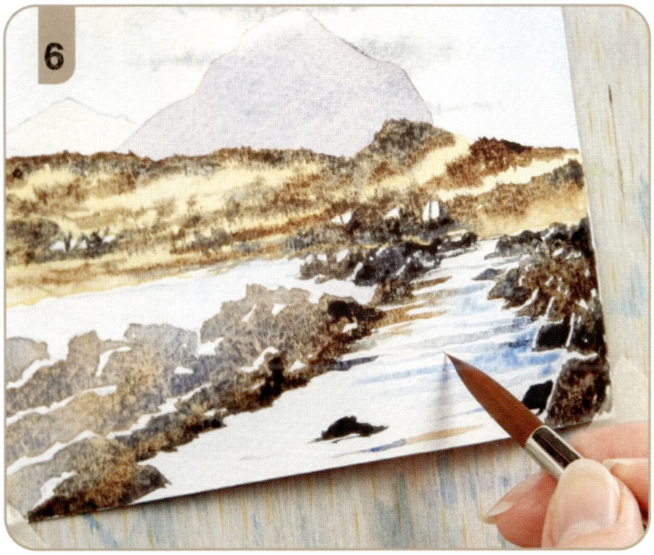

5 Ensure that you have a reasonable amount of French ultramarine and burnt umber mix, then begin to paint the rocks. Vary the strength and proportions of colour to give variety, and keep the foreground rocks on the left-hand side generally lighter.

6 Add medium and darker tones to the water using cobalt blue, French ultramarine and a little burnt umber. Soften the colour in here and there with a damp brush, to suggest reflected colour. Darken the riverbank on the left.

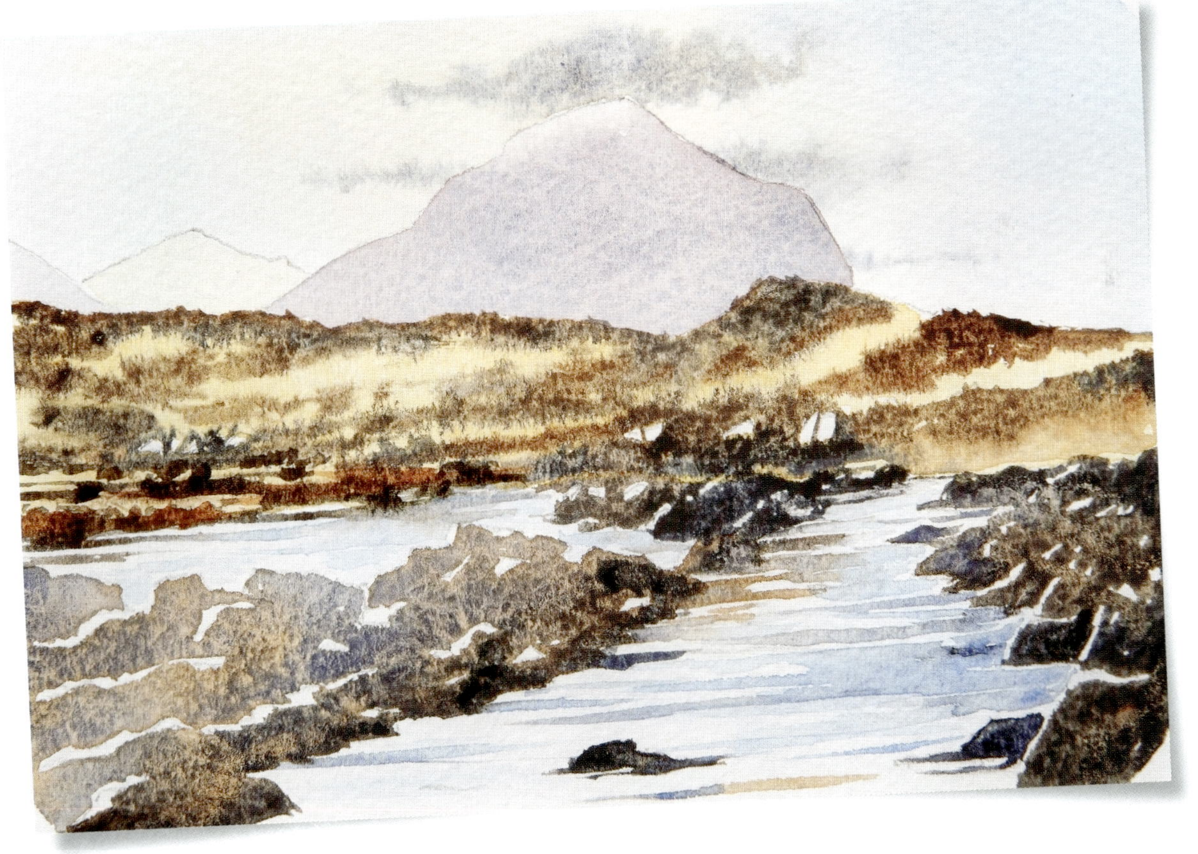

Simply tranquil

YOU WILL NEED

Paint colours: Winsor yellow, permanent rose, Prussian blue

Brushes: size 10 round

Other: tracing number 16

Part of the appeal of watercolour is its luminosity, and mountain scenes can work beautifully as semi-abstract mood pieces, rather than super-detailed representational pieces. In fact, this approach offers some rewarding challenges. The skill you will learn with this project is simply when to stop – and being able to do this means you will truly understand your watercolours. When transferring the tracing, copy just the top line of the mountains. This ridgeline is highlighted in a bolder line on the tracing to help make things clear.

I've chosen transparent colours for this exercise as they're less likely to create 'mud'; try other colours at some time and see how they differ. When you put plenty of paint to paper, you will often get a crisp, fine, hard edge, which works well here.

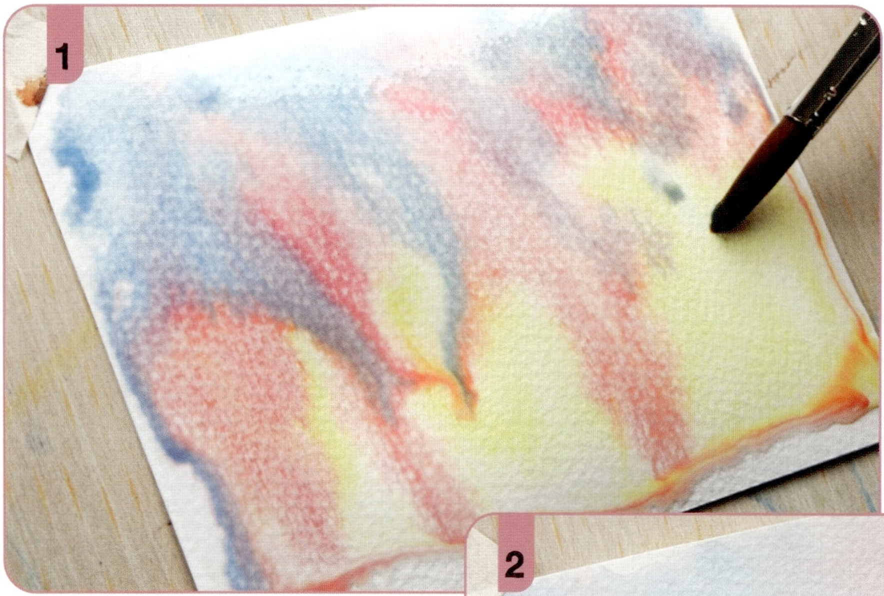

1 Wet the paper all over and drop in each of the three colours in turn. Allow them to run into one another and down the paper. Only tip the paper if the colours really need persuading to go in the correct direction.

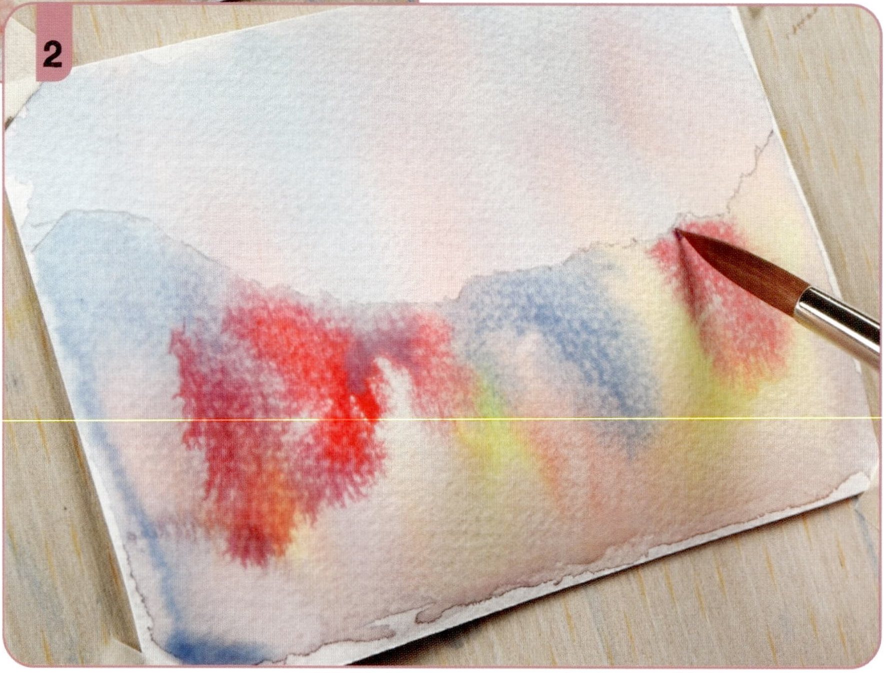

2 Once dry, re-wet the mountain area only and drop in the colours again.

Technique: Knowing when to stop

Only two steps? It really can be that simple; knowing when to stop is a skill to nurture.

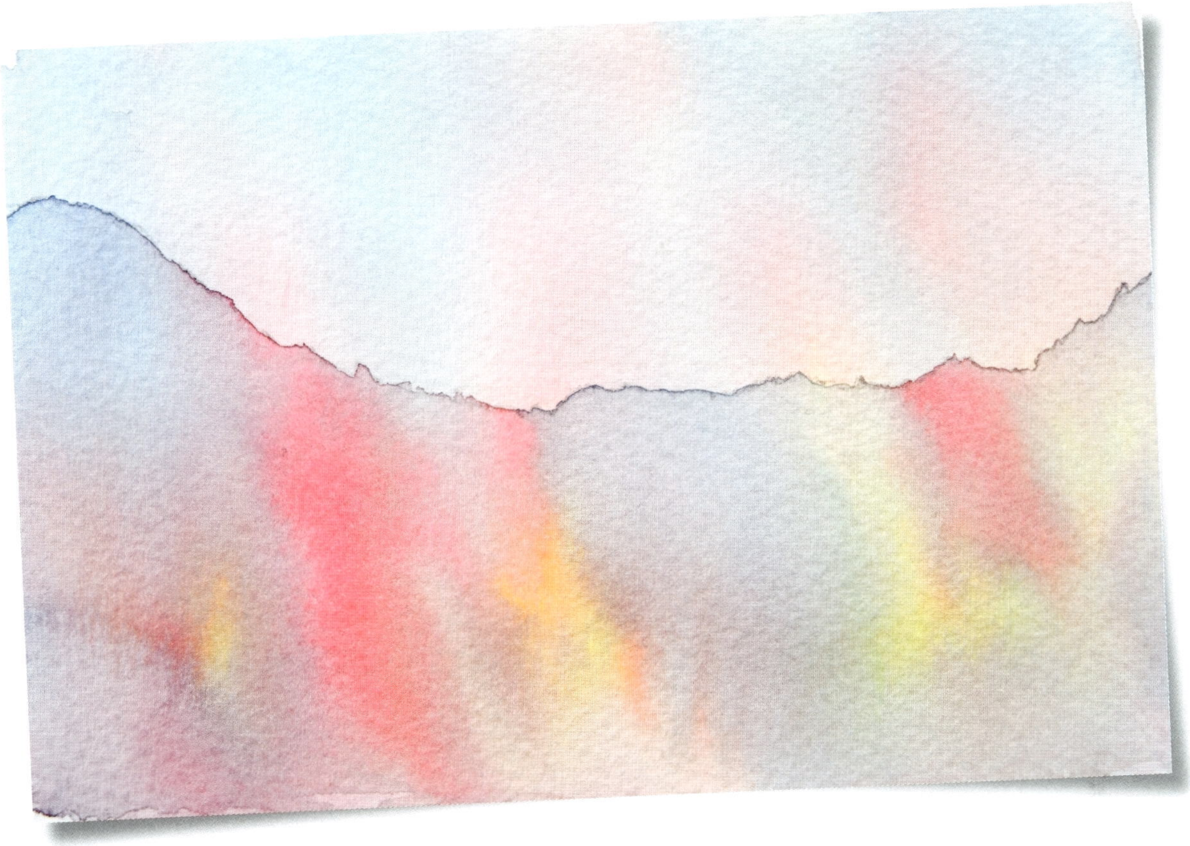

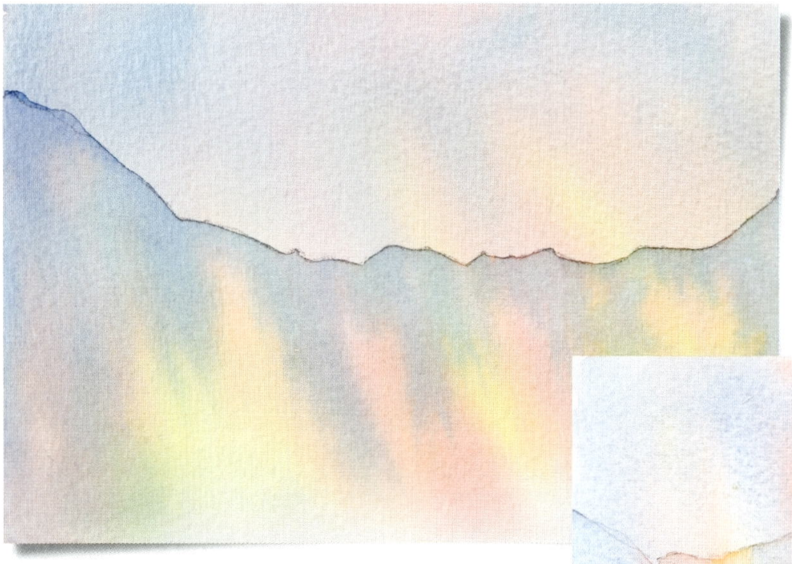

This is such a quick project that you have time to try out some other combinations. The example to the left was made using the same colours as the main project, but in different proportions.

The example below uses raw sienna, scarlet lake and cobalt blue, and I used a different tracing (21, from pages 72–73) to give me the initial line. Try this yourself – pick a tracing and just follow the top line.

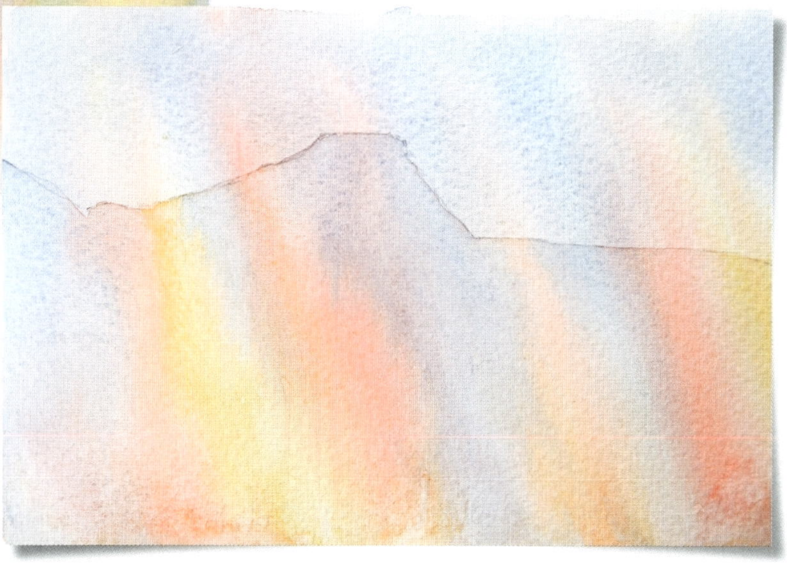

ADDING THE OUTLINE LATER

If you find the pencil line gets washed away by the first wash, try re-tracing the outline after the first wash has dried.

When you're more practised at this you could instead try making the wash first before tracing the line. See which method suits you better.

SNOW SCENE

See tracing number 28

This painting uses a detail of a distant peak of snow-laden mountain tops on a cold but sunny day. The peak was sunlit but the valley was in deep shade and did nothing to enhance the scene so I used a little artistic licence in order to make a more successful painting. This is another example of a very limited palette.

The following techniques were used for this painting: wet on dry, wet in wet, counterchange, lost and found edges, softening and negative painting. The projects on pages 20, 24, 78, 82 may help you.

The scene was simplified by 'zooming in', taking the view of the sunlit peak alone. Surrounding it with swirling dark clouds added a little mystery. We have no indication of how high the peak might be, as the lower slopes are lost in the clouds. Placing the peak high on the page might suggest to us that it's quite tall, but it is merely a suggestion.

The bright sunshine, indicated by the light and shadows on the hill, contrasts with the moody brooding clouds; where colours were dropped into the wet sky and allowed to blend. We all know that dark clouds indicate bad weather, but the mood is kept light with the sunlit peak protruding through them.

When making your own version of this painting, know when you've done enough. With this type of work you're unlikely to get exactly the same as the reference painting, because wet in wet isn't completely within our control. Practice will make it more so, but the joy of using watercolour is that something exciting may happen. If you try to control it too much you may well spoil it; so embrace what happens.

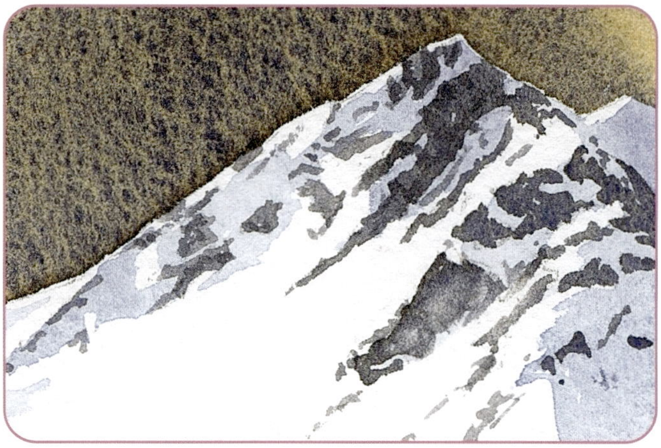

Just three tones are used for the shadows on the snow and rocks. This helps to keep them fresh and colourful.

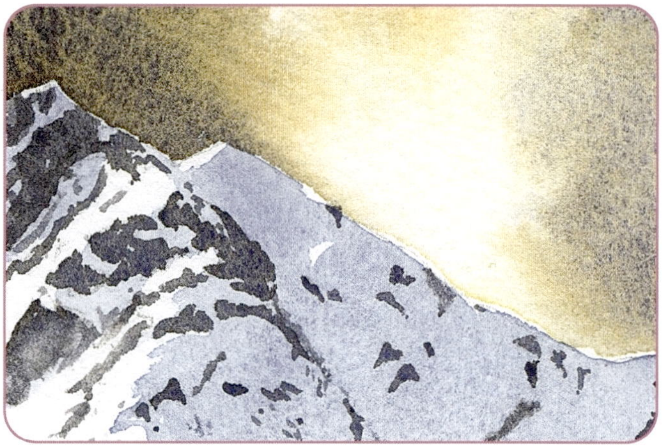

Here, warm sunlit cloud contrasts with the cool blue shadow. A change of tone heightens the effect.

Use of wet-in-wet techniques combined with granulation results in plenty of variation in tone and colour.

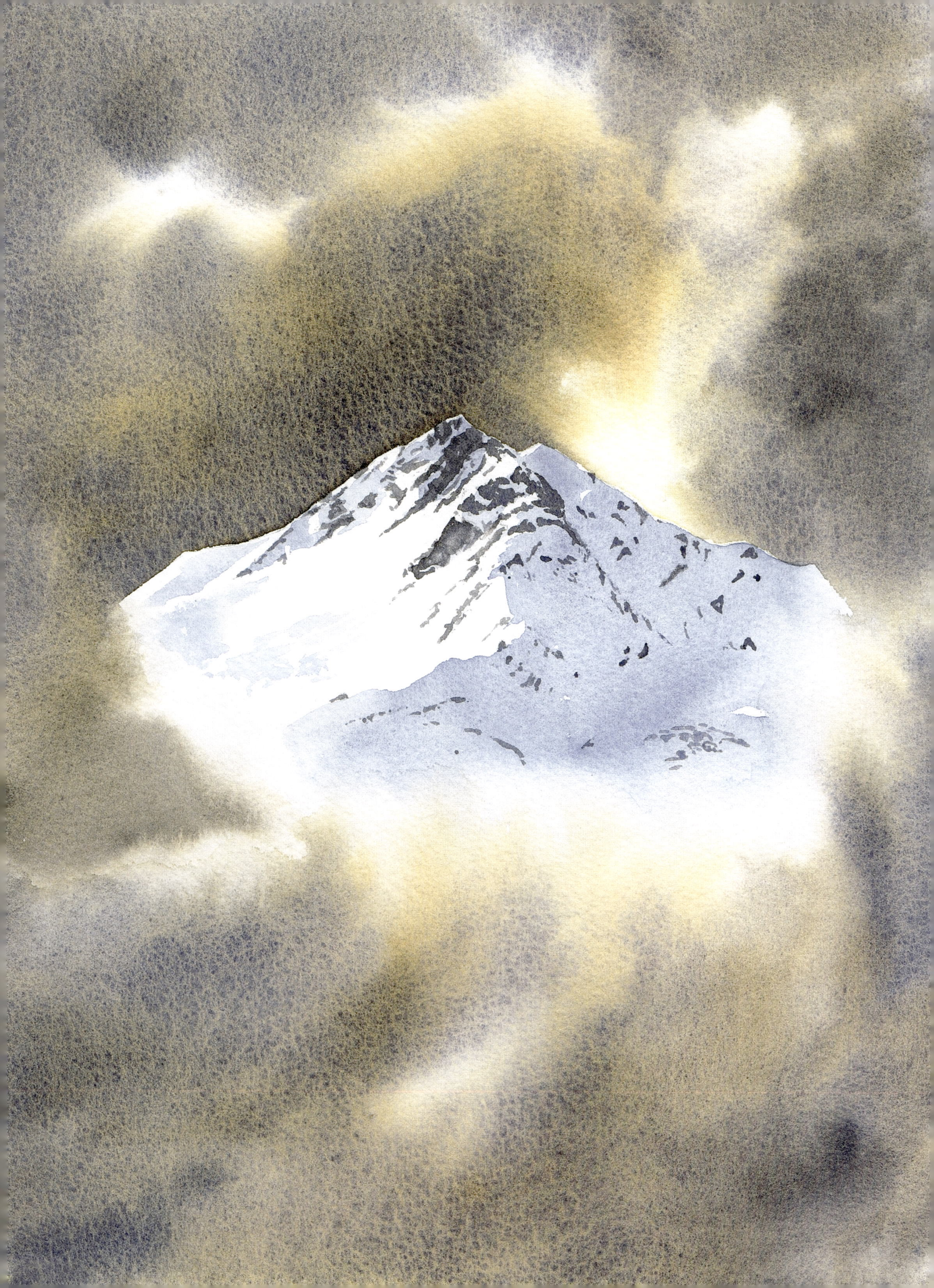

MOUNTAIN AND LOCH

See tracing number 29

Low autumn or winter sun features in many of my paintings because this type of lighting appeals to me. Here the sunlight bleaches the sky on the left and casts the hill on the right into deep shadow; which itself contrasts with the sunlit foreground hill. The blue sky reflected in the loch adds foreground brightness. A dark background feature here – the hill – breaks the rules of having pale colours in the distance, but this is the appeal of this scene, and without it the rest of the painting loses its impact.

In selecting this scene, I took an area from a much wider landscape, omitting a large area of shadow on the left which would have dominated the scene. The remaining shadow areas provide contrasts with sunlit ones.

In terms of mood, the low sun creates tonal variation from one side of the sky to the other, and illuminates the underside of the clouds. The sunlit moorland golds provide a warm glow to set off the cool blues and purples of the shadows.

This painting requires a little more planning than the one on the previous pages. Consider your choice of colours – there are probably fewer than you think. The techniques used include wet in wet, wet on dry, softening, negative painting and counterchange, as you have practised in projects on pages 20, 22, 24, 30, and 78.

While this is a more controlled painting than *Snow Scene,* don't be tempted to paint too much detail – we only need to suggest it. Allow the washes to dry thoroughly before attempting wet on dry; the reeds will not be crisp fine lines if the paper is damp.

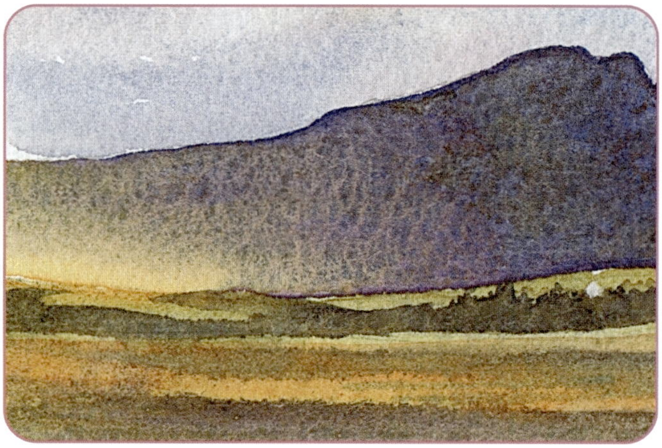

Soft wet-in-wet transitions run from light to dark and from warm to cool on the hill. These contrast with the hard-edged change from the dark hill to the sunlit moorland behind the tiny white house (on the right).

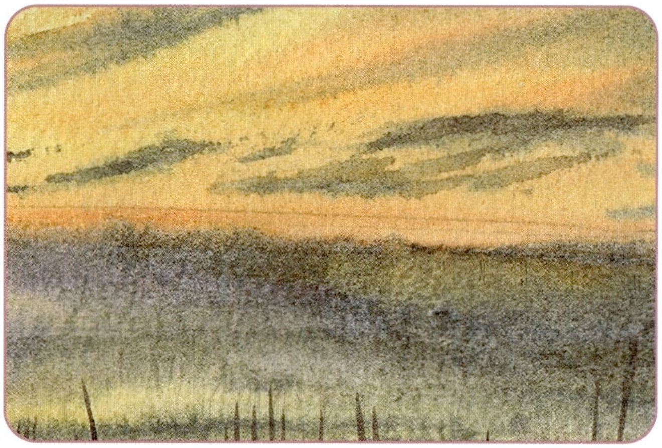

Wet-in-wet blends of golds, greens and purples are used here, with just a few touches of wet on dry to add more texture to the moorland.

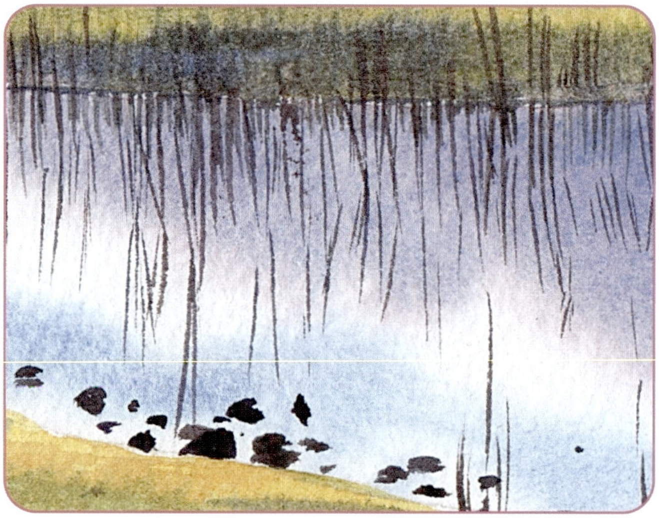

A fresh, clear wash for the loch and a few simple lines are enough to give an impression of still water. Practise thin brushstrokes for the reeds so that you can paint them with confidence.

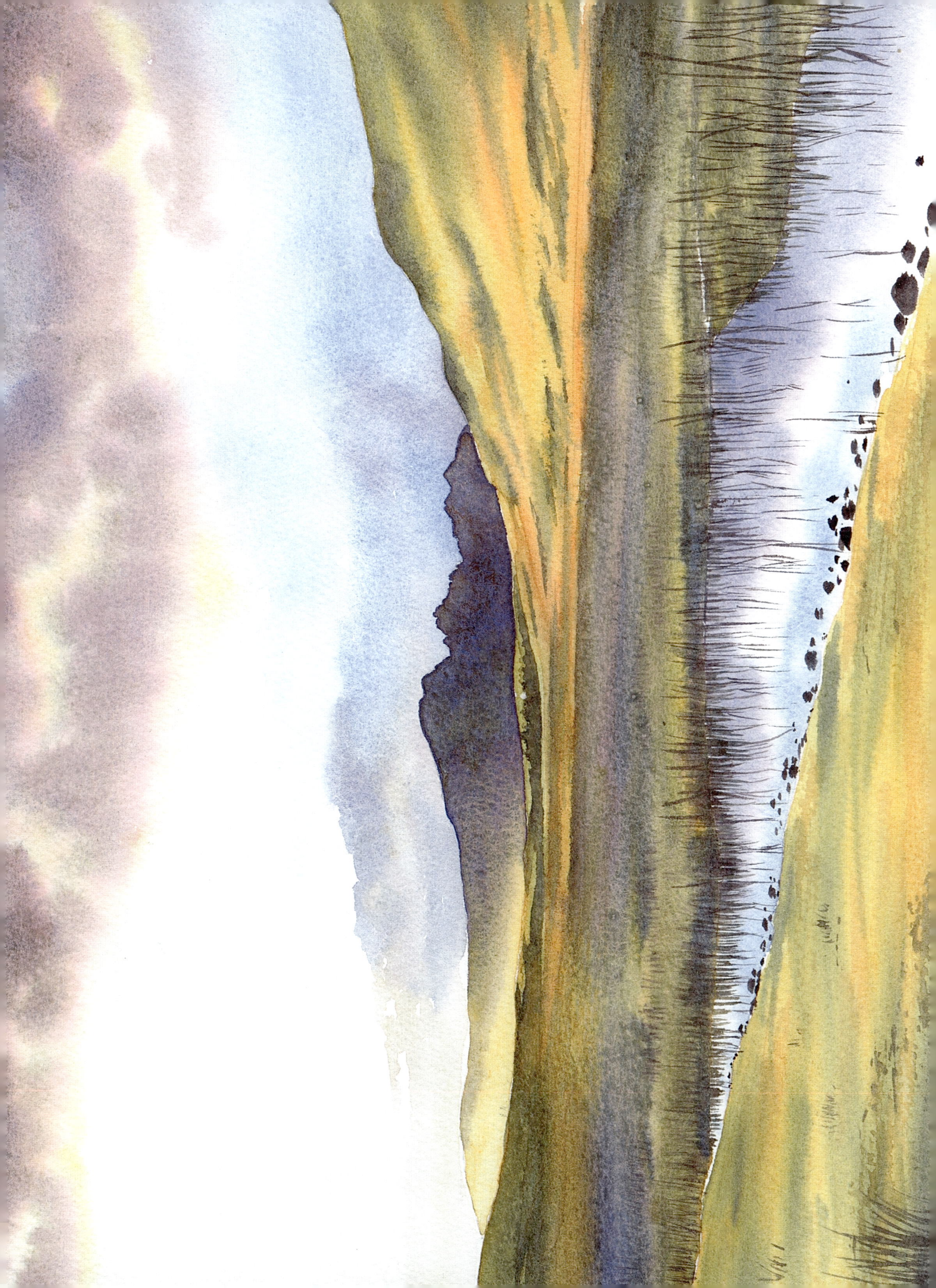

WATERFALL

See tracing number 30

This winter landscape uses a limited palette of blues and browns, with golden moorland grasses against dark heather. Although this scene takes in a great distance, it focuses on quite a narrow area of the waterfall, where the sparkling water contrasts with the darks of the rocks and shadows. The low sun from the right casts shadows which add interest through describing the contours of the hill and the foreground rocks. These shadows make up a large part of the foreground, and the detail in this area will keep you busy with a mixture of wet in wet, glazes, negative painting, and crisp wet on dry detail. The techniques explained on pages 30, 54, 66, and 86 will help with this one.

The real interest, however, is the waterfall, where the shadows bring the water to life. Because there is a lot of detail in the foreground, we have to resist the temptation to do too much to the moorland: this would reduce the effect of distance and make the scene too flat and too busy. The minimal areas complement the detailed ones.

Most of the rock in the stream is actually one piece and can be painted as such; the rocks appear slightly brown where they're in the sun, more blue or neutral in the shade – just vary the amount of blue or brown in the mix, and note that the shadows aren't black.

If you paint over a water droplet, it won't matter – the water is moving, after all, so no-one will see the scene exactly as you do. However, do try to preserve a few sparkles as these really make a difference. The shadows are important as they set the scene and make flat shapes appear three-dimensional: the whiteness of the water is enhanced by the darker tones around it.

Don't be intimidated by this project. It is simply more of what you have done already. if it helps you to be more confident, you might try practising painting in sections first. Do take breaks, step back and evaluate; better to consider 'Does it need more?' than think 'I wish I'd stopped sooner'. This painting is best done over more than one session, otherwise you may work the paper when it needs to dry or overwork the painting.

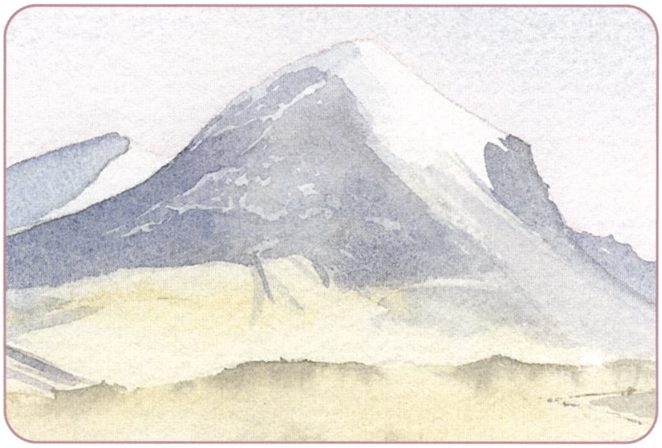

The distance has been painted simply, using soft colours, mostly wet in wet. Soft washes of subtle colours are used for the distant hills, the pale golden slope contrasting with the blue-purples.

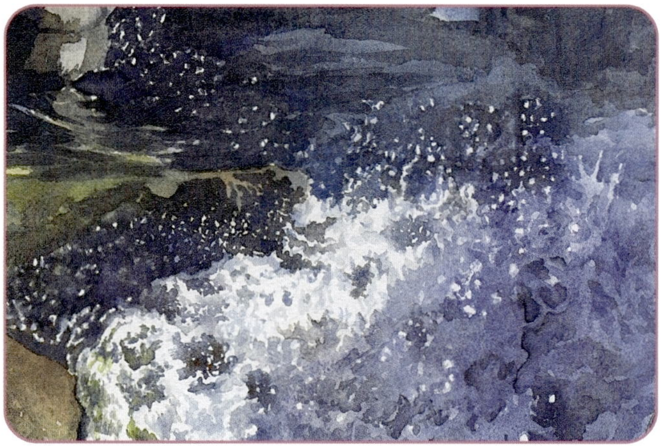

Lost and found edges are used as rocks and water merge. Shadows on and around the whitest areas of waters serve to increase the brightness of the white.

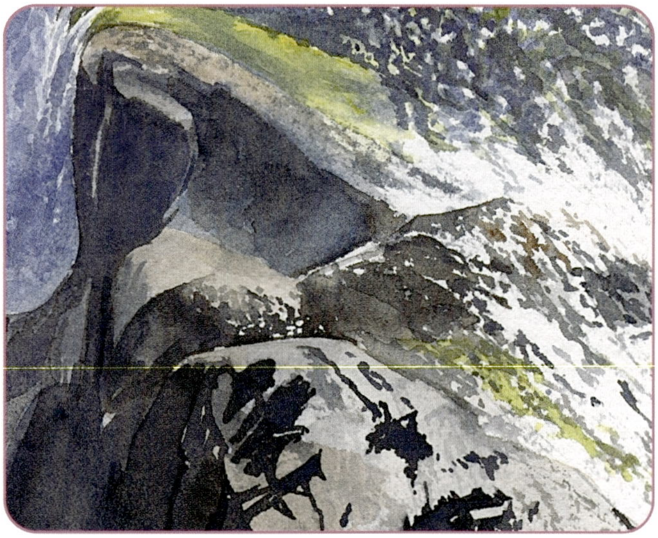

Crisp shadows contrast with the sunlit areas, and splashes of colour increase the impression of sunlight on the water.

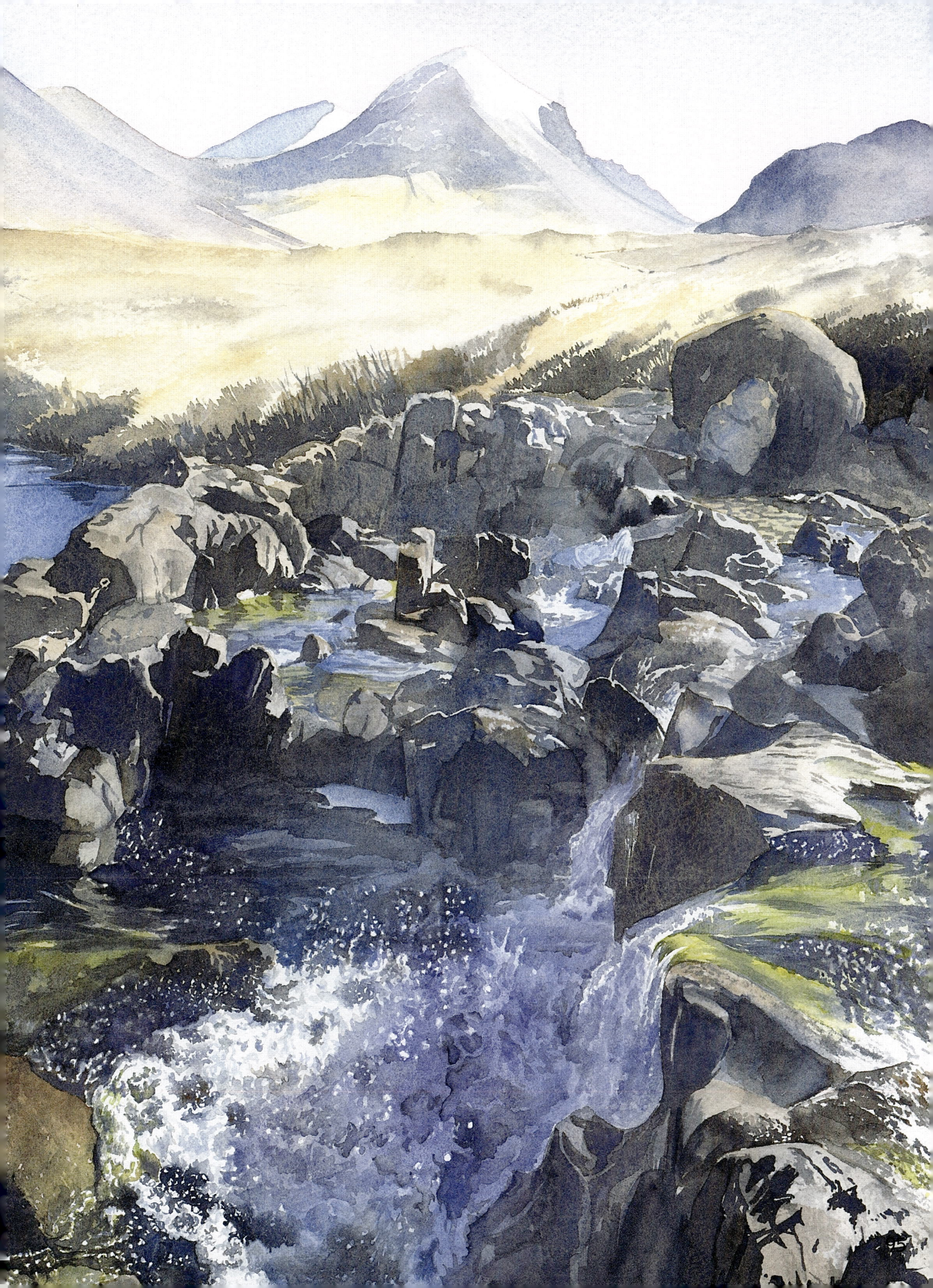

INDEX